Property of

That, excepting in rare cases, you might as well send to the foundling hospital and borrow a baby as to borrow a book with the idea of its being any great satisfaction. We like a baby in our cradle, but prefer that one which belongs to the household. We like a book, but want to feel it IS ours. We never yet got any advantage from a borrowed book. We hope those never reaped any profit from the books they borrowed from us, but never returned.—

* * *

Don't worry your friends BY borrowing this book. Buy one.

* * *

For sale by all book dealers or by mail on receipt of price by publisher.

Peschel Press ~ P.O. Box 132 ~ Hershey, PA 17033 ~ Email: Peschel@PeschelPress.com ~ www.PeschelPress.com

Fed, Safe & Sheltered

Fed, Safe & Sheltered

Protect Your Family & Thrive Amid Tough Times

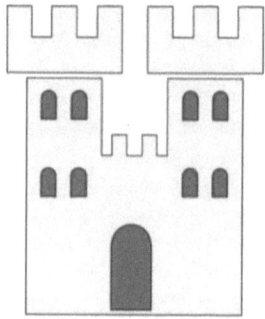

Teresa Peschel

PESCHEL PRESS ~ HERSHEY, PA.

FED, SAFE & SHELTERED: Protect Your Family & Thrive Amid Tough Times. Copyright 2017 Teresa Peschel. All rights reserved. Printed in the United States of America. No part of the notes or essays may be used or reproduced in any manner without written permission except in cases of brief quotations embodied in critical articles or reviews. For information, email peschel@peschelpress.com or write to Peschel Press, P.O. Box 132, Hershey, PA 17033.

Formerly Titled Suburban Stockade
Cover and book design by Bill Peschel.

Sign up for our newsletter at www.peschelpress.com

ISBN-13: 9781950347254

Library of Congress Control Number: 2017906650

Second Edition: October 2020

Table of Contents

Introduction: Making a Bargain With Omelas   10

1. Mission Statement   17

2. Goal Setting   19
How to Set Your Goals — Choosing Your Goals — Getting Your Honey Onboard — A Lifetime of Goals

3. Everyone Agrees That You Need To Do These Things   24
Get in Shape — Get Out of Debt — Get Your Paperwork in Order — Quit Your Addictions—Keep Food on Hand — Reskill, Reskill, Reskill — Improve Your Health — Fix Your House — Grow Some of Your Own Food — Store Water — Pay Attention — Form a Community — Get Started

4. Spouse Conversion; or, Becoming a Team   32
Can This Marriage Be Saved? — Train Your Spouse — Training By Example — The Why of Being Prepared — Explain and Praise

5. Financial Independence and Thrift   40
The Best Thrift Books — The Debt-Free Road Map — Riding the Debt Snowball — Building Your Thrift Library

6. Fixing the Work-Life Balance   44
Racing to the Bottom - Your Company Is Not Your Family - Your Time Is Precious - The Work-Life Illusion - Your Money Or Your Life - Learning to Say No

7. Swimming Against the Tide   50
Lies Our Culture Tells Us - Bad Housing Advice - The Student Loan Lie - College Is Not for Everyone - Feeding the Stimulation Monkey - Life Outside the Bubble — Navigating Our Culture

8. That Pesky Time Management   56
The Power of Goals - Keep Track of Your Life - Recognize Your Limitations - Organize Tasks Around the Calendar

9. Managing Your Television   60
Television Is Never Free - Television Is Educational - Television Has No Sense of Proportion - Television and Children - Fine-Tuning Our Culture

10. The Domestic Economy   64
What Is a Homemaker Worth? — Anyone Can Do It - Living With Less

11. Buying a Home   69
The Achievable American Dream - House-Hunting with Map and Camera - What to Look For In a House - What Else to Look For In a House - How Much Land Do You Need? — A Walk Through Our Yard - Buying the Right-Sized Home - The Value of Home Renovation - Avoid the Money Pit

12. Food Gardening   92
A Recipe for Storage - Why Garden?

13. Home and Personal Security   96
Locking Down Your House — Upgrading Windows - Signs for Emergency Personnel and Delivery Guys - Protecting Garages, Tool Sheds, and Porches - Keeping Your

Vehicle Secure – Emergency-Proof Your Vehicle – Dogs as Alarm Systems – Know Your Neighbors – Keeping Yourself Safe – Be Prepared – Know Where You Are – The Problem with Common Sense

14. Operational Security   120

15. You and Your Arsenal   122

16. Hedges and Fences: Or, Hiding From the Neighbors and Google Earth   125

Fencing For Beginners – Hedging Your Fence – The Problem With Privet – Planting by Direction – A Brief History of Our Yard

17. Enhancing Natural Light   134

Cleaning Windows – Window Treatments – Paint and Color Magic – Painting Walls – Closets — Cabinets – Floor Coverings – Light Fixtures – Mirrors – Interior Windows – Shrubbery – Basement Lighting – Windows, Solar Tubes, and Skylights — See the Light

18. The Window Dance   152

How to Dress Your Windows – Sealing Windows – 'Shall We Dance?' – Made In the Shade

19. Energy Efficiency   163

The Heterodyne Principle – Understanding Jevons' Paradox – Changing Your Behavior – Staking the Energy Vampire – Keeping Out the Weather – Appliances and Cars

20. Organization   175

Using the Martha Wall – Corralling Your Material World – Redoing Your Closets – Kitchen Storage

21. Home Self-Sufficiency   186

The Skill of Reskilling — Reskilling in Practice — Managing Your Time and Energy — "But I Don't Know How to Do Anything"

22. Your Home and Public Libraries   192

Where to Find Books – Building Shelves — Public Libraries — A Tale of Two Libraries — More Than Books — Build Your Library (At Taxpayer Expense)

23. Hanging Laundry   200

Lines and Pins – How to Hang Clothes – Winter Laundry – Differences In Hanging Laundry – Racking Laundry

24. Mongo and Obtainium   212

Stalking the Wild Trash Collector — Leave It Better Than You Found It

25. Soil Building   215

Turning Dirt Into Soil – Feed First, Then Plant – Living Off Compost – Handling Leaves – How To Start Building Your Soil – Growing Cover Crops – Put Your Soil To The Test – Soil Types

26. Water Storage   226

Emergency Storage – Efficiency and Cutting Water Waste – Fixing Faucets, Toilets, and Pipes — Getting On a Water Diet — The Three Types of Water — Collecting Water — Long-Range and Long-Term Water Storage

27. Diverting Water From Your Basement   238

Solving One Problem Revealed Another – Attacking the Problem From Outside –

The Magic of Drylok – The Return of the Seepage – Sticking the Landing — Give Your House a Checkup

28. Grocery Shopping and Food Storage   249
Your Ideal Grocery Store – Learning How to Cook – The Recipe For Beating the House – Keeping a Price Book – Relying On the Pantry Principle – The Truth Behind Food Expiration – Basic Grocery Shopping – A Typical Shopping Week – The Devil In the Small Print – Playing the Showcase Game – Win Friends at the Service Desk – Getting Gas – Jedi-Master Shopping – Protecting Yourself – A Place For Your Food – Kitchen Cabinets – A Fresh Look For the Pantry — Rethinking Space

29. Cooking From Scratch   277
The Curse of Uncrustables – Scratch Cooking – Learning How to Cook – Expanding Your Repertoire – Not All You Cook You Will Eat

30. Sewing and Mending   289
The Way We Used to Sew — The Price of Cheap – The Case For Sewing – Start With Repairs – The Next Stage: Creative Sewing – Making Clothes – Sew What? – The Hunt For Fabric – Sewing As Personal Expression – Why You Should Sew

31. Sleep   308
The Need for Sleep – The Best Way to Sleep – The Problem With Partners – More Ways to Fall Asleep

32. Exercise   317
Getting Serious – Adding Exercises to Your Chores – Time to Exercise – Is a Gym Worth It? – A Year Later – Another Year Later

33. Dental Care   329
How to Brush Your Teeth – Visit the Dentist – Your Teeth and Your Future

34. In-Depth Goal Setting   333
Bibliography
About the Author

Introduction

Making a Bargain With Omelas

THIS BOOK BEGAN AS A SERIES of blog posts. I called it *Fortress Peschel* as that amused me. Every Saturday, another section was posted online for the world to ignore.

When I wrote those posts, I did not go into detail about my religious beliefs; my feelings about the world being greater than what we see around us, that unseen world just around the corner that you can never quite reach. The world, that is, on the other side of the mirror, here and yet not here, a world that has to be taken on faith.

I think about it daily. Those beliefs color the philosophical underpinnings that make up *Fed, Safe & Sheltered*.

More and more, as I get older, I want less and less. I do not feel the need to backpack through the Himalayas. I don't want to own multiple houses. I have no desire to jet around the world, seeing quaint, indigenous natives displayed for my entertainment like zoo animals. They lead their own lives and do not need me staring at them.

I like a simpler life. I want less, I use less, and I need less. This can be freeing. In the immortal words of John Michael Greer, known online as the Archdruid: LESS. Less energy, less stuff, and less stimulation.

Having LESS means I can pay more attention to what matters, and I can enjoy what I have rather than wanting more than I need. Supposedly, one of the secrets of happiness is to learn to be happy with what you have and what you can achieve.

If I cannot be happy unless I'm batting clean-up for the Yankees, then I will never be happy. Batting clean-up for the Yankees, like being a prima ballerina, an astronaut, or an opera singer, will never happen for me.

If I want things I cannot have, I am going to be very unhappy. I'll make myself miserable, and I won't enhance the happiness of the people around me. However, if I can be happy with my quiet life of writing, sewing, gardening, and living in my small town with my family, then I have a very good shot at being happy.

The problem is that we are encouraged to be unhappy with what we have. Our economy demands that we buy more stuff, consume more services, and throw away perfectly good items. Our society belittles saving money and rewards broadcasting our status via our purchases whether they are the tea we drink or the vacations we take.

All of that stuff saps our energy and that of the world. It takes energy to make, energy to ship, energy to buy, and energy to work to earn the money to buy more stuff. Then it takes more energy to use our stuff, store it, maintain it, and finally, the energy to say, on holding up, say, that old-fashioned, outdated cell-phone – the one that doesn't allow you to talk to people on Mars – "I need a new one but what will I do with this one?"

Think about that cell phone. If you get a shiny, new smartphone, what happens to the old one? It still works. Recycle it? Sure, why not. Just drop it off at the recycling center when they do Electronics Collection Day and forget about it.

But where does the old cell phone go? This object, that was once so new, is made of hundreds of tiny parts. It cannot be repaired easily or updated, and it cannot be easily disassembled.

This object, like so many others in our lives, was made by slave labor in China, under the filthiest of conditions, polluting their land in a way that would never be acceptable in the United States. It is made of complex materials, many of them rare earths that were mined with picks and shovels and heavily laced with the blood of those miners, and devastating the environment now and for generations to come.

Garments are the same. Clothing used to be valuable, expensive, carefully repaired, and passed along. Now, we throw an unwanted shirt away, unworn, with the tags still on it.

Why is clothing so cheap? Because it is made essentially by forced labor. I know damn well how long it takes to make a button-up, long-sleeved collared shirt. It takes hours. Sewing the thirteen buttons on the placket, collar, and cuffs takes me a good half-hour alone.

How can that shirt cost less than $25?

If I were to make a shirt, starting with cutting out the pattern pieces from fabric, it would take me four or five hours. If I sewed shirts on a regular basis, I'd get faster at piecing the sections together and attaching the collar, cuffs, and placket, but not that much faster.

Garment factories have specialized cutters and machine operators who each do one task. They're very fast. They are paid about 39¢ an hour. In the United States, we'd like to make at least minimum wage, say seven or eight bucks an hour.

We'd also like bathroom breaks, a lunch break, and to work on a factory floor that isn't a health hazard. We'd like a sick day or two, even a vacation day. We'd like to work in a clean factory that doesn't poison the neighborhood.

However, our economic choices dictate that it's too expensive to manufacture clothing and other products under those conditions, pay people a living wage, and offer reasonably safe working conditions, so we export those jobs overseas. In return, we get back clothing, electronics, and all kinds of other stuff, for far less than it would cost to make here.

Isn't that wonderful? We spend so little to fill our houses and our lives with stuff, but we never count the cost. After all, nobody wants to pay more than the rock-bottom minimum, and nobody we know works in those factories.

I first learned this lesson in the early 1980s in the drapery department at Boscov's department store. We sold gorgeous embroidered sheer panels at two price ranges. One was very expensive. One was astonishingly cheap. I would routinely have customers ask me about the embroidered panels. They would balk at the price. They would ask for cheaper ones. Then they would ask which ones were made in the United States.

It was the more expensive ones, of course; the ones made by workers who had clean, safe working conditions and were paid a living wage. The other ones, just as pretty and one-third the cost, were made by Chinese prison labor. I and the other sales staff always told the customers this.

No matter what people said about preserving jobs in the United States and buying American-made, when they stood at the cash register, they bought the Chinese prison labor panels. They chose the short-term goal of lower cost for themselves over the job security and happiness of workers who they did not know.

They made their Omelas bargain.

Don't get me wrong. I like modern life. I like wearing clean clothes and living in a house that keeps the winter winds and summer heat at bay. I like driving somewhere in twenty minutes that would take hours to walk to. I like eating food that other people have grown, shipped in from across the country and the world.

Those are very pleasant options. I've read Ruth Goodman's *How to Be a Tudor* and the amount of work those people did every day just to eat is astounding. I don't want to live like that. I like many things about our lives. However, I try very hard to not lose sight of the underpinnings that support our lives of comfort and plenty.

This is where the Omelas bargain comes in. I learned about Ursula K. Le Guin's story from the Archdruid's weekly blog post (www.ecosophia.net). A historian of the first water, he can be very, very conservative, in the old meaning of the word: when you needed a compelling reason for changing what you were doing since something new and shiny and untested might have bad consequences. Traditional peasant cultures were very conservative. When you have little margin for error, and every spring brings with it the risk of famine beyond the routine hunger, you learn to be careful about changing what you know works pretty well.

The story, "The Ones Who Walk Away from Omelas," concerns the citizens of the shining, perfect, beautiful city on the hill and the bargain they make to keep their wonderful, easy lives. In exchange for this perfection, one chosen child is tormented daily almost to death; a child that begs for release, cries for mercy from its captors and receives none.

The citizens of Omelas know about this and most of them are okay with one child's permanent misery paying for everyone else's happiness. The needs of the many outweigh the needs of the few, right? Not everyone can swallow this bargain, and those are the people who walk away. Interestingly, the citizens who walk away don't do anything to help that miserable child. They just go somewhere else.

If you are a fan of *Doctor Who*, you've seen the Omelas bargain in action. The second episode of the fifth season, "The Beast Below," appears to be inspired by Le Guin's story. Matt Smith, as the good Doctor, comes up with a solution to the problem, which the residents of Omelas never do. Unfortunately, we do not have the Doctor in his blue box coming to our rescue. We have to clean up our own mess.

There is no avoiding the Omelas bargain in our culture. We're surrounded by the fruits of other people's labor made under dreadful conditions, but since they take place far, far away, we don't feel for them. So what do you do: embrace the bargain or leave?

We find a third way, and that is to use LESS: less energy, less stuff, and less stimulation.

The third way is to question why I should be mindlessly buying. The third way is to not waste the resources I use. The third way is to give my time and resources so others can share in the wealth of the United States. The third way is to garden and landscape so that I provide habitat on my quarter-acre city lot for my fellow critters. The third way is to shop locally, so my money stays in my community. The third way is to buy locally produced items, so those jobs stay in my community.

Does this mean I buy less? It does. Do I avoid much of our consumer culture? I do that too. Not having a television hooked up to the outside world helps.

Does this contribute to our goal of Financial Independence? It surely does. Spending less means more money can be earmarked towards more important goals.

Does using less make the environment around me a touch better? I think it does. If our one car is sitting in our driveway rather than being used for random errands, I am not polluting the air with its emissions, I'm not clogging the roads, and I'm not burning precious fossil fuels.

It's like that story, "The Star Thrower," a 1969 essay by anthropologist and educator Loren Eiseley, about throwing starfish back into the ocean after the storm. You cannot save them all, but you can save some.

Does this moral stance make life worse for sweatshop workers in the Third World? I don't know, but I'm sure not helping by buying disposable fashion, either. The price I pay does not translate into money for the seamstresses, and it wastes huge amounts of resources.

Whenever you hold something that was manufactured outside the First World, you can bet the conditions under which it was made were horrendous and that few Americans would tolerate them.

Interestingly, we have Third World conditions in the United States. Think of the fieldworkers picking those strawberries, packing those tomatoes, harvesting that fresh spring mix. Agricultural work is hard, stoop labor. To get those amazingly cheap prices you see down at the grocery store for fresh produce, you have to use plantation labor. People my age may remember Cesar Chavez and his grape boycotts. I do not believe he would be impressed by the improvements in working conditions.

Your local farmer's market is less likely to have those issues than the giant mega-farms that supply supermarkets. At least you can ask about working conditions and when you buy from the farmer, you put more money in his pocket so he can pay his pickers a bit more.

That unending race to the bottom, to pay the least possible amount, drives wages down. Unending population growth and open-borders immigration drives wages down as more people compete for fewer jogs. Automation drives wages down as more people compete for still fewer jobs. Off-shoring factories drives wages down as the jobs get fewer still for the people left behind who need them.

It isn't a good idea for a country to have a growing population at the same time that jobs get fewer and fewer. This is why I refuse to use self-checkouts. I go into the bank and use a teller. I use the call lines rather than the internet when I have a question or a problem with a company. Every time you use a self-serve line, you are sending a message to corporate headquarters to get rid of another job.

I understand that their employment affects what I pay. I understand, boy do I, about pinching every penny. However, if I need less, then I can spend just a little bit more to buy my paint at the local paint store instead of the big box hardware store.

The Omelas bargain never ends. How much of your life has to be supported on the misery of unseen others across an ocean? There is no good answer.

This is where we, as a culture, decide that we want what we use to be long lasting and repairable. The problem with that decision is that less money changes hands. If I buy a toaster that lasts twenty years, then I'm not buying another and another and another.

However, if everything is made to be long lasting and repairable, even if it costs more upfront, it saves money and resources downstream. If we choose to use less, to not replace our dishes on a regular basis, then we need to spend less money over the long haul.

If we rework our tax laws to reward businesses for hiring people and punish them for automating jobs out of existence, then we would have more jobs. That would certainly be a good thing, as people need to work and have a purpose in life.

Sitting on one's ass on the dole doesn't turn many of its recipients into musicians, artists, and poets. Think about trust fund babies. You read about the dissipation, drug use, and mental illnesses among those heirs who never had to work a day in their lives. The scions of the rich don't seem to become musicians, artists, and poets, yet those people get more education and opportunities than most of us will ever see.

Would spending much less money on products because they last a long time and can be repaired change the economy? Oh boy would it ever.

As I mentioned earlier, our economy is built on dissatisfaction. Why else would you replace your dishes? A set of china should last, barring dropping them on the floor, until the next ice age. Dishes don't go bad. They don't wear out. Why do you replace your dishes? Usually, because you're tired of your old ones, that's why.

I did replace my dishes many years ago, and I wrote about it in the chapter on organization. I replaced my old mismatched dishes by adding to the set we already had. I did not buy new ones; I bought old ones from a china match service.

Life under a sustainable economy would be very, very different, but I believe it is necessary. We should employ people and not machines. Automation should be used to make the job safer and less backbreaking, but after that, why use robots when people need jobs? Robots don't need jobs.

Robots and automation are a choice our corporate masters make, aided by the politicians they buy with campaign donations, so they don't have to accommodate the needs of human beings. They choose profits over people, when it should be the other way around.

If we all did this, there would be more jobs for people, products would last longer, and wages would rise a bit. Seamstresses in China getting 39¢ an hour might receive 49¢ an hour, a 25% increase in pay. They might even work in cleaner factories and get a sick day now and then.

I cannot save the world, but I can make my little part of it better and greener. I can try hard to use my share more sensibly without making it worse for someone else.

What I won't do is pretend that my choices are consequence-free and cause no harm. I won't pretend that my green life is green, when the pollution generated at the rechargeable battery factory is out of sight in China. That pollution is still there, and it will be for a long, time. The people who live and work there get to suffer so I can have a nicer life. All I can do is to use less and use what I have responsibly.

1

Mission Statement

*F*ED, SAFE & SHELTERED: *Protect Your Family & Thrive Amid Tough Times* is intended to help you prepare for a decline in America that has been accelerating since the recession of 2008.

Fed, Safe & Sheltered is primarily a collection of essays about my philosophies and thoughts. It is not a how-to guide about raising and butchering chickens, nor do I spend time on what kinds of guns to buy. There are far more knowledgeable people out there who cover those topics in depth. I will, however, list a few of my favorite resources to use during your journey to become more self-sufficient.

I am more interested in talking about why you should make your life stronger. I want you, dear reader, to be more motivated about getting off the couch and getting to work.

It is very easy to read about what to do. Getting up and doing those tasks is harder. I have plenty of books on sewing, quilting, cooking, and gardening to prove that reading is easier than doing. It is safer too. You are so much less likely to make mistakes. You don't get dirty. You don't waste (too) much money.

When I do write a "how-to essay," it will be on topics that I have not seen addressed elsewhere: how to maximize your home's natural light, the specifics of placing hedges and fences, or how to perform the Window Dance.

My hope is that after you read *Fed, Safe & Sheltered*, you'll be more motivated to do things you've been thinking about doing.

Do not wait too long. The winds of change are picking up. They are growing into a storm of biblical proportions that will affect every one of us and our families. We don't know what the future will bring except that it will be more challenging, more difficult, poorer, and harder in every way.

The question you should always ask yourself is: What do I want to do to make sure my family, my friends, and my neighbors get through these storms, relatively intact, and pass to the other side? You will not survive these storms unscathed. You can try to limit the damage.

So let's get started! I have a mission statement to encapsulate what I want to achieve.

The goal of Fortress Peschel is to be:
- Energy efficient
- Cost effective
- Financially Independent (so important we capitalized it!)
- Self-supporting
- Part of the community
- True green (not a greenie weenie)
- Sustainable
- Able to age in place
- Prepared for zombie attacks, because if you are ready for zombies, you are ready for anything!

To quote that famous crazy fascist poet Ezra Pound in his *ABC of Economics*:

"The minute I cook my own dinner or nail four boards together in a chair, I escape from the whole cycle of Marxian economics. I know, not from theory, but from practice, that you can live infinitely better with a very little money and a lot of spare time, than with more money and less time. Time is not money but it is almost everything else."

You don't have to be a weatherman to know that the wind is blowing. Act on that knowledge now rather than wait for the tempest.

2

Goal Setting

How to Set Your Goals — Choosing Your Goals — Getting Your Honey Onboard — A Lifetime of Goals

GOALS ARE A ROAD MAP TO THE FUTURE. We spend a lot of time at Fortress Peschel considering them. While sitting on our salvaged couch in the Florida room watching the fireflies come out, we discuss our hopes, fears, and concerns.

If you do not set goals, you drift like a leaf in the stream.

So if you want Financial Independence, a smaller ecological footprint, the ability to cope better with any disaster including economic turmoil, a house you can age in, and to set a good example for your children, then you had better get planning.

Failing to plan means you plan to fail.

Of course, plans can and do collapse upon meeting reality. Don't make that your excuse for not planning. At least you thought about what might happen. Failure is always an option because the universe does not care about what you want. No one plans to have a tornado strike or cancer or a car accident. The rain falls upon the rich and poor alike, but the rich have better roofs.

Planning ahead gives you breathing space when bad stuff happens. This means considering what-if scenarios and role-playing possible responses. What if your area suffered an earthquake or a tornado? What if you lost your job? What would you do? The idea is that you should hope for the best and plan for the worst. Experience taught us that what happens will be somewhere in between.

HOW TO SET YOUR GOALS

Mindfulness and awareness should be your mantra. Is what I am doing in accordance with my goals, both short- and long-term? Do my actions agree with my values? Will I be better or worse off if I don't do them? If what I am doing or not doing makes my life tougher, why am I doing it?

Goals are easy to say but hard to achieve. We struggle with it every day. But it is still worthwhile, because any progress makes us better off.

Let's look at our goals again:
- Energy efficient
- Cost effective
- Financially Independent
- Self-supporting
- Part of the community
- True green (not a greenie weenie)
- Sustainable
- Able to age in place
- Prepared for zombie attacks, because if you are ready for zombies, you are ready for anything!

These goals interlock and support each other. Being energy efficient means less money spent. Less money spent means getting closer to Financial Independence. Less energy used means being greener and more sustainable. Needing less money means it is easier to be self-supporting.

Everything we do ourselves means less money spent and more useful skills learned and being more self-supportive. Being able to age in place means less money is needed for expensive nursing home care. Being involved in the community through social groups and pass-along networks means more support and security for us.

True green means doing the hard work: turning down the thermostat (less money spent, less $$ sent to terrorists), growing our own fruit and veggies (less money spent, fewer carbon miles, more sustainable), staying off airplanes and visiting faraway places (less money spent, less air pollution, less climate change).

I considered my list of goals carefully. They all had to build upon each other, reinforce each other and lead, eventually, to Financial Independence. Dear Husband and I spent a long time talking about what we wanted as a couple. Then we figured out what to do to get there.

For example, when we moved into our latest (and I hope last)

Goal Setting

home, we knew we wanted to refurbish and renovate it. We created a long master list of home improvements, yard upgrades, and financial goals. As projects were finished, they were checked off. Attic insulated? Check. Raised beds built? Check. Lever doorknobs installed on every door? Check. Savings plans in place? Check. Kitchen cabinets repainted and D-handles installed? Check. New sheet vinyl on the floors and in the cabinets? Still on the list.

The lesson here is not to make a list for everything, but use the list idea for tasks that need them. For example, if you want to save money through your company's 401(k) program, all you may need to do is tell the HR department. That goes on the list. They do the work.

CHOOSING YOUR GOALS

Here is a thought experiment: Consider these questions. Warning: these are unpleasant. These are the thoughts that wake you up at 3 a.m., or pursue you after the hammer has fallen and you lost your job, or your spouse wants a divorce. But here and now, safe in your home, employed, healthy (I hope), even optimistic, ask yourself:

Are you living the values you say are important?

Do you have a will? Have you stored in safety deposit box paperwork such as marriage and birth certificates, titles to your cars, and the mortgage to your house? Can you easily find your bank statements, insurance policies, and retirement paperwork? Do you have copies in your home filing cabinet, and in Ziploc bags in your freezer (if your house burns down, the freezer will probably survive). If you die unexpectedly, the executor of your estate will thank you for making their job easier.

Do you have a week's worth of food in your pantry? How about a three-day minimum of stored water at a gallon per person per day?

Do you have good relationships with your neighbors? They will be the ones to phone the fire department when you're away and your house catches fire.

Do you vote? Do you send emails and letters to your congresscritter or local representative telling them what concerns you? They keep track of their mail.

Do you participate in your community? Even small, kind acts such as driving at a safe speed, keeping your sidewalks clean of snow, and clearing the debris from the storm drain in front of your house improves everyone's life, as well as sparing damage to the infrastructure (paid for by your taxes).

Are you debt-free? Do you have money in the bank and emergency savings if you lose your job? How is your retirement fund?

How much exercise do you get? Do you take responsibility for your health? Do you watch your diet and floss your teeth daily? Your health matters as you cannot take care of your family if you don't take care of yourself.

Have you learned new skills instead of playing *World of Warcraft*? Pushing your mind into unfamiliar areas keeps it sharp and lively.

Is it damaging to your life if you cut back on the booze, tobacco, gambling, pornography, and drug abuse?

Can you distinguish between needs and wants, and do you know when to say no?

Will doing the above make your existence worse? Or will your life be easier to manage when problems arise?

Hour by hour and day by day, our actions build up to where we are today.

GETTING YOUR HONEY ONBOARD

However, to get everything done, you and your partner must pull together as a team. A reliable, hardworking partner who shares your goals should be cherished and appreciated.

Unfortunately, not every couple thinks alike.

If you and your spouse have radically different dreams – you want a paid-for house and he wants a new car every other year plus expensive overseas vacations – you will have many problems. Unless you are very, very rich, there won't be enough money for those wonderful luxuries. Trying to have it all, paying for everything on credit, and then becoming a debt slave is a terrible solution and not one that will improve your marriage.

Or do you not know your partner's mind at all? If not, it is time to find out. You must have these conversations with your partner or you risk working at cross-purposes and never going anywhere except divorce court.

What do you do if your spouse won't cooperate?

Spouse conversion is possible but not easy. I have a chapter on the subject so I'll just say here that the key is in how you phrase an issue. Your partner doesn't care about climate change? He may care about spending less money. Is your partner indifferent to energy efficiency? She may care about sending fewer $$$ overseas to fund terrorists. Is your spouse afraid of looking and feeling poor? Becoming a debt slave to Visa may change that mind.

Emphasize the positive side of your goals. Where do you want to go with your life? To be snowbirds, to travel the world, to retire at age 53, to never have to set foot off your property again unless you want to?

If they're amiable to talking about it, pick your long- and short-term goals and figure out what you need to do to accomplish them. Write them down and post the list where you can see it every day.

Once they're up, you will be able to decide which ones to tackle first. Some tasks are easy and quick, such as diverting ten bucks automatically from your weekly paycheck into a savings account. Other things take time: building soil, learning to garden, and then learning how to cook, eat, and preserve your harvest. Checking jobs off as you complete them will show your partner that you are making progress.

A LIFETIME OF GOALS

With your goals established, do not expect the skies to open up, angels to descend and the road home to be paved with gold. Some days, a big project will be finally finished. Most days, you will tread water and put out fires, and take only tiny steps towards reaching a goal. If the best you can do is basic maintenance, congratulate yourself on at least doing that.

Be patient. Over time, and as you complete tasks, you can cross off old goals and add new ones. Then you can look over your list of finished tasks and see that you have taken control of your future. You'll feel amazingly good about it, and that will encourage you to press onwards.

3

Everyone Agrees That You Need To Do These Things

Get In Shape — Get Out of Debt — Get Your Paperwork in Order — Quit Your Addictions—Keep Food on Hand — Reskill, Reskill, Reskill — Improve Your Health — Fix Your House — Grow Some of Your Own Food — Store Water — Pay Attention — Form a Community — Get Started

THERE ARE A LOT OF THEORIES OVER HOW the world will end: economic disaster, electromagnetic pulse (natural or manmade), zombies, asteroids, super-volcanoes, foreign invasion, nuclear war, the next ice-age, massive earthquakes, pandemics, the moon crashing into the earth, or all of the opposite sex disappearing at once. Whatever the disaster, someone somewhere has written a novel about it.

Every politician and activist on the political spectrum has their fears about the future and the dreadful events that might happen if "they" don't take control, keeping us safe. And yet, there is a surprising amount of agreement on what people should do to be prepared for any disaster, even zombies. After all, if you are ready for zombies, you are ready for anything! There is actually a website that advocates for disaster preparedness in case the undead arise. Learn more at the Zombie Squad (www.zombiehunters.org), including the location of the nearest zombie-hunting chapter.

So what does everyone agree on?

GET IN SHAPE

If you are in poor physical condition, you cannot cope as well with problems. If you never walk farther than from your car to your TV chair, you will not be able to evacuate a building quickly when terrorists fly an airplane into it. Whatever shape you are in now, you can improve your physical fitness. Start slow, start small, and walk a little farther each day.

Although I am still overweight, after several years of exercising, I am in much better shape than I was. I started with five sit-ups a day, and I worked up to 150 crunches every day. I walk daily with my dog. I do a mix of the Royal Canadian Air Force exercise program, along with yoga, back exercises, and running in place.

Gym rats may sneer, but my program works for me. Despite what you read in health and fitness magazines, the best exercise program is the one you are willing to do every day.

GET OUT OF DEBT

It does not matter what dreadful event falls upon your household. They are easier to manage if you do not have to worry about bills and money. Car falls apart? Daughter breaks both legs? House burns down? Get laid off? No debt and money in the bank make everything easier to cope with. Do not believe for one minute that the collapse of the world economy will make your debts disappear. If zombies appear, debt collection agencies will hire them to collect from you.

Start with *The Complete Tightwad Gazette* by Amy Dacyczyn and any of Dave Ramsey's money books. Save dollars with Amy and then use Dave's debt-snowball program to pay off everything you owe. Cut your expenses enough, and you can work on food storage and weather-stripping your house while still paying off your debts.

GET YOUR PAPERWORK IN ORDER

Do you have a will? Where is the title to your car? The deed to your house? Birth certificates for yourself and your children? Marriage license, insurance policies, 401(k)s, Roth IRAs, pension plans, divorce papers, discharge forms from the military, websites and passwords, copies of all your account numbers, both for bills you pay and for places where you stow any form of money?

Can you put your hands on these papers?

Keep the originals in a safety deposit box — above the flood line as victims of hurricanes Katrina and Sandy will attest — and copies in your go-box so you can prove identity and ownership if you need to evacuate. You may also want copies in your filing cabinet and in a Ziploc bag in the freezer. Tell trusted family members where to find them so if you die suddenly, they don't have to go on a scavenger hunt. If you have gold, diamonds, or big wads of cash hidden in the heating vents, make sure the treasure map is also in your safety deposit box.

QUIT YOUR ADDICTIONS

If you absolutely have to have something, whether it is coffee or cocaine, then you need to prepare for a time when deliveries are cut off. Whatever happens, your fix will be harder to get. It will certainly cost more. Alcohol, tobacco, gambling (including lottery tickets), drugs, or pornography do not make you healthier. They waste money you could be spending on debt repayment, insulation, and food storage.

If you are considering growing tobacco or brewing beer after the apocalypse, do not get hooked on your product. Also, think about the desperate people who will want it. People with addictions will let their children go cold, hungry, ragged, and barefoot rather than give up that bottle or needle. Folks with addictions may not be reliable, upstanding citizens who will work hard to make life better. Is this behavior you want to encourage in your community?

Think about this before you start growing poppies (*papaver somniferium* to be precise) in your back garden to sell as opium to the neighborhood and herbalist for pain medication. Addicts may visit your house, too.

KEEP FOOD ON HAND

Every time the blizzard or hurricane comes, the grocery stores are mobbed and their shelves stripped. A typical grocery store carries only a few days' worth of food. They are resupplied daily from huge warehouses. Do not be that person standing in line with your hungry children, waiting for the National Guard to throw you a bag of MREs.

Keep a week's worth of food on hand *that you and your family will eat*.

Build up this surplus by buying a few extra cans every week of soup, beans, peanut butter, and cereal; the food you eat every day.

Once you regularly keep a week ahead on the groceries, move up to keeping two weeks ahead. Then three weeks. Aim for a month's worth of groceries. If a family member is laid off, you can still put food on the table for a few weeks while you make plans.

RESKILL, RESKILL, RESKILL

The more you know how to do, the easier you can cope with unexpected problems. If your sole cooking technique consists of calling for takeout, then you need to learn. If you throw away a garment because of a split seam, you need to learn how to sew. If you hire someone to replace a doorknob, you need some home handyman skills.

Can you check the fluids in your car? Put air in your tires? Change a tire? Use a handsaw, pliers, and screwdrivers? Can you get up on a roof safely, lay down a tarp, and re-tar after a storm has ripped off all your shingles? You may not be able to reroof your house, but you should be able to keep the rain out until you hire a roofer.

Think about what your grandparents knew how to do. Think how you would manage if your income was cut in half. Being able to do more tasks yourself means having to lay out less money for others to do it for you.

IMPROVE YOUR HEALTH

This goes hand in hand with getting in shape and quitting your addictions. Many health problems are related to lifestyle. Obesity, being sedentary, and tobacco and alcohol abuse contribute to poorer health. Eat a better diet with more fruit and veg and fewer Cheetos and soda, and you will feel better.

Second, get enough sleep. For most people, this is about eight hours a night. Sleep is vital to your health, both physical and mental. Poor sleep or not enough sleep will make everything harder to manage.

Ask your doctor what you could be doing to get healthier and then do it. If you take prescription medication, ask what lifestyle changes you could make to reduce this need. Struggling with diabetes? Arthritis and joint pain? High blood pressure? Exercise and weight loss will help them all.

Take care of your teeth. Like your eyes and ears, your teeth never get better. They only get worse. Dental pain can be never-ending and even life-threatening if you get a bad abscess. Get your teeth fixed now and commit to rinsing, flossing, rinsing, and brushing after every meal.

Have your eyes checked and get a spare pair of glasses for when the first pair breaks. Some people prefer wearing photo-gray lenses that act like built-in sunglasses to protect their eyes. Wear safety glasses when doing anything that might injure your eyes. You can't get a replacement set down at the hospital.

FIX YOUR HOUSE

Your house should be safe, secure, paid for, contain space for food production and storage, and be well sealed against the weather. If you are a renter, think about where you want to live permanently and start saving money for a house. If you live in an unsafe neighborhood far from reliable family and friends, then you need to consider why you are living there.

The goal of basic home security is to get the casual smash-and-grab burglars to go elsewhere. Like most people, burglars do not want to work hard; they will rob the easier houses. Don't let your home be one of them. For more information, see the chapter on Basic Home and Personal Security.

GROW SOME OF YOUR OWN FOOD

You can cut back on many expenses, but eating isn't one of them. You also don't want to wait until disaster strikes. The worst time to learn how to grow food is when your children are starving.

You do not have to grow everything you and your family will eat; you can easily supplement your grocery store purchases with your lettuces and tomatoes. Work up from a few herbs and peppers to as large a plot as you can manage, either on your property or in a community garden plot. Anything you grow will add nutrients and variety to your diet and improve your gardening skills.

STORE WATER

Even more important than food is water. You cannot live without it. Keep on hand at least the Red Cross minimum: one gallon of water per person per day for a minimum of three days, plus extra for your animals. If you have the space, store more. Keep your water cool, dry, and in the dark.

Once you have the minimum stashed, look into catching and storing water in your topsoil, rain barrels and cubes, even cisterns and ponds if you're ambitious. Can you drill a well on your property?

A well and a hand pump equal permanent water security.

PAY ATTENTION

Know what is going on around you. Look at your surroundings, and see what is happening. I walk my dog daily and watch for changes in my neighborhood. I find money on the ground and reusable items for my home. I interact with my neighbors. If I were plugged into an iPod, this would not happen. People have been hit by trains because they were too focused on their smartphones. Don't let this happen to you.

Pay attention to weather reports. Nobody should be surprised by a hurricane or a big winter storm. The National Weather Service gives several days' notice when a big storm is on the way. This gives you time to board up your house, stock up on supplies, and fill the gas tank. This is much more important than paying attention to Kardashians.

Watch the news. Is there trouble in the Middle East? Gas prices may jump so you want to be prepared for the extra cost. Bank runs? Keep cash on hand. Freezing weather in the coffee plantations? Store extra coffee and ride out the price spike.

The universe tends to punish people who drift. Car accidents, kitchen disasters, home-improvement mishaps, and industrial accidents: Anything can happen because of someone's inattention. Don't let that someone be you.

FORM A COMMUNITY

Everyone needs to be part of a group. Life is much easier when you can call on family and friends to help you. Get to know your neighbors. They don't have to know the size of your pantry or your arsenal, but they should recognize you as belonging in the neighborhood.

Encourage your family and friends to be better prepared. Even if all they do is follow the minimum Red Cross guidelines, they will be better able to cope. That makes it easier on you, when you don't have to assume a dozen people will show up unexpectedly. To start the conversation, a very nice Christmas gift could be the book *Just in Case* by Kathy Harrison.

Are you part of a church group? A fraternal order? A sewing circle? A civics group? A scout troop? Are you an active part of your community? That will help when disaster strikes, as the people living in your town are most likely to help you.

With family, friends, and co-workers, the topic of what to do in a disaster may come up during conversation. Use this teachable moment to talk about how to prepare for a big winter storm, an earthquake, or a hurricane. Don't mention zombies or economic collapse, however, if you suspect they'll start seeing you in a tin-foil hat.

Let preparedness flow from you like a wave: you, your immediate family, your relatives, your friends, your neighbors, your co-workers, your community, and your country. The more people who have food storage, skills, fewer addictions, and more resilience, the easier it will be for your town to recover from a disaster.

GET STARTED

At some point, you'll have to stop reading and thinking about what you are going to do. It is time to get your hands dirty and go to work. Recognize that you will fail sometimes. All skills have learning curves and require practice. Projects that work on paper may not work in the real world. You try and you try and you try and often, you fail. Then you get back to work and try some more.

So this is what everyone agrees on. It does not matter what awful things might happen or which group of nuts you are most concerned about. Get started on your life changes, and you and your family will be better off.

Finally, remember that list of disasters I ticked off at the beginning of the chapter? If you are wondering "who writes those kind of books?" check out the examples I like below.

Alien invasion: *The Puppet Masters* by Robert Heinlein (1951) and *Footfall* by Larry Niven and Jerry Pournelle (1985)
Asteroids: *Lucifer's Hammer* by Larry Niven and Jerry Pournelle (1977)
Economic collapse: *Noah's Castle* by John Rowe Townsend (1975) and *Into the Forest* by Jean Hegland (1996)
Electromagnetic pulse: *Last Light, The Reformation* series by Terri Blackstock (2005) and *One Second After* by William Forstchen (2009)
Foreign invasion: *Tomorrow, When the War Began* by John Marsden (1993) and *How I Live Now* by Meg Rosoff (2004)
Grain blight: *No Blade of Grass* by John Christopher (1956)

Massive earthquakes: *A Wrinkle in the Skin* by John Christopher (1965)
Moon crashing into Earth: *Life as We Knew It, The Last Survivors* series by Susan Beth Pfeffer (2006)
Next ice-age: *The Long Winter* by John Christopher (1962)
Nuclear war: *Alas, Babylon* by Pat Frank (1959) and *Warday* by Whitley Strieber and James Kunetka (1984)
Opposite sex vanishing: *The Disappearance* by Philip Wylie (1951) and *Y: The Last Man* by Brian K. Vaughan and Pia Guerra (10-volume graphic novel, 2002)
Resource depletion: *Ill Wind* by Kevin J. Anderson (1995), *Last Light* by Alex Scarrow (2007) and *Slow Apocalypse* by John Varley (2012)
Pandemics: *Earth Abides* by George R. Stewart (1949) and *The Things That Keep Us Here* by Carla Buckley (2010)
Super-volcanoes: *Supervolcano* series by Harry Turtledove (2011)
Zombies: *World War Z: An Oral History of the Zombie War* by Max Brooks (2006) and *Rot and Ruin* series by Jonathan Maberry (2010)

4

Spouse Conversion; or, Becoming a Team

Can This Marriage Be Saved? — Train Your Spouse — Training By Example — The Why of Being Prepared — Explain and Praise

Dear Husband and I have done as well as we have because we work very well together as a team. We have similar goals, needs, wants, and desires. We agree to spend less than we earn to reach financial freedom. We want stuff, but not so much that it chokes us. Most importantly, we want to be able to choose the work we want to do. Heading in the same direction makes the life journey much smoother and easier.

We also do not have any of the killer bad habits and behaviors. Here's a partial list: gambling, pornography, alcoholism, drug addiction, adultery, abusiveness and anger management issues, control freakiness, spendthrift and shopaholic behavior, chronic meanness, pettiness, and disdain for each other, spitefulness, and contempt.

We don't avoid conflict, but we don't consider fighting a recreational sport, either. We like to talk and boy, do we! We consider ourselves very lucky to have found each other.

Being able to form a mutual support and admiration society has made our life infinitely easier. I have read advice columns for some forty years, and I am amazed at the neglect people will put up with from their partners and how spouses will undermine each other.

I wonder how anyone could believe that they could treat their family and friends as doormats and punching bags and then be surprised when family members estrange themselves and friends walk away forever. How can you belittle your partner and expect them to support your goals?

Spouse Conversion; or, Becoming a Team

As we move deeper into an uncertain future — the Long Emergency as James Howard Kunstler called it — being part of a reliable support network will become even more important.

Disaster preparedness groups such as FEMA and the Red Cross will tell you that the first person to come to your aid in a disaster is likely to be a family member or a neighbor. The bigger the disaster, the longer it takes for outside responders to ride to the rescue. Enormous disasters such as Hurricane Katrina overwhelmed the resources of professional responders and some people could not be helped for weeks.

As for the family sized disasters, you'll be on your own. If you and your partner got downsized and the benefits have run out, FEMA won't be there for you. It will be your relatives, if you are still on speaking terms with them.

It is easy to think that a disaster will be a hurricane or tornado or an earthquake. Yet the most likely disaster to happen to a household is economic or medical, such as job loss and debt, or sickness and injury.

Being at odds with your partner will not make any disruptions easier to manage. A partnership, which is what marriage should be, means you work together as a team towards a common set of goals. That's hard to do if you look at your partner and see that lazy bastard lounging on the couch or that bitch stomping around in the kitchen.

Are you working together? Or are you at loggerheads over the basic issues of spending, debt management, and trust? Are you somewhere in between?

CAN THIS MARRIAGE BE SAVED?

If you are dealing with the four A's of adultery, abandonment, abuse, and addiction, then you should be thinking very seriously about *why* you are spending precious life energy with this person. If you are the abuser, addict, adulterer, or abandoner, then you should not be anywhere near decent people until after you have fixed your behavioral and psychological problems.

If your problems are not as extreme as the four A's, then there is maneuvering room. Advice columnists advocate making a list of good and bad qualities leading to the decision of "am I better off with him or without him." Why did you pair off with this person? There must have been some reason. Look for it, and see what has changed. It may have been you. Do you look at your spouse with rage and contempt? Does she belittle your every action? Does he treat you with disdain or ignore what you're saying? Do you want to change, for life to be better, or do you just want out? What does your partner want? Do you know or are you guessing? Serious problems like this may require outside help.

Marriage counselors and therapists have helped many, many couples. Ministers and priests provide this service as well. You may have a friend or family member who is a good listener. Keeping a private journal of thoughts, fears, and concerns can help some people. These actions are considerably cheaper than divorce and far less traumatic. They also require effort and change on your part as well as that (maybe) of your spouse.

You cannot change your spouse. You have to give him or her reasons to change their behavior. Then they have to do that hard work.

You can only change yourself. Changes in your behavior can encourage changes in your partner's behavior. If you are dealing with a sane person and not an abusive psycho, then behavioral changes are possible and your relationship can get better. You can start pulling together as a team.

TRAIN YOUR SPOUSE

Think like a good dog trainer. They know dogs will work very hard for praise and a pat on the head. Cats, on the other hand, are motivated strictly by food rewards and only if they feel like it.

The key to effective dog training is consistency, clear expectations, repetition, and praise, praise, praise. Each learned behavior builds on previous learned behaviors. Complex actions are taught in increments. To learn how to lie down, the dog has to be taught to sit. After that, the dog can also be taught to stay and to offer its paw. Teach the dog how to lie down after that, and it can learn to roll over.

This isn't difficult to do, as long as you are willing to spend a lot of time and on an ongoing basis. You have to be clear in your expectations and not confuse the dog by asking it to obey too many commands at once. *You* have to be consistent in your actions and commands. "Sit" should only be used to get the dog to sit, not "down," "wait," "hold up," and "stop, dammit, I *mean it now!*" If you cannot be consistent, patient, and methodical, you will frustrate the two of you and the results will not be nearly as good as they could be.

People training is similar. Treat your partner (and your children, co-workers, family members, friends, etc.) with care and concern. Be considerate. Make your expectations clear. Practice what you preach. Follow through on your promises. Lead by example. Don't expect any member of your household to do any work you refuse to do.

Is this hard? Oh, God, yes. It also can be endlessly frustrating, especially when you can't seem to explain what you mean and no one listens because they are busy, tired, overwhelmed, and full of unresolved feelings, just like you.

Dog training is much easier. Dogs tend not to have mental issues like people do. They don't multitask. They get enough sleep and don't stress out over whether their fur is in season or if their doghouse has the latest game system. Dogs don't have mile-long to-do lists, jobs, homework, or commutes.

The only issue a dog has with training is you, your inconsistencies, and your poorly expressed expectations.

Since people do have all sorts of impediments to training – not the least of which is suspecting that you are using dog-training techniques on them – should you try? Of course! Do you want to be part of a successful team or not? Clarify in your own mind what you want out of your life and how you want to be better prepared to meet an uncertain future.

Start with how you handle money. So much cannot be done if there is no money, such as buying insulation or building a pantry. Debt means more stress and pressure, and if you or your spouse loses a job, you just multiplied the stress.

TRAINING BY EXAMPLE

Now comes the hard part of fixing or at least modifying your spendthrift spouse's ways. It is hard to change someone else's behavior without coercion and even harder to change someone's way of thinking.

You can modify your own behavior much more easily.

First, don't expect anyone to do what you won't do yourself. If you leave your clothes all over the floor, why should anyone else pick up theirs? If you buy whatever strikes your fancy, why should your partner rein in their spending?

If you are disorganized, random in your habits, refuse to plan trips to save on gas, won't reheat and eat leftovers, and turn up the thermostat in the winter to 70 degrees, then don't expect your partner to pick up the slack because *you* are concerned about resource depletion and waste.

If you want tidiness and refuse to tidy up yourself, the message being sent is that you are a control freak jerk who wants other people to clean up after you. This is not the message you want to send to your family.

If you want to cut down the debt load and build up the savings, first curb your spending. Set up an emergency fund if you don't have one and funnel savings into it. If your partner spends every extra penny on comic books and overpriced shoes, you may have to take over the bill paying.

An easy trick to show how money can add up is to get a gallon-sized glass jar and drop change into it, every day. Keep it out of sight. Find out how much your spouse spends daily on vending machine snackies and store-bought coffee. Put that amount into the jar, too. When your partner moans that she needs spare cash, present the jar, count the amount, and show how little expenses add up. Use the saved change to pay off a bill or stock the pantry.

This method can be surprisingly effective because many people have no imagination. They cannot understand until they see before their eyes that a dollar or two a day can add up to lots of dollars.

If you're a couple who keep your paychecks, bills, and other monies separate, then focus your energy on paying off your debts and building your emergency fund. Keep a ledger to prove that you succeeded at getting debt-free by not spending and saying no to temptation, and not by winning the lottery and hiding the money from your spouse.

While you are getting your financial house in order, stop ragging on your partner for their spendthrift ways. It doesn't work and creates resentment. Instead, mention in passing that you are cutting your spending to pay off your student loan.

Then, when the transmission falls out of your car, pay for the repairs out of your emergency fund rather than using your Visa card. When your spouse asks how you did this, tell them you stopped shopping for recreation and planned for just this eventuality.

THE WHY OF BEING PREPARED

The goal behind planning for the future — saving, getting debt-free, reskilling, becoming self-sufficient, being energy efficient, improving your health, and bettering relationships with other people – is long-term security for you and your loved ones. If you don't care where your future meals and lodging are coming from, then you might as well drift along. It is a lot less work.

Does your partner know and understand why you want to turn down the thermostat and put on a sweater? You must lay out your reasons and not in an accusatory, unpleasant way. Unless your spouse is a mind reader, then he won't know why you want a fully stocked pantry.

You should explain to him that you want to be better prepared for disruptions at the grocery store because of hurricanes like Katrina and Sandy, tornados, earthquakes, blizzards, ice storms, and other natural disasters. Your list of natural disasters will vary depending on your location; no one in Florida will believe you are prepping for an earthquake, but they understand hurricanes. Any area with a winter is vulnerable to ice storms and extended power outages.

These are easy reasons to explain and easy for most people to understand. "I want our family to be better prepared, just like the Red Cross and FEMA recommend."

If your partner has trouble even conceiving that anything bad could ever happen, then you can turn to the media. Seeing or reading detailed scenarios can really clarify to the non-imaginative person why you want to store extra food. Disaster movies, TV shows, and novels can be great teaching aids for disaster preparedness. Observe and comment on the poor communication skills and lack of preparedness being shown and ask your partner if they would know what to do if the power went out for a week in January. A good novel like William Forstchen's *One Second After* can illustrate what-ifs in an easy-to-understand way. The author's scenarios more than compensate for your partner's lack of imagination.

But what if my spouse says that preparing for problems invites them to happen?

This is magical thinking. It's like saying that you don't won't make a will since if you don't have one, you can't die.

This kind of thinking is really a fear of the future and a fear of not having control.

You can explain that having money in the bank and food in the pantry does not invite problems into your home. It means you can still put food on the table when the grocery stores are closed or you have to take an unpaid furlough at work. Having savings and no debt gives you more options if you are laid off. Your household won't collapse into bankruptcy; you have time to find work while still paying your bills. It may help to show your spouse that you are not one paycheck away from disaster, but two, four, or even twenty paychecks away.

Would knowing this make your spouse feel more secure? More willing to not buy those expensive shoes? That radial-arm saw that will never be used? Point out that the long-term security of your family is your main concern, not playing tit for tat over spending habits. Prove this by your actions.

Another way of illustrating the need for disaster preparedness is to use insurance as an example. Why do you have homeowner's insurance? It isn't because you expect (or want) your house to burn down. It is just in case. Why do you have life insurance? Same reason. You don't expect or want your partner to die. However, if they meet the Mack truck at the red light, it would sure be nice to have money to take care of the kids. A big cash payout won't lessen the grief, but it will provide breathing room while the family recovers.

Why wear a seatbelt? In case of an accident. Why lock your doors? To discourage burglars. Why floss your teeth faithfully? To prevent expensive dental problems.

We do this, not because we think we will have a burglar or an accident, but "just in case." "Just in case" is the purpose of disaster preparedness. Use "just in case" when talking to your partner about stocking the pantry, learning how to garden, taking a martial arts class, and exercising every day. It may make why you are concerned about the future much clearer.

It can be depressing to contemplate disaster, both short-term like a tornado and long-term like a decades-long economic collapse. If your partner is overwhelmed by an uncertain future, then your actions can show how your household can stay in control.

You want to demonstrate that planning ahead and doing "just in case" tasks can make your lives better and safer. Show how your savings can add up. Show how the emergency fund paid for a car repair. Show how a full pantry kept your household eating when the stores were closed. Show how insulating the attic lowered heating bills. Show how a vegetable garden put fresh salads on the table.

EXPLAIN AND PRAISE

Remember that your spouse won't do a blessed thing if you don't act on your beliefs. Model the behavior you want to see in thrift, exercise, preparedness, reskilling; anything you believe to be important.

Read (and leave lying around) books on thrift *(The Complete Tightwad Gazette)*, disaster preparedness *(Just in Case: How to be Self-Sufficient)*, gardening *(Gardening When It Counts and The Resilient Gardener)* and health improvement *(You: The Owner's Manual)*.

Be precise in your discussion. Explain why you are doing what you are doing. Repeat as necessary. When your partner picks up a hoe to weed the garden, then praise, praise, praise! Praise every effort and ignore as best you can the unwanted behaviors. Stop the belittling and demeaning remarks. They don't help.

Spouse conversion can take years, so better start now. Never forget, you cannot ask your partner to do anything you wouldn't do yourself.

5

Financial Independence and Thrift

The Best Thrift Books — The Debt-Free Road Map — Riding the Debt Snowball — Building Your Thrift Library

Live within your means, never be in debt, and by husbanding your money you can always lay it out well, but when you get in debt you become a slave, therefore, I say to you, never involve yourself in debt ...
— Andrew Jackson
Seventh U.S. president

FINANCIAL INDEPENDENCE MEANS LIVING the life you want to live. Here at Fortress Peschel, that means never, ever having to set foot off our property unless we want to. Not "I *have* to work at a hated job." Not "I *need* to work to pay off debts incurred years ago." Not "I *must* make more money to keep the collection agents at bay." But "I *want* to go to the county fair and see the quilt show."

How can you achieve this wonderful state? By not owing anyone money. This includes your mortgage. You also cannot owe money on credit cards (which should be called debt cards), vehicle loans, boat loans, student loans, and personal loans.

The only expenditures you should have are for taxes, utilities, food, health care, and other basic goods and services. Ideally, these should be cash transactions and minimized as much as possible. The less money needed for necessities, the less money needs to be earned.

THE BEST THRIFT BOOKS

I have read dozens of thrift and saving money books over several decades. These are not the same as financial management books. Those books are about stocks, bonds, annuities, insurance plans, and other money games. Don't play those games unless everything else is paid for and you have the cash to do so.

Thrift books are about saving more and spending less, sometimes a lot less.

By far, the best author on the subject is Amy Dacyczyn. She wrote a wonderful newsletter called *The Tightwad Gazette* in the early 1990s. When she had said everything she needed to say on the subject, she quit. Most of that material was repackaged as *The Tightwad Gazette* volumes I, II, and III, later combined into *The Complete Tightwad Gazette*. This is the only book I recommend that you buy at full price.

If you cannot cut your spending after reading *The Tightwad Gazette*, you don't want to. Some of the material is dated – check out those Clinton-era prices – but the advice never grows old. Keep a copy handy to study, make notes in, and refer to often. Think of it as your bible on thrift.

THE DEBT-FREE ROAD MAP

Another very good book is *America's Cheapest Family* by Steve and Annette Economides. If you can afford only one book, buy Amy's and get the Economides' book from the library. Later, as your savings increase, you might want to spring for this title.

The best piece of information I got from the Economides is their priority list on spending. Here it is, slightly modified based on my experiences and studies.

First, establish a budget. You can't do anything else unless you do this first. Then, follow these 10 rules:

1. **Pay off all consumer debt**, including family and personal loans.

2. **Build up your emergency fund.** Aim for $1,000; more is better.

3. **Set aside savings for regular big expenses**. Car insurance and taxes are not emergencies! They are costs that come on a regular schedule.

4. **Pay off your cars** and start saving for their replacements.

5. **Pay off your student loans.**

6. **Evaluate your life insurance needs.** Can you use less? Term insurance is usually the best choice, but do your homework.

7. **Pay off your house.**

8. Save up six months to one year of salary. If you lose your job, this and being debt-free will make life easier.

9. Invest in IRAs or 401(k)s. If your employer matches your contribution, fork over the money up to the maximum match and no more until your consumer debt has been erased and you have a savings cushion. Then, maximize your contributions to the full amount.

10. Save for your kids' college expenses.

Any money management book will tell you how to set up a budget. The hard part is sticking to it. If it helps, call it a spending plan. Go through your credit slips, bills, receipts, checkbook registers, and bank statements, and calculate how much you spend every day. List (be honest!) *all* your debts, including the money you owe friends and relatives.

Next, look at your income compared to your spending. Is there cash left over or are you ending every month in the red? Amy Dacyczyn and the Economides give hundreds of ways to cut back on spending.

I repeat: If you cannot cut your spending after reading their books, it is because you like owing money more than you like saying no to every whim.

RIDING THE DEBT SNOWBALL

Now that you know how much you owe, it's time to buckle down to work. I like Dave Ramsey's debt-snowball method, and he has nice worksheets on how to do this in his money management books.

Here's how it works: List your debts in order from the smallest to the largest. Make the minimum payments to all of them, except the smallest one. Focus every extra dollar on that account until it is paid off. Then devote this amount to the next-smallest bill, adding it to the minimum you are already paying. Focus every extra dollar onto this bill until it is paid off. Repeat until all of your debts are paid off.

Two points to keep in mind: This won't work unless you *stop adding to your debt load,* and you must still make the minimum payment to every debt.

Don't think of not being able to use your credit cards as denial. Remind your covetous self how nice it would be to not be a debt slave. Focus on the positive: You're striking a blow for your freedom.

While you are getting the debt snowball going, you need to set aside money for an emergency fund, for when your car breaks down, your daughter sprains her ankle, or your cat needs emergency veterinary care. If emergency dollars get spent, you may have to slow down the debt snowball while you replenish the account. When it's back up to full, go back to pushing that snowball.

When working on your money makeover, remember that your salary may not be your sole source of income. Money from heaven – gifts, tax refunds, bonuses, eBay sales, inheritances — can be put toward debt repayment (including the mortgage), home improvements or infrastructure, and savings.

Using your bonus to pay for a vacation trip is fun, but so is the peace of mind when you use that extra money to beef up the emergency fund or pay down another bill while enjoying vacation time at home.

BUILDING YOUR THRIFT LIBRARY

Hundreds of books have been published on thrift and saving money. The topic goes in and out of fashion with the publishing industry as the economy goes up and down. Any library of any size has at least one or two books on the subject, and copies can be found at yard and library sales, used bookstores, and thrift shops. Online, eBay and ABEBooks.com are a great source of titles.

Using these sources, I have slowly built up a decent library of thrift books. I reread them regularly to refresh my memory and remind me of my goals.

Thrift books vary wildly in quality, so request a book from the library before you lay out hard cash. Thrift shop purchases are usually cheap enough that you can take the plunge.

You won't win the lottery, but you can win at money management.

6

Fixing the Work-Life Balance

Racing to the Bottom – Your Company Is Not Your Family – Your Time Is Precious – The Work-Life Illusion – Your Money Or Your Life – Learning to Say No

WORK HAS TO BE DONE, NO QUESTION. People need to work. It gives meaning and structure to our lives, knowing that we are useful, and that we add value to the world. The question is: How much work do you want to do? What kind do you want to do? What kind of a life do you want to live?

Work and life can be compatible, but it requires hard choices. No matter what the news media and the women's magazines say, you cannot "have it all." Having a life is diametrically opposed to having a modern job.

RACING TO THE BOTTOM

We live in a capitalist society in which 99% of the working population is employed to create a profit for the 1% who own businesses. It is in their interests to direct their underlings – your bosses – to cut costs, any way they can. This creates a race to the bottom in which companies in every industry compete to use the cheapest materials, demand the highest productivity, and use the fewest workers to create their products.

Ideally, what bosses really want are golems. Golems don't eat, drink, breath, or have any messy biological functions including families. If you can't get golems, get slaves. If slavery is unacceptable, get serfs. The least desirable is employees, since they have to be treated like human beings. However, as soon as possible, replace people with robots. When you see ATMs, self-checkout machines in grocery stores, driverless vehicles, and machines in restaurants that take your order and your money, you are also seeing fewer jobs for humans.

There is a great incentive for the culture to teach you to work harder and longer hours. Silicon Valley promoted this idea when it portrayed young programmers working sixty to eighty hours a week, sleeping under their desks, and eating junk food as heroes, not exploited victims. It made sense to spend your life energy for a small company with a great idea in the hopes of becoming a millionaire through stock options. But why are you expected to do that at Facebook, where you're not going to get rich anymore but you're still expected to put in long hours, to the point where engineers are on call 24/7? Where when you reach thirty, you're married and starting a family, they will cast you aside for younger, hungrier programmers (particularly those imported from overseas on H1-B visas, because of course there are not enough programmers in this country).

When you are caught in corporate games like that, you're trapped. You can't agitate for a union; you can't complain to the government. The only way to win is not to play.

YOUR COMPANY IS NOT YOUR FAMILY

Your company does not love you. You may love working there, but the feeling is not returned.

No matter what your supervisor tells you – or you tell yourself — everyone is replaceable. Graveyards are full of people who thought they were indispensible at work. Someone else replaced every one of them, even CEOs and company founders. Steve Jobs is moldering in his grave, and Apple still puts out products.

Your company does not love you. If you fell deathly ill and had to go home permanently, would your co-workers miss you? If you died, would they grieve? They might visit you in the hospital – if they can take the time off – but they'll bitch about having to take up your slack. Your co-workers and your boss would attend your funeral – depending on the workload – but during the eulogy they'll be thinking about who will replace you or fretting that they will have to take on your duties so the company can save a few bucks on a new hire.

Your family will grieve; if you spent time with them while you were alive. Your friends will grieve; if you made the effort to keep them in your life. Not your co-workers. Not your boss. Not your job.

YOUR TIME IS PRECIOUS

Every day has twenty-four hours. You never get less, and you never get more. Nobody, no matter how rich they are, gets more than twenty-four hours a day.

But doesn't it seem that some people get more done than you? That is because they outsource many of their daily chores. Your productivity rises enormously when you buy someone else's life to clean your house, cook your meals, chauffeur your car, run your errands, tend your children, monitor your social obligations, perform civic duties, go to school activities, walk your dog, wash your laundry, maintain your house and garden, stand in line at the DMV for you, shop for you, ghostwrite your memoirs, nurse your aged relatives, and perform any other chores that take time away from your career.

The only things you can't outsource are exercise, oral hygiene, sleep, eating, and eliminating your body wastes. If you are rich enough, you can even have someone else wash your hair while minions give you your manicure, pedicure, leg waxing, full body scrub, and read aloud the daily news. Even pregnancy can be outsourced using surrogates.

There is nothing like plenty of money and good time management to free up valuable hours for more work.

You and I cannot do that, so we have to use our twenty-four hours wisely. I break it down like this:

Sleep: You have to sleep. You think that you can squeak by with five or six hours a night for years on end, but you'll more likely spend part of each day in a haze of fatigue and fuzzy thinking. Allow at least seven hours a day for sleep.

Basic body maintenance: This covers cleanliness, exercise, oral care, eating, and personal hygiene. Probably three hours a day. You are now up to ten hours spent per day.

Work, commuting, and lunch: You'll work an eight-hour day, plus one hour for lunch (which you work through, of course) plus an hour of commuting each day. That's ten more hours gone.

That leaves four hours left to spend with the family you say you love, the friends you say you want, the animals that need your care, the aged parents who need you too, household maintenance, and any recreation or hobbies you use to rejuvenate yourself.

But wait! We forgot the weekend, jam-packed with the deferred grocery shopping, chores, maintenance, and errands you didn't have time for during the week. Don't forget the email alerts on your smartphone that demand answers and the work you brought home which simply must be done and no one else can do it but you.

THE WORK-LIFE ILLUSION

The work-life balance is only a problem if you want a life. Thanks to the internet and smartphones, work will fill every available hour if you let it.

However, the dirty secret is that there will never be enough time to get everything done. Even rich people with staffs have to pick and choose what they can get done. It is the curse of Parkinson's Law: Work expands to fill the available time. If you can be reached 24/7, then that space will be filled with work as well.

Technological advances mean that today you cannot escape your job. When you needed a secretary to type your memos and letters, you could only work when the secretaries were on duty. Now, everyone is their own secretary, their own receptionist, and their own janitor. Why pay for low-level staffers when the magic of technology can make those jobs go away? The work remains, of course.

Your smartphone, your netbook, your Wi-Fi access: They are your permanent electronic dog leashes.

You try to cope. You tell yourself that you can multitask your way out of the problem. At the mandatory company training session, you are told the answer is not to work harder but smarter.

Nevertheless, you learn you can't be in two places at once. Trying to play with your kids while taking a meeting via speakerphone just means you do both poorly. Can you watch your son's school concert and scan your email on your smartphone? Where is the pleasure in that? Checking email at dinner with your spouse tells them that work matters more than they do. To appreciate this, let's reverse the roles: You're revealing something important about yourself and look up at her. You are talking to the top of her head. She is scanning Facebook posts.

How would you feel?

Very few people say on their deathbed that they wish they had spent more time at work. Most people regret those lost opportunities to see their families and friends, to dance, to play, to be true to themselves, to eat more ice cream and fewer rutabagas.

There are those rare few who do wish they had spent more time at work. Isaac Asimov was asked what he would do if he knew he was going to die tomorrow. His answer was "I would type faster." Not see his children. Not see his wife.

Are you going to say, as you lay dying, "I wish I had spent more time at work"? If so, then own your decision. Get rid of those pesky obstacles. Divorce the spouse, dump the kids, drop the animals off at the kill shelter, and estrange yourself from your relatives and friends. Move into a condo, hire a housekeeper, and eat every meal from a takeout container or the freezer. Stop exercising, don't date, and medicate as needed to avoid sleep. You will sure get a lot more accomplished. Think of the praise! The accolades! The warm fuzzy feelings and maybe, more money, more recognition, and more challenges! And more work to fill the time.

You will have achieved the capitalist vision of a perfect work-life balance.

If you don't want this brave new world, then you will have to make the decision to say no. No to the bigger house, the second home, the vacations to places other than the vacation home, the boat, the wardrobe of vehicles; no to possessions and luxuries that cost time and money but aren't necessary to a full and satisfying life.

How do you determine what path you want your life to take? Let's find out in the next section.

Your Money Or Your Life

The Complete Tightwad Gazette gave me the tools to achieve Financial Independence, but my thinking was first changed by *Your Money or Your Life: Transforming Your Relationship with Money and Achieving Financial Independence* by Joe Dominguez and Vicki Robin.

The book's lesson is simple: We trade our life energy for money. You could boil it down to a formula:

MONEY = LIFE ENERGY

Your Money or Your Life advocates calculating how much you really earn per hour by factoring in all of your job-related activities. This includes job-required clothing, dry cleaning costs, day-care, lunches out, convenience products and services, and anything or anyone you pay to keep your job or that you can't do yourself because of the job.

Start with your after-tax salary, subtract the expenses, and divide by the total time spent working (including commuting time). What is left is your true hourly wage.

That tells you how much life energy you have to expend to afford what you want. Let's say you take home $10 an hour. See that beautiful Coach handbag on sale for only $150? It is so stylish, so long-wearing. You will have to work fifteen solid hours to pay cash for it. Is that Coach bag worth fifteen hours of work?

This calculation works for anything. An expensive meal out costing $30? Three hours of your life. A $5,000 motorcycle to park alongside your combat commuter? Five hundred hours, plus more each year for insurance and maintenance.

Seen through that lens, you will quickly determine if something is a need or a want.

LEARNING TO SAY NO

The more Dear Husband and I used the Money=Life Energy formula, the easier it became to say no to all kinds of wants. The fewer wants we had, the easier it became to meet our needs. When they were met, it was easier to say no to offers of overtime and yes to taking holidays instead of working them for more pay. Our home life was more important to us than the extra dollars. We want a life of our choosing more than vacations, premium entertainment packages, meals out, boats, travel, second homes, and the other trappings of success. Work supports our life. It is *not* our life.

You get twenty-four hours a day, never more and never less. Time passes, whatever you do. You will never get the time or life energy back that you spend at work. If you had a choice, would you be at work or at home with your family?

There is not necessarily a right answer. If the status toys are more important, then admit it. Spend more time at work earning more money and stop complaining that you cannot afford to spend more time at home with your loved ones. Apply yourself to what is important and ignore what doesn't matter. This is how you can find your life-work balance.

7

Swimming Against the Tide

Lies Our Culture Tells Us – Bad Housing Advice – The Student Loan Lie – College Is Not for Everyone – Feeding the Stimulation Monkey – Life Outside the Bubble — Navigating Our Culture

We are not mainstream at Fortress Peschel. I stay home to run the domestic economy (a fancy way of saying housewife). Our lone television is not hooked up to the outside world. I do a lot of things manually: knives vs. food processors, and clotheslines vs. dryers. I mend clothes. I patch sheets.

When Dear Husband worked at the newspaper, he packed homemade lunches. He brought beverages from home instead of buying from coffee or soda machines.

We planned our car trips to minimize gas usage. We had two vehicles for three licensed drivers. Now we have one. I don't shop for recreation. We take stay-cations where we relax and work on home improvement projects. We visit the grandparents in Delaware. We go to movies maybe once a year. We rarely eat out.

Does this make us boring, dull people? It certainly means that we do not consume, consume, consume goods and services as economists say we should. It may be better for the economy if everyone shopped till they dropped, but that is not better for the individual household.

LIES OUR CULTURE TELLS US

Listen to the news, and you would think that economists rule us. The health of our economy is reported with an eye towards growth. If the economy is doing well, they imply, we're doing well. We're happy.

But they're wrong. Our culture encourages us to make choices that hurt us. We don't see it because we're like fish who don't notice the water they swim in. It's all around us, so it becomes invisible.

Take the Gross Domestic Product. It measures the monetary value of the goods and services produced over a period of time, usually a quarter of a year. A higher GDP is supposed to be a good thing, right?

But by that measurement, a highly productive member of society would be a long-term cancer patient undergoing a divorce. New Orleans was an economic powerhouse because Hurricane Katrina spurred a building boom.

I don't believe even economists would admit that the cancer patient or Louisianans were very happy with their circumstances.

Americans are wallowing in debt, whether for homes, cars, college educations, or last night's dinner at McDonald's, yet any attempt to pay off that debt risks an economic downtown, which is bad. So we continue to spend our future income (in the form of debt) to pay off our past purchases.

By that logic, we should be borrowing money to buy more stuff. Instead, we don't owe any money to anyone. Our mortgage is paid off. We own our car. Our one credit card is paid off every month. Hardcore thriftiness is letting us reach our goal of Financial Independence. We work hard, every day, and still have time to relax and have a life. We're happy. The economy will have to live with that.

BAD HOUSING ADVICE

The news is full of financial advice that sounds good but is not. During the housing bubble, we were advised to get the biggest mortgage we could qualify for on the biggest house we could find. As salary rose, the argument went, the mortgage would take up a smaller percentage of income, plus it was tax-deductible. In addition, when you sold, the constantly raising price would take care of any little issues such as how much money you still owed.

But what if you didn't get those regular pay raises? When the bubble burst in 2007, companies cut back hard. Workers were laid off or forced to take furloughs. Those who went heavily into debt for that McMansion, instead of putting the cash into savings, lost their homes.

Then some "experts" argued that you should never buy a home. You were supposed to rent. This let you live where you wanted, move when you wanted, and during the first few years of the mortgage most of your payments went to interest anyway. So why bother?

Again, this is where the needs of economists and people clash. You have to live somewhere, even if it is under a bridge. Your home is not an investment. It is where you live. People can be deeply rooted to an area and family; a concept that is not factored into the formulas of economists.

If you want financial security and independence, a better strategy would be to minimize the cost of your dwelling place. A smaller house with a smaller mortgage that you pay off early shelters you from job loss. You will still have your utilities, groceries, insurance, and taxes, but the mortgage is gone.

Renters pay forever. Serial movers and refinancers pay forever. Both are good for the economy, but not good for people's peace of mind.

THE STUDENT LOAN LIE

For the longest time, financial advisers told us we should borrow money to finance our children's college education. After all, the little darlings will pay off those loans by getting the great job the degree promised them.

We know how that turned out. Students were getting degrees in fields that didn't pay enough to cover the debt. They got degrees in fields they turned out to dislike, such as law. Some flunked out, which left them holding the debt bag. Like back taxes, student loan debt cannot be discharged through bankruptcy. You owe them until you pay them off or you die.

If you are old enough to go to college, you are old enough to do basic math and estimate future earnings as compared to your college debt load. If these numbers do not match, it is time to rethink your plans.

As a parent, I do not believe you are doing your children any favors by saying, "Don't worry. Do what you love and the money will follow." What drivel. Life and the universe do not care if your child adores philosophy. Money will not appear. They will be astounding the customers at Starbucks with their knowledge of Wittgenstein's theory of private language and its effect on meaning while living in Mom's basement.

You are also not doing your children any favors by picking up the tab for their expensive college education. Are they going to work harder, knowing that you sacrificed *your* Financial Independence? Maybe. Maybe your student won't party hearty through four or five years to get that BA. Then when they get the good job, you can move in with them.

This inability to connect current desire with future costs leads to financial problems. Part of growing up is learning that everything has to be paid for, one way or another. Do not send your children into the world ignorant of that fact.

COLLEGE IS NOT FOR EVERYONE

Not everyone is college material. It is heresy to say so, but it is true.

In high school, students get used to lots of handholding, encouragement, rah rah rah, and follow-up to make sure they show up and do their work. Colleges do not care. Their only concern is that the check clears. Students are supposed to be adults who show up on time, do the work, and hand it in when it is due.

As a parent, look at your student. Is he or she going to work hard without supervision? If they cannot do it now, for free, why will it be better 500 miles away supported by a truckload of borrowed money?

If you are contemplating college for yourself, then you need to be honest. Are you studying hard in high school, taking advantage of the free education offered by people who want you to succeed? Are you stretching yourself with the fullest course load that you can handle? If you are not, get your head out of your ass and get to work.

If you are unsure about your further education, start at the local community college. The cost is infinitely less; you can live at home and hold down a part-time job to cover some of the costs. It accustoms you to college-level demands.

College will not be better, easier or more rewarding than high school if you are lazy and shiftless. If you do not have a career path in mind, then take the widest array of classes you can while still in high school. Taste everything to see what you enjoy and are good at. Work hard, ask questions, and get the best education you can while it is free. If nothing else, the highest GPAs lead to potential merit scholarships that can cut your college costs drastically.

FEEDING THE STIMULATION MONKEY

Another message our culture sends us is that we need constant stimulation. Do you need your smartphone on and your ear buds in place constantly lest you accidentally hear the people around you? Why are you more involved with your phone and ignoring the people sitting beside you? You know, the ones you claim to care about deeply.

Isolation in a technology bubble means you get what you want when you want it. You don't have to interact with pesky, live family members who might misunderstand you or want you to do something you do not want to. Boring, dreary Mundania; who wouldn't want to avoid it?

But when they go unused, your social skills, your people skills, and your real world abilities to do and achieve do not improve. They atrophy. It becomes harder to cope with messy, irritating humans and their petty wants and needs. If you are genuinely concerned about the difficult future bearing down on us, then cut the electronic apron strings and rejoin the real world.

LIFE OUTSIDE THE BUBBLE

We succeed by not playing. Our television is not connected to the outside world. It can only play games and DVDs. This reduces the impulse to turn it on when we're bored. We have to make an effort to use it; we have to decide what we want to see, so it doesn't get used that much. It is never left on to play to an empty room.

As for the online world, I don't do social media. I have no Facebook page, and I don't tweet, Snapchat, Instagram, or whatever is the current, newest thing. Whatever time I spend online is divided among my favorite news sites. Dear Husband has a Facebook account he neglects and a Twitter account he rarely uses. He maintains PlanetPeschel.com and PeschelPress.com as platforms to promote his writing and mine.

Our household has a smartphone. My sister insisted we have one, and she pays for it. I use it when traveling to say I am on the way home.

I hear people say they do not have time to cook, garden, sew, make home improvements, exercise, be thrifty, get organized, or volunteer. Stop spending several hours a day with your TV, your social media, aimless surfing, and hunting Orcs online, and that time will magically appear.

Which option will make you stronger and more resilient: playing games on Facebook or learning how to darn socks and grow food?

Subtract out what you have to do and then decide how valuable the remaining time is to you. Use it to learn and grow or fritter it away. You choose.

Does avoiding electronic time sucks make us boring and dull? I am pretty well read and reasonably up on current events. I can walk into a kitchen, cold, and turn out a meal for five. I can repair almost any piece of clothing and make it last longer. I exercise and improve my fitness and health. I write books. I walk my dog and meet my neighbors. I volunteer with the Derry Twp. Environmental Action Committee. I think I can hold my end up of any conversation.

NAVIGATING OUR CULTURE

The culture around us, the water we swim in, is formed by our families, our beliefs, the area we live in, and our country. Each group brings its values to the table. Human beings are extremely flexible thinkers, and that is reflected in the enormous range of cultures throughout history.

But it is only in this past generation that, thanks to technology and the internet, we can pick and choose what we value most. We can even discard values such as blind consumerism, celebrity worship, and indulgences in time-wasting activities that leave us feeling empty.

Examine your life. Is it what you want it to be? You can choose to swim against the tide and improve your life. But you have to be mindful, aware, and willing to work to succeed. It does not happen on its own.

8

That Pesky Time Management

The Power of Goals – Keep Track of Your Life – Recognize Your Limitations – Organize Tasks Around the Calendar

TIME MANAGEMENT IS EASY TO UNDERSTAND and difficult to execute. Like everyone else, I have too much to do and too little time to do it in.

I could be writing the adventures of Dez and Jaxim in *The Steppes of Mars* series, sewing any one of the hundred projects begging for my attention, particularly the beautiful coats, tackling the mountain of boring, mundane but useful mending, weeding the yard so it resembles a planned, natural garden and not an unkempt, neglected wilderness, researching stormwater management, doing more cooking from scratch, learning how to preserve the garden harvest, maintaining close ties with family, friends, and neighbors, and walking Muffy. The list is endless, and I don't work outside my home!

As I said earlier, everybody gets twenty-four hours a day. Once we subtract from it all the tasks that have to be done, we are left with about four hours a day to do what we want to do.

Is it possible in those four hours to maintain close family ties, cook slow food like Michael Pollan and Mark Bittman recommend (do they really do this on a daily basis? I doubt it), exercise, garden, learn new skills, sew your own clothes, train your dog, be involved with your children's school, participate in the neighborhood watch, be politically active, run some of your church groups, etc., etc., etc.?

It is exhausting, overwhelming, and never ending, but not impossible. It helps to consider your options rationally. Here are some ideas to think about.

THE POWER OF GOALS

I do not believe anyone can do everything they want to and should do. You have to say no. If you try to say yes, yes, yes, then you end up not sleeping enough, which eventually makes you unhealthy, overweight, psychotic, and suicidal, as well as ensuring you do the things you want to do in a half-assed, lick-and-a-promise fashion. This is how it worked for me.

To accomplish what you want to do, you have to set goals. Then you look at an activity on your list. Will doing this help you reach your goal? If the answer is yes, then it needs to be done. If the answer is no, then you need to ask why you are doing it.

If your goal is to become financially independent, out of debt, and owing your own home, then shopping for recreation has to come off the to-do list. If you leave it, you are saying that you don't want to be financially independent. No matter what you tell yourself, your actions speak the truth about what you value.

Want to improve your job skills to make more money? Take classes, ask for help from people who you want to emulate, and ask the boss what needs to be done. Study, pay attention, focus. Learn how to do better, whatever you are working on. Drifting aimlessly says you do not want to do any better.

Every goal is like this, whether community activism or intensive gardening. You have to work at them, or they remain castles in the air.

KEEP TRACK OF YOUR LIFE

It helps me to write my tasks down in a daily log. My logbook reminds me, it provides a written record of what I have accomplished, and it helps me stay focused. In addition, I make lists of various projects and estimate if they are short-term, long-term, or nice-to-do if money and time allow.

I also use my logbook to keep the family focused on their jobs. I receive, as you can imagine, a lot of resistance from them. But I persevere, as my kids would do even less if I let them. My family (including the pets) is a part of my time management problem as I use some of *my* time to keep *them* focused and on the job.

Having a clear idea of my goals on a daily, weekly, monthly, yearly, and lifetime basis helps me prioritize. Removing aimless behaviors and time sinks is the only way I can make time to tackle those objectives.

RECOGNIZE YOUR LIMITATIONS

While the above advice is effective, it still does *not* give me anything close to enough time to accomplish what I want to do. That is just the way it is.

One problem comes up when you have two goals you would like to accomplish. I like to cook, but if I am going to write *Fed, Safe & Sheltered* plus the fiction and edit Dear Husband's writing, then I cannot spend several hours a day cooking.

I have wonderful ideas but I don't have the time to execute them. One of them is to make insulated fabric bags lined with ironing-board material. This is an updated hay box in which you bring your homemade soup to a boil, then put the pot into the heavily insulated bag so it can cook slowly with residual heat all day. At dinnertime, the soup is ready without heating up the kitchen — good in summer — or spending precious dollars on cooking fuel. Boy, does that meet some of my goals. It will not cost me anything to make as I have a salvaged metallic ironing-board cover, wool batting, and a lifetime supply of fashion fabric for the exterior. All it would cost me is time.

I cannot spare this time now, even though this insulated cooking bag will, eventually, save me time and money babysitting soup or stew.

This great idea ran up against the Winter Arts and Crafts Festival in November at Hershey High School. Dear Husband and I sell our books there every year. I was inspired to make tote bags of heavy fabric and sized to hold groceries. They would be worth selling on their own, making us some money, and make ideal gifts for customers who bought three or more books.

The original plan was to sew a set of bags, then work on another sewing project such as a wonderful velvet coat, then tote bags, then the insulated cooking bag, then tote bags, then tackle the mending mountain, tote bags, a lined jacket, and so forth.

That plan went by the wayside when I discovered that in order to make enough tote bags in time for the show, I could not sew anything else. I had to choose. Being financially self-sufficient was more important than making wonderful clothes for me. My velvet coat – a '50s vintage swing coat with a funnel neck – will have to wait. So will the jackets, the mending, the stylish tops, and the insulated cooking bag. They are still waiting.

With sewing and writing taking up my time, I had to accept limitations in other areas. The garden has largely gone by the wayside. Most of the cooking has been turned over to Dear Daughter, and Dear Husband can be convinced to cook pancakes and bacon or pizza for dinner. The other dream tasks have to be set aside for now.

ORGANIZE TASKS AROUND THE CALENDAR

We have learned over the years that certain jobs have to wait for good weather. Sewing and writing can be done anytime. Painting is best done in spring or fall when we can do it outside (for doors) or at least open all the windows. Building the patio using pieces salvaged from rebuilding the front sidewalk is a spring or fall job. Insulating the attic is a fall, winter, and spring job. You do not want to be up there in July when the temperature is 125 degrees. Insulating the pipes in the crawlspace or basement should be done in the summer.

Some tasks have no "best" time, because they are routine. Cooking has to be done year-round. Laundry and basic housekeeping have to be done daily or else you end up with mountains of work piling up.

Time management is so difficult. I'd like to say that practice makes it easier, but I don't know about that either. I look around at everything I am not doing and wonder: What am I missing? What is going to jump up and bite me, saying, "You didn't do me, and now you will pay! Bwah hah hah hah!" *Arghh.*

It will always be a challenge, but it is a worthwhile challenge. Establish your goals, try to instill better habits in yourself, compare what you are doing to what you say you want to accomplish. Say no, adapt, and say no again. Keep out the tidal wave of media, stuff, and everything else that is trying to come in your front door. Reassure yourself that you are doing what you have to do to fulfill your dreams. Say no some more. This is what time management is.

9

Managing Your Television

Television Is Never Free – Television Is Educational – Television Has No Sense of Proportion – Television and Children – Fine-Tuning Our Culture

SOON AFTER DEAR HUSBAND AND I got married, we became television-less. Our one, lone TV had broken down. We looked at our bank account. We did not have the money to replace it. Because he worked eves, and I had never gotten into the television habit, we rarely turned it on. Unfortunately, our Oldest Child (OC), a tot at the time, was finding it difficult to do anything *but* watch TV. It zombified him, and we didn't like that. So we decided not to replace the set. OC found other things to do, and the money from cancelling the cable bill was put to better uses.

To our family and friends, we might as well have told them we were shaving our heads and joining a guru in Oregon. How could we live without a television?!?! It wasn't for ideological reasons. We just didn't need it as much as, say, clean air or good food. Once in awhile, someone would offer us a TV they did not need, and we would say thanks, but no.

Years passed. The kids grew up; we had more free time, so we accepted from a friend both a TV and a PlayStation II. We also made the command decision to keep the beast isolated from the outside world. We bought a DVD player and haunted the bargain bin at Wal-Mart, looking for old movies we wanted to see again.

Except for upgrading the gaming systems, that has been the situation ever since. The TV can only play movies and shows that we select and games we choose. This has saved us thousands of dollars in cable bills, even counting the movies we have bought. It probably saved us even more money because we, and our children, were not bombarded by ads for products we wouldn't have needed until we saw the ads.

People have an abusive relationship with television. It sneers at us, neglects us, talks down to us, and still we come back to it. It's been this way ever since Uncle Miltie wore a dress on *Texaco Star Theater*. Must-see TV does not change this paradigm.

TELEVISION IS NEVER FREE

Economists teach that there is no such thing as a free lunch. Someone has to pay, whether it is taxes that go to pave our roads, or wars fueled by debt that will be paid by our children (and children's children).

Same with television. Much of it is paid for by advertising, which is designed to make you dissatisfied with what you have. Advertising is the pick-up artist, and we are the lonely girl seated at the bar at closing time. Only instead of saying "Desperate?" in that smirking I-don't-mean-it-but-maybe-I-do tone, it is suggesting that your car must have looked good when your grandpa drove it, that you should hang on to your clothes because that look will be hot again in a few decades and is it the light here or are your teeth always that dingy?

The purpose of TV is not to entertain you, but to sell you stuff. The shows are just to hold your attention so you will watch the ads. Often, they are for products you don't need, are not good for you, or formulated to make you crave more. That is why there are far more ads for potato chips than potatoes.

TELEVISION IS EDUCATIONAL

In TV Land, life is full of happy, happy, joy, joy; no consequences or costs are ever associated with the beyond-thrilling lives you see. Your life is drab by comparison, and there are no witty writers feeding you clever, cutting lines. No one listens to your life story or wants to reward you by making over your kitchen or shoving a camera in your face.

This leads to dissatisfaction. Why isn't your spouse as attractive as her TV husband? Why aren't your children as clever and cute? Everyone is better dressed than you are and lives in a better decorated home. Their problems are solvable, often within 23 minutes.

Every second of television is educational. Is this what you want your family to learn?

TELEVISION HAS NO SENSE OF PROPORTION

How often do you see a car chase through your town? Or a massacre? Or a tragedy? Turn on the news, and it will seem like disasters are everywhere. If you are not worried about violence, how about the threat of the day: killer bees, SARS, Ebola, and (for now) Zika.

If you are not worried about your health or the health of your loved ones, then how about a nice moral panic? *Dungeons & Dragons*, Satanism in day cares, Harry Potter, rap music, and even Pokémon have been the object of well-meaning, ill-informed, and sometimes damaging crusaders.

Blame the need to fill the news hole 24/7. The media overestimates the dangers of our modern lives by pounding a story at you until something bloodier comes along. It underestimates the pleasures of people who live regular, bill-paying, responsible, considerate lives. Those are dull and do not make for good storytelling.

To get a better idea of the effect television can have on your life, try turning it off for a few days, a week, if you can bear it.

What happened? Did you find yourself bored for awhile? Could you detect the passage of time? Maybe you got a few chores done. When you turned the TV on again, you may have discovered that the world was still there, that you didn't miss anything, and that what they're telling you doesn't matter to your life. It may even annoy you.

TELEVISION AND CHILDREN

Breaking the cable habit changed how our children grew up. They are all readers. They like playing video games, but they are not addicted to TV shows or movies. It is easier to pick up a book or a graphic novel than to choose a movie from our collection, turn on the power strip, and find the remote. It was easier and quicker to play outside or draw or read.

Not having the TV also meant never hearing a lot of "I want this" and "I gotta have that." You don't just save the money from the cable bills; it is also all the junk being advertised that creates a need that was not there before. We used the money to buy products the kids wanted, such as art supplies, Legos, K'nex, and electronic kits.

FINE-TUNING OUR CULTURE

With our set-up, we have the best of both worlds. We see the movies and TV shows we want, just not when everyone else does. We wait for the library to buy it. Do we miss a lot of must-see TV? You bet we do. We've missed *Seinfeld, Friends, Breaking Bad, The Sopranos, Mad Men,* and *Desperate Housewives.* We've read about the shows, and caught clips on YouTube, but did we really miss anything? No more than missing Oscar-winning movies that we wouldn't have wanted to see. With so many entertainment options, everyone is missing something cool.

Does this free up oodles of time for other activities? Oh my, yes. Every hour you spend in front of that set is an hour you are not doing something else (unless you're like me and do a lot of mending or needlework while watching TV).

If you are looking for a way to cut back on expenses, disconnecting your TV from the outside world may be the ticket. Add up your TV-related costs for a year, both in dollars spent and hours per day. Think what you could do with that money. Think what you could do with that time.

10

The Domestic Economy

What Is a Homemaker Worth? — Anyone Can Do It – Living With Less

I DO ONE OF THE MOST RADICAL, UNFASHIONABLE jobs there is these days, and I have since our kids were tiny: I stay home and work hard at not being a consumer.

It started when I calculated that the cost of putting three kids in daycare was astronomical. It wasn't worth it to work a minimum-wage job forty hours a week, then turn around and give the money to a child-care facility.

What was the point? To work for free so I could earn Social Security? Since I don't believe that I will ever see any money from Social Security, this didn't seem like a good enough reason. Should I work for free so that I could stay employable in case Dear Husband met a younger, blonder cookie and abandon me and the kids? He is not that type. I've read advice columns since I was twelve, and DH never showed any of the red flags that columnists talk about endlessly. Should I work for free so if my Dear Husband died, we wouldn't be left penniless? This is why term life insurance was invented.

Should I work because I have no family or friends to turn to and may God save us from asking for help from the people who love us because that would show what candy-assed weaklings we are? I am not a big fan of the current line of thought that says we – a species that evolved in tight family groups – should be atomized as much as possible to show how independent and unneedy we are.

I've done my time in the work world. I have an art education degree and after doing my student teaching, realized that I would never set foot in the public school system. I would rather tip my hat to the brave men and women who perform that thankless, underpaid job.

I've worked retail at a few chain stores. It's tough work, and it is no longer rewarded after the bean-counters destroyed the idea of a career at a department store. You remember, when you could find a thirty-year veteran in the appliance department who knew everything about the washing machines and stoves he sold.

I was in the Navy for almost ten years. I learned that I didn't want to command a ship, so when they offered me money to leave, I did. Now I'm captain of my household, which I run as a tight ship.

Based on my time in the work world, I fail to understand how a job is fulfilling, demonstrates your worthiness as a human being, and allows you to self-actualize.

Humans need to work. When we don't have worthwhile work, we drift into dissipation and despair. People on the dole, loaded with free time, do not turn into artists, musicians, and entrepreneurs, unless they were born that way.

However, there is work and there is work. A job is what you do to earn money so you can live your life with the people you love: your spouse, your kids, your family, your friends, your neighbors, and your community. If what you do to earn money makes you feel worthwhile, then my hat is off to you. You are contributing to the betterment of the world, and this essay may not apply to you.

This is a roundabout way of saying that the domestic economy is far more important than it is given credit.

WHAT IS A HOMEMAKER WORTH?

I have never met anyone who didn't appreciate a clean, comfortable, beautiful house. I have never met anyone who didn't like eating meals prepared from fresh ingredients and eaten with family and then the washing-up gets done afterward. Everybody likes wearing clean, mended clothes. Dirty laundry that disappears and then reappears clean, folded, and put away is a delight. What is not to like? Do you enjoy climbing into bed at night between fresh sheets and aired bedding? I do. Everyone does.

However, someone has to perform those tasks.

Then there is the support a spouse at home can give. It mattered very much to my children that when they were sick, they could stay home and lay on the couch instead of being heavily dosed with Tylenol and shipped off to school or day care. I'm sure that made the staff happier too, along with the other parents who didn't have their children exposed to whatever my children had.

Because I stayed home, neither of us had to make the dreadful choice of who got to beg for time off from an unforgiving boss ("If we wanted you to have kids, we would have assigned you some") nor did we have to take unpaid time off to do so. Dear Husband went to work, and as far as his job was concerned, he didn't have a messy, inconvenient family.

A major difficulty with the work world is that it, along with the school system, is still set up as though there is always an adult at home to cope with snow days, weather emergencies, illnesses, household chores, paperwork management, car troubles, everything! The work world is very unforgiving of human frailty and human needs.

So many people are desperate for any kind of income-generating work that they will put up with the worst treatment from bosses. People who are at the top of the corporate structure, not down at the bottom, processing chicken carcasses at minimum wage for eight hours a day, write all that silly chatter about work being a joy.

Because DH worked for a boss, I made sure he didn't do much of anything when he returned home. He spent his workweek earning the money. I spent my workweek on household chores and stretching that money as far as possible.

Larger projects or ones that required skills I didn't have were divided between us. He built the stone walls and the raised beds and laid the sidewalks. I painted the house and sewed the draperies.

We discovered that running our domestic economy efficiently gave us more freedom than a second, low-wage job ever would have. It gave us the flexibility of time. I do all those cost saving, time-intensive tasks such as growing some of our produce and serious scratch cooking.

According to the government, an "average" family spends about $2,000 a year on clothing. I doubt if we spend $200 a year. I make some of our clothes, using bargain fabrics and buy the rest at Goodwill or at yard sales. Not much is bought new. I also mended our clothes, squeezing every last bit of wear out of them. Second-hand shopping is a terrific way to save money on clothing and household goods, but it, like mending, takes time, which I have.

I didn't pay someone to paint every room in my house with elaborate patterns. I did it myself for the cost of paint and plenty of time. I don't pay someone to clean my house. I do it myself. I don't pay someone to maintain my yard. I do it myself and what I don't do gets assigned to one of the offspring.

ANYONE CAN DO IT

It sounds like I have the skills of a master chef, master carpenter, and master organizer, but none of these tasks were hard. Anyone can learn to cook, to garden, to shop effectively, to knit socks and quilt window panels, but they take time. It takes time to teach kids to read or to do household chores, and it takes time to sit and listen to your neighbors as you get to know them.

What is challenging is dropping out of society. At Fortress Peschel, we have lived on the fringes of society for many years. We are used to it. We aren't doing anything special, either. Everybody used to do this, including our parents.

For example, we have one car for our household. Since we now both work from home, one car is all we need. This saves us a ton of money. Even when DH was working at the newspaper, we made do with one car. Technically, we had two but Oldest Child was living at home and had a job. He used the second car, so we rarely drove it. This meant I had to plan my usage of the car. This sounds like a lot of trouble, but it wasn't. Jobbing all my errands into one trip saved me money, time, and depreciation on my vehicle. It forced me to be more efficient. How is that bad?

It all comes down to Financial Independence. If you do not control your money, you cannot control your life. Do not think that having money in the bank and no debt makes your problems go away. It doesn't. However, it is easier to manage everyday life when you know that you can throw money at emergencies instead of nearly maxed-out credit cards and storefront loans.

Everything works together for us. The gains we realize from one area spread into other areas as well. My money management skills let me stay home. The time I gained staying home let me hone my money management skills still further. The time I spend exercising helps my health and mental well-being, making me easier to live with. I have time to sleep which certainly makes my life better and absolutely makes the life of my family better.

The domestic economy of running a household matters to the well-being of the family. But my staying home also did something else. It meant that the job I passed over went to someone else, someone who needed it more than I did.

LIVING WITH LESS

If I can manage on the money we have, then why do we need more? Why do I need to do a job that I wouldn't particularly like? Should I take the food from someone else's children because society says I should be gainfully employed?

I don't think so.

This is very radical thinking. Our economy is built on consumption, encouraging us to live with more possessions, rather than living with less.

I absolutely believe that we will all be living on less in the future, because we will have to. There will be less money floating around, fewer resources, less choices available, less of everything, except work and hunger and cold. There will be more of that.

By dropping out early and learning to live on less when it is easy, you learn the skills to manage when it gets harder. If you start turning your thermostats down when you can afford to pay for more heat, you save money upfront for other uses and you learn you don't need to heat your house to 70 degrees in January. Every year, we went a degree lower and now we heat the house to a toasty 64 degrees during the day. If we need to warm up, there are robes, hot tea, and even a space heater for the basement office.

If we had to, we could go lower, to 63 or to 62 degrees or even less. Every degree-tick down saves money on heating oil, but it also shows us that we can manage acceptably on less.

The future ahead of us will be challenging in many ways. We will all have to have someone home full-time to do the heavy work that our grandmothers and great-grandmothers did.

Male or female, it doesn't matter. Whoever goes out into the work world should be the one who earns the larger salary or who hates it the least.

The partner staying home to manage the domestic economy should be taking that job seriously. You don't get paid in dollars; our culture does not value taking care of the family. You make your money by making what you do have go further and learning how little you really do need to be happy.

11

Buying a Home

The Achievable American Dream – House-Hunting with Map and Camera – What to Look For In a House – What Else to Look For In a House – How Much Land Do You Need? — A Walk Through Our Yard – Buying the Right-Sized Home – The Value of Home Renovation – Avoid the Money Pit

AN AWFUL LOT OF PEOPLE CONCERNED about the future think that you should have a large property way out in the country; a second home to run away to when your current home, close to your job and relatives, is overrun by the Cossacks.

This can be a worthwhile goal, *after* you have dug yourself out of debt, built up your emergency food supply, learned a lot of skills, got in shape, and did everything else we've talked about. Oh, and you need to be able to pay all the bills for the place you live in now *and* for the place way out in the woods that you will only visit from time to time.

I think this is unlikely for most of us.

Owning a second property is pretty damn expensive. It has its own set of bills just like your main home. There are taxes, utilities, homeowners association or other residency fees, insurance, and a mortgage.

A moment's thought also brings up more issues. For example, who is going to mind the store when you are not there? What if burglars target your home? Vandals? Storm damage? Fire? Burst water pipes in the winter? Everything that can happen to your main home can happen to your second property, and you won't be there to keep a small problem (missing shingles on the roof) from becoming a big problem (wind storm tears off roof, house is flooded by rain, contents of house ruined).

If you plan to bug out in an emergency, how will you get to your safe house? If you have tried to leave town in a hurry on Friday afternoon on a three-day weekend, imagine what it will be like during an emergency evacuation. You are going to spend a lot of time sitting in traffic.

Then there is the question of your new neighbors. Can you trust your caretakers or neighbors – whom you barely know – to take care of the place and call you if there is trouble? Will the neighbors who don't know you from Adam welcome you to the community with open arms?

Here's an alternative plan: Since you should own your home and it should come with land, find the best possible place you can afford as your *main* home. That is, the place you live in as opposed to the one you daydream about.

THE ACHIEVABLE AMERICAN DREAM

The ideal place is a single-family house sitting on a tenth of an acre or more, in a small town with no more than a thirty-minute commute to work. This will be your first home, your main home, your only home. The place you live with your family until they roll you out the door feet-first.

This is an achievable goal. You get land, security, and family and friends nearby for support. Since you have to live somewhere, why not choose a house that makes your life easier?

As an aside, one of the benefits of owning your home, lock, stock, and barrel, is that it is harder to lose your house. If you are having significant cash-flow issues and you own your house, you can choose to drop your house insurance (very risky), or delay paying your property taxes. The state doesn't foreclose nearly as fast over unpaid property taxes as a bank will over an unpaid mortgage.

I don't recommend either option, as they can make other problems down the road even bigger. But if you are still paying a mortgage, you don't have these options at all.

My father firmly believes that you should go into retirement with a paid-for house, no debt, a paid-for, late model car, decent health, and money in the bank. This way, you have a margin for error when bad times come.

The house you choose can strongly determine whether you can meet this goal. Select too much house, and you will never be able to pay off the mortgage ahead of time and still meet the taxes, insurance, utilities, pay for all the maintenance, pay off your other debts, and build up your savings.

An affordable house means, eventually, a place to live that you don't pay for, other than taxes, insurance, and utilities.

As for housing options, I think a single-family home is the best choice. Townhouses, row houses, duplexes, and condos mean you share walls and roofs with other people. Your happiness depends on their behavior and vice-versa. If the neighbors have roaches, you'll have roaches. If they have wild parties, you're invited whether you want to attend or not. If the neighbor above you teaches tap-dancing or the neighbor alongside you gives tuba lessons, you get to practice right along with the students. If the neighbor neglects to clean their dryer vent and their house catches fire, so does yours. Their water damage is your water damage. Their mold is your mold. Their termites are your termites. Their rodents, pets, and children become your varmints, critters, and annoyances.

There are advantages to townhouses. They are good uses of land, allowing high-density neighborhoods that mean a better chance of finding more services with walking distance. Townhouses give you a little land for food gardens and privacy. Sharing a party wall means you share heat in the winter. You have close (very close) neighbors who may keep an eye on the neighborhood and help you when you need it. Townhouses tend to be more affordable than single-family residences, enabling you to live in the ideal small town that you cannot otherwise afford.

This ideal small town has services like a hospital, decent schools, grocery stores, retail stores selling essentials, library, churches, banks; everything you need for daily living. You know your neighbors and they know you. You participate in the community via church, school activities, local government, scouting, whatever you and your family likes to do. You can walk or bike to much of what you need to do. You spend your money locally, keeping the community economically healthy.

A healthy community, of which you and your family are a known and valued part, goes a long way to being stronger and more resilient in an uncertain future.

Having a short commute means that you have more money left over and more time to spend on want you want to do. A short commute also means you have a prayer of getting home if you are forced to travel on foot. Very few of us are up to walking more than ten or fifteen miles in a day. If your job is much further than that from home, think about how to get home if you could not use your car. Closer is better.

Therefore, if you are thinking about relocating, this is what to look for: a single-family house with some land in a decent school district, with services nearby and within a half-hour's commute from the main breadwinner's job.

HOUSE-HUNTING WITH MAP AND CAMERA

How do you find such a dream property? You start with a map. Purchase or print out one that has a small scale, i.e., local or county level versus the state.

Take your map and put a pin into it where the main job is located. Get your compass and draw a twenty-mile radius around it. Look for property inside this area. A twenty-mile radius is forty miles across, giving you hundreds of square miles of houses to choose from.

If you must have two jobs to bring in enough income, then draw a twenty-mile radius centered on each job location. Your target area is where the circles intersect. If they do not intersect, then either draw bigger circles until you get a joint area, or one of the two jobholders should consider changing jobs to spend less time commuting. You should also seriously consider cutting back on your living expenses.

Your long-range goal should always be Financial Independence. Cut back, cut back, cut back, and use the second job to pay off your debt. Then, when your household is debt-free, use the second job to build a fat cash stash. When you reach this position, it's time to think about ditching the most-hated job.

The house you eventually choose, like the spouse you choose, can help you reach Financial Independence, or it can ensure you remain a wage and debt slave your entire life. If your job situation is uncertain and you must rent, then you should still draw your circles and look for rentals in the magic area. The goal, always, is to reduce your costs.

Amy Dacyczyn of *The Complete Tightwad Gazette* wrote about looking for her dream house. She and her husband chose their area and looked at 176 houses before they bought #177.

They discovered that the more properties they looked at, the more they educated their eyes. They learned to spot flaws before they even went into the house; they saw potential problems that took houses off their list; and that made it easier to spot a great bargain when they found it.

This takes time, so much that you have to rent while you house-hunt. Yet is that bad? You learn the area, where the services you want are located, and which neighborhoods meet your needs.

You cannot learn this by buying a house sight unseen and in a hurry. My sister in Florida sold a house to out-of-town buyers. It was a charming house with great curb appeal, but only out-of-town buyers would have bought this place. The locals knew that twice a day the street it was on turned into a 55-mph speedway. Only local buyers knew that the neighborhood was becoming unsafe.

I remember some of the houses I've looked at over the years. A house I saw in Norfolk had a view of the Elizabeth River from two different spots: from the roof with a pair of binoculars and underneath the pallets that lined the unfinished basement floor. I also didn't buy the house in the obviously skeevey neighborhood where you needed two husbands and a big dog to feel safe in your kitchen.

A house we looked at in Hershey showed the importance of being your own building inspector. On the outside, it looked like a charming house on Granada Street in the center of Hershey. It was within easy walking distance of the schools, the library, many restaurants, and even Hersheypark.

A closer inspection revealed suspicious stains on the ceiling and walls below the second-floor bathroom. The bathtub had caulk thickly swirled around the edges like cake frosting. The basement had been subdivided into a warren of tiny, dark cells. The addition on the back of the house sagged. Floors seemed uneven. The kitchen needed a lot of work.

We seriously thought about buying the house. We could fix the problems, but we had to add the cost and hassle factor to our offer. We offered Mrs. Granada a price that was deliberately low, to see if she would come down on her price. She said no, as we expected, but she also didn't make a counter-offer. We walked away.

I've been grateful ever since that Mrs. Granada wouldn't make a deal. She saved us tens of thousands of dollars and a lot of aggravation. Years later, we met the new owners of the house, and they confirmed that, if anything, we grossly underestimated how much work and money the house needed.

We only looked at houses in our price range and in our target area. We saw, both me and Dear Husband, separately and together, many, many houses, but probably not 177 of them.

We did not buy the house that had the shaking floors and bedrooms that doubled as hallways into the next room. We did not buy the house that was surrounded by freeways on three sides. We did not buy the house where the sewage and water lines had to be installed by the homeowners. We didn't buy the houses out in the boondocks where you had to drive ten miles for a gallon of milk. We didn't buy the houses located next door to an all-night Kwik-E-Mart or the no-tell motel.

We didn't buy the Harrisburg house in a flood zone. It was a gorgeous house, with original tile, parquet floors, and high ceilings. It had everything a house junkie could want and the price was well below our maximum limit. It was also located on a one-way street that turned into a four-lane, 55-mph speedway every day at rush hour. Harrisburg has one of the worst school districts in the state. Moreover, we *knew* the city had flooded during Hurricane Agnes. Most of Harrisburg flooded! Would this property flood again? We don't *know*, but we can guess that it did. Years later, Hurricane Isabel blew through in 2003, followed by Hurricane Ivan in 2004. They both flooded much of Harrisburg. Then, Tropical Storm Lee in 2011 flooded much of the midstate again.

We also avoided houses in the Harrisburg neighborhood called Shipoke that is so low-lying that it floods after especially heavy rains. People buy houses here regularly and are then surprised when they get the flood insurance premium and complain that the basement is full of water.

At one house, I didn't even get out of the Realtor's car. We drove up to the edge of a cliff. All you could see was the plunging driveway with its mailbox and newspaper tube alongside it. You could not see the house; God knows where the photographer stood to take the picture for the real estate brochure. I thought about trying to drive up that driveway in a Pennsylvania winter of ice and snow.

We kept on looking in the magic circle.

WHAT TO LOOK FOR IN A HOUSE

Look at school districts, services within walking distance, and the size of the yard. Is the house in an area ruled by a homeowner's association? Run away, run away, run away if you don't like what you see.

Look at road maps. Is the house on a country road between two larger areas? Is it a state or federal numbered highway? Expect that road to be widened in the future giving you less front yard and more high-speed traffic.

How isolated is the house if you need fire, police, ambulance, or snowplow services? Does the house have access to gas lines, and electrical, cable, telephone, water, and sewage hook-ups? Is it on a newspaper delivery route? If you want them and they aren't available, you will have problems and major expenses.

Plenty of people around here get their water from a well and dump their sewage into a septic tank. These need to be spaced far apart or your well might pull in water that passed through your septic field. Make sure you find out where they are. Get the well water tested for bacteria to be sure of its purity.

What can happen next is that the sewage lines are extended as the area grows and the homeowner is required by the government to pay to install water and sewage lines. It won't matter that you're using a well and septic tank.

Did you know that septic tanks need to be pumped regularly? Did you know that even if the septic tank is regularly pumped empty, the leach field eventually fills up and the septic tank and its accompanying pipes will need to be moved to somewhere else in the yard? And that this work is done at the homeowner's expense? A contractor who told me that wondered what people would do when there was no place left in the yard to relocate the septic tank, particularly if the water came from a well. Install a new, more expensive system, no doubt.

Train your eye to spot damage and potential problems. Visit houses with a pair of binoculars, a flashlight, and a heavy marble. Use the binoculars to look at the roof for uneven ridgelines, leaning chimneys, and missing shingles and flashing. Use the marble to see how uneven the floors are. Use the flashlight to look into every dark corner, cabinet, attic, and basement. Look for water damage such as discolorations or paint flaking off cinder-block walls, mold, missing insulation, insect damage, and suspicious stains. If you don't like what you see, move on to the next house and save yourself the cost of a home inspection.

Take plenty of notes and photographs as you look at houses. They will help you remember what you saw, and you can show them to your partner if they were not along on the tour.

How clean is the house? If a home seller cannot clean up for you, the prospective buyer ready to hand over a bag full of money, then this person probably didn't do routine maintenance, either. It's like going into a restaurant and facing dirty bathrooms. If the part they let you see is unsanitary, would the food preparation areas be any cleaner?

When you zero in on a house, test the commute by driving out to it from your job at your usual time. I did *not* buy a townhouse in Virginia Beach for this very reason. When I went with the Realtor to look at the house at 11 a.m., it was a quick, quiet drive. When I drove out a few days later at 5 p.m., that twenty-minute drive took nearly an hour.

Next, ask about any damages to the house from radon, mold, asbestos removal, flooding, murder, meth labs, and anything else you can think of. Not every municipality requires full disclosure of any past problems so you have to ask. Find out about the school district. Ask about the crime rate at the local police station. Are new developments or shopping centers being planned nearby? Is the road behind the house being turned into a limited-access freeway? You may not get answers, but you certainly won't find out if you don't ask.

Use your eyes and look around. Visit the house at various times of day and night. Does it seem like a quiet, safe, low-key neighborhood? Do you hear screams, sirens, and gunshots? Are there vegetable gardens? People on the street who seem to know each other? Are the properties well maintained? Or do you see broken glass and litter?

Does the house belong to a homeowner's association (HOA)? Some people really like this option. But if you are serious about food gardening, chickens, compost bins, wilderness gardening, landscaping other than grass, small-scale power generation via solar panels or windmills, clotheslines, running a home business, even putting up the American flag on a flagpole, then do not buy in an HOA.

An HOA is a private organization. When you buy into one, you give up many of your rights. The Supreme Court said so. Most HOAs take extremely dim views of anything that looks messy, threatens property values, or lets the homeowner show any individuality whatsoever. In exchange for the dubious advantage of someone else watching over your life, you are subjected to a laundry list of dos and don'ts.

So read the HOA manual very, very carefully before you buy. If you don't like the rules, then don't willingly inflict them on yourself or your family.

Since this house will be your permanent home, the one you get carried out of feet first, it is worth taking the time to do it right. Just like selecting your spouse, you do not choose the first likely looking person you meet. Get to know them first and meet their family and friends, too. Pay attention to those red flags, whether it is the boyfriend being abusive to waiters or the house with cracks in the foundation. These problems do not get better by themselves.

WHAT ELSE TO LOOK FOR IN A HOUSE

So what else do we look for when buying our one and only homestead?

Some people say they won't buy anything old, as they don't want someone else's problem. Other people prefer them because they may be better built. A house built before 1960 will be far more likely to have windows all around and in every room. No air conditioning meant that every single room *had* to have natural ventilation. Windows might be lined up to provide a through breeze, allowing the house to better cool itself.

Older houses are more likely to be built with nails and solid wood as opposed to glue, staples, and oriented strand board (wood-like panels made of shredded wood glued back together). Older houses may be built of real brick or concrete block. They tend to be in older neighborhoods, more walkable and closer in, with mature trees that provide shade in the summer and allow the winter sun to warm the house. Hardwood floors and solid-wood windows are other pluses.

Newer houses tend to have better insulation and wiring. It is not easy to add insulation to an existing house, nor are they easy to rewire to meet the demand of computers, gaming systems, or Ultra HD 4K 60-inch televisions. It can be done, and the contractor will be happy to work with you on improving your house. If you do this, study up before you sign any contracts. Make sure you are sitting down when he tells you how much it will cost.

You can fix many house problems. Roofs can be rebuilt, insulation and storm windows installed, kitchens improved, and storage shelves and pantries added. Outside, gardens can be planted, fences erected, and trees and hedges grown to regulate the sun and wind.

But it is impossible to fix the location. Realtors say the three most important considerations about a house are location, location, location, and they are absolutely right.

While you're looking around and saving as much money as you can for the down payment, make lists of what you want your house to do. Do you need a home office? A sewing studio? A greenhouse? Room for a swimming pool? Extensive food gardens? Clotheslines? Chicken coops? Garage and workshop space? Storage space for a year's worth of groceries? Space for a home-based business? Every house you see should be evaluated with what *you* want in mind. Also, take notes and photos of great ideas you run across, like a solar tube, that you can add to your list.

If you end up in the lovely position of being able to choose between several equally good houses that you can afford, then you have to make decisions.

Do you want the least-expensive, smallest house? That leaves more money left over to pay off the mortgage and other debts. You can achieve Financial Independence sooner.

But, will the smallest house help you? Is there enough space for extensive food gardens and pantries? Does the house have any kind of supplemental heat like a wood-burning stove? Is it heavily insulated? Will you have to make extensive renovations that will burn up the money you saved on the price? Is there a source of water nearby? Are you allowed to harvest rainwater? Do you have enough space for a home-based business? Will the zoning allow for small livestock like chickens or rabbits? How is the commute? The schools? The walkability to local services? The neighborhood?

Do you want the biggest house? Bigger houses allow more room for options like home offices, studio and workshop space for home-based businesses, libraries, extensive food storage space, or the renting out of rooms to bring in money (and is that legal in the neighborhood?). A bigger house means you can have relatives who can contribute to your domestic economy live with you and you can better take care of elderly or challenged family members.

Bigger houses also take more money to insure, to heat and cool, to furnish, to maintain, to reroof, and to pay taxes on. If you are concerned about always having money left over every month, the size of your house matters.

Do you want the house that is furthest out in your twenty-mile radius? That means more privacy, fewer intrusive neighbors, and usually, more land.

It also means that you have to be better organized, when every single item you run out of means a trip into town to get it. Either you learn to do without said item, you maintain extensive supplies of whatever you use routinely or you keep very careful shopping lists that you continually update.

Farther out means more commuting time and its associated costs of money and wear and tear on your body and your vehicle. More commuting time means less time spent at home. Farther out means fewer neighbors who can watch over your house and help you when you need it. Farther out means that every single time you need something or you have an appointment, a school or church function, or you meet someone for lunch, you have to drive to do it.

Do you want the oldest house? The one with the solid red-oak floors, the extensive woodwork and moldings, the solid-wood doors, and the slate roof, mature landscaping, and decent ventilation that cools the house in the summer. This may be the house that needs to have insulation blown into the walls, a new roof, re-wiring, and termite removal and treatments.

Do you want the newest house? It has decent insulation, up-to-code wiring, walk-in closets, and at least one bathroom on every floor. It may also be made of chipboard, staples, and glue, with the very cheapest of everything from kitchen cabinets to carpeting. Since it is new, the assumption is that you will run either the air conditioner or the furnace to cool and heat the place. Opening all the windows won't naturally vent the building as they were not lined up by the builder to do this. Some rooms, like bathrooms, may not even have windows. Hope you have alternative lighting for those spaces when the power goes out.

HOW MUCH LAND DO YOU NEED?

Do you want the house with the largest yard? A larger yard means space for extensive food production, fruit and nut trees, berry bushes, tool sheds, bicycle storage, chicken coops, rabbit hutches, beehives, clotheslines, compost bins, rainwater storage, patios, and outdoor kitchens.

A larger yard means you can spare the space to run a yew hedge around the perimeter for privacy. You have space for wilderness areas to provide habitat for predatory insects and birds. If you should ever need to build an outhouse, you have the room.

A larger yard may have a well and a septic system, which can free you from those kinds of utility bills. Your well and septic system will also give you another system to maintain.

A larger yard will cost more when you install a six-foot chain-link fence around the perimeter, and more yews and cedars to plant as a screen. A larger yard takes more time to mow.

Do you want the house with the smaller yard? A careful layout of almost any yard will allow space for raised vegetable beds, clotheslines, compost bins, outdoor living areas, and even ornamental and wilderness plantings.

A smaller yard is much easier to maintain and keep track of as you can see it all and walk through it quickly. However, you need to plan the layout carefully. It isn't easy to relocate raised beds, compost bins, and patios if you change your mind.

Smaller yards mean saying no to some things such as chicken coops. Smaller yards mean choosing semi-dwarf fruit and nut trees. Smaller yards mean that every plant should be doing double duty: producing food, attracting pollinators, screening out the neighbors, providing wildlife habitat, and beautifying the neighborhood. This means that you cannot go down to the nursery and buy what looks pretty. You will have to do research to get the best use of your space and money.

Do you want a yard at all? Absolutely. Even if you end up with a duplex or row house, you need yard space. It's room for your kids, your dogs, your laundry, your outdoor living, and your garden. You cannot harvest rainwater or make compost without it.

Yes, you can sign up for a slot in the community garden. However, it is far easier to grow and then use tomatoes and lettuces when they are steps from your kitchen door, rather than a fifteen-minute drive away. Even a 100-square-foot walled patio (10 feet by 10 feet) will permit room for vegetables, flowers, a lawn chair, and a birdbath.

You do not need acres of land to grow food. A small set of raised beds, managed closely, can be extremely productive. Look for books like *Square Foot Gardening* by Mel Bartholomew and *How to Grow More Vegetables Than You Ever Thought Possible On Less Land Than You Can Imagine* by John Jeavons.

If you *have* to grow some of your own food, a slightly larger parcel of land – say a quarter-acre – may be better simply because you can allow parts of the yard to lie fallow every year under a life-restoring layer of green manure. Don't be lured into thinking that you need to buy a mini-farm to grow a pile of vegetables. You can manage on as little as a tenth of an acre.

A WALK THROUGH OUR YARD

When I walk Muffy through the village of Hershey, we cruise the alleys to admire the back yards. There are many tiny yards that are closely managed and they produce, clearly, plenty of produce. By the way, this is yet another reason for a fence with a privacy-enhancing hedge. You may not want to have your food production efforts on display for the world to see. And touch. And take.

I compare these yards to mine and marvel at the many ways every inch of space is used. We have about a quarter of an acre (8/32), including the footprint of our house and driveway. Subtract the house and driveway and you move down to about 6/32 of an acre. Subtract the wilderness-y screen across the front yard that provides privacy from Google Street View and habitat for wildlife, and the total acreage I can grow food on goes down to, maybe, 5/32 of an acre.

This space is our fenced-in backyard lined with yews and thujas to act as screening. There is a hedgerow of blackberries and other shrubs on the north side with hardy kiwi trellised along the fence, a tool shed and compost bins, a climbing gym overgrown with hops and weeds, clothesline space, a "back forty" to retreat to, a thicket dead center to provide wildlife habitat containing shagbark hickory trees, a row of persimmon trees and gooseberries, a rise of hazelnuts, a bed of three kinds of currents, a row of twelve columnar apple trees, and some grassy areas. This is a lot of potential food production.

Then there are the extensive raised beds, some with built-in trellises, paved walkways, and the two permanent beds of perennial vegetables (rhubarb and asparagus). These beds, if I managed them better, have the potential to provide much of the vegetables and fruit we eat.

I would not have to buy very much produce, other than citrus and bananas. It would even be possible, although challenging, to reduce my produce purchases to zero. I would have to change my cooking to reflect what I can grow in my climate, train the family to eat it, do four-season gardening, *and* preserve it for the winter.

To do this, my gardening would have to be much better thought out. If I improved my container-gardening skills and made better use of the natural winter light, I could grow citrus and peppercorns inside. According to the Logee's catalog, I could grow bananas, coffee beans, and other tropical goodies.

If I wanted to, I could transform the abandoned climbing gym into a chicken coop. That would net us eggs and manure for soil enrichment and meat for the pot. I would remove the hops — I don't think we will ever brew our own beer — and replace them with grape vines. The fruit would be more useful than the hops, and I suppose we could make our own wine.

We have enough room that we could house rabbits for meat. The difficulty would be Muffy wanting to eat the rabbits before we got to them. The other hard part would be slaughtering and prepping the chickens and rabbits for the table. But I could learn. Plenty of people do this.

If I wanted more meat than what I could raise, I could take advantage of Pennsylvania's game lands. There is a season on some kind of game animal virtually the entire year. Deer hunting is so big here that the first day of deer hunting season with a rifle is a day off from school. It is traditionally the first Monday following the Thanksgiving break, so we get a five-day weekend for the holiday. The Reese factory down the street has an empty parking lot on the first day of the season. Plenty of people in the state fill their freezer with game meat. We could do that too.

If I wanted to add more to the workload, I have the space for a beehive or two. That means better pollination for the garden, honey for the table, and beeswax for candles.

These possibilities exist on a quarter-acre lot in town. More land is not necessarily needed.

Now that we have considered how much yard we want and the sliding scale between privacy deep in bear country versus a shorter commute and more services and conveniences in town, we come back to the house itself.

BUYING THE RIGHT-SIZED HOME

How much house do you *want*?
How much house do you *need*?

They are not the same thing.

A lot of us lower-to-middle class people grew up in 1,200-square-foot, three-bedroom ranch houses. This is what our family owned in South Carolina. Three bedrooms (parents, boys, and girls), one lone bathroom, kitchen, small dining area, living room, laundry corner, furnace and hot water heater tucked in somewhere. No basement. A carport. No pantry. Tiny closets. There was very little storage space and most of it was in the accessible-by-ceiling-ladder uninsulated attic.

There are plenty of these houses around. Ones built before 1960 tend to have actual 2-by-4 stick construction built over large, heavy joists you don't see any more. Pre-1960 ranch houses also tend to have windows arranged so you can cool the place during the summer. Since they are small, they usually cost less to buy, less to insure, have lower taxes, and lower utility costs. Are they worth a look? If the location and price are excellent, then you should certainly include them in your search.

As noted earlier, it is impossible to fix the location, but you can fix the house. In the small 1959-vintage ranch house I grew up in, my dad remade the carport into an insulated family room and installed a potbelly stove for supplemental heat. He installed shelves everywhere. Redid the bathroom. Fixed problems. Insulated everything he could reach. He made that house more functional in every way and the current residents are still enjoying those improvements fifty years later.

In our 1954-vintage ranch in South Carolina, we ripped out the carpet revealing the red-oak floors, added a closet in a bedroom, and turned an enclosed porch into a home office, half-bath, *and* pantry. We rebuilt the kitchen, added ceiling fans throughout to improve the airflow, installed shelves, and insulated the attic and crawlspace. If we had not moved to Hershey, we would have renovated the carport into a family room.

Our current 1955-vintage ranch reveals what can be done while staying within the footprint of the house. It has, unlike the other two, a full basement. The previous owners finished off about 3/5th of the basement into living space with a small bathroom. They added a Florida room to the back of the house, and a partial second floor with a fourth bedroom with its own large walk-in closet and private bathroom. There is still plenty of attic space left for dead storage.

We repainted, added shelves, rebuilt the pantry to triple its usable space, insulated, insulated, insulated, added solar tubes for free lighting, built in a home office, rebuilt the closets, and added storage organizers of every kind to every possible corner. This does not include the extensive work we did in the yard, starting with the four-foot chain-link fence and the hedges.

Did this house have issues? It most surely did. However, we could afford it, its daily maintenance, and its renovations while still paying extra to the mortgage. We are in town in a great school district, Dear Husband did not have a bad commute, we don't live in an HOA, and we can walk to restaurants, stores, downtown, even the library if need be. We also have a world class (they tell us this regularly so it must be true, da?) hospital two miles away in the Penn State Milton Hershey Medical Center and in the other direction, we have Hersheypark, the Giant Center, Hershey Theatre and other forms of entertainment.

When Dear Husband spent six months house-hunting up here, he focused on finding enough space for all five of us and all our animals. We wanted a yard for the kids, the dog, and a vegetable garden. We wanted the best school district we could afford. We wanted space for storage, our library, our home office, and my sewing area. We wanted a basement. We wanted to live in town with an easy commute within twenty miles of DH's job. In fact, the commute turned out to be ten miles for many years. When the *Patriot-News* moved its offices, the commute doubled, but was still within the magic twenty-mile radius.

DH was renting an apartment up here, while I, three kids, four cats, and a big dog stayed behind in South Carolina doing the *Dress Your House for Success* program trying to sell our house. It was not easy but we did it. And it was worth it. He got us a house that we could afford. In addition, six months after the sale, we got a lovely piece of validation for all the work we put into the house in South Carolina. The new homeowner sent us a thank-you note saying how much she loved the house because it "made her organized." Wow.

So take your time and look over the houses you see. Look at location and price first. Then evaluate how much of your money and life energy it will take to turn the house into what you really want. Some extra space is absolutely worth paying for, but be realistic about how much that extra 2,000 square feet will cost you in life energy.

There are other factors to consider.

A basement is very nice.

We use most of ours as finished living space, including my sewing area and our home office. There is a finished bathroom with a shower stall so we have overflow space for guests. We rebuilt the shoddy pantry shelving into finished storage that was triple in volume compared to what we started with. The unfinished portion of the basement contains the washer and dryer, a workshop, the mechanicals, and plenty of dedicated storage space. A crawl space could not have been easily repurposed into usable space like this. A slab foundation would not even give you the option.

A carport or garage is very nice.

My dad, as mentioned above, turned our carport into finished living space by himself. He even built in a desk for a tiny home office. If we had stayed in South Carolina, we would have enclosed the carport in much the same way. A garage might be even easier to finish as it already has walls.

An attic you can stand up in is very nice.

Attics can be finished off, either into living space or dedicated storage space. The hard part is arranging for a permanent staircase rather than one of those awkward pull-down ones, or worse, a hatch accessible only with a ladder. In my parents' current house (a Victorian farmhouse that had been remuddled into a duplex), my dad took advantage of the two parallel hallways on the second floor. He removed both pull-down staircases and turned one hallway into a permanent attic staircase with a closet built underneath it.

An attic that you have to crouch in or that is full of trusses cannot be finished off into living space, and it will be very difficult to repurpose as storage space.

Porches can be very nice.

A porch can be left as-is, giving the option of fresh air and outdoor living; or it can be enclosed, allowing more heated, year-round space. My house in Norfolk had a porch that had been made over into part of the house. I used that space as a sewing room. Our house in South Carolina had the same thing. Someone, years ago, enclosed it and tied it into the heating system. We finished the job, installing a home office, a much-needed half-bath (a second toilet is a huge luxury), and a walk-in pantry.

An extra room can be very nice.

This space can become a home office, a sewing studio, a guest bedroom, or dedicated to storage.

Space for a dedicated workshop is very nice.

You should have some place to put the tools, the screws, the paint cans and their brushes. A built-in workshop means you can more easily do basic home repairs. A bigger workshop means room for bigger projects, like library-style shelving and an upgraded pantry.

Closets can be added to rooms. Existing closets can be upgraded via the miracle of ClosetMaid, almost doubling the usable space. Add shelves, add hooks, and in the kitchen cupboards add pullout slides for knives and upright storage for cookie sheets. We have done all of those jobs, and each one made the house a better performer.

Add insulation. We knew, going in, that the house had a smidgeon of rock wool insulation in the attic. Dear Husband insulated, insulated, insulated, and insulated some more. He installed reflective foil in the attic to keep the heat at bay. Younger Son then covered the fiberglass batts in the basement ceiling with white foam panels. Not only did this improve the insulating qualities and made the ceiling more light reflective, it kept the cats from eating the fiberglass and requiring expensive trips to the vet.

Insulating the house, a job that we did entirely by ourselves, paid for itself long ago. Each winter since, we spend far less money to heat the house than we otherwise would have. This awful, horrible job made us more financially independent.

THE VALUE OF HOME RENOVATION

One way to get the most out of your home-buying dollars is by buying a rundown home and fixing it up. Home renovation is not for sissies but the payoffs include a rising home value, more comfort for you and your family, and an intimate knowledge of your home's condition. You can hire people to do it for you, but it has been worth it to us to do as much as we can ourselves. This saves us huge amounts of money and vastly improves our skill sets. But it's your choice; only you know your tolerance for sanding walls and laying fiberglass batts in the attic.

There are many kinds of home renovation projects out there, and you will see all of them as you house-hunt inside your magic circle.

The best kinds are disguised as handyman specials but are really cleaning-lady specials. The house is so messy that it *looks* like it needs major repairs, but when you remove the junk, clutter, grime, and filth, you discover a nice house underneath. You have to have a good eye to see under the built-up crud to spot the solid bones underneath.

Almost as good are the home-renovation projects where all you need to do is repaint the walls, install ClosetMaid shelving in the closets, upgrade the storage space in the kitchen, pantry and bathrooms, add ceiling fans, and install bookcases.

Then there are the true handyman specials. The roof is damaged. The windows need to be replaced. The carpets needs to be ripped out and the solid oak floors sanded, stained, and polyurethaned. These jobs don't change the layout of the house and very handy homeowners can do much of this work.

The next step up are contractor specials, where the kitchen has to be gutted and rebuilt, moldy bathrooms have leaking pipes, the foundations are cracked, and the layout is so bad that walls need to be rearranged. All the wiring may have to be replaced to keep the house from burning down. These tasks are far more costly and aggravating to fix. This kind of house needs fantastic benefits to make it worth buying.

Still bigger home renovations can mean adding a second floor or a new wing. If the house is bought and paid for, expanding in place *may* be a better choice than selling and moving. Contractors for this level of work should be very carefully selected. This is not just because the contractor and his crew will see you in your bathrobe at 7 a.m., but also because you'll be living with them for months and the results of their craftsmanship for years afterwards.

So when you evaluate houses, decide if you want to do the work of upgrading a particular house to its full potential.

Any house can be improved, but is it worth doing?

I am thinking of one house in particular: the gorgeous Victorian castle in Steelton, built by a Bethlehem Steel executive. Solid mahogany everywhere, a slate roof, huge and varied rooms with ten-foot ceilings and eight-foot windows, a full basement with nine-foot ceilings. It was less than $100,000! Nevertheless, just from the walkthrough, I could see it needed another half-million dollars in renovations and repairs, starting with repointing four stories of brick walls and replacing the slate roof. This project would take decades and truckloads of money. The end result would have been a stunning castle for our heirs, located in the dying town of Steelton.

However, home renovation does not just mean fixing problems or making the house more modern. It can also create your dream home, helping your house meet the daily needs of your family.

If you want space to store a year's supply of food and a few thousand gallons of water, you will have to build the storage for it.

Are you a serious gun collector? You'll need a secure, dry place to store your arsenal.

Do you collect art? You need miles of blank walls and storage space for the rest of the collection.

If you want to harvest rainwater to water the garden in the summer, you need gutters and places to put your rain barrels. If you really need to collect every drop of rainwater to provide for every household need for a year, you'll need to install a 10,000-gallon cistern and a hand pump.

If you need to reuse every drop of your water, then you need to install and maintain a gray-water reclamation system.

Want to generate your own power? A few homes come with solar panels and battery storage space but not very many. Is the roof big enough? Is it oriented correctly? Is there space for the battery banks? Can you go passive solar with hot water heating, Trombe walls, and stone floors that act as heat sinks? You won't find many houses with these elements already in place. You will have to install your own wind turbines as well.

If your home business is car repair or fine woodworking, then you need more extra space than a writer does. A woodshop needs hundreds of square feet of well-lit space and miles of workbenches. You also need to look into local government regulations and zoning restrictions to be sure you can legally run this business from your home.

If you own a 10,000-book library, then you need to evaluate the amount of blank walls you have. Should they all be lined with bookshelves or would it be better to turn a spare room into a dedicated library with stacks?

If you want your house to light itself, then you paint every ceiling white and every wall with pastel high-gloss paint. You clean every window; install new windows, solar tubes, and skylights; and mount mirrors opposite every window.

Are you serious about bicycling everywhere? Where will the bikes live so they are easily accessed when needed? They have to be kept secure and dry, so parking them under a tree is not the best option. Where will you put their spare parts?

Are you a serious ballroom dancer? Then you need to add a

2,000-square-foot addition with a hardwood floor that is kept empty so you have plenty of space to rehearse your routine. My sister did this with her house in Florida. She absolutely loves the space, and she would never have found a house with this kind of renovation in place.

There are dozens of specialty uses that houses can do, with the proper renovations: art studios, yoga studios, dance studios, sewing workrooms or taxidermy workshops. Evaluate the houses you look at with this renovation in mind. Many of the uses can be income-generating home-based businesses.

Many people think of a home as a temporary place. They fear making changes because, in their head, it'll make the home more difficult to sell. But if you're planning to stay there for the rest of your life, you're free to do anything you want.

AVOID THE MONEY PIT

Our culture encourages going into debt, and nowhere is that more apparent than in real estate. This is because there is often a wide range between the price you're comfortable paying and the price the Realtor says you can afford. Realtors are paid a percentage of the home's selling price. The more expensive the home, the bigger their paycheck. It's in their economic self-interest to get you into an expensive house.

Being able to afford a house means not just covering the monthly mortgage payment. It means the taxes, utilities, and insurance as well. Most real estate ads display only the price, and do not include those added costs. If you have to foreclose because you cannot afford the payments, or you lose your job and you don't have enough money saved, the Realtor doesn't have to give their money back.

So insist on seeing houses only in *your* predetermined price range. Otherwise, you will be shown whatever the Realtor thinks you can afford.

When you are judging a potential home, even one in your price range, think about the true costs. Affording a house means being able to pay for the heating, cooling, lighting, landscaping, furnishing, and decorating bills in addition to the mortgage, taxes, and insurance. Some costs are ongoing, such as the heat. Other costs are one-time-only, like installing a four-foot chain-link fence around the perimeter. Can you afford a new roof? A new kitchen? Repaint the walls that are now in various shades of mustard and dirt? All that work takes cash you cannot spend on the mortgage or anything else.

Estimate what you can pay and then shop for houses that come in well under that price. Doing this allows money left over to pay for maintenance. It also means that if your income is cut for some reason, you have a better chance of being able to stay in the house. Realtors love telling you that buying a house above your means is a stretch now, but it won't be in years to come as you get those pay raises. However, pay raises may not come. You can never count on future income. You can only count on what you earn now.

Put as much money towards the down payment as you can safely manage since the bigger the down payment, the smaller the mortgage payments. Smaller payments are easier to make and they are easier to double up on. Then there is private mortgage insurance. Some lenders require a PMI policy until you pay off 20% of the home's value. A large down payment will save you the cost of those premiums.

Throughout the process, keep this fact uppermost: *YOU LOSE ALL YOUR NEGOTIATING POWER WHEN YOU SIGN THE CONTRACT.*

Up until that point, you have all the power, so long as you are willing to walk away. If the price is too high, walk. If the contract isn't what you want, walk away. If no one will explain the contract to you so that you can understand it, walk away. This applies right up to the day of closing, when you make the final walkthrough of the house before signing the contract. Even at this point, issues can arise, such as the homeowners not fulfilling their part of the bargain. Speak up and get it fixed before you sign! If the homeowner doesn't follow through, walk. There is always another house.

Repeat this mantra to yourself: There is always another house.

When you get your mortgage written up, make sure you can make extra payments towards the principal. Some contracts will penalize you for doing this, so read those documents carefully and do not sign the contract if you don't like it. A thirty-year loan is set up to pay for the house two, three, or even four times over, depending on the interest rate. Each payment is divided into principal (the money you borrowed) and interest (what the bank earns). The payments are divided on a sliding scale so the first few years on a $500 monthly mortgage payment mean a principal payment of $10 and an interest payment of $490. That is right: during the first year or so, you may pay less than $200 towards the truckload of money you borrowed.

Get an amortization schedule and read it carefully. An extra $100 a month in principal during the first year can chop many years off the total life of the loan. Putting extra dollars towards the mortgage faithfully can turn a thirty-year loan into a twenty- or even a fifteen-year loan. Does this take self-discipline? Oh, God, yes. But the payoff is well worth it.

Plenty of financial planners tell you that you should be putting your extra cash into the stock market via your 401(k) plan. They will tell you that you don't know if you are going to be living in that house for very long so you shouldn't tie up your savings.

But if you are in an area for the long haul, with all your relatives nearby, with the services and amenities that you like, then why would you move away or rent? Unless you live under a bridge or you permanently couch surf, you have to live somewhere. Make it your own place, paid for in full, instead of paying rent on the same property for fifty years to a landlord. I had relatives who did this in North Dakota. They were forced to move when their long-term rental was sold out from under them.

A carefully chosen house can help you reach Financial Independence. Houses and spouses, spouses and houses. Choose wisely, and you will always be grateful. Choose poorly, and you will never stop paying.

12

Food Gardening

A Recipe for Storage – Why Garden?

IT IS TOTALLY WORTH GROWING AT LEAST SOME of your own food. If nothing else, you'll appreciate how hard farmers work and how nice it is to go to the supermarket and buy clean, insect-free produce.

With time, you can learn to grow a lot of food for your family. Some people do so well that they grow much of what they eat and then branch out into small livestock like chickens, rabbits, and bees.

There are mountains of books out there on raising vegetables, so I am not going to repeat their advice. Since I like raised beds, I will just recommend books by John Jeavons and Mel Bartholomew as being the bibles for this method. Instead, I want to focus on what gardening books do not talk about.

It is not difficult to grow lettuces and tomatoes. As you get better at it, you get more enthusiastic. You plant more varieties, and then you find yourself with a larger garden than you had anticipated.

That's the problem not usually addressed in books explaining how you can grow more vegetables than you ever dreamed. What are you going to do with them all? Why did you grow those items? Will anyone in the family eat them?

The key to effective food production is planning and management. It's a waste of time, energy, and resources to grow more food than your household will use.

We keep running up against this problem at Fortress Peschel. It is easy to grow fifty pounds or more of tomatoes. But what do you do with them, especially if they ripen all at once? You can give only so much away to the neighbors. The rest have to be dried, frozen, or canned, which takes time, or they rot in place. At least that puts organic material back into the soil. Then the preserved tomatoes have to be used up during the rest of the year. If you don't use them up before next year's harvest, your pantry shelves will be groaning with still more preserved tomatoes.

The obvious solution is to grow less; much, much less.

This requires being honest about how much cooking you're going to do and if you're growing food your family will eat. It is really easy to grow twelve tomato plants: four slicers, four cherries, and four plums. They don't take up much space. It sounds like such a small amount. Yet twelve plants give a *huge* amount of tomatoes that have to be dealt with. You may be better off with only six plants, two of each type, or even less than that.

This is what we discovered when we planted a lot of beds without thinking ahead to the harvest. We grew peppers, which freeze well; lettuces which had to be eaten fresh; cucumbers which were better than the supermarket cukes, but were still cucumbers; carrots which were hard to grow well and cheaper to buy; and Swiss chard, which no matter how we cooked it, tasted like dirt and, my God, the enthusiasm with which it grew. One year we tried tomatillos, which were best used as a sort of lemony jam as no one would eat them any other way. The sweet potatoes grew vigorously but the weather was uncooperative so we couldn't cure them well, and we didn't use them up at nearly the rate we should have. Younger Son wanted to grow peanuts and discovered that the amount of work involved in harvesting and shelling them made supermarket ones much more attractive.

We tried onions, which turned out, after the first very good year, to be never worth the effort again. Our onions from seed didn't grow well and onion sets from the hardware store came pre-inoculated with onion maggots. Egyptian walking onions grew with such joy that they took over the yard but as they are mainly a substitute for leeks and green onions, how many do you need? Not as many as we harvested, that's for sure.

The kale grew beautifully but we didn't use it up. The spinach was excellent but grew sparsely and grudgingly. We tried New Zealand Malabar spinach, sold as a heat-resistant spinach substitute. It grew fine, but bore very little resemblance to actual, delicious spinach. Rhubarb grows with vigor but how many rhubarb pies can you eat and then it is back to that damn kitchen again to preserve it all for the winter. Bleah.

A RECIPE FOR STORAGE

Once I learned to grow the stuff, then came cooking with it *and* learning how to store the bounty for the winter.

For us, preserving the harvest had a steep learning curve in both the preservation skills and the using-them-up-in-the-kitchen skills. When you start preserving food, you have to have storage space. This varies depending on your preserving method.

A freezer takes space, costs money up front to buy, and uses electricity to run. This means they're also susceptible to power outages, which can be a significant drawback. But some veggies store better in a freezer than anywhere else.

If you favor canning, then you must have sturdy shelving, both for the supplies and the filled, heavy jars.

If you dry, pickle, or ferment foods, then you need storage space for the solar dryer and crocks, plus cool, dry, dark storage space for the preserved food.

Other vegetables are best stored in root cellars, packed in sand, or wrapped in newspapers. These spaces have to be checked regularly for varmints and signs of rot.

There are plenty of books on a wide variety of food storage methods, but I recommend *Putting Food By* as a good overview. Other titles focus exclusively on canning, drying, fermenting, or using a root cellar.

These storage methods have a learning curve, but the one thing they require is space that's cool, dry, insect-free, and in the dark. Everything lasts longer when you follow those rules.

The next challenge, after you have learned to grow and preserve vegetables and fruit, is feeding them to your family. Learning how to cook, especially to master new recipes, takes work. This is why, as you learn, you should go slowly, take your time, and be honest about what you choose to grow.

If you live with a family of vegetable haters, they won't eat that Swiss chard, no matter how pretty or fresh it is. There is no shame in sticking only to tomatoes for sandwiches and lettuce for the salad when you are just starting out.

WHY GARDEN?

So why should you even bother with this hassle when the grocery store does it for you and you have a handy farmer's market or a Consumer Supported Agriculture group nearby?

(Consumer Supported Agriculture, or CSA, links your dinner table with local farms. You sign up for a share in a participating farm's bounty. You pay for a set number of deliveries in advance and then you learn to cook and eat everything they grow and give you. A CSA can be a good way to try a huge variety of vegetables that you would otherwise never go near or see in your local supermarket.)

You should learn to grow your own vegetables because you may need to in the future.

Grocery stores are at the end of a long and intricate system that delivers food from all over the world, fresh and beautiful, to you at a ridiculously low cost. This system ignores the seasons, which is why you can get strawberries in December and apples in May. Most of the produce comes from hundreds to thousands of miles away; moved by boat, train, truck, and airplane.

I expect that system to break down due to rising energy prices. I expect food prices to rise and that astonishing wealth of choice to get much more limited.

Prior to the invention of refrigerated trains, most shipped foods were dry like grains or beans, or shipped easily like potatoes and other root vegetables. You only got fruits like strawberries that were locally grown in season.

You learn to grow your own produce to supplement the rice and beans you buy at the store. Homegrown produce supplies variety, taste, and much needed trace vitamins and minerals to supplement that boring diet of grains and legumes.

It takes time to get your soil up to par and to learn how to grow vegetables and cook and preserve them. We have had our share of failures and anyone who tells you that they can take a jar of preserved seeds and grow a successful garden after the zombie apocalypse is delusional. They will starve while waiting for those seeds to produce something edible.

Now is the time to practice growing sweet potatoes and regular potatoes when there is no risk if you fail. Now is the time to expand the variety of vegetables you and your family are willing to eat.

The time to learn how to grow and cook beets is not when your children are hungry. It is when they have full tummies and you have a full pantry.

13

Home and Personal Security

Locking Down Your House — Upgrading Windows - Signs for Emergency Personnel and Delivery Guys - Protecting Garages, Tool Sheds, and Porches - Keeping Your Vehicle Secure - Emergency-Proof Your Vehicle - Dogs as Alarm Systems - Know Your Neighbors - Keeping Yourself Safe - Be Prepared - Know Where You Are - The Problem with Common Sense

GOOD SECURITY IS TEDIOUS, EXPENSIVE, INTRUSIVE, and demands constant vigilance. You have to be right every time. Burglars, terrorists, and other nefarious people have to be right only once.

However, there are simple methods you can use, both active and passive, that will improve the security of yourself and your household. You won't be bulletproof, but you will be more secure. Some suggestions are easy to implement, such as keeping your doors locked starting now. Others are harder, such as growing that six-foot-tall thorn hedge.

LOCKING DOWN YOUR HOUSE

If someone really, really wants to get into your house, they can do it. A sledgehammer will take out your picture window in a second. A kick next to the doorknob will splinter the frame. A brick can shatter a sliding door.

But burglars, like most people, prefer easy jobs to hard jobs. The harder or more dangerous-looking the house, the greater the chance they will look elsewhere.

The first line of defense is to keep your doors locked, even when you are home. A typical burglar tactic in towns where houses are cheek-by-jowl is to walk down the street, checking each door. A locked door means move along; an unlocked door says come on in. Even though we live in a suburb, we never leave the front door unlocked unless someone is using it.

Next, make it difficult to look inside. During the day, it's hard to see into my house. Not only is it much brighter outside than in, the semi-sheer lace panels on my windows obscure the view. The windows also have shades that are pulled down to block the summer sun and heat, and at night, the drapes are closed. If I am cooling the house in the evening, then the drapes are left open and the shades raised far enough to expose the screens. The rest of the glass is covered, blocking the view inside.

This seems obvious, but when I walk Muffy in the evening, I see many houses with their lights on and a clear view into their rooms. I see the glow of giant TVs and computer monitors.

Don't do this for two reasons.

The first is security. At night, not only is it easy to see into a room, the light is so bright it catches your eye, ensuring you notice.

Secondly, if light is escaping, then so is heat. On my walks, I've seen many houses with screened windows improperly closed in cold weather, some even with box fans installed. That homeowner is literally paying to heat the outside. As soon as the sun goes down, close the windows and put up the window treatments. Trap your heat, and keep out potential prying eyes.

Your outside doors should have working locks. The doorknobs should be exterior grade and lockable. Many years ago, Dear Husband worked for a company that housed him in a farmhouse owned by its CEO. He discovered that the side door had an interior doorknob. It was installed so from the outside you could see the latch, and it could be forced back with a butter knife. Never assume, especially with older houses, that the homebuilder did it right.

But a lockable doorknob is not enough. The door also needs a separate deadbolt. Install it yourself if you are handy or hire a locksmith to do the job.

Are you the home's first owner? If not, consider having your locks rekeyed so that you are the only one who can open them. You have no idea how many keys had been distributed to family members, neighbors, or secreted under a forgotten rock in the yard. A locksmith can change the tumblers and give you new keys. If you are using a separate key for the front and back door handles, he can also change them so both will open with the same key. If you are renting, have this job done yourself rather than wait for the landlord to do it. You will have to give a key to your landlord but again, you will have more control over how many keys there are.

So buy a heavy-duty exterior-grade doorknob. We use the lever-style knobs instead of the round models; it is far easier to work these when you are tired, carrying bags, or in a hurry to get inside. A strong lock is your first line of defense.

As for deadbolts, they come in two styles: single key, which has a turn-knob on the interior side, and double key that requires a key to unlock both sides of the door.

The double key makes the door more secure, but in an emergency, such as a fire in the middle of the night, you may not live to regret scrambling in the dark to find the key, jam it in, and turn it while you're in a near panic and your eyes are stinging from the smoke. Some people keep the key on a hook by the door. If you are going to do that, you might as well get the knob-opening single-key style.

A double-key deadbolt might be effective in doors with a glass sidelight that a burglar can punch through. If you use a single-key deadbolt, the way to foil the burglar breaking the glass and unlocking the door is to install a chain bolt. Get the heaviest one. Do not install it above the doorknob within a burglar's easy reach. Install it at the top or the bottom of the door, as far from the windows as you can get. The longer the intruder is slowed at the door the greater the chance you or your dog will notice, and you can call the police.

Here's a handyman tip: When you install the locks and strike plates, don't use the screws that come with the lockset. Get the longest screws that will fit through the strike plate. Something three or four inches long will go through the frame and into the house. They'll be hard to screw in, so spray a little WD-40 on them first, drill a pilot hole, and use a power screwdriver rather than brute force for this job.

While you are upgrading the screws on the strike plate, upgrade your hinges as well. Get the heaviest hinges and screws longer than three inches. This will support the door better and make it harder for someone to kick it off the hinges.

Look at your front door. Is it solid, heavy oak? All steel? Is there a peephole or a small, high window so you can see who is outside? All-glass front doors look lovely and let in tons of natural light and anyone can get through in seconds with a brick. Get a solid-wood door and a beautiful, all-glass lockable storm door. That will let light in during the day if you need to and leave two layers of locked doors at night. A storm door also cuts down air infiltration and protects your solid-oak door from the elements.

As long as you're in a renovating mood, consider these upgrades as well: weather-stripping, a loud knocker that can be heard anywhere in your house, and a peephole. As a final touch, install shopkeeper's bells on the inside. When the door is opened, they make noise, alerting you and your dog to someone coming in. A cheaper alternative is to hang jingly bells from a loop and hang them on a cup hook mounted at the top of the door. Put the bells on every exterior door, including back doors and French doors leading to your patio. Use stick-on or suction cup hooks to mount them to patio sliders.

UPGRADING WINDOWS

Next up are those big holes in your home's walls called windows. Because they are made of glass, they are vulnerable to a rock being thrown through them. You may think a burglar is unlikely to smash a window because of the noise. Unfortunately, your neighbors are unlikely to investigate the sound of breaking glass, particularly if they are tucked away in their homes with the air conditioner running.

Burglars sweep through your home quickly, most times in less than ten minutes. They will head for your master bedroom first, looking for jewelry, money, and electronics, and in your bathroom, prescription drugs. If you proudly display your collection of hunting rifles, your big-screen TV with its game consoles, and your framed rare coins on the wall, and this is easily visible at night from the street for everyone to see, you've made them inviting to burglars as well.

Not only should you harden your windows against burglars, you need to see your home as a criminal would. Walk around your house during the day. What can be seen from the street? Do it again at night when the inside lights are on and the curtains pulled back. This is what a burglar sees.

To counter this, I highly recommend a layer of lacy semi-sheer panels at each window. All patterns work the same; they make it harder to see into the house during the day without blocking the free sunshine, and they add another layer of insulation at night. The thicker or heavier the pattern, the more light they block and the more they conceal. Choose what works best for your situation; more lightweight panels on a rod will equate to fewer heavy panels as the added bulk of another panel compensates for the thinner fabric.

Layers and layers of window treatments are also a little harder for an intruder to struggle through than a single set of vertical blinds.

The Window Dance chapter tells you how to dress your windows for heating and cooling; it also works for security. If your prized possessions cannot be seen, there is less chance you will lose them.

Next, check your window locks. Every window should have a locking mechanism. The lock makes it harder to open from the outside and keeps the window tightly closed against the elements.

If you have old wooden double-hung windows, most hardware stores carry replacement locks. They also carry a special lock for a wooden double-hung window that lets you open them a few inches at night and no more. Get the heaviest brass ones you can afford. Mount these air-venting locks so the window goes up about two or three inches from the sill. More than that is a judgment call; you get more cooling air but it's easier to pry up the window from the outside.

If you have new-fangled double-hung windows of vinyl or aluminum and the cheapie, fragile built-in air-venting locks don't work, got broken, don't exist, or you don't trust that flimsy tab of plastic, use ½-inch oak dowels as a substitute. Cut a 3-inch section of dowel, insert it under the open window and close it. Measure the space between the top of the lower window and the top of the window opening. Cut the second dowel to fit. Working together, both dowels will keep the window from being opened from the outside with anything other than a brick. If your windows are large, use two sets of dowels per window, one set per side. When you place the dowels, tuck them into the frame where the molding will conceal them.

Just like your doors, if your windows are not in use to air out the house, they should be kept locked. Make sure your family knows this and knows how to operate the lock in case of fire.

Your windows should have screens for airing out your house and storm windows as well. If you can, get screens that cover the entire window. Those that cover half the window are easier to slide aside. A full screen lets you vent the room better and keep out bugs.

Storm windows get opened and closed with the rain and the seasons; fully closed against the winter night, they offer another layer to get through. If you are running an air-conditioner, make sure the

Home and Personal Security

storm windows are tightly closed to trap that expensively cooled air.

When you close your storm windows, the outermost pane of glass is at the top and over the lower, inner pane so the window sheds rainwater. If you reverse this, rainwater can leak inside. This seems like a minor point, but I routinely see incorrectly closed windows when I walk Muffy. We also see open storm windows in the dead of winter, depriving the house of both heat and security. This is such an easy fix.

If you have to replace windows, ask about security features and make sure your new ones come with locks and full-size screens. There are also plastic films that you can adhere to the inside of the glass that will make your windows less breakable. They will probably let in a little less free sunlight, but then, so do sheers.

If you live in a hurricane zone, then storm shutters would be invaluable. Their cost is sure to be less than that of rebuilding your house after the storm, and they would be easier to use than storing, installing, and removing sheets of plywood. Their presence may also give you a discount on your homeowners insurance. Closed storm shutters at night would be very secure.

SIGNS FOR EMERGENCY PERSONNEL AND DELIVERY GUYS

Take another walk around your house and, in particular, look at it from the street. Are the house numbers large, readable and clearly visible day and night and in all seasons? If not, put a set on the house, the mailbox, and on a reflective sign at the street end of the driveway. If your growing shrubbery will obscure a house number, move it or put up another set. Make sure it can be seen from both directions.

Why do this? Your mother, your friends, and the mailman know where you live, but paramedics, police, and firefighters do not. People have died while the ambulance tried to find them. Houses have burned to the ground while firefighters looked for the house. When seconds count, don't make it hard for the EMTs to find you.

Proper identification on your house can benefit your neighbors. Emergency crews keep track of the address signs they pass. If every third or fourth house is marked so the firemen can find it, then they can find the ones in between more easily.

We learned this from our Oldest Child when he delivered pizzas. He routinely saw what paramedics see: no house numbers, confusing house numbers, illegible house numbers, dark brown numbers on black siding, white numbers on cream siding, numbers twenty feet off the ground, numbers painted on the curb with cars parked over them, numbers so small they can't be seen from the street, and numbers that appear to have been installed at random locations.

Correctly placed numbers benefit everyone trying to find your house. The pizza guys can deliver your hot food faster. The ambulance guys gain precious seconds that could save your life. The FedEx and UPS guys want to find your house quicker, along with the police, plumbers, electricians, paper carriers, and furniture delivery crews.

House numbers are available at hardware and big box stores in a variety of designs. Look in particular for the ones that are readable at night in the rain.

The best house numbers are reflective signs that you mount on a post at the end of the driveway. Check with your local rescue group or fire station; many sell these signs as a fundraiser. If you work with a local group such as the scouts, you may want to suggest this as a way to raise money. I think the bright blue reflective sign is more visible, day or night, than the green reflective sign.

PROTECTING GARAGES, TOOL SHEDS, AND PORCHES

The rules about valuables apply to a driveway, carport, or garage. Leaving something unsecured and theft-worthy in plain sight is asking a casual thief to stop by. Keep your carport or driveway clean and clear of bikes, lawnmowers, and yard equipment. You will have more room for your car and less incentive for someone to help themselves.

If you have a garage, open the door only when you are entering or leaving. There is no reason to show off your expensive woodworking shop for the world to see. If your garage door comes with a lock, use it, particularly when you are on vacation.

The door between your house and your garage is vulnerable because many homebuilders treat it like an interior door. If someone forces his way into your garage, that door is all that stands between your family and a home invader. Treat it like your front door: Replace it with a heavy, exterior-grade model, mount it with extra-long screws, and install the proper hardware and locks. Be sure to have it keyed so you can open it with your front-door key.

Your toolshed should have its own lock. Even if you only use it when you are on vacation, it can protect your lawnmower, weed eater, chainsaw and other easily pawned tools. If your toolshed is large enough, it can store items like patio furniture and gas grills while you're away. Lock up everything you don't want to lose.

Porches are lovely for sitting on and keeping you out of the rain when you are unlocking the door. Don't leave anything there that you don't mind disappearing. Several streets over from us, a homeowner had a pair of heavy concrete dwarf statues sitting by his front door stolen. Each one weighed about seventy-five pounds. He bought another set and chained them down. In some cities, you have to chain down your shrubbery! If I lived in a place where I had to guard my azalea bushes, I'd move.

As for your spare key, for heaven's sakes, don't put it under the doormat. Burglars know all the typical hiding places, including fake key-hiding rocks, flowerpots, and turtle statues. If you're feeling tricky, put a false key under the mat and store the real key elsewhere. Probably the only safe place is inside your German shepherd's doghouse in your fenced backyard. If your dog isn't using his doghouse – because he is in the kennel – then don't leave a key hanging around. A trusted neighbor is a better choice.

As part of your household security, every evening when you lock up for the night, make it a point to check your doors, windows, garage doors, etc. Get your kids to bring in any bikes or sports equipment they left on the lawn or driveway. Don't make it easy for thieves.

Remember, most burglars are looking for easy pickings. Don't give it to them.

KEEPING YOUR VEHICLE SECURE

First and foremost, keep it locked! I frequently see a car at a convenience store or in the driveway with its engine running and left unattended. That driver is wasting gas and begging someone to steal the car. If you must run the engine to defrost the car, then either do it while scraping the windshields or get a second set of keys and lock the vehicle while the engine is running.

Don't leave your car unlocked, unless you are loading and unloading, not even when it is parked in your own driveway. Even if your car isn't stolen, a casual thief can get in and steal change, phone chargers, gloves, anything portable, even the personal identification such as ownership papers, insurance cards, and registration from the glove box. Don't make it easier for someone to steal your identity.

Just like with burglars, car thieves look for opportunities by walking down the street, testing doors to see which fool left their auto unlocked. Don't be that fool.

Keep your doors locked while driving. Most late-model cars automatically lock the doors at a certain speed. Get in the habit of locking the doors yourself as soon as everyone is in the vehicle. Don't wait for the car to do it for you. That way, when you are still moving slowly in the parking lot, it will be that much harder for someone to open your door and rob you. Don't make it easy for potential carjackers.

Don't store anything in sight that you would mind being stolen. Keep your interior empty and clean; this sends the message that there is no reason to break into the car. If you have a trunk, use it to store your purchases. If you don't have one, you may have a built-in panel that pulls across the back of the vehicle. If not, tuck your packages on the floor in the backseat or cover them with a blanket.

If you have a GPS unit on your dashboard, cover it with a ball cap when not in use. No burglar will waste time on a dime store ball cap.

This is more of a safety tip: Back into the space when you park.

This is a very worthwhile skill to learn. Backing in makes it easier and quicker to drive out; you can see exactly what you are doing and if anything or anyone is in the way. Pull-through parking spaces work well too, even if it means being a few spots further away from the building. It is much easier to get out fast.

When you park at home, you still want to back into the driveway and for the same reasons. Taking a few extra moments to back in saves you time when you are leaving in a hurry for work or an appointment.

There is another benefit to backing in. After you pull in and park, children have a tendency to leave stuff in the driveway behind your car. This creates a nasty surprise the next time you back out and over those trikes, jump ropes, and other car-damaging junk. By backing into the space, you will be able to see what is laying in wait in your driveway when you leave. That also makes you less likely to run over a toddler.

EMERGENCY-PROOF YOUR VEHICLE

When you park, especially for a large event or in an unfamiliar place, look for identifying signs so you can find your car quickly when you leave. Back in or pull through; either method will make it faster and safer to pull out of the parking lot and leave. Parking further away from the front door and closer to the exit will also allow you to escape the parking lot faster as you do not have to watch out for other cars and pedestrians quite as much. If you know you are going to be in that huge lot after dark, park near a street light. Then you can see if anyone is hanging around.

If you don't feel comfortable, ask building security to escort you. That is what they are there for. Practicing vehicle safety doesn't work if you're mugged in the parking lot.

Get a cell phone charger for your car and use it. Cell phones only work when charged, so you might as well use the time spent driving for this purpose.

Whenever your gas gauge goes below halfway, fill up the gas tank. This prevents the emergency (power outage, weather, etc.) where you can't get gas. If you are running on fumes and can't buy gas, you are stuck where you are.

Once upon a time, cars were much less reliable. When you pulled into a gas station, the attendant would pump the gas, check your oil and tires, wash your windows and make sure that you could drive on safely. Gas station attendants are a thing of the past. Even if you faithfully get your car serviced at the dealership, it doesn't hurt to know a few techniques to keep you from ending up by the side of the road.

This is not just protection against an uncertain future. In January 2016, a blizzard swept through Pennsylvania. Tractor-trailers on the turnpike became stuck on a hill, causing a backup several miles long. Motorists were stranded in their cars for more than 16 hours and the National Guard was called out to help them.

Here are some basic rules for the road that will help you keep rolling.

Check your vehicle's fluids – windshield wiper fluid, oil, radiator, brakes, power steering, transmission fluid, and tire pressure on a regular basis, weekly if possible. This will catch problems while they are still small and ensure you don't run out of windshield wiper fluid when that truck sprays your windshield with mud.

Follow your vehicle's maintenance schedule. Changing the oil regularly can add years to the life of your vehicle as does changing air, oil, and fuel filters. The maintenance schedule is not there to make money for the dealership. It helps keep your car running better and longer. If you feel handy, get a Chilton's guide for your car and do this work yourself.

Get road maps for your area. Know how to read and use them. Yes, you have a GPS. Sometimes, they don't work. They've been known to make mistakes. Sometimes, you want an alternative route because of accidents or unbelievable traffic jams as everyone flees the city to escape the overturned chlorine tanker car. When you drive in your daily routine, take alternate routes. This makes your mental map of your driving area larger, more complete, and more flexible *before* you need to know where that gas station is.

Carry basic supplies in your trunk. Get a milk crate and fill it with a quart of oil (check your vehicle's manual for the type), anti-freeze, windshield wiper fluid, brake fluid, powered aluminum, fix-a-flat in a can, dry gas, a tire gauge, space blankets, a flashlight, a poncho, water and snackies. Carefully packed, they will fit into a standard milk crate. Make sure your spare tire is full of air and while you're at it, do you know how to change a tire? Do you know where the jack is and the tool to raise and lower it? Is the car's manual in the glove box?

The powdered aluminum is used to fix tiny radiator leaks. If you discover your radiator is losing fluid rapidly during a trip – and I mean over a half-hour or an hour – pour the powder into the radiator and refill it. Drive the vehicle for a while and recheck the fluid level (be very careful; the water will be scalding). The powder should fill in the pinhole long enough to drive home safely.

We learned this on a long road trip from Delaware to Charlotte, N.C. The radiator light lit up in the hills of Virginia. We pulled into a truck stop, where the clerk enlightened us about the magic powder. The fix worked so well that it lasted for fifteen years, until we scrapped the van because it was collapsing from old age.

The fix-a-flat can keep a tire going without you having to change it. The tire will be ruined, but you can get home or to the garage safely. The dry gas treatment will remove water condensation that may be in your gas lines. This can make your car drive poorly, especially in the winter. The poncho lets you change a tire or check fluids in the rain. The flashlight helps when it is dark and raining. The space blanket traps or repels heat depending on which side is out. If you have to stay in your car, in the winter, it can be a lifesaver. It is the size of a deck of cards, costs a few dollars and can be found in a store's camping department. Get one for each person who routinely rides in your car.

Water and snackies are for that emergency that leaves you trapped on the road for hours. You can buy U.S. Coast Guard-approved bags of water and emergency food bars. They are very expensive but they are made to be stored in all kinds of weather in the trunk of your car (or boat) for years. You can substitute water bottles and granola bars, but the bottles can break or leak in the winter and the bars should be swapped out regularly.

Keep your car washed to keep corrosive road salts from damaging the finish and causing rust. The glass on your headlights will become cloudy. There is a buffing compound at auto parts stores that will polish out some of the scratches. This will help you see better at night. Doing the taillights means other people can see you better.

What does this have to do with security? A well-maintained auto is far less likely to leave you stranded at the mercy of strangers.

The final and most important piece of car security is to pay attention!

If you drive on autopilot, checking your smartphone, you will miss seeing the accident that is about to happen. Carelessness is a big cause of accidents, just like fatigue, recklessness, and substance abuse.

You may think that talking to passengers would be just as distracting as talking on your cell. It isn't, simply because your passenger will scream that a truck is headed right at you whereas your cell conversation partner has no idea that a pick-up truck ran a stop sign and is about to T-bone you.

And don't do anything that distracts you from the road: texting, eating, reading, applying make-up, reaching around behind you to swat your mouthy kids, driving while drinking, getting high, or being blurry with fatigue.

Not paying attention leads to unlocked doors and someone opening them at a red light. Not paying attention means leaving valuables in the back seat and wondering why you were targeted for a smash-and-grab. It is hard to be mindful and harder to train recalcitrant family members to do the same. Nevertheless, their safety depends on you seeing that SUV blow through the red light in front of you.

DOGS AS ALARM SYSTEMS

Electricity is a wonderful thing, but I don't like using more than I have to, and I don't like having vital systems depend on its presence. Electricity can and does go out due to bad weather, cars running into electrical poles, trouble at the sub-stations, or terrorists or hackers knocking out the grid (unlikely but it could happen). An alarm system is dependent on electricity. A small to medium-size dog can be far more useful than any alarm system.

We have Muffy. She is a forty-five-pound German shepherd/unknown terrier mix and a valuable upgrade to our home security.

First of all, she is here. She barks to warn us if someone is approaching the house. She roams free in our fenced backyard. I have cowbells on each gate to make noise when someone enters. Muffy barks and races to the gate to see who is there.

I walk Muffy through my neighborhood, meeting my neighbors. Muffy likes to say hello to everyone, so not only do I get to know my neighbors, they know me and know that we have a dog.

Burglars hate dogs of any size. Even the tiniest ankle-biter will bark, sometimes a lot, when someone enters their territory. Word gets around. Many years ago, I had an acquaintance at church tell me that in her old neighborhood, they were the only people who never had their house broken into. They had a big Siberian husky. Two weeks after the dog died, their house was robbed. Word got around.

However, you don't need a hundred-pound Rottweiler to improve your home security. In fact, unless you can handle, train, and work daily with an aggressive dog like that, you shouldn't get one. Almost every dog, no matter what its size, will know its territory and make a racket when someone enters it. That is what you want: a mobile, loyal alarm that does not need electricity.

However, having a dog works *only* if the dog is with you, in your house. This is especially true at night.

If you're planning to keep a dog chained up in the far corner of your yard and only see it to give it food and water, get an alarm. Not only is that incredibly cruel and unfeeling towards the dog, but if your dog barks at a prowler, how will you know? And why should the dog bark? Dogs show loyalty and love to the people who show loyalty and love to them.

If you do not want to care for another member of the family – and a dog *is* a member of the family – then don't do this. There are far too many neglected, unwanted, abused dogs out there. Don't add to the problem.

If you do get a dog, then learn basic doggy obedience training. The vet, the humane society, the local kennel club, the pet supply store, and the groomer can recommend a dog trainer. The better trained you and your dog is, the happier everyone will be.

You do not have to get a particular breed of dog for home security. Almost every dog, purebred or mongrel, will be territorial enough to be a watchdog.

While a watchdog instinctively warns you of an intruder, a guard dog tries to handle the problem. If you cannot control the guard dog, you lost control of both the dog and the problem.

Guard dogs and attack dogs are usually certain specific breeds. They *require* extensive dog-handling experience and regular training to be safe around your family and effective in performing their duties. Unless you know what you're doing with aggressive dogs, don't do this to yourself, your family or the dog.

To get a dog, start with the local humane society. Every humane society runs a shelter with plenty of dogs that need good homes. Stop in regularly, get to know the staff, and meet the dogs. Spend time with them and see who works well with you. Every family member should meet the dog prior to adoption.

If the paperwork seems intrusive, it is because every dog at the SPCA was abandoned by someone. The staff wants a forever home for each dog and a good match means they will not have to take back a dog that's more traumatized because worthless humans let the dog down, again. Before you bring your new family member home, have your house ready with dog food, leashes, beds, and a vet visit lined up.

If you want a specific breed, study up to learn their strengths and weaknesses. A great book to start with is *Paws to Consider: Choosing the Right Dog for You and Your Family* by Brian Kilcommons and Sarah Wilson.

After you read up on breeds, visit dog shows to see the breed in action. It is very different reading about a breed and seeing the dog for real. Any veterinarian, pet supply store, and the local SPCA will know about the local shows.

Dog owners are generally happy to tell you all about their wonderful dog breed. They will also be honest about the challenges that the breed presents. For example, I originally wanted a Newfoundland. They are great big dogs and extremely gentle around children. I liked everything I read about them. The books did mention, in passing, that Newfies shed and drool. Indeed they do. However, it is not until you see the dog in action that you can appreciate that Newfies are the size of ponies and look like black bears.

Nor did I truly understand what shedding and drooling meant until I saw at a dog show that every Newfie left a trail of black hair, even after they had been groomed to a fare-thee-well, and their owners were draped with towels to mop up the rivers of drool. They ate like horses and shat like elephants.

We do not have a Newfoundland.

If you've decided to adopt a purebred dog, you have several options. Start by avoiding a dog from a puppy mill. They tend to be the pedigreed breeds sold in pet shops. These dogs may have papers but that does not mean that they have good, healthy genes. Many puppy mill dogs develop severe health and temperament problems.

If you want a purebred, go with a breeder, local if you can, who cares enough about the dog to work with you. A reputable breeder will take the dog back if there's a problem. They guarantee health and temperament (assuming you don't abuse the dog). They can recommend local trainers and obedience schools. They let you see the parent dogs and inspect the kennel. Puppy mills don't let you do any of this.

Another excellent source for a purebred dog is one of the many breed-specific rescue groups. Nearly every breed has one. Like the humane society, rescue groups will investigate you to ensure a forever home for the dog. Rescue groups don't care about your privacy; they care more about finding a happy, permanent match for their dog. There will be fees of course, because like the SPCA, these groups spend plenty of money on dog food and vets.

Muffy came from Castaway Critters. She has been a wonderful addition in our life. She is always up for a long walk, allowing me to thoroughly explore my area and improve my fitness.

She has also proven her worth in the backyard. We do food gardening, with vegetable beds, berry bushes, and fruit and nut trees. Groundhogs and rabbits were eating everything in sight. Rabbits crawl under the fence and groundhogs can waddle up a four-foot chain-link fence to get to your beans. They are also pretty damn fast, so you will never catch one.

We no longer have a problem with rabbits or groundhogs. Muffy patrols faithfully, and she has killed or severely injured four groundhogs so far. The rabbits seem smarter and stay out of the yard. Muffy, of course, uses the yard to do her business. Her urine advertises to all sorts of critters that a predator lives here. It also seems to keep raccoons, possums, and skunks out of the yard.

To let everyone know you have a dog, put up a "Beware of Dog" sign on every gate. Get them at the hardware store for a few bucks each. Make them last longer by laminating them with plastic or clear contact paper. Use sturdy wire to hang them on your fence, and they should last for years.

Avoid getting cute with your signs, like those that say "Cave Canem" (Latin for "beware of dog"). No one will know what that means. You want to be clear that you have a dog on patrol. The best sign I saw had a silhouette of two Dobermans and the line "We can reach the fence in 10 seconds. Can you?"

We installed a dog door in our Florida room to make it easier for Muffy to get in and out without us manning the sliding doors. We keep them unlocked, and even if we did lock them, I suppose a skinny burglar could shimmy through the dog door. However, dog doors generally mean dogs and most burglars know this. More than one prowler has gone through a big dog door into a house and met the Rottweiler on the other side. If you have a dog door but no dog, then close it off.

Your dog can also make it easier to hide a spare key on your property. Put the key on a hook inside the doghouse that your Great Dane sleeps in. Not many people will risk their hand to reach in.

So if you like dogs and are willing to do the work, a furry friend can be a terrific upgrade to your household security. They are the only alarm that can also act as your companion, garden patrol, deterrent, exercise machine, and neighborhood explorer. Dogs do it all.

KNOW YOUR NEIGHBORS

The next easiest step in home security is getting to know your neighbors. If there is any kind of disaster, the people around you are the most likely to come to your aid. The bigger the disaster, the longer it will take for the cavalry in the form of FEMA and the Red Cross to arrive.

This does not mean that you need to – or should – treat your neighbors as your dearest friends. It does mean you should get to know them, so they'll see you as a neighbor. You are not a stranger squatting in one of the foreclosed houses. You belong.

Walking Muffy regularly and at different times of the day means that I recognize many of my neighbors on sight. They can certainly recognize me. They may not know my name, but they know that we have a dog. I always smile, say hello, and make general conversation about the weather or gardening.

Muffy allows me to thoroughly explore my area without appearing to be nosy. I don't look like a suspicious person walking up and down the alleys looking into other people's backyards. I am just walking my dog. I am not looking over trashcans for possible mongo or piles of scrap lumber. I am just walking my dog. I am not looking for low-lying areas that flood, potential food sources from unused apple trees, or like-minded preppers as evidenced by their extensive food gardens and water-storage devices. I am just walking my dog.

Muffy allows me to map out a two- or three- mile circle around my house in the most innocuous way possible. I blend right in as I learn the ins and outs of my area. She even pays for a can of dog food now and then with the change we pick up.

There are other ways of getting to know your neighbors. If someone holds regular get-togethers, start attending them. Meet people. Be part of the group. It could be the crotchety retiree with the big vegetable garden who calls the fire department when your house starts smoking while everyone is away. Or the nosy dog walker who calls the police when she sees that something isn't right at the home where the lights are on, the mail is piling up, and the grass isn't being mowed.

Be civil, be polite, and ask questions about how their tomatoes are growing. If you are starting a garden yourself, most of the long-time gardeners will be happy to tell you all about the soil, and from which nursery they buy their plants.

If you hear of a break-in, spread the word! If your car gets its side mirrors broken by the trash truck, tell your neighbors. It shows that you care, and someone may have had the same issue as you and knows who to call to complain.

This kind of contact can lead to neighborhood watch organizations. If you have a group in your neighborhood, join it. If you don't, and petty crime seems to be rising, you may want to start one of your own.

What neighborhood watch groups are supposed to do is watch. Not guard. Not defend. They are extra eyes and ears to see what is happening from day to day. If someone's walking down the street testing house or car doors, then call the police. Get a description of the offender and any vehicle associated with him. Be the security you want to see.

Are there beer bottles strewn along the roadside? Did your dog find the guts of a deer in the grass median? Are there missing stop signs and street signs? They should be noted and reported to the police. It never harms the security of a neighborhood to have a patrol car drive down it a little more. Word will get around that there are eyes on the street and criminal activity will be noticed.

As you get to know your neighbors, opportunities may arise to talk about disaster preparedness. The better prepared each house is, with stored food, water, etc., the safer overall the neighborhood will be. Hurricanes, ice storms, and the like are great opportunities to talk about the importance of flashlights, batteries, and sleeping bags. This does not mean you need to go into detail about your year's supply of rice, your gold coins, or your arsenal. That is nobody's business but your own.

But don't push the prepper talk too much. Be seen as a reliable, upstanding, law-abiding citizen, not that kook in the tin-foil beanie. Clued-in, responsible neighbors are more likely to be told about potential problems, such as the house down the street that is turning into a drug den and teenage hangout. Helpful and reliable neighbors are more likely to be listened to when they suggest basic disaster preparedness such as what FEMA and the Red Cross recommend.

KEEPING YOURSELF SAFE

You can enhance your own personal security by following a few rules.

The first and most basic tip is: **Pay attention**.

Know where you are and who is around you. Listen to the sounds around you and not to the music on your smartphone. People have stepped in front of oncoming freight trains because they were plugged into their tunes. They stepped in front of cars and trucks for the same reason. Ear buds do not provide a force field against a ton of rolling metal.

If you wear ear buds while driving, walking, bicycling, etc., at least turn down the sound so you can hear the sirens of emergency vehicles, horns of trucks, whistles of trains, barking of dogs, and whatever else is happening around you.

The same goes for cell phones. If you are paying close attention to your conversation, you are not paying attention to your surroundings.

Pay attention when you walk through a parking lot or down the street. If you are leaving the mall late at night and you don't want to walk through the dark parking lot with strangers hanging around, ask mall security for an escort. They do it all the time. What concerns you more: your perceived toughness (*I don't need an escort*) or not being mugged?

Pay attention when you exit a 10,000-person performance. Pay attention when you get in and out of your car. Pay attention when you unload groceries and other purchases from your car. Who is watching you?

If a situation doesn't feel right or safe, it might be because it isn't safe. We get bad vibes for a reason. Sometimes, it may be paranoia. Sometimes, it isn't.

In his best-selling book *The Gift of Fear,* Gavin de Becker theorizes that millions of years of evolution determined that people who noticed their surroundings were less likely to be eaten by tigers and more likely to reproduce. There are still plenty of tigers around, but now they are two-legged.

Don't do stupid stuff. Yes, you should be able to get so drunk you are on the verge of blacking out and then stagger to the automatic teller at 3 a.m. to get cash for that skeevey all-night diner and be perfectly safe from predators.

But life is not like that. Our society is so safe that most of the time we think we will never be harmed. So we lose control of our body and senses and invite someone else to control us. Sad? Wrong? Unfortunate? Criminal? Sure. Get over it. This is what your mother meant when she said stop looking for trouble. Ask for trouble, and the universe will give it to you.

Predators look for the weakest prey in the herd. They don't care about your political correctness. They look for victims. Don't make it easy to be victimized.

Does this mean you shouldn't have a good time? Well, if you only have a good time when you are drunk or stoned, you have a problem.

The more high you have to be to have a good time, the bigger the problem you have. If you are realio and trulio serious about a scary and difficult future, you need to address this issue. Addictions won't make your life easier.

Do you drive recklessly? Don't wear a seatbelt? Ride a motorcycle without a helmet and leathers? Climb mountains with no food or water, in shorts and a T-shirt? How about leaping the fence into the tiger's cage at the zoo? Dropping a rock from the overpass into the traffic below? Thinking for thirty seconds about the consequences of your act can save you a lifetime of regret.

In short, **Don't do stupid stuff.**

Stop handing out personal information. There you are, in the park, yapping away at top volume into your cellie about how you'll be out of town for two weeks. Who is listening to you? Which bystander will follow you to your car, write down your license plate number, find out where you live, and rob your house while you are away? It sounds farfetched, but people are robbed this way.

Do you talk on Facebook about your family heading for a concert that night? Who sees this information? In the case of one Indiana woman, as reported on CNN, it was a childhood friend. While they were at the concert, he and his partner entered their home, and stole a 50-inch television, jewelry, and computers. Her recently installed security cameras captured the crime.

Everything you put onto the internet is public access. Even on closed Facebook groups, it only takes one person to screenshot those photos of you, drunk in that Cancun strip joint, and email them to your boss. The rule is simple: If you don't want to read about your activities on the front page of the *Washington Post*, don't put them online. Do not assume privacy, ever.

This goes double for loudly revealing your address, your credit card and banking information, your SSN, and anything else you don't want public.

You even reveal information about yourself and your household via your trash. Did you buy a new 60-inch flat screen TV? You do not know who sees the now-empty box at the end of the driveway waiting for trash pickup. Flatten those shipping boxes and recycle them discreetly.

Your trash is a goldmine of personal information for identity thieves. Both thieves and law enforcement agencies know that trash bins tell everything about their owners. They'll pull on their latex gloves and sort through it to get your personal data.

Putting paperwork into the recycling bin does not make it disappear. I have picked up people's pay stubs in the street, complete with name, address, job data, and SSN, blown out of a bin by the wind. If you don't want someone to see it, shred it. Use a crosscut shredder; strip-shredded documents can be pieced back together. When the shredder bag fills up, compost the paper. No one will ever be able to read those documents. Also, shred your documents yourself. The minion shredding your personal papers is capable of reading them as they get fed into the shredder.

Just like your trash, your online presence reveals plenty about your household and your lifestyle. If you are serious about you and your children's privacy, then don't use social media. I don't have a Twitter account, Facebook page, or any other social media account. I don't want to do them, so I don't. This frees up a lot of time for more productive activities.

Even something as simple as looking at a book online at Amazon or searching for information will get you tracked. I recently had to sell a junker car and did some online research. For weeks afterwards, I saw targeted ads at Weather.com for selling junk cars. Yes, my DH practices safe computing, installs plug-ins that are supposed to repel tracking cookies, and we still get tracked, traced, and recorded.

It is possible for people to know more about you than you think. You can safely assume that if you don't know how an online site is making money, it's doing so by data-mining your life.

Take your buying habits. Did you buy a mouse-shaped laser pointer? You might have a cat. Buy Ever Clean kitty litter in bulk at Amazon? You definitely have a cat; probably more than one. Pregnancy test kits? Birthday party supplies? Books on locksmithing? Hair dye by the case? Insulation by the pallet? That custom AK-47 with the Hello Kitty design? The complete works of Ayn Rand? Every one of these purchases says something about you. Taken in aggregate, they say a lot more. Do you want to reveal yourself to strangers who may not have your best interests at heart?

Shopping in the real world with cash saves you money. Studies and real-life experience show that you spend less when you have to part with real money instead of checks, debit cards, or credit cards. More importantly, it makes it harder for someone to learn what you bought. Your credit card receipts reveal where you were, when you were there, and what you bought. Think about your life being on display every time you use your magic plastic card. Paying cash means never getting your credit card data stolen by hackers like at Target (and also in 2016: Neiman Marcus, UPS, Goodwill, Home Depot, and others).

Consider having two credit cards from two companies, such as a Visa and a MasterCard; or a Discover and an American Express. Use one only in the real world and the other in the virtual world. If suspicious charges show up — such as $8,000 in airline tickets to Jakarta — it will be easier to figure out how the card was compromised, and you'll have a back-up card in place. Remember that when your credit card marches off with the restaurant waiter, you don't know who else sees it. If nothing else, this can make it harder for someone to know everything about you. They will only see that half of your life.

Don't forget that your phone calls, particularly cell phones, can be tracked, too. The NSA could be listening to you right now.

Get in shape. Your physical condition serves multiple purposes. When you are in the office on the 42nd floor and the fire alarms go off, the elevators will stop working. Can you run down 42 flights of stairs? In the dark? If not, it is time to start walking.

Being in better shape will let you evacuate a building more quickly, help other people get out, stay out of the way of rescue personnel, and you won't be the unfortunate soul who has to be carried down 42 flights of stairs by firemen. If you have a heart attack from the stress and extreme exercise, you may not even make it out alive. You don't need to be strong enough to run a marathon, but you should be able to walk briskly for a mile or two. We'll talk more about getting in shape in the chapter on physical fitness.

Once you start your fitness program, keep at it. Your security can only be improved by being able to walk farther with less pain and stress. Being physically fit helps your mental toughness; you may be less inclined to panic if you know your body won't fail you in a crisis.

Be prepared. Keeping safe in the workplace means being prepared for an emergency, such as an evacuation caused by a fire alarm. Most of the time, it will be a drill. However, not all of them are, and being prepared can make a bad time easier to handle. So don't ever assume that a drill is just a drill. Sometimes, it isn't.

Here's an important tip if you have to evacuate a building: Grab your bag before you leave; the one with your wallet, keys, ID, and cash. You don't know when or if you will be allowed back into the building. If you have your bag, you can go home. If you don't have your bag, you get to stay there until you are let back inside or someone rescues you.

If you want to kick up your preparedness a notch, do this: If you work in an office and wear impractical footwear, then keep a pair of sneakers and socks in your drawer. Before you run down those 42 staircases, change out of those high heels. Keep a jacket, a bottle of water, and granola bars in the same drawer along with some cash. If you have to get out in a hurry, you have weather protection, water, food, and money. Keep this stuff in a small tote bag and grab it, along with your purse or wallet, when you run out the door.

Keeping yourself secure applies to whenever you set foot outside of your house. Consider where you are going and who will be there. Does your household know where you will be and when they expect you to return? Do you know how to get to your destination? Are there alternate routes in case of accident? Do you need gas for your car? Will the weather be bad? If you are going to be gone for hours, do you have water and snackies for you and the kids? Winter coats? Sun hats? Something that will make the wait more bearable because of that ten-car pile-up on the interstate?

When you enter a building, pay attention to the exits, the fire alarms, and the emergency stairwells. Public buildings are often required to have fire escape maps on the walls. Take a look at the map when you enter the building and see where the fire exit is in relation to where you are going.

If you are on a plane, listen to the safety briefing and look for the exits. Count the number of rows between you and safety so you can get out if the plane is full of smoke.

If you are on a boat, pay attention to the lifeboat drills if they have them. If they don't, as on a ferry, then find out where the boats and life preservers are. If you can't find them, ask a crewmember. They will be glad to help. Better-prepared passengers make their lives easier.

Do your children know where the exits are in their school, without a teacher to tell them what to do? Kindergarteners may not be able to do this, but by the time your kids are in middle school, they should be able to read the "you are here" map and find a way out.

We live in a small town, and although my kids ride the bus in the mornings, they can walk home in the afternoon. They know the way so if they miss the bus, they can still get home.

KNOW WHERE YOU ARE

Every time you go somewhere, as a driver, passenger, bicyclist, or pedestrian, read the street signs. Know what street you are on, what direction you are headed, and your destination.

Travel different routes whenever you go anywhere rather than always going the same old way. Build up a big mental map of your area, both walking and driving. You don't know when you will have to avoid a fire scene and a bigger, more complete mental map will make it less stressful if you have to change your usual route home.

In addition, knowing where you are means that you can tell 911 that the chemical truck overturned in front of you is at mile marker 125 on U.S.30 West near the Salunga exit. If you don't know where you are, you get to say "duh, duh, duh," while rescue personnel waste precious time trying to locate your cell phone signal. Make it easier for them, and you won't have to wait as long.

THE PROBLEM WITH COMMON SENSE

If this strikes you as basic common sense, you are right! And yet, common sense is rare. Why is this?

Mathematically speaking, half the population is below the median for intelligence. (I would say that more than half the population is below the median except that this is mathematically impossible.) The bulk of the population is clustered around the median and the numbers become less and less as you head towards the imbecile and genius ends.

So what is the problem? These suggestions have one thing in common: They require you to pay attention.

The solution is to establish good habits, such as always locking your doors or never letting your car's gas tank go below one-half; habits that keep you safe. Being mindful of your surroundings takes effort but it only takes a second to have an accident that will leave you disabled for life. Be more mindful. Pay more attention. Be safer.

14

Operational Security

OPERATIONAL SECURITY IS A MILITARY TERM, commonly abbreviated as OPSEC. OPSEC has plenty of real-world value, so it should be added to your daily living toolkit.

Basically, OPSEC means don't tell people what they don't need to know.

How does this apply in normal, daily living? Let me count the ways.

OPSEC means shredding your personal documents, especially those with bank account numbers, SSNs, credit card numbers, and other ID numbers. Carelessness with this information leads to identity theft.

OPSEC means using two credit cards, in case one of them gets hacked.

OPSEC means paying cash. You'll spend far less money and your spending habits can't be tracked.

OPSEC means not using E-ZPass, the automated toll-payment system. Every time you pass through the scanner, it takes a snapshot of your movement. This information, compiled with your credit card statements, shows clearly where you have been and when.

OPSEC means being careful about online searches and trying to keep your computer clean of cookies.

OPSEC means being careful with social media. You should never consider anything you do online as being private.

OPSEC means emptying your mailbox promptly and always stopping the mail and the newspaper when you travel. Alternatively, you could have a trusted neighbor pick up your mail and newspaper. Either way, you don't alert burglars to an unattended house.

OPSEC means routing your mail to a post office box in another town when you don't want that vicious ex-husband to find you.

OPSEC means being careful what you order online or from catalogs and have delivered to your home. Your mailman knows what magazines you subscribe to, what catalogs you buy from, and who writes to you. If you regularly order stuff, so do the UPS guy and the FedEx guy. The Postal Service has a program where law enforcement agencies with a warrant can track your mail. The postman writes down the return address and other identifying information for each piece of mail that is sent to and leaves from your home. You never see a difference in your mail delivery.

OPSEC means breaking down the boxes that your big-screen high-def TV came in, along with the boxes for ammo and guns, fancy gaming platforms, high-end computers, and anything else that signals, "I got good stuff! Rob me!"

OPSEC means not leaving mail with the address visible in your car.

OPSEC means asking for identification of anyone entering your home to do work on it. OPSEC is the reason you stay and supervise those workers. Most contractors, cable installers, furnace repairmen, electricians, and plumbers are honest, but it only takes one dishonest person to ruin your day.

OPSEC means not showing anyone pictures of your arsenal and your year's supply of food.

OPSEC means closing your shades and drapes every night so people walking by don't see into your house, noticing what you have waiting to be stolen.

OPSEC means discussing with friends and neighbors how to prepare for an uncertain future.

OPSEC means thinking, every day, "Do I want the bigger world to know this part of my business?" Good OPSEC isn't easy, but it can be learned. It can become a good habit that helps you and your family stay safer.

15

You and Your Arsenal

THIS CHAPTER WILL BE SHORT. I CANNOT recommend firearms for your situation. I don't know enough about them to speak authoritatively.

Guns aren't like Financial Independence. Everyone should work towards Financial Independence no matter what their situation, and it is always done the same way: cut your expenses, pay off your debts, increase your cash flow, distinguish clearly between needs and wants, and say no a whole lot of temptation.

Guns are tools. They can be useful, and they can be misused. The difference between an axe and a rifle is you can kill more game animals or people faster with your Winchester, and you don't have to get nearly as up close and personal as you do with an axe. The same is true of your car, machete, baseball bat, cast-iron skillet, and chef's knife. Every one of those items, useful as they are, has been used to kill people.

So if you want to arm yourself, what should you do? You should go into it, knowing in advance, that gun safety is paramount. Plenty of people have shot themselves with guns they were sure were unloaded. Good gun safety assumes that the gun is always loaded unless proven otherwise. Every person in your household must be taught gun safety, starting and ending with your kids. Take refresher courses regularly. It is easy to get complacent and forget what you learned.

Part of good gun safety is storing them correctly. Make sure your family understands what proper storage is. It isn't a good idea to store your prized Hello Kitty AK-47 in a glass case over the couch where potential burglars can see it through your living room window.

A good gun safety course should address this issue. Ask plenty of questions and follow through on the answers. It doesn't help you to learn that you need a locking, closed cabinet to put your shotguns in, if you are going to leave them lying around because you haven't the

You and Your Arsenal

time or the money to install one.

In fact, you may want to start by taking a gun safety course first. Using any kind of gun means learning how to use it properly. TV and movies are not the way to learn. You can find out if gun ownership is right for you, and what may be the right gun for you, before you spend any money. The NRA offers gun safety programs, or ask at the police station, gun shop, or sporting goods store.

Once you have learned the basics, you still have to practice. Taking the classes and going to the range a few times will not make you an expert, nor will you be comfortable with handling and maintaining your firearm. It may make you overconfident instead, leading to mistakes. Just as with driving a car or knitting socks, if you don't practice a skill regularly, you will forget what to do.

Using a handgun or a long gun is no different. If you want to hit your target accurately every time, put in the hours on the shooting range. If you want to hit your target in the dark during a home invasion, you *really* have to practice. Stress and fear do not improve your aim.

How much time, weekly, should you spend on the shooting range? That depends on how proficient you want to be. Like with everything else, you have to put in the time to train your mind and body. As with riding a bicycle or playing the piano, you have to teach your muscles what to do until doing the action becomes automatic.

This is why professionals practice, practice, and practice some more. They still make fatal mistakes. Don't assume you will do better, with a few hours of training under your belt.

Don't get caught up in the idea that having a Glock will make you safer, healthier, or more resilient. Your gun collection is one more tool in your toolbox of skills. Having an arsenal with plenty of ammo does not mean you can skip learning how to cook, paying off your debt, working in your garden, getting active in the community, or insulating your house.

If you have the idea that you will purchase a gun collection so you can take stored food and water from your more careful neighbors, stop right there. This is not just theft. It is behavior that, in a crisis, will get you killed. Then your family will be at even greater risk of bad things happening to them *and* your arsenal may end up with the person you tried to rob.

A common saying in the prepper community is "beans, bullets, and bandages." Notice that food is listed first. Before you start your gun collection, start your food-storage program and your vegetable garden. Learn to cook what you grow and preserve the harvest. Your food needs always come first.

If purchasing guns and ammo will put you into debt, or keep you from paying off debts, then you need to revisit your budget before spending any more money. You need the emergency cash cushion more than you need another rifle.

Guns, like everything else, have associated costs. Without plenty of ammunition, they are awkward clubs. You also need storage lockers and cleaning equipment. Depending on where you live, you may need extra insurance or annual licenses. Lessons cost money. You may have to pay to use the range. These costs have to be paid, so don't forget to include them in your budget.

You also have to have your spouse onboard. If your partner objects to having firearms in the house, you need to listen. Some of the objections may be based on fear and ignorance. Is having a gun worth straining your marriage? This is the time for gun safety courses, taken before you lay out any money on purchases. Take them with your spouse. Knowledge can go a long way towards relieving fears.

The other common objection to starting a gun collection is cost. Again, if you have debts, no emergency fund, and no food storage, then the gun collection needs to take a backseat. Take care of those issues and objections to buying a rifle may go away.

Buying a gun could be the right choice for your household, but do your homework first and get your family onboard and trained prior to your purchase. Guns have a learning curve like everything else and they require regular practice, safe handling, and maintenance to be a useful tool. Earn the right to bear arms.

16

Hedges and Fences: Or, Hiding From the Neighbors and Google Earth

Fencing For Beginners – Hedging Your Fence – The Problem With Privet – Planting by Direction – A Brief History of Our Yard

WHY DO YOU NEED A FENCE *AND* A HEDGE? Because they work together. The fence acts as a placeholder while the hedge grows up around it. The fence tells people where the property line is. The fence corrals kids and dogs. When the hedge grows up around it, the fence still blocks access through gaps in the hedge and makes it harder to push through the shrubbery.

We moved into our house many years ago, and like many houses with small yards in small towns, it had little vegetation and no fence. It was exposed to the streets, the surrounding homes, and eyes in the sky. The tree cover consisted of two Norway maples next door that were subject to being cut down or pollarded and beyond our control. We had an ugly forsythia hedge on the north side that provided cover for birds but no habitat or food. The south and west sides were bounded by neighbor's privet hedges that were routinely pruned to below waist height.

We were surrounded by two-story houses that overlooked our yard. Lots are narrow and deep, so side-yards run from about twelve feet wide to much, much less. A few hundred feet to the south is a four-lane divided highway. Several hundred feet to the west is the Reese factory, clearly visible from our backyard. Like the highway and the dentist's office, it has annoying lights on all night long.

We suffered from noise issues, light pollution, a lack of privacy, and no fence to corral our toddlers and our much-missed 70 lb. dog, Fido.

Much work needed to be done. So where to start?

FENCING FOR BEGINNERS

If you are in a similar situation, first, install a fence on the property line. Enclose as much of the property as you can, especially the backyard and any side-yards up to the front of your house.

Many locations won't allow you to fence the front yard at all. However, we'll discuss ways to keep your yard from being accessible to passers-by.

If you intend to plant shrubbery along the property line (and you should), install the fence first. Your installer will thank you, or at least not curse you as they try to retrofit fencing into a dense hedge.

When you have the fence installed, if you have the space, get a double gate facing the street. This will allow a vehicle into the backyard to transport garden or renovation materials.

Get people-sized gates as well. We have two, one on each side of the property. The standard gate comes with a lift-up latch that can be secured with a padlock or held closed with a carbineer. This will keep tots in and make it harder for someone to accidentally open the gate and let your dog out.

While a fence can be made from any material, we recommend aluminum chain-link. It is utilitarian in appearance, but for its cost, it will last forever and is maintenance-free.

Wooden fences have to be regularly stained or repainted and rotted posts and sections replaced.

Vinyl fences look very nice, at first. Sadly, we have seen on our neighborhood walks that after a couple years, the fence breaks down. The sun turns them brittle. They crack when you run a lawnmower into a post. Unlike wood fences, vinyl cannot be repaired, only replaced.

Wrought-iron fences are beautiful, and they can last for decades. They must also be repainted every couple of years. They are stunningly expensive.

For those deeply into privacy, nothing beats a six-foot masonry wall topped with broken glass set in concrete. Even if we could have afforded this gaspingly expensive option, the township would never have allowed it.

Therefore, we came back to chain-link. Get a four-foot high fence, higher if you can afford it and your municipal code permits it. You might be allowed to run a six- or seven-foot-tall section along the back of your property if it runs along a road or wilderness area. In our township, we had to get chain-link with a green vinyl coating. I wasn't happy paying the extra cost but the fence disappears from a distance, and it vanished into the hedges far better than regular aluminum would have.

Install the highest fence you can. It makes it harder for your 70 lb. dog to leap over it and your toddlers to climb out. A higher fence says keep out.

HEDGING YOUR FENCE

Fences and hedges work as a team, providing the maximum of privacy and security.

Start by drawing a scale diagram of your property on graph paper. Work out the orientation of your site in each direction — north, east, south, and west — note the views you want to hide - factory, highway, dentist office - and other sights you want to screen, such as the neighbor's second-story balcony in the narrow side-yard. Look at the power lines. Where are they? How high up are they? What is the path of the sun over your house? Where do you need to plant shade trees to cut your air-conditioning bills? How do you feel about committing to a regular, four times a year - or more - pruning schedule?

All of this will help determine your hedge plants.

Tip: Start by lining the northern side of your yard with evergreens. Yews, pines, cedars, thuja, boxwood, holly, junipers: anything that will keep its needles all winter long. This will provide a permanent screen against those frigid winter winds screaming down from Canada.

If you are starting with a barren rectangle, you will have plenty of freedom in choosing your landscape. You won't have to cut anything down, and your hedge can be mixed-use, providing screening, security, and food production.

Plant the hedges as soon as the fence is in, *and* you know what plants you want. Hedges take time to grow, so don't wait until a need appears. Plant the hedges when you move in next door to that quiet old lady. When she passes the house onto the loud, hard-partying, drug-running teenagers, your tall green wall will be in place.

Any shrub can be planted in a row to make a hedge. Many will give you bonus flowers, fruit, nuts, and fall color. Even better, many shrubs come equipped with thorns. If you want to keep people out with an attractive screen, a tall, thorny hedge of roses works very well.

Spend time studying up on shrubs and ask questions at the nursery. A mail-order catalog like Musser Forests (www.musserforests.com) is a terrific resource. It has a fabulous selection and competitive prices, and it will tell you the approximate mature height and spread of each plant along with an idea of its shape.

I really like Hicksii yews (taxus). This particular variant grows as a column about three to four feet in diameter and ten to fifteen feet tall at maturity. A row of Hicksii planted three feet on center (meaning three feet from the center of one plant to the center of another, in a straight line) grows into a dark green wall that stops below most power lines. Yew tolerates pruning very well so if it has to be topped, it won't kill the plant. We have had our yews for at least ten years, and we have never had to prune them.

A word on yews: They come in every shrub shape and size there is. Whether you want meatballs, cones, cubes, pillars, or chocolate drops, there is a yew that will grow in approximately that shape. Purchasing the correct variety of shrub means you should have very little pruning in your future.

THE PROBLEM WITH PRIVET

You may ask: why not use privet? You see it everywhere because it is easy to grow, easy to find, long-living, very traditional, and it takes to shearing and pruning with enthusiasm.

However, privet also wants to mature to a height of thirty or forty feet with a fifteen- to twenty-foot spread. If you don't want your privet hedge this big, you *must* prune regularly. If you let it grow into the power lines, you'll risk freezing when they bring them down after an ice storm, or watching the power crews topping them and possibly sticking you with the bill. I never recommend privet to anyone who doesn't want to get out the pruning equipment four to six times a year.

Instead, choose your hedge by the *mature* height and spread of the shrubs. If you don't want to prune, don't plant something that wants to grow fifty feet. Save yourself the trouble. If you want a four-foot-tall hedge, choose plants that don't grow taller than four feet.

Hedges and Fences

Once they are planted, check on your shrubs routinely to ensure they are growing as expected. Being living things, shrubs are capable of not growing like the catalog claims they will. Named varieties of shrubs from a reputable company like Musser Forests will come close to doing what the ad copy says they will, so long as your soil is good, your light levels are adequate, and you take care of them. If you don't, your expensive shrubs will die. The nursery will provide planting and care instructions. Follow them to the letter.

So, study catalogs and choose your shrubs. Any shrub that grows as a column or pillar will make an effective wall/hedge without too much fuss or requiring too much elbow room. Shrubs that want to spread out can also make a hedge, but they either need lots of space or you will have to prune them regularly.

Keep in mind that you are not restricted to one plant type. You can alternate thuja and taxus for a vertical striped effect. Mix tall and short shrubs for an undulating horizontal line. A ten- to fifteen-foot wide planting strip inside the fence provides loads of room for a hedgerow if you plant in multiple rows or a wave pattern. A hedgerow will give you lots of privacy, amazing wildlife habitat, even fruit and nut production depending on your selection. This will also shrink your yard area as hedgerows eat space.

You don't have to use evergreens, either. You can grow a hedge by lining up tall ornamental grass, *clumping* bamboo, or even columnar apple trees. The main advantage of evergreen hedges is they provide a year-round living wall.

Plant the shrubs so that they have growing room between themselves and the chain-link fence. Cedars and yews will grow up to the chain-link and then through it. If needed, you can shear yews back to the fence. Cedar doesn't like pruning and only the new growth should be removed. The combination of an 8-foot-tall wall of yews growing into a high chain-link fence is hard to see through and harder to climb through.

When I talk about what to do — starting with a barren rectangle — I'm talking from experience. Over the past 17 years, we learned through trial and error how to create a green, enclosed space that requires little maintenance and as little mowing as we could manage.

We made our share of mistakes. For example, along the north side of the yard, we had the aforementioned forsythia hedge. We cut it down and replaced it with a mixed hedgerow of 6-inch high native shrubs. I had a 50% failure rate due to inadequate soil preparation and those freezing, desiccating winds. I was amazed at how much wind that loose, open line of forsythia blocked and how it had improved the yard's microclimate in January.

I kept trying to make the new hedgerow work when I should have widened it, moved the survivors into the yard, and lined the fence with yews. I would have had the privacy and a permanent windbreak. Instead, we have a messy hedgerow of mixed native shrubs, Jerusalem artichokes, volunteer goldenrod, mixed weeds, and blackberries. Much of this dies to the ground in December, leaving us with no screening or windbreak.

Alongside the fence, Oldest Child installed three salvaged A-shaped frames from the old swing set. He lined the open tops of the eight-foot-tall As with scrap fencing and now Arctic Beauty Kiwis are struggling up them. I am also trying to grow Castle Spire and Castle Wall hollies to fill in the gaps and block the wind.

Despite our mistakes, we keep trying to make this work. I wanted the hedgerow to act as a screen against winter winds, to provide wildlife habitat, to give privacy, and to supply food production. It isn't working out very well. More and better planning and a year of soil preparation would have saved me time, money, and aggravation.

If the columnar hollies don't make it, then I will have to plant yews and retrofit them into the existing plants. That will be a messy, dirty job, particularly as my back is fifteen years older than when we started this evolution.

The west side of the yard faces the Reese factory. There is also the neighborhood's main power line about fifteen feet up. Reese is a twenty-four-hour operation so there is always light and noise. This location demanded a wall and Hicksii yews fit the bill beautifully. They grew so eagerly that I had to widen their bed and move the underplanted daffodils and daylilies; the yews were shading them out. The yews are about eight to ten feet tall and still have room to grow. They have filled out to about three feet in diameter. The combinations of our yews and the neighbor's hedge created an impenetrable wall, reinforced by the chain-link fence between them.

At least it did when I wrote the first draft of this chapter a few years ago. Recently, the landlord cut down their privet hedge. Chain-sawed it right to the ground. My yews are fine and appreciate the additional light on that side.

Hedges and Fences

The moral is that neighbors change and so do how they treat their hedges. Before we showed up, the original neighbors kept the privet hedge to three feet. After we installed the fence and the yews, new neighbors moved in. They let the hedge go and pruned it back once every few years. Then it was hacked back from eight feet to four feet tall, and it lost a lot of thickness as well. Now, it is gone; just a line of stumps to remind us of its existence.

So don't rely on your neighbor's hedges for the screening you want. Consider those hedges as bonus thickness and barriers. They can and do go away.

The south side of the yard faces the highway with the dentist's office at the southwest corner and the two-story neighbor's house at the southeast end. The noise and light from the highway never stop. The dentist has twenty-four-hour security lights. The neighbors have a second-floor balcony and the slope of the land puts their property several feet higher up than ours. The narrow side-yards put the houses close together. Their house blocks a lot of morning sun. This is okay in the summer but very bad in the winter and affects how we perform the Window Dance (see Chapter 18). There is also a low power line that ties the main line to their house.

This complex setup demanded multiple strategies. The back third of the fence got more Hicksii yews. The middle third got arborvitae (thuja) that grows as very narrow cones and top out at eight to ten feet. This comes in under the power line, as it gets closer to their house.

The front third was the most difficult. We got the least privacy where we needed it the most, as the change in elevation between yards was highest here. This gave their porch almost as good a view into our yard as their second-story balcony. Each house's side yard is about fifteen feet wide. Their side is a rental property so the tenants change regularly. Larry the landlord insists on the privet hedge being clipped to four feet. I needed as tall a screen as I could get that was two feet wide – the yard was so narrow, I didn't want to sacrifice more space – and let in the summer sun to light and warm the house. That meant a deciduous hedge that would provide shade in summer and drop its leaves in winter.

The first attempt was ornamental grass. Two varieties were tried and neither was satisfactory. Even when the catalog says columnar forms, the stuff is grass and will spread into a fountain. Both varieties took up way too much horizontal space. I could have lived with this, but they weren't tall enough!

In addition – I did not know this at the time – ornamental grass has to be hacked back to the ground every spring for it to grow well. So every spring, we had no hedge for weeks and weeks until the grass grew back.

Back to the catalogs.

A field trip to Longwood Gardens led me to columnar apple trees. These get really tall — twenty feet — and grow no more than three feet in diameter. As a bonus, you get flowers in the spring and you may get apples.

Oldest Child dug out the dozen clumps of ornamental grass, and they went to the school district for their landscaping projects. The columnar apples went in and are coming along nicely.

The trees were about four feet tall when they arrived from Stark Brothers' nursery and have grown past eight feet tall. They leaf out well, but do require trimming at the graft. They produce a mix of crabapples, red apples, and green apples.

The crabs set flowers and fruit. The red and green apples are more variable and took longer to mature and set fruit. The apples are very small and hard. Since I mainly want the screen, I don't care.

They screen us beautifully spring, summer, and fall. When the leaves drop, the screening value goes down tremendously, but we get the warming winter sun as compensation.

If the apples fail – although it looks like they won't – I might have to go to evergreens or clumping bamboo. The bamboo would certainly give me height; some forms can grow to 100 feet tall. However, bamboo can be extremely aggressive and you must make sure you get the type and variety you want. Don't go cheap and get a running form that will swarm your neighborhood. You and the neighbors will regret that decision forever.

Now we come to the front yard. Front yards don't usually get fenced, nor do they usually get tall hedge walls. Many jurisdictions won't let you install any kind of fence in front other than a low picket fence.

I wanted the yard to look normal from the street. This side faces east and has a lot of solar gain; bad in summer and good in the winter. This has led to lining the street edge of the yard with a wide bed planted with carefully spaced trees, and an underplanting of shrubs.

Hedges and Fences

There is no fence.

The flowerbed alongside the driveway is full of mixed perennials, some five to seven feet high. This gives a pretty good screen between the house and the street. It is much better in the summer, of course, when all is grown and thick. In the winter, these perennials are cut down to the ground.

Even in the winter, we still get screening from the branching trees and shrubs. They do not make a formal hedge, rather a loose, flowing, fluffy mass of greenery and flowers. It is kept weeded and edged and the lawn area is mowed. That sends a signal that the yard is maintained as a naturalistic garden and not allowed to run wild.

This part of the yard takes more maintenance than the other three sets of hedges combined, including the hedgerow on the north side.

The alternative was to plant and neatly clip hedges trimmed to about four feet tall. I don't like pruning, so I went with the loose, fluffy mass of shrubs. If you don't want a low hedge in the front yard and dislike the loose mass of mixed shrubbery with taller trees, you are back to a picket fence or wrought-iron.

Whether you choose hedges or trees and shrubs, mark your street side property off with *something*. Low walls of brick or stone look great and can be built a little at a time as you get time and money. Rows of ornamental grass, tall daylilies, herbaceous borders, anything but a bare expanse of grass will give you a boundary at the street. Shrub roses are very pretty and come with vicious thorns. No one could ever object to a row of rose bushes, and no one will ever walk through one either.

This advice becomes even more important with the popularity of Google Earth and Google Street View. If you don't want to be on display for satellites and roaming picture-takers, you need screening trees and hedges. Google cannot take a picture of your yard through a fully leafed-out oak tree.

So study those catalogs, talk to the gardeners at the plant nursery, ask homeowners about that attractive hedge they're growing and think about your need for privacy, food production (blackberry bushes with thorns), security, pruning tolerances, light and solar gain as the seasons change, wildlife habitat and space limitations. Your needs will determine the plants you choose.

17

Enhancing Natural Light

Cleaning Windows – Window Treatments – Paint and Color Magic – Painting Walls – Closets — Cabinets – Floor Coverings – Light Fixtures – Mirrors – Interior Windows – Shrubbery –Basement Lighting – Windows, Solar Tubes, and Skylights — See the Light

REDUCING THE USE OF ELECTRICITY FOR LIGHTING is a terrific goal: You get to stop sending money to the power company and become greener. However, you don't get there by substituting candles, oil lamps, propane fixtures, or active solar. Those alternatives still require fossil fuels and money to make, purchase and operate.

Candles – other than beeswax or solid bayberry – are made from petroleum derivatives and are expensive if you use a lot of them. Oil lamps and propane lanterns need continuous sources of fuel ($$$) and, like candles, produce soot and are fire hazards. As for solar panels, do you want to be your own engineer? Active solar can be costly, has a steep learning curve, and when you need it the most – those dark days in January – you get the least sun.

Electricity is very, very nice. It is cheap, convenient, and, so far, always available.

The objective then, is to get the largest possible return on your lighting dollars no matter how that light is generated. Do not expect your costs to fall, unless you stop using light fixtures and get up and go to bed with the sun.

The strategies below range from quick and cheap to harder and expensive. Nevertheless, they tend to be permanent improvements requiring only routine maintenance. You spend your money once. Even if you are renting, you can still follow many of these suggestions.

Enhancing Natural Light

CLEANING WINDOWS

Don't laugh! Free sunlight cannot penetrate dirt very well.

Wash every window inside and out and vacuum the screens. Do not use Windex and newspapers to wash windows, particularly ones that haven't been cleaned in years. In my experience, this method doesn't work that well.

This is what I do. You need a vacuum cleaner, two buckets, plenty of hot and cold water, a little dish detergent, a single-edge razor blade, a stepstool, and a stack of terrycloth cleaning cloths. I use bar mops. These are ribbed terrycloth towels, almost square and a little smaller than a hand towel. I use them for everything cleaning-related and wash them with the regular laundry. Get some or make your own by cutting up old bath towels.

The first bucket is for the cleaning water. Use the hottest water you can stand to put your hands in and add a squirt of dishwashing liquid. The second bucket is filled with cold water for rinsing. The rinse bucket keeps your detergent bucket clean. When the rinse water gets dirty, dump it and refill with fresh water. You will do this a lot.

Now, let's get cleaning. Do one window at a time before going onto the next. This way, any removable parts like storm windows and screens aren't mixed up.

Vacuum the window, including the frame, to remove loose dirt, dust, cobwebs, dead insects, cat hair, etc. Use a broom on the outside of the house to knock off loose stuff. Remove the window screen (if you can) and vacuum both sides, top to bottom and side to side. The screen may actually change color. Take down the storm windows and set them on a towel in the bathtub. Scrub both sides, rinse them, and dry. While the storms are in the tub, vacuum the tracks.

Wash, rinse, and dry the window. You may get both sides from inside the house. If not, close the window, and go outside with a stepstool and buckets. While washing the window, get the frames and sills as well. If you see paint spatters, decals, or stickers on the glass, wet the razor blade and scrape them off.

The first cleaning is the most involved. You will undoubtedly be removing decades of grime. The second time around is *much* easier. If your window glass and screens are as dirty as mine were, you may double the light coming into your house.

Clean *all* the windows, including attics, basements, garages, and patio sliders. You may be able to clean only the removable parts and the insides of second-story windows. This will still greatly improve your light-gathering.

After this first, mammoth effort, wash the windows and vacuum the screens every year or so to maintain them. Cleaning the windows will allow you to inspect for broken glass or missing putty, caulk, or mullions. Do the repairs before winter comes to stop drafts and trap your heat.

If you discover painted-over sidelights (those narrow windows that flank doors), transoms (windows on top of doors), or basement windows, you will have to make a decision. A previous owner probably painted them over for privacy. Scraping off the paint will let in free sunlight, but possibly let people peek inside. If that bothers you, install very narrow curtain rods and sheers in sidelights. Transoms should be too high for anyone without a stepladder to look in, so scrape away.

Basement and bathroom windows can be covered with either frosted Contac paper or etched in place. You can get frosted Contac paper at Walmart; Martha Stewart will tell you how to etch glass. Both techniques create translucent panels that let light pass through while blocking prying eyes. If the glass panes are broken or replaced with plywood, buy fancy patterned glass replacements and give yourself privacy and light.

WINDOW TREATMENTS

Windows let in the light and views. The curtains and drapes you choose and how you hang them will enhance or minimize that light. Closed draperies occupy a huge amount of wall space so their color matters. Pastel fabric will reflect lamplight back into the room, while a darker fabric will absorb the light, and making the space darker.

When you hang your drapes or curtains, expose as much glass as possible without showing the wood trim. The space your curtains occupy when fully open is called the stack back. Mount the curtain rods so the stack back barely covers the glass when the drapes are completely open. The valance should cover the trim and an inch or less of glass. Any covered glass blocks free sunlight.

Insulating drapes that are lined and interlined are so heavy that they will pull the mounting hardware out of the wall. Unless your trim is very wide, install the hanging hardware on the walls. You may have to reinforce the wall to support the weight of the drapes and their hardware. Mount a square of plywood, (quarter- to half-inch thick) with glue and screws to the wall. Be sure the screws are going into the studs. Make the squares three or four inches across to allow room for the drapery hardware. Paint them to match the walls and they will disappear when the rods and drapes are in place.

Mounting the hardware on the walls with the drapes covering the trim has the added advantage of making your windows look larger than they really are.

If you want added insulation to accompany maximum light, then extending the drapes well beyond the trim and covering more of the walls along with the windows will help cut down on drafts. A valance mounted to the ceiling will block more drafts and so will drapes that barely brush the floor.

Do not puddle your drapes on the floor like you see in magazine photos if you have kids or animals unless you really, really like extra work.

If privacy is a concern, add a layer of sheer curtains like lace or net closest to the glass. This will block some light when the main curtains are open, but they will obscure the view into your house from the street. Add properly fitted room-darkening window shades, and your windows will be much more energy efficient both when opened (via solar gain) and closed (via insulation and draft control).

See the next chapter on the Window Dance for more details.

PAINT AND COLOR MAGIC

Have you ever wondered why some rooms feel like caves, even at high noon? The answer is color choice. Correctly chosen paint can work wonders. The lighter the color, the brighter and lighter the room will be. This is also true of wallpaper and paneling.

Ninety percent of a quality paint job is proper preparation. Libraries are full of helpful books on how to paint a room. Get one and follow the directions, particularly about cleaning, spackling, sanding, and priming. Don't skip the priming step; primer is *not* the same as paint. And don't use cheap paint! Read *Consumer Reports* for details on paint brands, or ask at your local independent paint store.

The price of doing a good job is not just the money spent buying paint and primer. It is investing the time to prepare the surfaces and do a careful job. Latex paint works very well and is easier to clean up afterwards than oil paint. Your paintbrushes will last for years if you are meticulous in cleaning them. Rollers take so much water to thoroughly clean them that I buy cheap ones and throw them out after each painting job.

Start painting a room is at the ceiling. The only correct color is white. It makes the room brighter and diverts attention to the decoration and furniture.

Most ceilings should be painted with "ceiling white." This is a standard, low-gloss thick white paint formulated for ceilings. It is easier to work with and will not spatter as much as regular white paint.

Bathrooms and kitchen ceilings need to be washable, so use a glossier white. I use as glossy a paint as I can find. Commonly called ultra-high-gloss latex enamel, this is normally used for trim. It is super washable, super reflective, and demands lots of surface preparation. Bathrooms get lots of moisture and kitchens get lots of greasy moisture, so make them easier to maintain by having cleanable paint.

Ceilings painted with "ceiling white" usually have to be repainted to clean them. If you have smokers in your home, your ceilings will end up a dirty yellow and you will have to repaint them more frequently to get them white again. Tobacco smoke works its way into the wall. When friends of ours renovated a home occupied by a long-time smoker, it took several coats of Kilz, a brand of primer formulated to hide stains, before the color and the smell went away.

PAINTING WALLS

Walls are the largest surface in a room, so they can have an outsize effect on how a room feels when you walk in. Light colors make the room feel larger as well as brighter. Careful surface preparation will ensure a better, smoother, longer-lasting paint job.

No matter what the can says, flat paint cannot be washed. It has a lovely, velvety, glare-free texture that will be instantly destroyed by a tot with a crayon. The glossier the finish — ranging from eggshell to ultra high gloss — the easier it is to wash. Each uptick in shine means more surface preparation as every spot you miss spackling and sanding will show. Careful surface prep and several coats of ultra-high-gloss paint will resemble a lacquer finish.

I painted every wall in my house with ultra-high-gloss enamel, and they reflect every bit of light. They are so shiny, they can look wet. I have had people touch the wall to see if it was dry. That shinier finish can let you choose a slightly darker color, but to maximize light, stick with paler tones.

As a side note, you may encounter resistance when shopping for paint. Each time I told a clerk I was buying gloss paint for my walls, they would try to talk me out of it. You'd almost think people were scared of it.

CLOSETS

Closets should be painted from top to bottom – trim, ceiling, walls, inside of closet doors – with ultra-high-gloss white and nothing else. No matter how pretty those jewel tones look in a magazine photo, in real life the closet turns into a dark hole. There's no need to treat your closet like a cave. Gut the space, paint it white, and install wire shelving that doesn't block light or airflow and see how bright your closets can be. It also makes it easy to find things, too.

Best of all, when the job is done, the closets need never be repainted, even if you change the room's color. At most, you may need to touch up scrapes and wash the baseboards and walls.

CABINETS

The insides of kitchen and bathroom cabinets should always be painted bright white. The shelves can be lined with light-colored sheet vinyl cut to fit and glued down with floor adhesive. This makes a permanent, wipe-clean, water- and bug-resistant surface. We use scrap flooring left over from other jobs. Thick, cushioned flooring quiets the noise when you store plates and glasses, too.

As for the exterior of your cabinets, it depends. If they are made of beautiful wood like solid cherry, it could be a sin to paint them. If the wood is dull and nondescript, then paint away. Remove the doors, clean thoroughly, sand lightly, prime, and paint. It is disruptive and takes a while to get an entire kitchen done, but you can do the work in stages. Just do one set of cabinets at a time.

All my wood trim and window frames are painted the same ultra-high-gloss white. They present a uniform appearance and can be easily washed. The interior doors are, very slowly, changing from dingy, dull tan lauan mahogany to the same bright white. Already the few finished doors bounce light down the hallway into dark corners.

Painting your house takes time and money. It lasts a long, long time if done right. Assume it will take a week to prepare a room and paint it;

one coat primer, two coats paint, plus ceiling and trim. Much of that time will be spent doing something else while the paint dries. It is tremendously helpful if you can send your toddlers to spend a week at Grandma's while you paint. It made the job easier for me when I did this. If you cannot enlist grandparents as free childcare, double the time you think you will need.

Look around and see how much of your house can be painted. With the right primer, almost *any* surface can be painted. Good, careful surface preparation ensures that the paint sticks well to less traditional surfaces.

For example, I painted the drop-ceiling panels in my finished basement. It was slow, tedious work. I'll go into detail below, when we come to the basement.

I painted over our dingy, fake wood paneling. Some walls had been painted over previously, some not. Very dark paneling may need more than two coats of paint over the primer. Our basement bathroom, for example, had fake wood paneling that was almost black. It took the primer coat and *five* coats of yellow paint to turn that dungeon into a cheerful space.

I painted the house's blue vinyl siding white in our Florida room. The paint is in its fifth winter and holding up fine. A fancy faux finish over the bright white turned the siding into an interior wall and gave us more living space.

The only surface I have not painted over is wallpaper. It is possible to do, but only if the paper is adhering tightly to the walls with no rips, tears, or bubbles. If you have those problems, it would be better to strip off the paper, clean the walls of any glue, and then paint. Reference books from the library will explain this process in more detail.

Painting is an easy, cheap and relatively fast fix. A little paint will hide a lot of sin.

FLOOR COVERINGS

Floors reflect light towards your newly white ceilings. As you might expect, paler or shinier floors create a lighter, brighter space.

When we had the hardwood floors sanded, I went with a high-gloss finish. I knew regular usage would turn it into a matte finish but until then, how it bounced the light around was amazing.

A few years later, I got lucky in the clearance corner at Ollie's Bargain Outlet and found a huge, cream wool rug. I knew it would make the living room instantly warmer and quieter. I knew with three kids, three cats, and a dog, it would not stay cream for long. But the price was so low ($175!) that it was worth the risk. I did not know that the living room would become instantly brighter, but it did.

In addition, at night, with the drapes closed and the lights on, the magic still worked. The pale rug bounced the light off the white ceiling and back again. It was like adding another light fixture.

Unfortunately, light-colored floors need more maintenance. Without regular vacuuming and cleanings, little kids turn white carpet into dirt-colored carpet.

If you change your floors, consider the color and reflectivity of the possible surfaces: carpet, hardwood, rugs, sheet vinyl, and tile. Each has its advantages. Your choice will affect your lighting and maintenance budget.

LIGHT FIXTURES

Light fixtures' design and their shades determine how much light you actually get from the bulb.

The first step is to thoroughly clean the fixture. Just like the windows, the first washing is going to be the hardest.

Lampshades (fabric or paper) should be vacuumed inside and out using the dusting attachment on your vacuum. A feather duster won't help much when the shades haven't been cleaned for years.

The light bulbs build up a layer of dirt, too. Take the cold bulb out of its socket and gently wipe it clean with a damp bar mop. Dry it off completely before reinstalling.

Compact fluorescents get especially dirty since they are so long-lasting and have swirly dust-trapping tubes. Take the bulb out of the fixture and carefully dust all over, using a feather duster, then work a dry bar mop to get in between the tubes. I don't like using damp cloths on these bulbs so they have to be dusted more often.

Glass shades (called fitters) have to be removed and hand-washed in the sink with warm water and dishwashing liquid just like any other dish. Dry them off completely before putting them back. It is amazing how much better they can look. Dear Husband was sure that the glass fitters on the ceiling fan light were yellow glass. They were not; washing revealed that they were clear glass.

Wash or dust every fixture. Even the ones that are closed collect dust and dead bugs. After this first go-round, do this every year or so to maintain them. If you need to change a bulb, take the time and clean the fixture.

If you have a fixture with crystal prisms, remove them and handwash them in the sink. They cannot be cleaned or dusted effectively while in place. Each prism is held in place by a tiny wire with a pinhead at one end. Twist open the loop and remove the wire before you wash the prism. Replacement wires and prisms are available at any good lighting store so you can replace missing parts of your chandelier.

Faithful, devoted dusting of chandeliers will postpone this tedious job, but not for very long. While the prisms are drying, vacuum the fixture and get all those cobwebs.

While you are washing your light fixtures, don't forget to wash the glass shades on hurricane lamps, oil lamps, kerosene lamps, and candleholders. Because of the soot, they get dirty even faster than electric light fixtures.

MIRRORS

Mirrors are incredibly useful for reflecting and bouncing light. I have them in every room in the house.

With the exception of the mirror backsplash behind the stove, all my mirrors came from yard sales, thrift shops, family members, or trash picking. If the silvering is still good, the mirror is worth picking up. I have several very large mirrors that used to belong to dressers.

SEE THE LIGHT BEFORE BUYING

When you buy a light fixture, look it over carefully before you spend any money. Many, many lamps are made for ambience, style, and looks rather than functionality. An electrical showroom will let you turn on the lamp so you can see how much light it releases.

When shopping, keep in mind that opaque glass lets less light pass through than frosted, and frosted releases less light than clear glass. Colored glass blocks and distorts light.

As for shades, dark, heavy, or thick lampshades made from paper or fabric will block most of the light. Giant drum shades cast a circle of light on the ceiling and another on the table and nowhere else. Wooden or metal trim won't let light escape at all. Ask yourself why you want to use a 100-watt light bulb and only get 25 watts of light out of it.

Dimmer switches are another word for sitting around in the dark.

They are hanging on the wall, just as if they had started out in life as a wall mirror.

For best results, place mirrors opposite windows and behind lamps to reflect and double your light. In several rooms, we have large mirrors hung on opposite walls so they reflect each other endlessly, bouncing ambient light into infinity.

Wall-mounted candle sconces really benefit from this treatment. If backed with a heatproof, washable surface, you get twice the light from each candle. The extra light and added fire safety is why so many traditional designs for candle sconces have a mirror attached to the mounting. If your sconces don't come with a mirror backing, hang a mirror directly behind the sconce or above the part that holds the sconce to the wall.

Unexpected places can provide good homes for mirrors. A mirror tile can be mounted in the far back of an awkwardly shaped kitchen cabinet so you can more easily see what is inside. Do this after you paint the interior ultra-high-gloss white.

In our last house, we built a fake transom window with mirror tiles left over from our wedding reception. The twelve-inch tiles fit perfectly between the ceiling molding and the trim of the extra-wide doorway. The tiles were separated by strips of cheap screen bead trim painted to match the molding. It made the space brighter. When we installed the "transom" on both sides of the wall, it even fooled a few people into thinking we had windows between the rooms.

As mentioned earlier, I have a mirror backsplash behind my stove. I wanted a wipe-clean surface that would double the light from the range hood. I had to buy this mirror, as it had to be sized to fit the width of the stove. It is mounted permanently with mirror tape, mirror mastic, and plastic clips.

I have a few upcoming mirror projects. I want to turn the drab lauan mahogany door in the hallway into a faux French door. Ultra-

---

NEW LIFE FOR OLD MIRRORS

You can revitalize a salvaged mirror with an awful fake-wood plastic frame. Lightly sand the frame, prime it, and paint it with leftover paint from other projects. The previous owners will never recognize their junked dresser mirror with its snazzy new flamingo pink frame trimmed in black and white and hanging on a wall.

high-gloss white paint, screen bead, and eight twelve-inch mirror tiles should work.

Another task is in the kitchen. The kitchen counter behind the toaster is like a small cave, even after the cabinets and walls were painted white. That entire corner would benefit from being mirrored. I have some salvaged mirror that could be professionally cut to fit. The hard, expensive part is cutting out openings for the electrical outlets.

So look around. Make your mirrors work for you. Keep them dusted and clean, and they, too, will give you more light for your money.

INTERIOR WINDOWS

Another way to spread light is through interior windows. Many older houses had real transom windows. These are the windows that are over a doorway, especially interior doors. They let light fall deeper into a house, and if operable, allow airflow without compromising privacy. If you are fortunate enough to have them, and they are painted over, you can easily strip the paint off.

Retrofitting transom windows is not a job for amateurs. You must be very sure it isn't a load-bearing wall, and you have to be a good carpenter.

You can also spread light, while maintaining privacy, by replacing solid-wood doors with ones with frosted-glass inserts. It is easy to get second-hand doors with glass inserts; the difficulty is finding one that fits your door opening.

The bathroom in our finished basement — the former dungeon with bright yellow walls — gets no natural light. We decided a frosted-glass door would let us use the space without turning on a light during the day – the family room would supply the light.

After one offered door wouldn't fit, I broke down and bought a beautiful door with a full-size glass insert. The glass is heavily patterned to allow light *and* privacy.

The cost for this kind of door varies wildly. Do you have a standard door opening or is it an odd size? Do you need to have it professionally installed or can you do it yourself? Shop around. Habitat for Humanity runs thrift shops for recycled building material, and you may get lucky.

Another way to shine light into dark corners is to add interior windows. After painting and replacing the basement bathroom door, it looked less like a cell but still didn't have natural light. Opposite the door was an interior wall built by the home's previous owner. On the other side was the unfinished basement with the studs left exposed.

We were in the middle of insulating and finishing that wall as part of the pantry rebuild, so we decided to add a window. Dear Husband cut a long, vertical hole between two studs. He framed the hole with a 2-by-4 at the top and bottom and painted it white. He added a pane of frost-patterned glass on the bathroom side and a piece of plain glass on the other. Trim was added to hold the panes in place against the top and bottom studs. A coat or two of ultra-high-gloss white paint and careful caulking ensured no air leakage or dust. The interior window lets light fall into the bathroom alcove from a nearby basement window.

When the bathroom door was replaced, I also replaced the door to the unfinished basement with a similar door. Depending on time of day, sunlight pours down the basement staircase and into the unfinished basement or light filters from the unfinished side into the finished living space. The door makes it much easier to walk around without having to turn on lights.

SHRUBBERY

I routinely see homes that have shrubbery growing in front of every window, up to the roofline and beyond. Our house, for example, had a row of cedars completely blocking two bedroom windows. Even at high noon, those rooms were gloomy caves. Cutting the cedars down to the ground instantly rewarded us with light and air. The previous homeowners had planted those cedars when they were tiny and let them grow. Unfortunately, those cedars wanted to be fifteen feet tall. With overgrown shrubs like these, you have two choices: cut them back hard to below the windowsill and prune faithfully or remove them.

If you want to prune faithfully for the rest of your life, first identify what is blocking your windows. Yews love regular pruning and can recover from the aggressive haircut you are going to give them. Cedar hates pruning and will likely die. If you prune back hard without knowing the plant, it may die, and you will have to dig it out anyway. Flowering shrubs have to be pruned at specific times of the year, depending on the variety, so you don't cut off the flower buds. A good, local nursery may be able to help you identify what you have – don't expect this kind of assistance at a big box store.

If you cannot identify the plant or have no taste for hard annual pruning, the better solution is to remove the offending bushes, roots and all. This is not a fun job. When your back has recovered, rebuild the soil, then replant with something with a mature height below that of your windowsills. Your nursery staff can help you find something or use mail-order catalogs like Musser Forests.

A well-chosen bush should never need to be pruned; it will naturally grow to fit the space. Yew, a very common foundation shrub, comes in a wide variety of shapes and sizes from little meatballs to columns to monsters thirty or forty feet tall with corresponding width.

When you choose your hedges to go with your fences, include your foundation plantings as well. Like them, foundation shrubs can fulfill multiple duties: privacy, looks, wildlife habitat, and the security of thorns.

BASEMENT LIGHTING

Basements demand multiple techniques to improve their lighting. First and foremost is cleaning any windows, including their screens.

Walls are the next step. White paint is the best choice. Anything darker than the palest pastels simply cannot compensate for the miniscule amount of natural light you'll get. Off-white and creams just look like dirty white.

The type of paint used – latex, cement, or Drylok – depends on the wall. Sheetrock or ugly paneling can be painted like any other wall (i.e., with latex paint). Raw concrete block, however, demands specialty paint. Interior walls or support pillars can be painted with cement paint. Foundation walls of raw, unpainted block should be painted only with Drylok. If they are already painted, look closely at their condition. If your foundation walls are chipping and flaking due to moisture, the paint could be scraped off with a wire brush and the walls covered with Drylok.

Drylok is formulated especially to seal the concrete and keep out moisture. Drylok won't hold back a river, but it will drastically cut back seepage and small leaks. Drylok *cannot* be applied over paint. It is designed to soak into the concrete, and it can't do that if there is paint in the way.

If the paint is in good shape and you have no water issues, use cement paint. If you have water issues, move on to the "Diverting Water From Your Basement" chapter before you do anything else there.

Because it is messy and time-consuming, the best time to paint basement walls is before you move your stuff in. Drylok every foundation wall, if they are raw concrete block, even if you don't have a moisture problem. This will save you wetness and humidity problems down the road.

Next, paint the interior block walls and pillars with regular cement paint.

Cement floors should be painted too. A light gray or tan color is the best compromise between hiding dirt and lightness. Use paint made for floors; it is tougher and will wear better. There are many choices in floor paints so ask about ease of application and durability. This is not a job you want to repeat soon and better quality paint will last longer.

Your window wells come next. The windows and screens should already have been cleaned. Dig out the dirt and rocks from the well down to at least six inches below the bottom of the foundation windowsill. There is no need to go below the bottom of the metal well. Sweep out the cobwebs and dust. Scrub clean the exposed foundation wall framing the window inside and outside the house. Paint the concrete inside the well with two coats of Drylok.

Wash the dirt off the rocks and remove any nails, trash, broken glass, and other detritus. Put back the clean, dry rocks but leave enough room to top off the salvaged layer with two or three inches of white marble chips. They will reflect far more light than the dingy gray and brown rocks. The new rock layer should stop an inch below the bottom of the foundation windowsill. If rainwater gets into the well, it won't immediately flood in through the window. The rocks permit drainage and keep everything dry.

Now for the final step. Clean the metal well walls and paint them with gloss white Rust-Oleum paint. This will probably take three coats for good coverage. Top with a clear plastic bubble or salvaged storm window to keep out the rain.

I have done this with all four of my window wells and my three-foot-deep light shaft in the Florida room. The difference was amazing. The gloss white paint bounces light into the basement and on sunny days, the wells glow.

The job was tedious, messy, dirty, and hard on the back. It took over a week per well, much of which was spent waiting for paint and rocks to dry. Cleaning out the wells was the worst part, but it was completely worth the work. Our basement was so dark that, even on the sunniest of days, you could not safely walk through it without turning on a light. Now, depending on weather and time of day, you get almost enough light to read by, especially after the walls and ceiling tiles were painted.

Once the job is done, the cobwebs and dust will need to be swept out every year or so. Do this when you clean the windows and screens and the light will pour in.

The basement ceiling comes next. If you are lucky enough to have a drywall ceiling, paint it over with ceiling white paint.

I was not that lucky. My finished basement has a suspended ceiling: a metal grid that holds insulated two-foot-by-two-foot panels. They cannot be painted in place with brushes and rollers. The panels shift so you cannot get an even coat, and when they dry, they glue themselves to the grid, and you cannot remove them to get access to the wiring and plumbing.

The tedious solution is to paint the grid very carefully, using either a narrow slant brush or a foam one, with a coat of primer followed by two coats of ceiling white. Try not to get paint on the panels as they are then harder to remove for painting. I used latex paint on the family room grid and, because of the rust issues, Rust-Oleum on the basement bathroom grid.

Next, tackle the panels. Set up a pair of sawhorses with an old door on top. Carefully remove two or three panels to make sure they're put back in the right place. Place them insulation-side down on the door. Prime and paint them with a brush. A roller was too large and tore apart the ceiling panel. The panels will suck up a huge amount of primer. Let them dry and then paint with ceiling white. You may need only one coat. Mine did. Let them dry completely before putting them back.

Keep track of the job as you go, as it is easy to lose your place. If you have fifty or sixty panels, it may take weeks or months to finish the job.

It would have been easier to replace the panels, but it would have cost ten times as much and the new panels still wouldn't be as white as possible. We priced replacement panels and even the cheapest ones would have cost hundreds of dollars. The paint cost about $60.

Enhancing Natural Light

If your basement ceiling is bare rafters and exposed subfloor, the best choice is to insulate it. There is no good way to paint the underside short of spraying, and that's a job for professionals. However, insulating is well worth the bother as you will be far more comfortable and save energy dollars. I have insulated the undersides of three houses — both crawl spaces and full basements — and in each case, it made a big difference in comfort and cost. It was worth every penny.

After you have installed insulation batts, you may want to take a further step. Our pink insulation was exposed to dust, cobwebs, and bad cats. I would find wisps of fiberglass here and there, some quite large.

I decided to try white Styrofoam insulating panels between the joists, over the pink insulation batts. Younger Son and I bought a package as a trial. The panels are about sixteen inches wide and four feet long and fit perfectly between the joists.

Younger Son slowly installed them across the entire ceiling, holding them in place by friction helped with slightly wider pieces of heavy wire dug into the joists. Cut-up wire coat hangers work very nicely. He cut and fitted some panels to avoid light fixtures, outlets, wires, and other impediments. The individual foam panels can be easily removed if we need access.

The job took him months, but the panels cleaned up the ceiling remarkably, and bounce light far more than the fiberglass. It seems to keep the house a little warmer, and bad cats have stopped snacking on the fiberglass.

Don't hesitate to turn every flat surface white in your basement. As each area gets painted or finished, the ambience will become lighter, brighter, and easier to maintain.

WINDOWS, SOLAR TUBES, AND SKYLIGHTS

There comes a point when mirrors, cleanliness, and white paint are not enough. You have to get more natural light into the house from outside. If you are willing to write whopping big checks to contractors or are a skilled handyman, you can get virtually anything you want.

These ideas are best reserved for the house you are going to live in permanently.

Examine your windows. If your house is old and has been renovated, it's possible that some heathen replaced the original big windows with smaller ones and filled in the gaps with wood or brick. Examine your walls, inside and out, for shadow markings, irregularities in siding, changes in style, anything that indicates that the current windows aren't the original ones. Look for transoms that have been nailed shut and sidelights that have been replaced with plywood. Old pictures of your house can be helpful. Get several estimates and see if reopening to the old window size and installing a new window is worth the cost.

The next option is to add windows where none existed. A hole can be cut into the wall and a window installed just about anywhere. Before you do this, consider the cost, the view, changes in privacy, the added light, the change in airflow, the added cost of new window treatments and how this new hole in the wall will affect your heating and cooling system. Get the most energy efficient windows you can.

Skylights can sometimes be retrofitted into a house. Nothing will let in as much light as a big skylight. They have to be seen to be believed. My friends have a skylight in their bathroom. When the door is open, the space is as bright as an operating room and light spills into the hallway, lighting it as well. If you are having extensive work done on your roof, a skylight might be a very good addition. However, they *must* be installed and flashed correctly or you'll have a big, leaky, drafty hole in your roof.

Easier and cheaper to install than new windows or skylights are solar tubes. These are tubes, ten inches in diameter or larger, that connect from a bubble on your roof to a glass plate in your ceiling. They can be installed anywhere you have open attic space between the roof and the room you want new light in.

Solar tubes come in two basic models. The easier to install and less costly one has a tube that looks like a giant metal dryer vent. It is very flexible and lets in quite a bit of light. The harder-to-install and more pricy design has solid sides of polished aluminum. There isn't that much difference in light output on a sunny day between the styles. The difference comes in on cloudy or marginal days. The mirror interior magnifies the captured light and gives you far more sunshine than the dryer-vent style.

We installed four solid-style SolaTubes. Each bathroom got a ten-inch tube and the kitchen got two fourteen-inch tubes. SolaTube has optional light and vent kits so you can ventilate your windowless bathroom. Get the biggest tube you can fit through your rafters without cutting them.

After the previous owners added a Florida room off the kitchen, only one of its three windows received sunlight, turning the room dingy. We always had the lights on, even at high noon. Courtesy of the tubes, this is no longer needed. The added light meant we could leave the fixtures off for most of the day.

True, I could buy a lot of electricity for the cost of the four tubes. But that doesn't take into account what they contribute to our happiness. Even the dreariest day in central Pennsylvania is brighter since the tubes were installed. The natural sunlight makes me feel better in a way that the fluorescent ceiling fixture never did. We even see changes in the sun through the tubes as clouds move across the sky. At night, when Dear Husband came home from work, he didn't need to turn on the lights. The moonlight made the tubes glow, softly lighting the space. During storms, lightning makes them flash.

Figure on spending several hundred dollars per tube. Light and vent kits increase the cost; enough so that a bigger plain tube may cost the same or less than a fully accessorized smaller one. Installing solar tubes is not a do-it-yourself project unless you are already skilled in the building trades. Keep in mind that it is a hole in your roof, just like a skylight would be, only smaller. The dryer-vent type is much easier to install, and if you have a tricky location with lots of joists to work around, you may not have a choice between it and the less flexible, more brilliantly sunny solid-side style. Either one will put natural light where you never thought you could get it before.

SEE THE LIGHT

You can bring more free, natural sunlight into your house. The work is hard and dirty, but the reward is more light, permanently. Clean your new, shiny surfaces occasionally and they will continue to work for you and lower your electric bill. Even if you accomplish only a few of these suggestions, you will see more light for your money.

Look around and see what other possibilities suggest themselves. Something as simple as replacing that dark shower curtain with a clear one will brighten up a bathroom.

Remember that lighter, shiny, clearer, and cleaner promotes natural light. Darker colors, dirt, dull finishes, and opaqueness will keep that wonderful, natural sunlight outside of your house. Get to work and maximize those lighting dollars.

18

The Window Dance

How to Dress Your Windows – Sealing Windows – Shall We Dance? – Made In the Shade

THE WINDOW DANCE IS WHAT WE AT Fortress Peschel call the daily routine of opening and closing draperies and windows. It may seem like a housekeeping chore of little value, but this is far more important than it seems. The Window Dance lets us control solar gain and heat loss throughout the year. The idea is to match the needs of the house to the weather by manipulating the windows and drapes: to catch warmth and light in the winter; to repel heat and trap cool air in the summer; and air out the house whenever possible.

In other words, you expend *your* energy to prevent writing big checks to the power company for *their* energy.

Windows and skylights should be considered to be holes in the house. Their insulating properties are measured in U-values. Insulation everywhere else — walls, ceilings, floors, and roofs — is measured in R-values.

Windows, and only windows, are measured as U-values because this hides the horribleness of their R-value. It lets you think that a U-value of a double-pane window is twice that of a single-pane window. Which it is. And that you have greatly increased your energy efficiency. Which you have not.

While a number of factors go into calculating a window's U-value, a rough determination of its R-value can be found by taking its inverse (in other words, by taking the number 1 and dividing it by the U-value). For example, if a window has a U-value of .25, then its R-value is 1 divided by .25 = 4.

An R-value of 4 is not very good when a standard exterior wall

The Window Dance

should have an R-value of 15 or 20 or more.

But we have to have sunlight, fresh air, and views. Otherwise, we might as well live in caves. So we compensate for the miserable R-values of our windows with window treatments and their correct usage.

There are three steps to the Window Dance:

1. Add window treatments. More layers mean more trapped, dead air to act as insulation.

To see what I mean, close your drapes one night. Turn on all the interior lights. Walk outside and around your house. Every bit of light you can see is the same as lost heat. The goal is not to have any light peeking past the drapes.

2. Open and close drapes, shades, quilts, and windows as the time of day and season demand. Once the window treatments are installed, they don't change but they do move. The dance changes every day, sometimes several times a day. The more careful and observant you are in doing the dance, the more energy you save and the more comfortable your house remains.

3. Plant deciduous trees to provide shade in the summer while allowing heat and light inside during the winter. A tree grown from a sapling will take ten to fifteen years or more to start working for you.

HOW TO DRESS YOUR WINDOWS

For maximum effectiveness, every window should be dressed in multiple layers. Working from the glass into the room, there should be:

* A *window quilt*, which fits the frame and hangs below the sill;
* A room-darkening white *window shade* that covers the window frame completely;
* Sheer lace or net *curtains*;
* Heavy *drapes* consisting of a muslin (or Roc-lon room darkening) lining, a flannel interlining, and the fashion fabric;
*And a *valance* or *pelmet*.

Let's break this down.

Window quilt: I made mine from old sheets and leftover quilt batting. Each quilt consists of front and back layers of plain fabric with a core of quilt batting. I always use white or cream sheets as this layer shows to the street. They hang in the window frame from a wooden dowel that hangs from a pair of cup hooks. The dowel slides through a rod pocket at the top of the window quilt. The dowel needs to fit easily within the window frame but the quilt should be wider than the glass by several inches and should be long enough to hang over the sill a few inches. The overhang will give a better seal to the window when the other layers are in place. The quilt does not touch the glass.

Window shade: This was the most expensive part of our set-up. We bought them from a local dealer and had him install them. It was absolutely worth it to get good quality, properly fitted, and installed shades that will last for years.

Do not buy cheapie install-it-yourself shades. They are difficult to fit precisely. The spring rollers wear out quickly, and then you have to replace the shades.

If you can afford them, buy honeycomb shades; the more honeycombed the better. They cost more, but they insulate far better than plain old shades. Honeycomb shades may also let you omit the window quilt layer. They do a good job of insulating on their own.

A word about other kinds of shades: Vertical blinds belong only in office parks. They do not insulate, room-darken, or allow you to open windows while repelling the sun. Horizontal blinds are marginally better but are difficult to keep clean and don't provide a solid barrier to heat loss. Heavy grass cloth roll-up shades take up a *lot* of room and their insulating and room-darkening qualities vary wildly depending on how tightly they are woven. Their very rough surface acts as a dust magnet. Insulated roman shades are nice (and expensive) and take up a lot of stack-back room up top when fully open. They can work well when you cannot have the other layers of fabric as in a bathroom or kitchen. Wooden plantation shutters are useless for anything other than firewood.

Have the dealer install the shades to cover the window frame from side to side with enough shade material to hang down well past the sill. Get white shades, preferably room-darkening, as those tend to be a little heavier. A clutch cord will make the shade mechanism last for years and it keeps you from touching – and having to clean – the shades.

Sheer lace or net curtains: I have made my own sheers for years, and it is an easy sewing job. In essence, it is a seam at the top and another at the bottom for each width of fabric. Any basic book on sewing window treatments gives the directions. They are easy to find and cheap to buy if you want to go that route.

The purpose of the sheers is to add another layer of dead air. More importantly, they screen you from the neighbors. When the other layers are open, the sheers stay closed. That layer of netting makes it harder to see your big-screen TV while still allowing in sun and air. Choose whatever patterns you like in white or cream. These hang from a rod-pocket-style curtain rod hung above the window frame and several inches to each side on the wall. Your sheers should be two or three inches shorter than your drapes.

Drapes: These will be large and heavy and need very sturdy rods for support. They are so heavy that wider windows will need Kirsch traverse rods to support the weight and make them easy to operate. Do your research to see what kind of rods you need and if you can install them yourself. I had my 16-foot wide Kirsch traverse rod installed professionally although I made the pinch-pleated drapes myself.

Narrower drapes are hung on heavy-duty standard curtain rods with center supports. The important thing to remember with drapes is their stack-back, the space outside the window where the fabric goes when the drapes are open. The stack-back should be sized so when the drapes are open, all of the glass is exposed to light the room.

This means that the rods *must* be mounted on the wall several inches away from the outer edge of the window frame and several inches higher as well.

As with the sheers, there are plenty of books on how to sew these drapes, including how to make pinch-pleated drapes. Two common styles, tab tops and rings, lose heat at the top so I do not recommend them. If you must use tab tops or rings, add a pelmet to block the heat loss.

Rod pockets work fine for windows that are less than four feet wide; after that you must use heavier rods and you always should have a center support. Pinch-pleats must have a traverse rod.

Drapes should have three layers.

Layer one is a lining facing the street made of muslin, old sheets from Goodwill, or, if you really need the room-darkening and can afford the cash and weight, Roc-lon blackout lining. Because the other layers of window treatment show to the street first (quilt, shade, sheers) this one won't be visible but the standard colors are white or cream.

Layer two is an interlining of flannel. Quilt batting is very heavy and has to be quilted in place or it will shred and sag. It also makes the drapes bulky and awkward to handle. Old flannel sheets can work for this layer.

The third and final layer, which faces the room, is the fashion fabric. This can be whatever you want. It should be heavy enough to conceal the interlining. That is, don't put lace over flannel. Heavier fabrics will block more air and heat than thinner ones. They will also weigh more, something to keep in mind when buying and mounting the hanging hardware.

The drapes should come close to the floor. How close? Draperies that puddle beautifully on the floor don't open and close easily which you will need to do daily. They catch every bit of floor dirt. Your children and animals will step on them, lay on them, or pull them off the rods. Bad cats may use them as a litter box. If you hem them so they're an inch above the floor, they will open and close easily without losing too much heat.

The hardest part of sewing drapes is dealing with huge sheets of fabric. My biggest set of drapes is made up of two panels, each seven feet high and sixteen feet wide. They are pinch-pleats, hung on a traverse rod, and I sewed all those damn pleats by hand.

Valance or pelmet: The valance is fabric hung over the top of the drapes. It consists of the lining, interlining, and fashion fabric. It should have an interlining of quilt batting as opposed to flannel; this stiffens the valance so it hangs better and traps more heat. Its purpose is to conceal the drapery hardware, but more importantly, slow down the chimney effect in which the heat rises to the top of the window.

This heat loss can be cut even more if you use a wooden framework called a pelmet or cornice instead. This is a four-sided plywood box mounted to the wall over the hardware. It has a top, front, and two sides and is covered with padding and fashion fabric. Because it is closed at the top, a pelmet completely blocks the chimney effect.

Mount the valance or pelmet high enough up so that all of the glass is seen when the drapes are open. Setting your stack-back over the walls and your valance up high makes your windows look larger, thus giving you all the sunlight you paid for. If you use roman shades, a pelmet may hide the stack-back better when the shades are open.

SEALING WINDOWS

Even the finest, heaviest window treatments cannot compensate for broken or leaky windows. If you have old single-pane glass windows, especially if they are true divided lights – small panes of glass set in a wooden grid – you need storm windows. Get the kind that is permanently installed with screens you can open and close.

Examine your windows. Replace any broken panes and make sure they're all set snugly with glazier's points and good putty that does not appear dry and cracked. This can be a DIY job, but there is a risk of injury from handling broken glass. If mishandled, even the edges of an intact pane of window glass can slice open your hand. Trust me, I've heard enough horror stories from craftsmen and contractors who handle glass, and they're pros.

The library has plenty of handyman instruction books that show you how to do this job. If you have to reglaze many windows, you'll find that after you're done, you'll want to redo the first ten or so with your newly improved skills.

Reglazing can make an amazing difference. In a previous house, I had twenty or so windows with true divided lights and old storm windows. Some of the panes were broken, and all were loose in their frames. A handyman replaced every broken pane, scraped out and reputtied every window, added glazier's points (small slips of metal that hold the glass to the frame), and tightened and trued up the storm windows. It was an amazing difference: no drafts, no leaks, less noise, and no rattles at night from the wind.

Based on personal experience, if you can preserve old, solid-oak windows, you should do so. Replacement double-pane glass windows vary wildly in quality and price. They don't seem made to last the lifetime of a house unlike old-fashioned windows. When the seal fails on your replacement double-pane glass windows, you have the equivalent of single-pane glass. Rehab those windows and get good storms. That will go a long way to improving the dreadful energy efficiency of single-pane glass. Otherwise, resign yourself to the fact that replacement windows will eventually have to be replaced themselves.

SHALL WE DANCE?

The Window Dance changes with the season and the time of day. It will be a rare day when you don't open or close something. We can break down the dance by season.

Winter: You want as much light and heat as possible from your solar gain, while losing as little heat as you can manage.

When you get up in the morning, after the sun comes up, open all the layers, starting on the morning sun side, and work your way around your house. The drapes are pulled back to the sides of the window, the shades are up, and the sheers don't move. The quilts are taken down, rolled up on their dowels, and stored. The windows stay closed. Even if it is heavily overcast, open the drapes. There is still heat from the sun.

At sunset, close the layers ending with the house snugly shut up for the night. Hang the quilts, spreading each one out to cover the frame with an air gap between it and the glass; close the shade so it hangs well below the sill; the sheers stay closed and the drapes cover the window and all the layers completely.

Make sure that the drapes touch the wall at the sides as you lose more heat there than at the center of the window. For a better seal, apply Velcro strips to the edge of the drapes and to the wall and press them together.

The only change to this routine in winter comes on very warm days when you can open a window to air out your house. Open the windows long enough to freshen the air and not drop the indoor temperature too much.

Spring: The goal in the first half of spring is to keep your heat. The goal in the second half of is to cool the house as much as you can before the blaze of summer. So, as before, open window treatments to follow the sun and close up at night.

Now is the time to open the windows themselves to air out the fug of winter. This is a careful balancing act: fresh air versus temperature change. Keep an eye on the thermostat as the day progresses. Trap enough heat to keep the furnace from coming on and no more. You want to start the summer with a cold house.

As spring moves closer to summer, you'll open the windows more often. The window shades now become important. While the process is repeated as before, you'll finish by opening the windows and pulling the white shades down to the top of the screened opening. The shade will reflect the sun's heat while still allowing air movement.

At night, depending on where you live, you may not close the drapes or windows, leaving them open all night to maintain the home's temperature. Adjust the shades to whatever opening you have your screens at and leave the quilts rolled up and out of the way.

This should be obvious, but I will say it anyway: If you open your screens, and then close all those layers and layers of drapes, you won't get any fresh air. You will still get all the outside noise.

Summer: Now we keep the heat outside. Start each morning with the layers closed. Don't open any until after the window no longer receives direct sun. Follow the sun around the house, opening the layers only as the sun moves past.

Depending on how cool it is at night — and how safe your area is — you may leave the windows open all night (except for the shade pulled down to the top of the screen) and close them in the morning.

Never raise your light-reflective shade when the window is in direct sun! You may discover that certain windows will not be opened at all: They always get solar gain, either directly or from reflected heat. For example, we have two bedroom windows facing the north. They only receive direct sun in very late afternoon. However, because of the bright white house next door, these windows are always hot, hot, hot, since they receive a full dose of reflected sunshine from dawn to dusk. This is nice in the winter but bad in the summer. The layers remain closed all day and are opened only at night.

We have a large picture window that acts as a heat trap. Both the quilt and the shade stay in place all summer long to block the heat.

The difficulty with keeping the drapes closed is you may need to turn on the lights because your house is dark. You have to decide: pay for the electricity or raise the home's temperature with the solar gain. I go back and forth on this one.

Fall: Now we want to air out the house after the hot summer and trap heat for the coming winter. As soon as the sun kisses a window, open every layer. Warm days mean open windows with warm air coming in. Watch your inside temperatures. Do *not* let the house cool off. If your windows are open and the inside temperature is dropping, close them. Heat up your house during the day. As the sun goes down, tightly close every layer to trap the warmth. You won't be leaving windows open at night anymore. You will lose too much heat.

Open the windows during the day only to catch warmer air. For us, this is limited to the mid-afternoon and only for two hours. Closing the windows at 3 p.m. lets the house catch solar gain for a few more hours before sunset. The warmer your house is going into the winter, the longer it will take for your furnace to kick on.

MADE IN THE SHADE

You can have the best windows in the world, but full sun in the summer means heat and lots of it. Shade in the winter means cold, cold, and more cold since you're blocking the sun's heat.

The solution is deciduous trees; that is, trees that shed their leaves in the fall and grow new ones in the spring. Evergreens have their uses, but supporting the Window Dance isn't one of them. They should be planted on the property's north side to act as a windbreak against the winter air pouring down from Canada.

Trees take between ten to fifteen years to get some size, so get started on this right away. Figure out how the sun passes over your house during the year. What windows receive full sun and when? As the sun moves, windows that were borderline for natural light in one season may receive more or far less in other seasons. The only way to know is through observation and record keeping.

The buildings and trees around you will influence your solar gain by reflecting light or providing shade. The best location for trees is not on the south side of your house, it is the east and west sides for morning and afternoon shade.

Consider how dense you want the shade to be. Tree varieties range from light, dappled shade (like honey locusts) to deep, dark shade (like beeches). How big should the tree be? How far away from the house? What shape should the tree be: vase-like or a tall, wide spread? Many trees at maturity will be well over fifty feet tall, although it will take decades to get there.

Read up on trees before buying any. One warning: *Do not buy trees from a big box store.* You will get a much better selection from a nursery or a mail-order catalog and better information about planting and maintaining the trees. Trees are living creatures and some will do better in some locations than others. Low-lying swampy area? Acid soil? Alkaline soil? A tree that likes one kind of soil will wither and die in a different kind of soil. A good nursery will help with these issues.

As we discussed with hedges, know the mature height and canopy spread *before* you plant the tree under the power line or in the narrow space between buildings. Give your trees enough room to grow, accommodating for their mature height, canopy spread, and roots.

The root spread of a tree tends to match its canopy size. Don't try to fit a tree that wants to top out at seventy-five feet high and seventy-five feet across in a four-foot-by-four-foot planting area. Eventually, you will have a problem.

Also, don't plant trees from only one species. A mixed planting of taller and shorter trees of different species will be healthier.

There are other factors to decide before you buy. First, do you want saplings or older trees? Saplings are small, young trees, only two or three years old. They will grow fast and soon catch up to the much taller and more expensive six- or eight-year-old trees. The older trees have the advantage of size right out of the box, but they don't transplant nearly as well, take years to recover, and cost much more.

Then there is the labor factor to consider. One person can plant a sapling or a whip. A ten-foot-tall tree with a heavy root ball the size of a big laundry basket will need several people or even professional help to plant.

Follow the nursery directions on hole digging, planting, mulching, and watering to the letter. Lawn mowers and string trimmers are deadly to trees so keep them away with a large circle of mulch about three inches deep. Don't pile the mulch up against the trunk. That encourages rot and varmint damage. No mulch volcanoes!

Try to keep your trees at least twenty feet from your house unless they are very small at maturity or columnar. Plant on the east *and* the west sides of your house, and then, if you find you need more shade, fill in on the south side.

In addition to providing shade, trees create a cooling effect from the leaves respiring. If your neighbors also have trees, you can enjoy outdoor living in a cooling island instead of a heat island of concrete and asphalt.

LIGHTEN YOUR SHINGLES

There is one more thing you can do to improve the Window Dance and that is to replace your roof. For most of the country, a white roof will be effective in reflecting the sun's heat. If your attic is properly insulated, this won't make a difference in the winter, but in the summer, you get a big payoff. You won't have as big or hot a mass of air sitting over top of your air-conditioned spaces. An attic with a ridge vent under a white roof will be 15% to 20% cooler than an attic under a black roof. When you reroof your house, get the lightest-colored shingles available, install ridge and soffit vents, and reduce your cooling dollars.

Fed, Safe & Sheltered

The Window Dance substitutes your energy, active and passive, for the energy from the power company. It catches free energy from the sun and makes your life more comfortable. Recognize your window treatments and trees as insulation. They will save you money when used correctly.

19

Energy Efficiency

The Heterodyne Principle – Understanding Jevons' Paradox – Changing Your Behavior – Staking the Energy Vampire – Keeping Out the Weather – Appliances and Cars

BEING ENERGY INDEPENDENT MEANS spending less money over the long run, and if prices rise through the roof, spending much less money than you otherwise would have. Being energy independent does not keep crazy people from blowing up oilfields and making the price of gas double overnight, nor does it keep the hurricane from flooding your basement, forcing you to replace your furnace years earlier than planned. It doesn't make the winters warmer nor the summers cooler.

What it does do is make it easier to cope with those predicaments. Every dollar you don't spend on energy costs is a dollar you can apply to something else and those dollars accumulate, tax-free. Remember, you get taxed on what you earn, not on what you don't spend. At least not yet.

THE HETERODYNE PRINCIPLE

We've saved a lot of money at Fortress Peschel by reducing our energy usage. It required us to spend money up front, do plenty of hard, dirty work, and make lifestyle changes.

Each job, each decision, seemed to have a small effect at the time. However, we learned that these tiny benefits worked together, feeding off of and reinforcing each other. To coin a phrase: they *heterodyned*. (Heterodyning is an electronics word where you combine two higher frequency radio waves to get a third, lower frequency one.) That is, if you heavily insulate your house, you will save money. If you lower your thermostat in the winter and put on a sweater, you will save money. If you do both, you will save *much more* money than by either action taken alone. Moreover, by wearing the sweater, you could drop the thermostat another degree or two because you insulated the house.

The heterodyne principle shows up elsewhere in surprising ways. If you cut your oil and gas usage, you have the pleasure of knowing that less of your money spent at the gas pump or heating your house ends up in the pockets of multinational oil companies. Turning lights off means the nation needs fewer polluting power plants.

This matters to me, so I hang my laundry on a clothesline year-round. It's non-polluting, totally free after investing in poles, clothesline, clothespins, and a bag to put them in, gets me out in the sunshine, and no money goes into the pockets of some global corporation I disapprove of.

Going through the trouble to buy, install, and maintain solar panels to power a dryer is a ridiculous waste. Use a clothesline and save the solar energy for a task you can't replace as easily such as powering your computer.

UNDERSTANDING JEVONS' PARADOX

Perversely, practicing energy efficiency has an unexpected side effect explained by Jevons' Paradox. William Stanley Jevons was a Victorian British economist who noticed that more efficient use of coal (as technology improved) did *not* lead to a drop in the use of coal. On the contrary, it led to the usage, and actual wastage, of more coal.

In short, as a product becomes cheaper, the less care we take in using it efficiently.

This is true today. Electricity used to be expensive and scare. People didn't use it for much as it cost too much. As the technology to create and deliver it improved, the cost dropped. More and more usages for electricity were developed and marketed until today we use electronic picture frames so we don't have to keep seeing the same boring pictures of our kids. The picture changes for you. Does each electronic picture frame use much power? Nope, but add up a few million, plugged in 24/7, and you are devoting the output of a power plant to run them.

While I'm ranting about electronic picture frames, don't forget that they consume a huge amount of energy to mine and refine the materials used in manufacturing the frames, energy to ship, warehouse and sell the frames, and to build the power plant to run them.

To be truly energy efficient, you need to wring out every drop of usefulness from a fuel source and then *still use less*. Switch to the most fuel-efficient car you can and then *drive less*. You don't get to drive *more* because you are doing it in a Prius. You don't get to turn up your thermostat in the winter because you installed the most efficient furnace. You still should turn it down and wear a sweater.

Conservation is just as important as efficiency. It doesn't matter how efficient you are in using your fuel if you use more than ever. So how do we do this? We improve our efficiency (to wring out every drop of power from a given unit), we cut waste (i.e., energy we carelessly spill on the ground), and we make lifestyle changes that let us use less overall.

We will cover lifestyle choices first as they cost the least and can be implemented immediately.

CHANGING YOUR BEHAVIOR

At the head of the pack is *turning off things you aren't using*. Are the lights and the ceiling fan on in a room you aren't using? Is your porch light on at high noon? Turn them off. For maximum energy efficiency and conservation, train yourself and your family to walk to the switch and turn it off with your hand rather than installing devices that do it for you; devices that will cost you money to buy, install, use, maintain, and require an energy source to operate 24/7.

Turn down (or up) the thermostat. Does the house have to be at 75 degrees year round? We set our winter thermostat to 64 degrees during the day and let it drop to 55 degrees overnight. Our air-conditioner is set to 81 degrees during the day; and at night, when the AC doesn't have to fight the sun; I drop it down to 76 degrees. If that is too extreme for you, change the thermostat by two degrees and see if anyone notices. You may be surprised.

If the weather outside is good, *open the windows*. Let in warm sunshine and air during spring and fall. Let out the heat overnight during the summer. I regularly see, while walking Muffy and it's 70 degrees out, houses shut up tight and the AC humming. On sunny fall days, I also see houses with the furnace roaring away with the blinds tightly closed to keep out the sun. The Window Dance chapter has a lot more information about how to use windows and window treatments to manipulate the temperature of your house.

Dress for the weather. In winter, I wear a sweater over a turtleneck, with long pants, knee socks, fingerless gloves, and I add a hat or a cardigan if I need to. I am the person in my household who suffers the most from the cold *and* the heat, and if I can do it, so can you. In the summer, I wear lightweight cotton shirts, shorts, and go bare foot. I drink plenty of cold water in the summer and in the winter, hot tea is very warming. At the change of seasons, I may change my clothes, adding or removing a layer to accommodate the weather. When a family member whines to me that they are cold, standing in front of me in a tank top and shorts in January, my response (and yours should be too) is *put on a sweater*. Don't turn up the heat.

Job together your cooking. If the main course is in the oven, what else can you cook along with it? A potato side dish? Cake or bread? You've already heated up the oven so don't waste that heat. Cook ahead for tomorrow if you can, so you can eat leftovers for several days.

Plan trips. I do as many of my errands as I can on the same day to minimize the time and gas spent driving around. I devise the most efficient circuit I can make so I spend less time as well as less gas driving back and forth. This isn't hard. It just means being thoughtful.

When you have many errands in the same location, can you park so that you can walk from one to another? This may take more time, but remember that it also takes time getting in the car and moving it from parking space to parking space. This time spent is more than compensated by the exercise you're getting, the reduced gas and wear and tear on the car, and the opportunity to see where you are rather than driving by. You don't know who you'll meet, or what you'll see when you are on foot. I find change lying on the street this way, along with mongo and obtainium.

Be thoughtful. Ask why you are doing something. Are you stopping at the gym on your way home from work to walk on a treadmill? Maybe you could come home, saving the time and gas and money, and walk around your neighborhood at a brisk pace. If you have a complex routine, could you exercise at home with DVDs from the library or use the Royal Canadian Air Force fitness program? Every gym has huge amounts of energy invested in it. Do you receive enough of a benefit to make membership worthwhile?

Be thoughtful. Are you taking advantage of services available to you? Many kids, including mine, ride the school bus. I don't drive my kids to school, and I don't pick them up unless they have an appointment. They also walk to the bus stop, while there are parents who drive their kids, park in the street, and leave the engine running while they wait for the bus. This is in a small neighborhood, too.

If you have to pick up your kids after school, consider parking your car and walking to the entrance. On the rare occasions I have picked up my kids, I see people sitting in the pickup lane, sometimes half an hour early, with the engine running. Save the time and gas. Park in the lot, walk up, get the offspring, then walk back to your car, start it and drive away. It doesn't take long, and it uses much less gas than sitting and steaming in the pickup lane waiting on everyone else.

Be thoughtful. Do you let your electronic equipment entertain an empty room? If you aren't watching or listening, turn them off.

Be thoughtful. Is the dishwasher full when you run a load? Do you wash partial loads of clothes rather than wait for a full load? Why are you washing a load of towels several times a week anyway? Give each family member a towel and have them hang it up to dry on the towel rack. Towels are not dirty after one use; if they are, you're doing something wrong in the shower. Hang them up to dry and use them again the next day.

Be thoughtful. Do you run water at the tap until it gets cold enough? Put a pitcher of water in the fridge and use that.

Be thoughtful. Do you take showers long enough to empty the hot water heater? It doesn't take that long to lather, rinse, repeat, and condition your hair, even long hair. Unless you work in the bilges of a ship, you aren't that dirty. It feels terrific to stand for twenty minutes in a hot, steamy shower, but that is a lot of water you're paying for to buy and heat that is going down the drain.

Be thoughtful. Evaluate everything you do. Do you need to do this? Are there alternatives that use less energy? The savings are there, and they are real. The problem is that the results aren't as apparent as thinking about every bite of food you put in your mouth is (if you are dieting) or the money you spend on a shopping trip. It's easy to cut your spending by 5%, even 10%, simply by paying attention to what you're doing and deciding if you really want that item. Planning your car trips may result in buying gas every twelve days instead of ten. The savings in energy and dollars are there, but they don't show up unless you are looking for them. Plenty of lifestyle energy savings are small — and there are plenty of changes you can make — but they do add up over time.

STAKING THE ENERGY VAMPIRE

The next set of changes addresses electrical waste, which only starts with the lights you leave burning in empty rooms. Every electrical device in your home that has a light, a digital clock, or a remote control is permanently on. It uses power 24/7, even if it is turned off.

It's a challenge to buy a coffee-maker that doesn't have a built-in clock. Do I need a clock in my coffee-maker? No, nor do I want to pay for both the extra cost to add a clock and the few dollars a year in electricity that it uses.

This power drain on your electrical utility and your wallet is called a vampire or phantom load. This is the standby power a device uses to stay awake so it can spring into action at the touch of a button. Each device – the TV, a microwave, or a coffee pot with a built-in clock — uses very little electricity. Add them up, across the country, and these millions of vampire loads add up to a power plant or two.

The way to counteract vampire loads is, first, to try not to buy them. This can be a challenge. If you can't, then make sure your devices are really turned off by unplugging them.

If you have a group of devices, such as a TV set, DVD player, and Wii game platform in one place, plug them into a power strip and turn them on and off there. There is an added benefit to using a power strip; many come with surge protectors that keep power fluxes from frying the equipment. Depending on how many devices you have and how much of a power hog they are, this can add up to tens of dollars over the years. This is not much electricity on a house-by-house basis. On a society-wide basis? As I said, a power plant or two exists so we can have digital clock readouts on our coffee makers.

KEEPING OUT THE WEATHER

Are you pouring electricity onto the ground while heating or cooling the great outdoors? If you haven't checked your home's insulation or weather-stripping, chances are that you are wasting your energy dollars. Weather-stripping your doors and windows is easy and cheap. Even renters can do this one.

First, check your home for leaks. One night, close your front door and lock it. Turn off the lights, inside and out. Have someone shine a

Energy Efficiency

flashlight around the door's edges. If you see light leaking through, then your heat (and AC) is leaking out as well. Simple weatherstripping kits are available at every hardware store. Install them at every door and stop losing heat. Then tackle the windows.

Look for cracks and light leaks wherever walls divide heated and unheated spaces. Upstairs, we discovered a leakage in the inside corner of the stairwell. From the stairs, nothing was visible. In the attic, you could see a line of light 1/8-inch wide and seven feet high. This was the equivalent of a fist-size hole pouring heat and AC into the unheated attic year-round. A line of caulk and insulation plugged the gap.

Insulate, insulate, insulate. It isn't hard to do, but it is persnickety, dirty, detail-oriented work. We've insulated basement ceilings with batts of pink fiberglass and covered them with pressure-fitted Styrofoam panels. We laid and cross-laid fiberglass batts in the attics.

The previous owners said they had insulated the attic. There was batting there, but it was thrown about, leaving huge gaps. Heaps of junk had been thrown over the batts, squashing them flat and destroying their insulating qualities. Don't pile anything on your insulation if you want it to work.

Working with fiberglass batts is tiring, itchy, meticulous work, but you can do it yourself if you're handy and wear proper gear, including clothes that cover your skin, eye protection, gloves, and a dust mask. If your walls need insulation, your best bet is either to take down the walls and install fiberglass batts, or leave them up and hire a professional to blow cellulose insulation into the cavities.

Our upstairs bonus room was added onto the house years after it was built. We have a partially finished basement, also done about the same time. In each case, the walls had batting in them. You could see the batts from the unprotected side. To add more insulation, Dear Husband nailed 1.5-inch thick foam insulating panels over the exposed walls. The rooms were instantly warmer in the winter, cooler in the summer, and quieter year-round. These panels were heavy, thick and made for this purpose. They come in several thicknesses and with a reflective side. If you have exposed walls facing an unheated space, the panels are ideal for covering up the fiberglass and the studs. The installation procedure is the same whatever the thickness. The cost is more for thicker panels, but the added insulation and quiet make it worthwhile to use the thickest panels available.

The other job Dear Husband did in the attic was to staple rolls of perforated foil to the rafters, leaving gaps at the top and the bottom. This trapped heat from the roof and encouraged it to rise to the ridge vent. Attics are not supposed to be heated spaces. The goal is to keep the attic's temperature as close as you can to the outside temperature. The heavy insulation in the attic floor keeps the heat (or AC) in the house. Venting and reflective foil keep the attic from overheating in the summer. A cooler attic in the summer removes that hot mass of air sitting over you and reduces demand on your AC.

After we insulated our attic, we discovered how much heat it had been receiving from below when the exposed pipes leading to the upstairs bathroom froze. These pipes are now wrapped in thick pipe-wrap, with fiberglass wrapped around them, and in an insulated box built from leftover foam panels.

We then attacked all the exposed pipes with pipe-wrap. These are heavy foam sleeves that you slide over the pipes, both hot and cold water. We've wrapped every bit of the pipes that we could reach. Hot water *always* gets the thickest wrap, cold lines the thinner wrap. Doing this job made hot water arrive quicker and last longer to the upstairs bathroom, the kitchen sink and the basement bathroom. These spaces always had a problem with getting the water hot enough and then keeping it that way. No more.

To finish the job, we also tagged out the plumbing so anyone working on the lines in the future has a fighting chance of knowing what line goes where and what it does. If you don't feel that thicker and thinner wrappings identify the hot and cold water lines enough, mark the pipes with colored tape: red for hot and blue for cold.

There are other insulating tasks that'll help make your house more comfortable.

A few years ago, I purchased a headboard for our bed. It came with a wicker insert that I didn't like. I shrouded it with foam padding and a fabric cover. The headboard separates our bed from the cold north wall. Put your hand between the headboard and the wall in January and that space is cold, cold, cold. The bed side? Room temperature.

Insulation also means adding down comforters to beds. Leave blankets and throws on chairs and couches so when you're reading or watching TV, you can cover up with a blanket rather than heat the entire house a few more degrees.

Energy Efficiency

Insulating and weather-stripping also cuts down on drafts. It's worth checking to see why you feel a constant draft in a corner. You may discover a hole, or a cracked window. Improperly closed storm windows can also give you cold drafts.

The great thing about insulating and weather-stripping is that once it's done, your insulation will keep working for you, day and night, and you don't have to think about it anymore.

APPLIANCES AND CARS

The last step with energy efficiency comes from choosing the most energy-efficient alternatives.

When you replace your roof, get the lightest-color shingles you can. Unless you live in Canada, a lighter roof will cut your electricity costs for AC by as much as 15%. A white roof reflects heat, making the attic cooler so your AC doesn't have to work as hard. Make sure your attic is also properly ventilated with vents in the gables, soffits, and ridgeline. This will keep the attic dryer too, allowing moisture to escape rather than get trapped in your fiberglass batts.

If you upgrade your ceiling lights, install ceiling fans. Moving the air around makes the room feel cooler. It is more efficient to run the fan in the room you're in than cool the house.

When you replace appliances, look for the Energy Star logo and get the most energy-efficient unit. You may pay a little more, but the energy savings should more than compensate. This is especially effective for products you use for years, such as your freezer, furnace or whole-house AC. However, wait until you have to do it. No matter how energy efficient a new stove may be, you still have to count the cost inherent in manufacturing a new one plus the hit to your wallet. An existing stove, like an existing house, is already built and paid for. A more energy efficient stove *may* save you $100 a year. Since the new stove costs hundreds of dollars up front, it will take years to pay that cost back.

To keep appliances lasting longer and running more efficiently, do the maintenance and keep them clean. Vacuum refrigerator coils and wipe down the gaskets. Get the furnace and the air-conditioner checked every year. Change their filters every month. It isn't energy-efficient to replace an appliance that would still be working if you had taken better care of it.

When looking over your appliances, think about whether or not you need them. Do you *have* to have that second fridge in the garage? Do you *need* a TV set in every bedroom, plus the family room and the kitchen? In this case, the most energy-efficient alternative is to get rid of them.

Clotheslines are a stellar example of this. A clothesline does what a dryer does: it dries clothes. It takes more time to use one, from a few hours to a full day. It requires planning as you cannot dry clothes as well at night. You are on the weather's schedule and not your own. Dryers are very nice and very convenient, but you pay for this convenience when you buy the dryer, the wear and tear it inflicts on your clothes, and the electricity to run it.

I'm not against appliances. I have a stove, a dishwasher, a fridge, a freezer, a washing machine, hot water heater, oil-burning furnace, air-conditioner, lamps, sewing machine, microwave, coffee-maker, a TV set (but no cable), some computers, and other small appliances. However, I think very hard before adding to the collection. I don't have gadgets like bread makers or pasta machines. I wouldn't use them, I don't have the storage space for them, and I don't have the money to buy them.

For each appliance you want, decide if you want to spend the money — up-front and over the long term — to use it. If the answer is no, don't buy it. If you aren't using something, get rid of it.

If my energy costs rise, the dishwasher would go first. It is damn difficult to run a kitchen without a stove and a fridge, but dishes can be hand-washed. I like my dishwasher. It's a huge timesaver. Nevertheless, I can live without one in a way that I can't live without the washing machine.

(This is why you shouldn't tempt the fates: Since writing this, our dishwasher died, and we're back to washing up by hand.)

I like my freezer a lot. It lets me stock up on grocery store bargains as well as freeze garden produce. If I had to, I'd get rid of the dishwasher *and* the dryer before I'd lose the freezer.

I very rarely use the dryer as I prefer the clothesline and the drying racks. The dryer would go, forcing recalcitrant family members (they know who they are) to work around winter weather more than they already do.

I could live without the microwave. It's convenient, and it doesn't use that much power, but I could live without it.

Every appliance in your home should be thought about in this

Energy Efficiency

fashion. Do you use it? Do you need it? Is it worth the space, mental, financial, and physical?

In addition, every appliance should be evaluated for the complexity it brings to your life. Do you *need* a fridge that makes ice and has a cold-water tap in the door? These models cost more up front, cost more to run, take up more food storage space, and have more features to break. I've had bad experiences with icemakers, so I never buy a fridge that does fancy stuff. A water pitcher in the fridge and ice trays in the freezer work fine and take up far less space.

This is true of all kinds of appliances. The more they do, the harder they are to repair and the more prone to breakage they seem to be.

Cars fall into the same category as appliances. When you have to buy one (never lease them!), get the most fuel-efficient model that will suit your needs. Don't buy a larger, more rugged vehicle unless it is needed for something other than satisfying your ego. If you sell stuff on the craft circuit, for example, you'll want a panel van or a truck to haul your goods. If all you do is drive to the office, then why do you need a big pickup truck? Ranchers need big pickup trucks. Contractors need big trucks. They haul tons of stuff frequently. Do you?

Evaluate your fleet of vehicles. I have friends; a household of four licensed drivers. They have a pickup truck (his), a motorcycle (his), a car (hers), a running car (son), a non-running car (son) and a car (daughter). Six vehicles for four drivers that have to be paid for, insured (except the non-running car), maintained, and stored. Think about every vehicle you pay for and know *why* you are keeping them, beyond saying they might come in handy somehow.

My Dear Husband and I both work from home. Dear Daughter has a license. Younger Son is working on his. We live in a small, walkable town. We share one car, a small sedan. A van or a truck would be very useful to haul sheets of plywood for projects, but we don't do that much anymore, so we manage without one.

A fuel-efficient car will tide you over when gas prices unexpectedly spike. As of this writing, gas is a little over $2 a gallon. However, fifteen years ago, it was less than a buck a gallon. Gas prices have gone up and down, but they have *never* gotten as low as they were, and they probably never will. A fuel-efficient car will never stop saving you cash at the pump, cash that you can put towards something else.

There aren't many households that can't cut back on their energy usage. We've cut back a lot, and unlike what my father recalls doing as a child during a North Dakota winter, we don't have to break the ice on buckets of water. We have appliances, we have a furnace and an air-conditioner, we have a TV, and we have a car. We also have much lower costs than most of the people I know. It can be eye-opening to cut back and discover how little you miss what you thought you needed.

20

Organization

Using the Martha Wall – Corralling Your Material World – Redoing Your Closets – Kitchen Storage

We do a lot here at Fortress Peschel to kep the old place going. It may sound like I never stop working, that I never sleep, that I never do *anything* other than what I must do to meet my goals. This is not true. I waste my fair share of time. You cannot stay focused every second. It's not possible and anyway, all work and no play makes Jack a management consultant.

What helps me do a lot is to have goals. This is a form of focused thinking. You can look at what you are doing, and if it isn't moving you towards one goal or another, then you ask why are you doing this? (I say this after yet another game of Spider solitaire. I love that game, and I'm good at it, too.)

Goals help us distinguish which task is most urgent. Some jobs have an end date, some never end, and some are in between. Some jobs require a lot of work upfront and then they're done, like adding insulation and paying off debt, painting rooms, and redoing kitchen cabinets.

Never-ending jobs include laundry, cooking, sleeping, and exercising. No matter how much laundry you wash, a few days later, there is more. No matter how much you exercise on any given day, the next day you have to do it again to stay in shape. I sleep eight hours a night, but every night I have to do it again. Every day, meals have to be made, eaten, and cleared away afterwards. These are tasks, and time has to be allotted for them.

Gardening fits the in-between category; the garden requires work now and then, but not all of the time.

Organization makes it easier to get the routine stuff done. For those of us without staff, an awful lot of life consists of boring and mundane maintenance. Nevertheless, it has to be done to keep the piles of laundry from turning into tottering, reeking mountains. Organization is the structure and skeleton of your life. It lets you get the routine stuff done and leaves time to accomplish tasks that move you forward.

Being organized does not come naturally to most of us, and it's used as an easy excuse. "I'm just not organized!" is heard everywhere except near one's boss. You have to be organized on the job, you have to complete the daily assignments, or you get fired.

We are very poor managers of ourselves. We are bad bosses when we accept empty excuses from ourselves, especially when we *know* they're excuses. We are bad employees when we tell ourselves that we don't have to do that boring, mundane task. This is why, no matter what kind of aimless life a person lives at home — messy and chaotic and never getting the house insulated or the garden beds dug — they do not do the same thing at work. Most work is accomplished through structure and routine. You need this at home, too, to utilize the little free time you have to move closer towards independence.

I cannot tell you exactically how to organize your home and time. I am not riding along inside your skin. What I can say is to review your goals. Know what they are. Then ask yourself as you are playing Angry Birds on your cellie again: Is this getting me to my goals? Or am I just wasting time?

I have some suggestions and examples to get you started.

USING THE MARTHA WALL

I use several tools to manage my time, starting with a year-at-a-glance calendar on the wall in our dining area. Appointments, meetings, trips, school events, and other time-sensitive information go on this calendar so I can see what is coming up. If anybody in the family, including Muffy and those useless cats, is expected somewhere, it is on the calendar.

The calendar is part of a special area Dear Husband built using an idea from *Martha Stewart Living*. Like many of Stewart's home projects, it combines beauty with functionality. It consists of a ten-foot-wide bookshelf mounted above three yellow-painted bulletin boards mounted vertically, with space left over for four wall-mounted file holders. The four sections are framed with poplar boards painted white.

All of the family's business is tracked here. The bulletin boards, made from Homasote, let me pin up notices, appointment cards, coupons, ads for upcoming events, and to-do lists. The bookshelf holds our cookbooks and other food and drink books. The wall pockets hold bills, school paperwork, garden information, and whatever else we need at the moment.

The great benefit of the Martha Wall and the year-at-a-glance calendar is that they are visible all the time. Everyone can check their appointments and write in things.

I also started keeping a logbook several years ago. I use a composition notebook, the kind that has eighty pages that they sell at Staples for 50¢ when the school year starts. I use a page a day and since each page is double-sided (160 days worth); a notebook lasts a long time.

In it, I list the usual daily events, appointments, chores to be done by family members, memorandums, and notes. Additional tasks are added as they happen as well as the events of the day that don't fit into the routine schedule. The logbook lets me open my Visa bill, notice a purchase at K-Mart, go to that date in the logbook, and find out what I bought there.

The logbook remembers upcoming events and past happenings. I would be lost without it, and I highly recommend using one. Is it work to keep up with? Of course it is. I leave it out on the counter with a pen by it — when a kid didn't run off with it — so I can stop regularly and keep it up to date. It is far less work than trying to remember everything that I have to do. Since it is non-electronic, I don't have to worry about batteries, mechanical failure, or upgrades. I can write in it in the dark with a flashlight and a pencil if I had to. Costing 50¢ and a pen, it's cheap, too.

It shows how routine my day is, but a routine-oriented day lets me be more efficient. A written routine can also show you what you do versus what you think you should do. I exercise nearly every day and my logbook lists this on the first line. I get it done, and I move on throughout my day. If I don't exercise, I don't check off those items.

I use a second logbook to record my bills, taxes, and other expenditures. I've been doing this since Dear Husband and I got married, when I learned how to do this from his mother. The money logbook remembers for me, and I can go back in time and track my spending easily for taxes, insurance, energy costs, and the like. Since I record every bill, its due date, its paid date, and how much, I don't make very many mistakes in getting bills paid. On those rare occasions when a company claims I haven't paid something, I can easily find the information to prove that I am right.

Only I use both logbooks. Other people can check them, but I am the person who writes in them.

In addition, I keep lists of all kinds: writing projects, home-improvement projects (huge), sewing projects, whatever I think I need to do. As tasks are completed, they are checked off. Some projects or ideas never get done, but I don't have many that slip through the cracks anymore. The lists – they can be multi-page – are pinned onto the Martha Wall or by my sewing area as appropriate.

As our lives change, lists evolve, grow, or go away. My lists, the Martha Wall with its year-at-a-glance calendar and bulletin boards, and the logbooks let me clear my head of mental clutter.

CORRALLING YOUR MATERIAL WORLD

Physical clutter has to be managed as well.

None of us have unlimited space, and very few have spacious, empty basements, accessible attics, a barn, and multiple outbuildings. You can store a lot if you have plenty of space, but if you cannot find something when you need it, then you might as well not have it.

As preppers, we want to store goods that are useful and hard to replace. How often do I use that OST planting bar and the bulb auger? Not very often — perhaps once a year or less — but when I need them, I want to know where to find them.

Start by putting things away when you are done with them. Find a place for everything and put everything in its place. Dumb and basic, right? How many scissors do you have? Do you know where they are? I've known people who have multiple pairs but cannot find one because they never put them back in the same drawer.

You wouldn't have your work files tossed into giant Rubbermaid storage bins, all mixed up, so why is your home paperwork of bills, statements, and receipts done this way? Documents at work are organized, unlike the cardboard boxfuls at home. Decide on a place for bills, official paperwork, and office and school supplies, then put them away when you are finished!

Put a small trashcan in every room and use it. The floor is not the

Organization

place to drop litter. Use your handy trashcans *at once* when processing any kind of paper like the mail. If you don't *need* that catalog or flier, toss it. Take the few seconds now instead of letting it hang around for days, occupying precious mental space. Do not hesitate as catalogs breed in corners. They also encourage you to spend money, another worthwhile reason to toss them at once.

Sort and store like with like. Our gardening tools go in one of two places. The big stuff is out in our small toolshed. It is lined up along the walls and yes, that space needs to have plenty of hooks and bins to make it easier to grab something. I also keep a bucket with my commonly used hand tools — such as a trowel, pruners, and forks — along with a pair of gloves by the back door. I can grab it easily for a quick weeding session.

Tools that are not gardening related are kept in the workshop. They hang on hooks or are sorted, like with like, in clear plastic boxes and bins *with labels*. This is vital for small stuff like nails and screws.

Do this with everything. Car parts? In the garage. Paint, varnish, and primer? All together on a low shelf under the workbench. Dog food — canned and dry — dog treats, cat food, kitty litter? All on dedicated shelves with a barrier to keep the cats out. School and office supplies? On shelves in the unfinished basement in labeled, clear plastic boxes. In the kitchen, pots and pans are kept together. My dishes are stacked neatly. The bedding for each bed is stacked on the top shelves of that room's closet.

Once you start sorting the piles, like with like, you will find out how much stuff you have. Next, make it easy to put them away. Basic, yeah? If you have to rearrange your collection of margarine tubs and give-away plastic drinking glasses every time you finish the dishes, those dishes will never get put away.

How do you make it easy to put everything away? Get rid of the stuff you never use. I've seen kitchens with large collections, numbering in the dozens, of those give-away plastic tumblers. They are never used. They take up space and collect dust, and they get in the way of the glasses that are being used. They are not souvenirs. They are junk. Get rid of them.

Food in the pantry? Sort them by type: canned soup with canned soup, baking supplies together, cooking oils, pasta, cereal; they all stay with their relatives. Like with like, so I can see what I have and use what I have.

Health and beauty products? Cleaning supplies? Again, like with like. Cleaning supplies under the kitchen sink, bathroom stuff in the bathroom, and the overflow in the downstairs pantry. When something gets used up, I check my pantry *before* I purchase more.

I also do not allow family members to dictate my purchase of toothpaste and hair care products. We all use the same tube of toothpaste, and we have few hair-care products in the shower stall: Dear Husband and Younger Son use the shampoo/conditioner combo bottle, Dear Daughter and I use the same shampoo and conditioner. At a friend's house, I counted twenty-three separate containers in her shower stall alone.

How should you address all these containers if you were in that situation? Empty them out, over time, and don't buy any more until after you have gone through what you have. I am not above pouring all the hand lotion odds and ends into one container, then rinsing the bottles to get every last drop out.

Those stacks of magazines and newspapers that you are going to read someday? The mail-order catalogs full of helpful products you could use? You never will, so recycle them now, saving time and money.

Books? Should you get rid of them? This is a difficult topic for me. We have thousands of books, and over the years, we have purged unwanted books, looking at each one and asking questions. Does it have useful information on gardening, cooking, first aid, research for one of the many books we write? It will survive the purge. If it doesn't seem useful, it may go off to the library sale. We are careful about discarding books, as we've sometimes had to buy them back from AbeBooks.com. We discuss organizing your library in the chapter "Your Home and Public Libraries."

The purging idea applies to other parts of the house as well. What about tools? Do you use them? Do you know how to use them? Does each tool have a dedicated home on your workshop pegboard or toolbox or are they thrown, jumbled up, into a Rubbermaid storage bin? If the answer is the storage bin, then you need to sort through the tools, figure out which ones you know how to use and find them a home. The rest may have to find new homes, or you have to learn how to use them.

We all own clothes and most of us have far more than we need. The classic approach is still the best. Take everything out of the closet

Organization

and dresser, look at it, and then decide: Do I still wear this on a regular basis? Keep. Will I never wear this again? Get rid of it. Is it damaged? Can I repair it and wear it? If yes, *repair* and keep. If no, get rid of it. Does this item still fit? If no, get honest and get rid of it.

Children's wardrobes should be evaluated yearly, as they grow so fast. It is disheartening to discover brand-new clothes that were outgrown before ever being worn. If your kid's closet and dresser are full to bursting, then this is probably happening to you right now. Kids will wear what is easiest to grab and never pay attention to the other stuff jammed behind them.

Go through your house, your vehicles, and your outbuildings. Evaluate everything. Do you use it? Is it worth the storage space? Is it stored so that it won't get damaged with the passage of time? Do you like it? If you hate that ugly vase, you've always hated that ugly vase, and everyone else in the family hates that ugly vase, then it needs to quietly disappear.

Once you have done the purges and put like with like, then it is time to look at your shelving. Let me repeat the lesson: You cannot organize your way out of clutter. Get rid of the excess junk and then organize what is left.

Don Aslett has written numerous books on clutter busting. He is amusing and accurate. He and other equally authoritative writers agree: Get rid of junk first and *then* install your magic organizers. Otherwise, you are just building bunkers for junk.

Like so many products, magic organizers only work if you use them. Complicated organizing systems won't get used. If you have to stack possessions "just so" to fit them into a cabinet, you won't do it.

Getting rid of things lets you consider what you do use. We did this with our dishes. When Dear Husband and I got married, we mixed our dishes, all kinds of plates and bowls and what not. They had to be stacked "just so" to fit into the cabinets.

I got tired of that so I decided to use the dishes his mother had given him as that was what we had the most of. I bought plenty of plates, cups, serving pieces, etc., from Replacements Ltd. and got rid of everything else. The lone exception was the cereal bowls as it was a poor, almost unusable design. I found a perfect design from Martha Stewart when she still sold her line of household goods through Kmart. I bought two dozen cereal bowls in plain white. We use them a lot, and twenty years later, still have twenty of them. They stack perfectly and take up very little space.

I did the same thing with the glassware. We own two sizes of Anchor Hocking glasses in their Tartan pattern: 16 oz. ice teas and 6 oz. juice glasses. I got rid of everything else. We no longer own mismatched glasses that don't line up smoothly, those dreadful tippy plastic tumblers, no souvenir cups of any kind, or family pass-alongs. Get rid of them all. I love the Tartan glasses. They are heavy, non-tip, the ribs make them easy to hold and less likely to slip out of your hands, and they don't want to chip or break. Tartan is the best glassware I have ever owned, and we will never buy anything else.

As for coffee cups, we have a wide array that we were given or found in thrift shops. These are hung up under the cabinet using cup hooks to take advantage of dead space. As for serving dishes, I got rid of everything that had to be stacked just so, paring the survivors down to simple designs that nested easily. I did the same thing with plastic food storage containers, canisters, pots, pans, utensils, and silverware.

All of this took time, effort, and money (especially to Replacements Ltd.) but this made my cabinets more organized and accessible. Family members were also more likely to put clean dishes away properly *and*, most importantly, it freed up valuable, limited space for better food storage. I have nineteen cabinets in my kitchen, some of them quite small. I use eight of them for dishes, pots and pans, or other non-food items. The rest are for food storage.

Look over your kitchen cabinets and see what you can do to better arrange them, cleaning out the unwanted junk and sorting your food by category. Do this first as your cabinets are what you go to first every day.

REDOING YOUR CLOSETS

There are vital places where organizers can be very, very handy. We love ClosetMaid's shelving systems. I've redone closets using their system in multiple houses, and it has always been worthwhile, with one change to their "closet in a box" system.

A ClosetMaid organizer replaces the single hang-bar and shelf. The closet is divided in half vertically, one side getting a hang-bar about halfway up the center support bar, allowing you to hang shirts. This hang-bar has another one hung above it, almost at the top of the closet. The other side has a higher hang-bar for dresses and pants.

Organization

The genius of ClosetMaid is that the hang-bars double as shelves so you can store stuff on them.

We modify ClosetMaid's design by replacing the higher hang-bar shelf (which stretches only halfway across the width of the closet) with one that extends the width of the closet. The additional shelf doesn't cost much more, and it doubles the shelving storage space.

For maximum efficiency, gut the closet and repaint the inside, top to bottom, with ultra-high-gloss white enamel to minimize the cave effect. Do this *before* you install the organizer. Another tip: ClosetMaid organizers are adjustable but you need a hacksaw or bolt cutters to do it. The instructions inside the box will tell you this; the box itself does not.

A ClosetMaid system will give you about a third more usable space in your closet. It works most effectively *after* you've purged all those ancient clothes that don't fit anymore.

Hooks are useful everywhere. We have hooks all over our house, to hang mops, brooms and cleaning equipment; to hang coats, hats, and scarves; kitchen items and workshop tools; belts and bags. If an item can go on a hook, it does, even if we have to add an eyelet, hole, or loop to make it so.

Books need to be on shelves, period. If you own a lot of books, you have to arrange for shelving. The cheapest alternatives are either melamine shelving systems using wall-mounted standards and brackets (you can take them with you when you move) or building bookcases out of plywood. We've done both. Commercial bookcases, besides being made out of particleboard, place the shelves too far apart for good book storage. We keep our fiction shelves about eleven inches apart to get the most books in the least space.

KITCHEN STORAGE

Kitchens benefit seriously from purges *before* you invest in organizers. I have installed hanging hooks, pullout racks, and hanging knife blocks. I also got rid of any appliances I didn't use. Bread maker? No. Espresso machine? No. Food processor? No. Pasta machine? No. Tabletop grill? No. The list is endless. The more stuff you get rid of that never gets used, the more room you have left in cabinets and countertops for the items you do use. Only you can decide if a waffle iron you use once a year is worth the space.

But if you keep stuff that gets used once a year, move it to dead storage. These are the spaces that are really out of the way. If you can, replace the soffits over your cabinets with cabinets that go up to the ceiling. That dead space is ideal for long-term, storage of little-used items. Unless you really enjoy cleaning, I don't recommend using the open space over cabinets for storing anything, particularly decorative accessories. Anything up there quickly becomes a greasy dust magnet.

While I'm on the subject, let me address open storage in kitchens. *Don't do this, ever.* It looks pretty in home décor magazines where stylists arrange everything perfectly. It looks so professional, just like a restaurant kitchen.

However, the reason why restaurants store everything on big hanging racks is that they use this equipment daily. The fish pots and asparagus steamers don't have a chance to get dirty. In a home kitchen, even when you cook every single day, you won't use all that stuff. When you finally do, you will discover that the pan has to be washed before you can use it.

But what about those fancy kitchens you see in magazines? The people who own those kitchens have Carmen and Guadalupe come in daily to wash all that stuff, whether it was used or not. Restaurants have cleaning crews that come in nightly. If Carmen and Guadalupe don't come to your house, guess who gets to clean all that stuff? You do.

Organizing makes your life easier, not harder. Store everything behind closed cabinet doors and keep greasy dust to a minimum. Don't install freestanding cabinets where you have to clean under and alongside of them. The reason why kitchen designers went to built-in, closed cabinets (starting with Catherine Beecher Stowe's book in the 1860s) was to make it easier for a woman without servants to keep the place in order. If you have servants, feel free to ignore this. Or make your housekeeper's life easier and store your kitchen goods in cabinets.

If you insist on seeing your kitchen stuff, use glass doors on your cabinets. Just remember that, if you can see it, so can everyone else. Stuff that is stored in the open needs to be neatly and attractively arranged. Otherwise, you'll look like a slob.

Keeping track of possessions is even more vital for long-term storage. If you cannot find it, you don't have it, whatever "it" is. If what you are storing is damaged by time, weather, critters, or any-

Organization

thing else, you don't have it.

These tips are just the beginning of organizing your home and life. Libraries are full of get-your-life-in-order books. Their advice boils down to these principles.

- Is what you're doing helping you to meet your goals?
- Mental clutter needs to be managed.
- A place for everything and everything in its place.
- Put things back when you're done with them.
- Get rid of everything that you don't regularly use or adore.
- If you can't put stuff away easily, you have too much stuff.
- If you don't like something, why do you have it?
- If you can't find it, you don't have it.
- If you say you want to do something, why aren't you?

21

Home Self-Sufficiency

The Skill of Reskilling — Reskilling in Practice — Managing Your Time and Energy — "But I Don't Know How to Do Anything"

I T IS IMPOSSIBLE TO BE COMPLETELY SELF-SUFFICIENT. No one is, and I don't believe anyone ever was. Early humans lived in small groups as hunter-gatherers, and they worked together for the good of the tribe.

Being completely self-sufficient also means a very limited life. Want salt? You need access to a salt mine and a pickaxe or the ocean and a tray. But where do those tools come from? Do you want cotton clothing? All you need is to grow the cotton, pick it, clean and comb it, spin it, then weave the cotton thread into yardage that you cut and sew – you made the needles along with the carding combs, spinning wheel, and loom, right? – to roughly fit your body. If you can knit and make knitting needles, you can skip the steps after spinning the fibers into threads.

Do you want a chicken dinner? Start with chickens, a coop to put them in, protection from predators – everyone likes a chicken dinner – a rooster so the hens can lay their replacements, a hatchet, the tools to clean, pluck, and draw the chicken so it is ready to cook, plus the stove on which you are going to cook it, the pans, and then all the sides: mashed potatoes, Brussels sprouts, butter (from your cow), biscuits (from the grain you grew in your wheat field), a cherry cobbler to enjoy afterwards, and wine to wash it down with.

The point of this thought exercise is to demonstrate that you cannot be self-sufficient. No one can be. But you *can* do many things for yourself to save money, make you more resilient, give you a better quality product than you could buy, give you more options in an uncertain future, and more ways to earn money or learn skills to trade for goods. Most importantly, knowing how to do many tasks makes you more confident that you *can* do something, and when you pay to have someone do it for you, you know what you are paying for (and what you are giving up).

THE SKILL OF RESKILLING

This accumulation of practical abilities is called *reskilling*. We're relearning some of the skills that our grandparents or great-grandparents did as a matter of everyday living. If our great-grandparents wanted a chicken dinner, they had the chicken coop and knew what to do with the chickens or they had the skills to trade for the chicken dinner.

The *Little House* books by Laura Ingalls Wilder are a fascinating set of books and worth careful study. Anyone interested even the tiniest bit in self-sufficiency should read them. The breadth of knowledge of Pa and Ma Ingalls, Laura and her sisters, is wide-ranging and necessary for their survival. It's also amazing how hard they work every single day without ever noticing how much they do. But they were used to it. This is the way life was. You could drop this family down virtually anywhere in the American Midwest – which Pa Ingalls nearly did because of his wanderlust – and they would eat, acquire clothing, and build a roof over their heads. They traded knowledge, skills, and time for their livelihood.

However, when you read the *Little House* books, you also notice that the Ingalls didn't do everything themselves. They were part of a web of relatives, neighbors, businesspeople, and friends. When they moved, they made a place for themselves in their community, trading for what they needed.

RESKILLING IN PRACTICE

When you consider self-sufficiency, you have to decide what and how much you want to do. I make some of our clothes, particularly pajamas, to get exactly what I want. I don't make every stitch we wear; it is *far* cheaper and *much* faster to buy it at the Jubilee Thrift Shop in Palmyra. Even if I worked at my sewing machine full time, and had my fabric and patterns given to me, I couldn't sew the wardrobe my family owns. It would take too long.

A basic set of pajamas takes me between five and six hours to cut out the pattern and sew the pieces together. Is this worth my time? Yes, it is. I get far better quality jammies for my money. I buy the fabric (on sale), use my 99-cent patterns over and over, and my time is free but we'll say I get paid $5 an hour. Twenty dollars worth of fabric plus six hours of my time at $5 an hour ($30) equals $50 for custom, flannel jammies. Not bad.

The real reason for sewing, besides that I like it, is that I can mend our clothes so we get maximum wear out of every item. Mending is very cost-effective and a skill everyone should have.

You can be more self-sufficient in many areas. We do all our yard work, except removing large trees and installing the chain-link fence, which were contracted out. Planting the hedge? We did that. Building the sidewalks and raised beds? That was us, and it took years, a little at a time.

We do much of our home improvements and repairs. Big jobs like reroofing the house and replacing windows are contracted out. Small jobs like painting the cabinets are done in-house. Working on our house makes us very familiar with its needs and idiosyncrasies. It also means that when I talk to Jake the Contractor about a job, I know what I am talking about. I firmly believe that a contractor notices when he has an ignorant fool for a client.

We used to change our vehicle's oil, but as our free time shrank and the cars grew more complex, we let the dealership handle it. Your auto mechanic can get a fair idea of how much or how little you know about your car when you describe a problem to him. Does it ensure better service from professionals if they think you know something about the job? Maybe, maybe not. But you won't feel as stupid when you describe the problem if you know the lingo. You also have a better appreciation of the time and skill the job will take. Professionals notice when you know this, too.

MANAGING YOUR TIME AND ENERGY

Self-sufficiency is always a problem of managing resources: your time, life-energy, skill-set, and money. Time is at the top of the list. Many of the most self-sufficient tasks such as knitting socks or braiding rag-rugs consume lots of time. The skills aren't that hard to learn, but it takes time to learn them, get better at them, and execute the project.

If you are working forty hours a week, plus commuting time, then you have less time to change the oil in your car or paint your house. That means you have to prioritize your free time to use it more efficiently. This is where self-sufficiency and goal-setting intersect. If your goal is to get out of debt, then which is the better hobby to have: shopping or knitting socks? Watching TV or food gardening? The answer is always the one that gets you closer to your end goal.

Hobbies are a terrific way to improve your self-sufficiency skills. Look over the *Little House* books and be impressed by what the Ingalls family had to do every day to survive. Today, cooking, sewing and gardening are hobbies. Then, they were vital skills that kept you alive. If they become vital skills in the future, wouldn't you like to be good at them before you need them?

If you don't know where to start, look at your life and decide what you are tired of paying for. Are takeout meals getting expensive? Do you want to eat better and save money? Learn basic cooking.

Tired of throwing out clothes with plenty of wear left because a seam split? Learn basic mending skills and rescue that shirt for the cost of half an hour of your time, a needle, thimble, and thread. This will save you money *and* time, as you'd have to replace the garment – spending money that takes hours to earn – and use more of your valuable time to shop for a replacement garment. Second-hand shopping is cheaper, but the cost in time is as high as going to the mall.

You don't even need a sewing machine for mending. A lot of repair work is in tight areas, and it cannot be done on a machine. A needle, thread in white, gray, and black, a thimble and a pair of scissors are all that's required.

Tired of wondering how careful the garage was when they changed the oil in your car? Many older cars were made to be worked on in your driveway. We routinely changed the oil, checked the fluids, put air in the tires, and changed air filters. These are all basic tasks. It took time, but it wasn't hard and the Chilton manual explained every step with plenty of pictures.

If you have an older car or a simpler one, you can learn how to do a lot of routine maintenance. You can even do a better job than the garage when changing your oil. Why? It takes *time* to fully drain the old oil. You have the time to leave your car on its ramps in your driveway for hours to drain every last bit of gunk out of the crankcase. The garage cannot afford to waste the service bay when there are ten more cars waiting to be serviced. You will also be careful when you tighten and loosen the oil filter. Will they be as careful?

Tired of wondering what was sprayed on that amazingly expensive mesclun at the grocery store? Mesclun is French for roadside weeds sold to dumb city slickers by savvy farmers. There is darn little produce easier to grow than leaf lettuces. If you let some of them go to seed every year, they self-sow so you don't even have to plant them anymore. We've pulled lettuces that self-sowed out of sidewalk cracks and eaten them. They tasted fine and were far, far fresher than any at the grocery store.

Food gardening is one of the most useful hobbies you can have. It encourages you to do your own cooking, and if you grow what your family will eat, it can save you money as well. Start with the easy stuff that you cannot get fresh at the grocery store, such as tomatoes and lettuces. You won't ever taste anything better. As your skills improve, add other vegetables.

You won't be growing the majority of your family's food. Few people do. Nevertheless, you can grow plenty of stuff that will supplement what you buy, turning those dull grains and beans into tastier, vitamin-rich meals.

Tired of those sagging cabinet doors? Learn how to tighten the screws yourself or replace the hinges. Cabinet doors don't stay shut? Hardware stores sell magnetic catches for just this purpose. You'll need a pencil, a screwdriver, a hammer and nail to start the hole, and time. Learn how to install the first cabinet latch and the rest will be easier and you will start building up your tool chest.

Faucets leaking? It isn't that hard to replace the cartridge in a standard faucet. The library will tell you how, and the hardware store will sell you the parts.

Heating bills getting high? Weather-stripping a door is easy to do. It is so easy, cheap, and effective to weather-strip a door that you should do it on rental property. (Check with the landlord first.) I've had apartments where you could slide a quarter through the gap around the exterior doors. The cold winter poured in 24/7 until I installed the weather-stripping.

Insulation and weather-stripping are like changing the oil in your car. They aren't *hard* to do, but they demand time and attention to detail to get them right. You'll put more time into making sure your insulation is tight than a contractor on a schedule will.

"BUT I DON'T KNOW HOW TO DO ANYTHING"

What we have learned over and over is that the more skills you learn for basic, everyday living, the more self-confident you become about tackling a bigger job.

We did not start out in life with these skills. We learned how to do them job by job, day by day, and year by year. We learned what we like to do: painting, gardening, sewing, and basic home repairs. We learned what we couldn't do: reroofing the house and installing solar tubes. We stopped doing some chores like oil changes when the car got to be too smart for us. We've learned what jobs are worth doing ourselves and that frees up cash for the jobs we cannot do.

The time spent reskilling means that if you *have* to do something, you have a fighting chance of being successful. When you have no money, you spend your time.

Reskilling makes us flexible. It gives us choices. Should we spend our time or our money? It makes us better consumers as we can look at a ready-built cabinet and decide if it is worth the money.

It means we are less likely to be flummoxed by an emergency like the pipes bursting. We know where the shut-off valves are for every sink, toilet, bathtub, and washer in the house as well as where the main valve to the house is located. While I'm calling the plumber, Dear Husband can shut the water off to the house, preventing further damage.

Reskilling and being more self-sufficient pays off over and over for us, and it can pay off for you and your family. Ask yourself every day: Do you want to spend your limited free time doing something that helps you meet your goals or not? Having practical skills at your fingertips makes the choice easier.

22

Your Home and Public Libraries

Where to Find Books – Building Shelves — Public Libraries — A Tale of Two Libraries — More Than Books — Build Your Library (At Taxpayer Expense)

WHY DO YOU NEED A HOME LIBRARY? Because books remember for you. Because you cannot possibly learn everything there is to know, that there was to know, and all that there will be to know.

Books let you learn what other people, societies, and civilizations have learned the hard way. Book learning won't make you into a competent butcher of home-raised chickens, but it will keep you from making as many mistakes when you are standing there, knife in hand, and wondering where to start.

Books have advantages over electronic media. They do not require electricity or batteries. They can be read aloud by one person while everyone else is darning socks by the light of a kerosene lamp. The words do not fall off the page after multiple readings. They can be traded or resold and the words can still be read. Best of all, depending on how you shop for them, no one knows what you have.

Books do not rely on advanced technology that is utterly dependent on the grid and the blood of Chinese miners. You may be able to run your Wi-Fi laptop off your solar batteries, but the internet is dependent on massive server farms, each of which uses enough electricity to light a small town. Your batteries use rare earths mined in China that are becoming more difficult to find and more expensive.

Books can be handwritten on the skins of sheep with homemade ink. You don't need specialized technology to read them. Learn Old English, and you can read medieval manuscripts. Lose the equipment to read old floppy disks, and they become dust catchers.

If you don't want a book, it can be traded for something else. Or you can hang onto it in case it becomes useful later. The book remains perfectly legible while waiting quietly on a shelf. Even those ranks of Readers' Digests condensed books have their uses: insulation, toilet paper, sound deadening, fire-starters, radiation barriers, and art projects.

So what books do you want? For fiction, pick titles that you would want to read over and over. Only you can decide on the re-readableness of James Patterson, or if you're interested in trying *Moby Dick* even once. Disaster and apocalypse novels can be interesting because of the what-if scenarios they pose. Alien attacks, comet strikes, economic collapse, electromagnetic pulses, pandemics, volcano eruptions, or zombie uprisings: whatever crises the author postulates, the characters should have stored more food and organized a neighborhood watch program before page 1. How many stupid, eye-rolling things do the characters do? These books can guide your contingency planning.

For non-fiction, I like how-to books. I cook a lot so I have a wide variety of cookbooks, particularly older ones. They have recipes that don't use fancy ingredients. I also like books about food-preservation techniques.

I sew so I have sewing books, both on general topics and on very specific skills like edge finishing. I don't know how to knit, but I have basic instruction books and someday, I might have the time to learn.

Gardening books on vegetables, fruits, seed saving, soil building, and permaculture are more important to me than titles on ornamental flowers. I also prefer books about food gardening in containers as opposed to ornamental houseplants.

There are plenty of works on home repair, disaster preparedness, thrift and money management, first aid, and keeping chickens; anything you think you might want to do or should learn.

If you think you eventually want to learn a new skill, buy the books (and read them) to decide if you really do want to keep pigs or build a solar-fueled hot water heater. We buy books for potential future uses, as we don't know if that title or subject will come up at the library sale when we need it.

Dear Husband is a writer and a book annotator so we have a huge selection of histories, references, and biographies about Hollywood, the Civil War, literature, and world and American history from 1875 to 1930. We found that it is easier to search our home library first for a reference work, then move on to the public library, and then Google and other sources online.

The internet is very useful for looking up information but what happens when the free sites vanish or begin charging for use? Will a site still be there when you need it again? That book on your shelf won't go away. You can also make notes in your copy to make it easier to find a topic again, scribble thoughts in the margin, and highlight important passages.

WHERE TO FIND BOOKS

We buy books from everywhere. We have bought a few new titles from Amazon. There are no independent bookstores that sell new books in our area, but we visit the area's used bookstores. Cupboard Maker Books in Enola, Pa., has a huge selection of fiction and non-fiction and cats galore. The Midtown Scholar in Harrisburg, Pa., is almost exclusively non-fiction. They have a nice little café and display local art as well. They even carry signed copies of our books!

Further afield for us is the Avon Grove Lion's Club book barn near Avondale, Pa. They have 50,000 books and often run sales of $5 for a bag of books. They have a wide range of books organized by subject. Perhaps a charity group runs a similar store near you.

We go to library sales. You never know what you will find there.

Do not skip checking out thrift shops and yard sales. The price is right and you won't know what will be lurking on the shelf. One of our odder finds was a compilation of *Madame and Eve* comic strips. This is a popular newspaper comic strip in South Africa, and we would not have known it existed if I hadn't found the book at Goodwill for $2. It is a fascinating view of South African life and culture, told with humor and character.

I have even picked books up out of trash bins and from along the curb. If we cannot use it, it gets passed along, one way or another.

If we run across a title through our reading that would be a good addition to our home library, but we don't get lucky locally, we turn to AbeBooks.com. This site lets you buy from used book dealers in the U.S. and Britain. They're especially good for locating offbeat or unusual titles. EBay and Amazon are also good sources for used books.

BUILDING SHELVES

As your library grows, you will need to consider where to put them all. Books require shelves. These are not hard to build, and any how-to carpentry book has instructions. You store books like you store your food: cool, dry, and climate-controlled. Damp, moldy basements will turn your boxes of books into silverfish motels.

Every room in our house, other than bathrooms, has bookshelves. We try to build them from floor to ceiling to use the space efficiently. A wall of books also gives you a layer of insulation and sound deadening. Dedicated paperback shelves fit nicely along narrower hallways. Shelves can also be built in the unusable space behind doors, particularly closet doors. My cookbooks fit on a very high shelf that runs over the kitchen bulletin boards. That was ten feet of new space.

Keep your books shelved, in order – by topic for non-fiction and by author for the fiction – and you will always be able to find the one you are looking for. A book that cannot be found is a book you do not own, and it is especially annoying to find the missing title after you buy another copy. At least we can trade the duplicate to Cupboard Maker Books for credit.

We have so much non-fiction that we break books down into large categories: religion and philosophy, sewing and crafts, cooking, home maintenance, preparedness, thrift, biographies, Hollywood and the media, and history. History is organized into a chronological line, from prehistory and ancient history to today.

Build your home library on every topic now, when books are easy to find, and cheap. As your library grows, you may need to refine it by passing no-longer needed titles to friends, a used book dealer, or the library sale. This generates both good will and books that are more useful to you.

PUBLIC LIBRARIES

One major goal at Fortress Peschel is to never spend money if we do not have to. We never had much spare hard coin floating around – it was earmarked for something the minute it showed up – and now that we are living off our savings as we make a go of Peschel Press, we have even less.

Public libraries are one of the best resources available to everyone. They offer services for free or at a very low cost. You can get reading and research materials, DVD movies, even video games and eBooks. Best of all, if they don't have something, such as a book or movie, the nice librarians will get it for you at no charge, at least in our state.

This is called the interlibrary loan program. Virtually every library has one. Dear Husband could not have researched and written the annotated versions of *Whose Body?*, *The Mysterious Affair at Styles*, *The Secret Adversary*, three volumes on the life and times of William Palmer, Victorian poisoner, and a series of period Sherlock Holmes fan fiction without the interlibrary loan. He does meticulous research, sending Denise, our library goddess, to the far ends of the earth to find the materials he needs.

We could *never* have afforded to buy these books, many quite old and printed in very limited editions. We have even gotten books on microfilm this way. Libraries send them long distances so you, dear reader, do not have to travel the world to read an obscure tome on, say, strychnine doping by Victorian athletes.

If you aren't using this program, visit your library and ask how it works. Getting a book through the interlibrary loan lets you preview it so you can decide if you want to buy it. This has saved us some real bucks, when a book we thought would be useful turned out to be a dud.

A TALE OF TWO LIBRARIES

We have two library systems available to us. We live in Hershey (the sweetest place on Earth) so we have the Hershey Public Library. It is tied to the Middletown Public Library so we can draw on both for resources. Anything I request via Middletown from the online catalog is delivered to Hershey for me to check out.

Hershey is in Dauphin County, so we also have access to the county's library system. It has a much wider array of books at its many branches than Hershey does. I applied for their library card and use my local branch in nearby Hummelstown as my pick-up and drop-off site. I request what I want from their online catalog, and it is delivered there. Like Hershey, the DCLS has an interlibrary loan system.

It is important to know if your library is tied to a larger system. If you look only at the shelves of your local branch, you might not realize how much more is available to you. Ask if there is an online catalog. If so, you can request a book and the system will deliver it. A library that has this system has far more books available than its small home contains.

You might have other resources in your area. In Dover, Del., we had a nice library, but it wasn't until I was in college there that I learned that the state had its own library. Its collection was radically different from the Dover library and, as a state resident, I could use it. If you live near your state capital, look for this option.

Some colleges open their libraries to the public. They may charge a fee to check out books, but even if they don't, you can still go in and do research. If you are taking classes at a college, even a community college, find its library and get a card. Their selections will be very different from the local branch, as they'll tend to have subject matter that is more technical and fewer fad diet books.

MORE THAN BOOKS

What else can you do with your public library besides research obscure topics? If you read popular fiction, you may want to borrow the library's copy instead of buying it. I buy fiction, but it has to be something I want to read more than once. But James Patterson? Danielle Steele? Nora Roberts? They are library fodder. Even if you want the hardcover, you could borrow the book, then buy it cheap at the next library sale. Libraries tend to buy enough books to meet immediate demand, then when that fades, dump all but a few copies. This applies to new paperbacks and trade paperbacks. Both of my library systems buy them, so if something on the grocery store's paperback rack looks interesting, I can often get it from the library.

When *Fifty Shades of Grey* came out, we wanted to see how a piece of recast *Twilight* fan fiction could have sold millions of copies. I am so glad I didn't lay out any cash. It was a terrible book, terribly written, with a limp dishrag for a heroine, and a sadistic freak for a hero. Save your money. If you must read it, get it from the library. In fact, if you have *any* doubts about a new author, try the library first.

Libraries also have a mountain of children's books, cookbooks, craft books, gardening books, sewing books, and do-it-yourself titles, along with the biographies, current events, philosophy titles, economics tomes, and diet books. Wander the stacks in even a small library, and there is treasure to be found.

Both of my libraries have extensive collections of audiobooks, both on tape and on CD. These tend to have the same checkout period as a printed book so you can check out an audiobook and listen to it during your commute and still return it on time. The audiobook collections also include language lessons so you could learn Spanish on your way to work.

I read many magazines, but I only subscribe to *Threads* and *Vogue Patterns*. I get the rest at the library. Most libraries will let you check out the back issues. It might mean that you are always a few weeks behind but this doesn't matter for gardening or home-dec magazines. I don't find that it makes much difference when I read *Time, Newsweek, Vanity Fair, Atlantic,* or *Maclean's* either. You may be amused to see how quickly top stories fade from memory.

My library subscribes to all the major newspapers, and has extensive music collections, ranging from show tunes to classical to whatever is current.

They have tons of DVD titles: movies, TV shows, documentaries, and educational titles. They don't charge for checking out DVDs, although their late fees can be stiff ($1.50 a day). Even with the potential late fees, this is a bargain compared to using Redbox.

Our television isn't hooked up to the outside world, and we cannot afford movie tickets, so the library holdings are a terrific resource for us. Our internet connection is ssssllllooooowwww, so we don't watch TV online. Making the effort to get our TV and movie viewing choices from the library has the added benefit of clarifying how we want to spend our time. We are saved from the habit of flipping on the TV without thinking.

Some libraries now have video game collections. If you are a gamer, or you have one in your household, this is a good way to preview a title before paying upwards of $60 for one.

Both of my library systems have a wide array of electronic resources, including access to online databases and even ebooks. Ask your librarian what they have and how their system works.

My libraries have extensive reference sections. These are the big textbook-type books, some of them in multiple volumes. Books of this type cost hundreds of dollars per set, so if you need to consult one for a research project, the library is the way to go. If your local branch doesn't have the one you need, ask if it can be sent via interlibrary loan.

If you have kids or you homeschool, the library doesn't just have books. Many run programs to encourage reading, along with general information and educational programs. Libraries often act as meeting places for public-interest programs run by local activists. The librarians will know what is coming up on the schedule. If your library has an online presence, these programs should be listed there. You may have to sign up, as seating may be limited, but they are usually free.

If you have only a small library in your area and it is not part of a larger system, it will be worth finding out if a larger system is nearby, one county over. If you work in a different county from where your home is, you may qualify for a library card. A county system can have a quite different selection from the library in the next county over.

BUILD YOUR LIBRARY (AT TAXPAYER EXPENSE)

Libraries are always buying new materials, so they have to make room on the shelves for them. This leads to another wonderful resource: the annual library sale. Hershey runs a huge one every August that lasts several days. We never miss it. They sell deaccessioned and publicly donated books, DVDs, video games, and CDs, as well as rare items that are sold Dutch auction-style. The selection is amazing and the prices cannot be beat.

The Dauphin County system does the same thing, with each branch running its own sale. The dates don't overlap so it is possible to hit a Dauphin County library sale almost every month.

Library sales are one of the best ways to build your home library, particularly in reference and how-to books. They are priced to sell, you never know what you will find, and the money goes to buying new books. While you are online looking for library sales, check out the ones outside your system. We regularly attend the sale in Elizabethtown, even though it is in Lancaster County. We've also gone to the sales in the city of Lancaster and in Cumberland County.

Consider your public library as the backup system to your home library. You pay for it with your tax dollars, so take advantage of it. Add it to your routine of errands, get to know the staff, and open up a world of reading, entertainment, and research.

23

Hanging Laundry

Lines and Pins – How to Hang Clothes – Winter Laundry – Differences in Hanging Laundry – Racking Laundry

WHY DO I HANG LAUNDRY ON A CLOTHESLINE when I could use my dryer? It fits the goals of Fortress Peschel: to cut costs, to be more sustainable, to be greener, and to be more energy-efficient. Clothes smell better when dried on a line. They last longer, too; that dryer lint you collect is abraded fabric. Clothing elastic does not like dryer heat and will last far longer when line-dried.

It sounds strange, but there are right and wrong ways to hang laundry. The object is to get the stuff dry, but you want it also to dry quickly, be mostly wrinkle-free, and easy to take down and put away. Drying quickly matters when the weather is marginal (cold, cloudy, threatening rain), there are multiple loads of clothes and limited line space, or if you are dealing with a large bird population or dirty, dusty air. Wrinkle-free drying eliminates ironing time, or more likely these days, makes it look as though you didn't avoid ironing. Clothes that are easy to take down and put away make it easy for someone other than mom to finish the task.

Briefly, here's how to do it: Most clothes should be hung as though they were being worn: i.e., in the same orientation as it was on the body. Shake out the washer wrinkles so the garment won't dry that way. Don't crowd clothing on the line. Give each piece enough space so the air and sun can get at it. If you can, spread clothing on a single line so that one item doesn't shade another. This won't matter in August with its long sunny days, but a little shade can make a big difference in January.

Other than pants and socks, wash garments inside out. This saves wear and tear on the fashion surface, especially on printed or painted-on designs. Keep garments inside out on the clothesline to reduce sun fading. They *will* fade in time, but why speed up the process? When hanging garments, fold as little fabric over the line as you can. Doubled-up fabric takes longer to dry and adds wrinkles and clothespin marks. Line up the edge of the garment with the clothesline and peg it in place with no folding over at all. On windy days, use more clothespins if it needs the extra securing.

LINES AND PINS

The style of clothesline matters a lot. Don't get a square model with lots and lots of lines close together. They work okay in August, but when the weather is iffy, the clothes shade each other out and hang too close together to dry quickly. It is also very awkward to hang towels, sheets, curtains, and rugs on this kind of setup. Square clotheslines are only suitable for the tiniest of yards.

Instead, get the big T-poles that hold three or four lines. Ask for these at a hardware store, preferably locally owned. A big box store is more likely to sell only the square kind. Pick a sunny, windy spot close to your house and set the poles in concrete thirty feet or forty apart. Do not put your lines under trees as this attracts bird droppings. If you are washing for an army, you may need a second set of T-poles. When you set the poles in their concrete footers, make sure the eyelets are at the right height so that sheets and curtains don't drag on the ground. Higher-up laundry also tends to receive fewer grubby marks from children and dogs.

For the clothesline, spend the money on vinyl-coated steel cable. Lehman's catalog (www.lehmans.com) sells it to the Amish, and it will last for years. Parallel lines of steel cable will support the biggest, heaviest comforters and blankets so they will dry completely. We've used our line for more than fifteen years before it broke, because Dear Husband ran a single strand through all three lines in an S-pattern. This created metal fatigue in the curves where the vinyl broke

As for clothespins, use the spring model. They work much better than those pegs you see used for crafts. Get plenty of them and a big bag that can be hung on the eyelet bolts on a T-pole. The metal frame that holds the cloth bag is more important than the bag. The cloth bag will eventually rip and have to be replaced. If you can sew, you can replace the bag yourself. A heavy metal frame will last forever; I am now using my fifth or sixth replacement bag. Some frames are easier to replace the bags on and some are more challenging. When you buy the clothespin bag, examine the frame carefully to see how hard it will be to replace the bag with your homemade, sturdier fabric replacement.

Clothespins and bags are sold at the hardware store you bought the clothes poles at or in any grocery or discount store. Very windy days will require more clothespins, so buy plenty and then get several more packs to be sure you have enough.

HOW TO HANG CLOTHES

So, let's start hanging those garments! Pants go up by the waist side-seams with a third clothespin in the center back. Open all the buttons and zippers. If the weather is chancy, either cold or threatening to rain, pull the pockets out so they can dry. Otherwise, push them into place, flat and wrinkle-free. Open the pants legs to allow airflow. This is vital with jeans in the winter. They will freeze in this open position and dry faster. Hang shorts the same way.

Skirts are hung by the waist at the side-seams with another clothespin at center back, adjusting the placement to avoid zippers. Open all zippers, buttons, or snaps. If the skirt is a wrap skirt or opens from waist to hem, open it up completely and use as many clothespins as you need to keep it reasonably flat on the line.

Pullover shirts can be hung two ways, depending on the collar. Open any buttons, zippers, or snaps and pull the front of the garment away from the back. Shake out the wrinkles.

Turtlenecks and cowl-necks must be hung upside down by the bottom hem. Hang them by the side-seams *without* stretching the bottom hem and use more clothespins spaced equally to support the weight of the wet garment without it twisting. Open the turtleneck to allow airflow. Tops with any other kind of collar can be hung this way *or* you can hang them up by the shoulder seams. A heavier top may need two clothespins on each side to support the wet weight.

Hang raglan- and dolman-sleeve garments as if the seams were in the usual places or hang upside-down.

I always hang sweaters upside-down. They seem to dry better, especially at the underarms. I use seven to nine clothespins on a sweater hem for better support and less stretching. If you are concerned about stretching a sweater out of shape, drape it over the clothesline at the underarm seams and peg it that way. It will take much longer to dry because of the thick layers of fabric.

Shirts and jackets that button or zip up the front should be completely opened and hung upside-down by the side-seams at the hem. A flat-bottom hem will need a few more pegs to spread out the garment. A curved, shaped hem just gets clothespins at the two side-seams and in the middle. Smooth and flatten pockets or pocket flaps and collars. Crumpled parts on a flannel shirt will dry crumpled and only an iron will fix the wrinkles. Unbutton and spread open the cuffs as well.

Dresses should be hung from the shoulder seams with one or two clothespins per shoulder, depending on the garment's weight. Don't put a clothespin on a shoulder pad; this deforms them. Work around them or take them out and hang them separately. If the dress has ruffles or ties, take a few minutes to smooth the wrinkles flat with your fingers. If the ruffles dry without doing this, the wrinkles will set in place and you will have to iron the dress. Any other details like big collars should be handled the same way. As always, open every button, snap, and zipper; pull the front of the garment away from the back and open up the sleeves.

Underwear should be hung at the waist side-seams without stretching the waistband elastic. This is very difficult to repair or replace so avoid damaging it. Men's briefs hung by a clothespin at the crotch will dry in August but not in January. Bras will last far longer if you wash them in a mesh bag after closing the hooks on the smallest setting and letting them air dry. Nothing kills bra elastic like a hot dryer. Unhook bras and hang them by the closure end. Open up each sock and hang them by the toe. Hang bathing suits by their shoulder straps (tops) or the waist side-seams (bottoms).

I wash second-hand shoes, especially sneakers and trash-picked footwear, and dry them on the clothesline. Open up the shoe, remove any laces, knock off the loose dirt and pick the Velcro closures clean with a corsage pin before throwing them into a cold-water wash. Wash the laces separately in a mesh bag with a warm or hot water load. Hang the shoes by the back and spread out the sides and tongue so they can dry better. If the laces come out clean, match them with their shoes. Depending on their condition, it may be better to replace them, particularly if the shoes come out really clean.

To take up less space, hang towels vertically, if they can dry out of reach of dogs and toddlers. Depending on the size and wet weight, you will need three or more pegs per item. Snap your towels hard, four or five times, before hanging them on the line and again, four or five times, when you take them down. They won't be as stiff when you use them.

Sheets should be hung in a single layer, not folded over. Even when the weather is too iffy to dry anything else, sheets can dry satisfactorily outside. Drape larger sheets over two parallel lines and use plenty of clothespins to secure them. The wind will treat them like sails and your kids will think you made them tents. Pillowcases can be hung at the closed, narrow end. Shake them open before you hang them so air can get inside.

Spread blankets, comforters, quilts, and rugs over two or even three parallel clotheslines to support their weight and get that air moving underneath. If you have to drape a blanket over a single line, the underside is not as likely to dry out. In the winter, flip them over after a few hours to dry the other side. Shake out or spread every wrinkle and crumple or the sheets, particularly flannel ones, will set up that way. If the weather is cold enough, they will freeze and won't dry out in the center of the wrinkle.

As for drapes and curtains, they may not need to be washed. They get dusty, but unless you have a household of smokers or people who throw juice on the drapes, they don't get dirty. Hang them on the line on a very windy, sunny day, and the wind will blow all the dust off them. Do this once a year and you may be able to avoid washing them or paying the drycleaner for processing the pinch-pleated, unwashable ones.

Hang curtains as though they were still hanging on the rod; top up and bottom down. Spread them out smooth to keep wrinkles away. Heavy drapes may have to be draped over parallel clotheslines. Valances will occupy a *lot* of space so you may have to hang them long-ways over the line. They get fewer wrinkles if they are hung in the same orientation as you put them in the window.

Kitchen towels, dishcloths, bar mops, and napkins should be hung smooth and straight. Hang tablecloths like sheets. Hang kitchen and bathroom rugs on a single line. They will need many clothespins; as many as one every six or eight inches for a wet, heavy rug. If the wind is very strong, drape the rug over two lines. Don't drape a rug over a single line or you may have to flip it over to dry the under side.

To make it easier for someone else to take the laundry down and put it away, sort the laundry when you hang it up. Yes, I do that. I'd rather spend another twenty minutes outside in the sun and fresh air first thing in the morning than try and match the socks at the end of the day when I am tired.

When you hang the wash, group all of one person's clothes: socks paired and hung up, underwear next, T-shirts, etc. If you have the line space, use one line per person. I go so far as to match up my kid's outfits with a shirt and pants, shirt and pants, shirt and skirt, etc., side by side on the clothesline. When someone else takes in the wash, it is already sorted. This is a big timesaver at the end of the day.

I hang my laundry outdoors year-round, in summer heat and winter cold. Technique really matters in the winter, when the days are shorter and there's less time to dry, which is why it gets its own section. But as long as the weather is windy and dry, daytime temperature doesn't matter. The sun doesn't have to be fully out, either. The laundry freezes dry in the wind. It is stiff and cold when brought inside, but it is rarely damp. Remind your laundry helpers: Cold is not the same as wet.

Here's another tip: Sort your wash in the house. Unbutton those buttons and open zippers so you can minimize handling cold, wet clothes outside. It is easier to manage the clothespins wearing thin gloves than heavier ones.

Because I do not want to use the expensive dryer, I bought a pair of extra-large wooden drying racks. Since I bought my racks, I have trash-picked several more, but my Amish-made racks are still the best. I hang laundry anytime it is not raining, snowing, foggy, or misting. Laundry that isn't dry gets spread out on racks in the living room to finish overnight. Even a few hours outside cuts the indoor drying time drastically. If I have to go directly to the racks from the washer, the laundry can take all day and overnight to dry. It is definitely worth it to me to hang stuff outside for three hours to save six or nine hours indoors.

The only exception is with sheets and big towels. Because of their size, they don't rack well, so I save washing them for better weather.

I also use my clothesline to prewash scavenged items. When I pick up blankets, rugs, or clothing along the side of the road, I hang them up on the line and let the wind and rain do a prewash. Very dirty blankets may need several hard rains to get enough mud off to safely wash them. Setting up more clothesline space than you think you need for your day-to-day needs frees up space for these kinds of finds.

It doesn't take very long to hang laundry on a clothesline, and it can save you quite a bit of money over the years. Dryers use a lot of electricity, and it's challenging to run one off your solar panels.

After paying for T-poles, lines, and clothespins, solar drying is free. Extra-large drying racks can be expensive — my pair cost $115 — but they pay for themselves in a few years. If you get lucky and find racks in the trash or as pass-alongs, they cost nothing.

A dryer costs hundreds of dollars upfront and then you pay more every time you use it. Dryers are hard on clothes; they wear out the elastic and rub off the fibers into dryer lint. Items like bras and bathing suits should never be put into a dryer. A good quality, well-maintained dryer will last for years. Steel powder-coated clothes poles set in concrete with vinyl-coated steel cable clotheslines will last forever.

The hardest part of using a clothesline is getting started early enough in the day so that you can get the wash on the line and catch all that free sun. I have put laundry on the line as late as 4 p.m. in July and had it dry. In winter, it has to be up by 10 a.m. It simply takes longer to dry with less sun and lower temperatures. I haven't done this, but I have read of people leaving the wash out for several days until it freezes dry. I like racks better.

Dryers are a convenience but do you want to pay for them? My dollars have better places to go than the electric company. I use my dryer perhaps a dozen times a year during those weeklong rains. With some planning and a clothesline, you can hang out most of your laundry, too, and put your dryer dollars to better use.

THE COST OF DRYING CLOTHES

Assume that each load of clothes dried in a dryer costs between 50¢ and $1. This varies depending on your rates, the wattage of your dryer, the amount and wetness of the load, and how long it takes to run a load. Seven loads of laundry a week equals $182 a year or about $15 dollars a month. If you wash more laundry or your electrical rates are higher, you will pay more.

WINTER LAUNDRY

When Dear Husband and I got married, I moved from my apartment into his house and for the first time in years, had a clothesline again. I started using the clothesline every sunny day. We lived in South Carolina, so there were many warm, sunny days, even in January. I did not have to use the dryer very much.

Then we moved up to central Pennsylvania. It is far colder in the winter and not quite as hot in the summer. It takes longer to warm up in the spring and cools off quicker in the fall. Winter days tend to be shorter with less daylight and sun. The clothesline season is not nearly as long as it was in South Carolina. I used my dryer frequently: When it was raining, when it was cold, when it was convenient, when I hadn't planned ahead, when I had a load of towels, and I wanted them snuggly soft. My electric bill went up. Then the rates went up some more.

I wondered how much I was spending drying our clothes. I turned to Amy Dacyczyn's *Tightwad Gazette* and calculated how much I was spending every time I used the dryer. To do this, you need to know how long your dryer runs, what its wattage is, and how much you pay for each watt used.

Electric utilities bill by the kilowatt-hour (KWH). A KWH is 1,000 watts used in one hour. Your dryer and other electrical appliances should have the wattage marked on them or listed in the instruction manual. Multiply the wattage by the number of hours you use it per load and divide by 1,000. This is your dryer's KWH usage. Multiply this by the cost per KWH found on your bill. This is how much it costs to run the dryer per load. Don't forget to add in the cost of any magic dryer products you use.

For us, it worked out to about 50¢ per load. Drying thirty loads per month costs us $15 a month in electricity plus a box of dryer sheets now and then. We won't count the wear and tear the dryer inflicts on clothing.

Since we are very, very serious about our goal of Financial Independence, this was an easy choice. I planned ahead and all the laundry went onto the line, weather permitting, in spring, summer, and fall. On rainy days and cold, gloomy winter days, I used the dryer.

This cut our electric bill noticeably, but not enough. I wash more laundry in the winter because we wear more and heavier clothing. What in the summer might be one load of shorts and T-shirts becomes two loads of long pants, turtlenecks, and sweaters. My costs are higher.

I became more aggressive about hanging out the laundry on iffier days. Gradually, I began using the clothesline any day that wasn't actually raining or snowing, or a heavy, humid mist or fog. Outdoor temperatures became immaterial, so now you see me in a parka putting wash on the line in 15-degree weather.

DIFFERENCES IN HANGING LAUNDRY

Hanging laundry in the winter is quite different from the summer. In July, it doesn't matter what time you hang it out as long as you get two or three hours of sunlight. In the winter, every hour of sunlight is precious.

You have to get outside with the laundry basket before 10 a.m. If you must do a second load, get started earlier and wash the heavier, longer-drying items first. Clothing like polar fleece and acrylic sweaters dry fast. Jeans, heavy wool and cotton sweaters, and bulky layered fabrics take a lot longer. That load has to be washed first so it can go on the line first. Then it has additional drying time while load two is being washed. This extra hour can make the difference between clothing being dry enough to put away and still-damp garments that have to finish overnight on the racks.

The rules for hanging clothes discussed above become even more important with winter laundry. Garments should be spaced so that there is airflow around every piece. Clothing or towels that are overlapped because you don't have enough clothesline space will not dry.

Sort your laundry inside the house! A pile of wet, tangled garments will freeze into a solid mass outdoors that is difficult and unpleasant to work with.

I keep a special pair of gloves by the door for laundry use. Heavy gloves get in the way of my hands, and I end up taking them off. Holding wet, frozen laundry in 20-degree weather is a good way to court frostbite, so find a pair you can live with. My gloves are a cheap pair of Joe Boxer two-layer knit gloves from Kmart. The pair consists of a full, inner glove of some cheap polyester knit and an over, fingerless glove of the same cheap knit. Worn separately, the gloves are poor at keeping the cold out. Together, they keep my hands from freezing while allowing me fine muscular control of my fingers so I can manage the clothespins. The other reason I like these gloves is that the fingerless portion (the over-layer) can be separated and worn while typing in our cold house.

After putting on my parka, hat, and special laundry gloves, I head outside. A full-sun day with a breeze will dry almost all laundry no matter how cold it is. Overcast and windy will work well too. No sun and no wind mean that the thin stuff like sheets will dry completely. Everything else has to finish on the indoor drying racks.

Fortuitously, my clothesline is at right angles to the prevailing north wind. We lucked out here; we put the clothes poles alongside the existing sidewalk. This means I, sometimes, get sun on the front of the garments and wind on the back. If the day is windy with no sun, I will hang the laundry from the back side of the clothesline so that the wind blows through the garments. This is especially helpful with heavy pants, to have the wind blow down through the legs. Any openings on garments like sleeves, necklines, legs, and pocket flaps should be hung into the wind. The wind will blow into them, separating front from back, and it will dry far faster.

As you hang everything up, shake out wrinkles and crumples and open up legs, sleeves, pockets, and the legs of socks. Two layers of fabric frozen together will take far longer to dry. Having that airspace speeds up the process.

Tops that are hung in summer by the shoulder seams are hung in winter by the bottom hem as the sleeves dry better, especially the armpit area. When a pullover is hung by the shoulder seams, the sleeves hang alongside the body and the underarm area won't dry. Sweatshirts and pullovers get four evenly spaced clothespins on the hem. I don't want to stretch out the hemline. Sweaters get seven or nine clothespins on the bottom hem to keep them smooth, well supported, and unrippled.

RACKING LAUNDRY

Putting the wash outside in the dead of winter cut my dryer bill substantially, but I wanted to do more. That's when I found, at Wilhelm's Hardware in Hershey, an array of Amish-made heavy-duty, solid-wood drying racks in various sizes. The biggest ones had nearly fifty feet of drying space.

The two racks I bought have been used for more than a decade and have held up beautifully. They see some use in the summer when it rains, but they really shine in the winter. A few years of use paid back their initial cost, and now they cost me nothing but time. Since purchasing my two lovely racks, I have trash-picked more and been given a few racks as well. None of them hold as much as my big racks, but they are used for overflow or smaller loads.

When shopping for racks, look for solid-wood construction. Anything else won't hold up. How the rungs are arranged can affect how much you can put on the rack. Tippyness is a big defect. My best trash-picked rack is solid wood and has closely spaced rungs to hang tiny things in a small space. It was clearly designed to hold underwear and socks, but I can also lay a sweater flat on one set of rungs.

Get the biggest racks you have space for. Underwear, socks, heavy sweaters, and pants take an amazing amount of rack space. Take into account that a big clothesline may have 150 feet of linear drying space. You will need several big racks to equal that. You also have to have storage space for the folded racks that is easily accessible but not in the way. You need some space to set up your racks.

To find racks, start with old-time, local hardware stores. They are more likely to have the well-made models than Walmart or Lowes, and they can use your business. Antique stores may have old wooden racks, too. Ask around; many people have a rack or two tucked away that they inherited when Grandma got her dryer. Solid-wood racks can be repaired with new dowels and rubbed down with butcher-block oil to restore them. If you have to rub butcher-block oil on a rack, let it stand for several weeks before using it so nothing gets on your clothes.

Lehman's (www.lehmans.com) and the Vermont Country Store (www.vermontcountrystore.com) sell wooden racks, but they are expensive and the shipping for a big one gets costly. A local hardware store may end up costing less when shipping is factored in.

Laundry that goes straight to the racks from the washer is handled differently from laundry that goes on the clothesline. Clotheslines have far more room and it is all in a straight line. Racks hold many garments in a very small space with rungs close together. The bottom-most rungs are only inches off the floor.

If I have two loads, I wash the smaller, lighter stuff first and fill the rack from the bottom up and the inside out. The second, heavier load gets hung on the top and outside rungs. Underwear, socks, and napkins go closest to the floor, and I will arrange and rearrange until everything is on the rack without overlap or crowding. Practice has made me a lot faster in loading a drying rack.

I wash most of my laundry inside out to keep the fabric from fading. The garments go on the rack inside out and then, at the end of the day, I turn the clothes right side out to finish drying overnight. Racks take more time to dry heavy clothes; far more than an outdoor clothesline would. Don't put away even slightly damp garments as they will develop a mildewy, musty odor.

I look at winter laundry as an exercise in mindfulness and goal setting. How serious am I at achieving Financial Independence? Do I really want to be able to never set foot off my property unless I want to? Am I willing to live my beliefs of caring for my environment and not sending dollars to organizations I disapprove of? Winter laundry is a way of saying my goals matter to me.

24

Mongo and Obtainium

Stalking Wild Trash — Leave It Better Than You Found It — Obtaining Obtainium

A MAJOR WAY TO CUT COSTS IS THROUGH the recognition and creative use of mongo and obtainium.

You get mongo and obtainium via trash picking, Freecycling, Dumpster diving, asking around, and recognizing the opportunities in front of you before you send them off to the trash hauler. No money changes hands.

Mongo is found stuff that is ready to use as-is. My large, framed Ansel Adams poster of a snowy tree? The neighbors two streets over were throwing it out, along with two seascapes and mirrored candle sconces. The rattan end table on our Florida room? Same source, different neighbors. The IKEA chair and footstool in our office? Ditto.

Candles, sheets, picture frames, fabric, canned food, mirrors of every kind, clothing, lamps, furniture, and fancy shower curtain rods: All were found on the streets. I won't say that you will find everything you need, and certainly never when you need it, but there sure is a lot of stuff out there going begging.

Obtainium is raw material that you repurpose. Pieces from a giant trampoline became an archway on which to train jasmine. The metal U's that held campaign signs in the last election — collected a week *after* the voting was over — support salvaged ceramic tiles to edge the garden beds. Mops and brooms become garden fence posts. Fancy drapery rods become fancy garden junk. Storm windows become window well covers. The broken-up front sidewalk is our back patio. Its fire-pit was built from two circular pieces of concrete drainage pipes left over from a flood-control project. The contractor was delighted to see us take them. I saved him the disposal fee.

STALKING WILD TRASH

How do you get this wonderful stuff? By knowing the hauling schedule of your trash collectors and keeping your eyes open. My neighborhood gets its trash and recycling collected every Monday, so I walk Muffy every Sunday evening and sometimes, Monday mornings. Dogs make excellent camouflage for this sort of prospecting.

If I want metal, like old trampoline frames, I *have* to get it Sunday evening, or as soon as it gets put out. Scrappers make a living by salvaging tossed-out metal and they hit the road by 5 a.m. and get every ironing board, storm door, fan, fluorescent ceiling light fixture, and washing machine long, long before the recycling truck comes by. Scrappers don't want clothes, pictures, mirrors, or most furniture so those items will be waiting by the curb Monday morning.

When you commute to work or run errands, look over those trash piles. If you see something good, grab it. It won't be there — like those oak filing cabinets that we still regret missing years later - when you come back.

The only exception I have found is big bags of leaves and yard waste. These *may* still be there if the recycling truck didn't get them first. However, you cannot count on this, so take that free soil builder and mulch when you see it.

Be cautious of mattresses and box springs as they may have bedbugs already installed. Big sofa cushions make excellent dog beds, and I have not had a problem with them.

LEAVE IT BETTER THAN YOU FOUND IT

There are important etiquette rules with trash picking:

* **Make sure it is being thrown out.** If it isn't trash day, then why is that dresser sitting alongside the road? It may be waiting for a Freecycle pick-up. When in doubt, leave it. If you really want that mahogany sideboard, knock on the door and ask.

* **A pile of stuff with a free sign** is an open invitation.

* **Clean up as you go.** When they move, many people leave their discards. As you remove what you want, neaten the pile. Don't leave a mess. Someone will have to clean it up, and they will not be encouraged to leave stuff out for prospectors if the result is a bigger mess.

* **Return the favor.** Put out scrap metal early with a FREE sign

on it for the scrappers. Anything I cannot use gets passed along to friends, neighbors, family, or the thrift shop.

The difficulty with trash picking is its randomness. You have to decide, on the spot, if you want that beautiful metal barstool. Can anyone you know use this barstool? Do you want to store this barstool until you decide? Do you have the space? What is your spouse going to say about yet another great find? Are you becoming a candidate for *Hoarders*? So the barstool stays, and you find out the next morning that Oldest Child's friend needed a barstool. You go back to look, and a scrapper got there first.

I pick up a lot of stuff on spec. When no use appears for the item, it moves on to the thrift shop. This makes up for the items I pass over and then later regret. It evens out.

OBTAINING OBTAINIUM

Obtainium is much harder to judge than mongo. Mongo in good condition is easy to pass along or even sell if you don't want it.

A pile of mixed bits of wood may be reusable for a project, but it has to be stored until you rebuild the toolshed. Nails may have to be removed, adding to the workload. It may not even be burnable if the wood has been pressure-treated with arsenic. Piles of construction leftovers should be handled carefully. They can be booby-trapped with nails and screws or the pile will slide on you as you yank out the concrete blocks. I keep heavy gloves in my car for just such opportunities.

Obtainium is easier to cope with if you have a barn in which to store your finds. Rain, snow, heat, and cold will not improve raw materials so if the toolshed is full, you may have to pass up that pile of shingles. Someone will excel with those folding doors I left behind.

So if you need something, and want it for no- to very low-cost, look around. Put the word out to everyone you know that you want boxes of unused ceramic tiles (garden edging), dead electric blankets (quilt batting), dead houseplants (soil building) and old TV sets (Younger Son's experiments).

Look through sites like Freecycle and Craigslist. Learn the trash routes around you and when the regular bulk pickup day is. Every item you save from the landfill, that *you* can use, will save you money and teach you new skills as you transform it into what you need. Mongo and obtainium can open your eyes to the possibilities around you.

25

Soil Building

Turning Dirt Into Soil – Feed First, Then Plant – Living Off Compost – Leaves and Grass – How to Start Building Your Soil – Growing Cover Crops – Put Your Soil to the Test – Soil Types

SOMETIMES, WE DO THINGS OUT OF ORDER. Gardening books tell you that soil building is important. However, they don't go into detail about how and why, and the overriding importance of starting soil improvements the day you move in.

Before you open your catalogs, draw the first garden layout on graph paper, figure out your solar orientation, the high and dry and low and soggy spots, the microclimates and the prevailing winds, you should be working on your soil.

We did not do this, and therein lies a story.

Fortress Peschel is my third house and Dear Husband's second in which we had yardage for an actual garden instead of a few houseplants.

My first home was in Virginia. I was stationed at the naval base in Norfolk and bought a house whose lawn was in poor shape. In my second home in South Carolina (with DH), the soil was heavy clay and also poor. In fact, I should not call what we had soil at all. What we had was dirt. Worn out, tired, beaten down, exhausted, and barely alive dirt.

Growing up, I had watched my mother garden in Delaware with almost barren sandy dirt, so I thought this was acceptable. I was wrong.

While dirt is normal, it is not what you want. What you want is *soil*. Soil starts with clay, sand, or silt, and you add life to that base with rotting organic matter that feeds a zoo of insects, fungus, microbes, worms, arthropods, and other multi-legged critters. Much of what makes soil alive can only be seen with a magnifying glass or a microscope. Your zoo of critters turns this rotting organic material into *humus*. Humus makes nutrients available to your plants and retains water without becoming soggy.

In other words, soil is *alive* and the healthier it is, the healthier your plants will be.

TURNING DIRT INTO SOIL

Without realizing it, I started learning how to make soil in South Carolina. It began with a desire to minimize mowing the half-acre lot that was a mix of lawn, trees, and shrubs. We raked the leaves into big mulch circles around the trees where it was too heavily shaded to grow grass.

A few years later, while raking around the trees, I noticed a thin layer of rich, humusy soil forming over the red clay. As the leaves decayed, built up, and decayed again, the dirt was coming alive. We accelerated the process by getting a few tractor-trailer loads of leaves from the town and raking them around the trees. We were letting these areas go a little wild, and free leaves made great mulch. By the time we moved to Pennsylvania, this soil was different compared to the hard red clay under the struggling grass.

I began to recognize what nature was showing me.

When we moved to Fortress Peschel, the property was a barren rectangle. In the tiny front yard were a green spruce and a Japanese maple. The neighbor's privet hedges lined two sides of the property, and a scraggly forsythia hedge formed the third side of the backyard. Otherwise, the dirt was dead. There were no worms in the soil. We didn't even have *slugs*. I would have said the dirt had been ChemLawned to death except the grass was in too poor a condition. The dirt was mostly clay and had been packed into concrete.

However, we had a plan. We wanted to grow a few herbs and vegetables, a hedge to shield us from the neighbors and the highway, and a mini-refuge for birds, squirrels, and other furry little animals.

The first year was spent settling in and getting the most necessary repairs done. Then it dawned on me to find out if the township offered free leaves as they did in South Carolina.

They did not. Instead, the recycling center collected leaves and yard waste and turned them into giant mountains of mulch and

Soil Building

compact mounds of compost. We could have as much as we could haul away for free.

Every weekend, Dear Husband would bring a dozen large containers and as many empty buckets as he could find and fill them up. We laid out vegetable and flowerbeds, hedgerows, thickets, and covered everything with thick layers of mulch or compost.

Over time, I learned to salvage leaves. I sent out Oldest Child or Younger Son with a rake and a lawn cart to collect the leaves the neighbors left at the curb. People rarely asked why a sullen teenager was raking up piles of leaves from their gutter and hauling them away.

In nearby Elizabethtown, residents used the bag system to get rid of leaves. In the fall, whenever I drove by the telltale brown bag of yard waste, I stopped to see if it was leaves and took them home. It's possible to stuff as many as ten bags into the passenger seat, backseat, and trunk of my Ford Focus sedan. I have never had anyone ask me what I was doing.

Now that I have a neighbor with a small lawn-care business, I can have pickup-truck loads delivered to my driveway. It saves Denny time and gas money to drop off his seasonal mountain of raked leaves mixed with grass clippings in my yard instead of hauling them to the township's recycling center.

I still collect bags of leaves when I drive by them and Younger Son gets sent out to harvest the local street leaves before the township gets them. We get compost and mulch from the township when needed and add to the mix our compost of food scraps, yard trimmings, and shredded paper.

Why don't we slow down? Because it is nearly impossible to add too much organic material to the soil. The organic material gets used up by the soil critters and plants. If you have a wilderness area, the falling leaves and dying plants will slowly, very slowly, continue to build up. Nature might build an inch of soil in 500 years this way. That may be okay in a meadow or forest, but not in a vegetable garden.

Vegetables are heavy feeders of soil fertility. Every carrot pulled from the soil takes with it nutrients that you have to replenish. If you do not use synthetic fertilizers – which are very damaging in a host of ways – your crop yields will drop and the soil will be exhausted. So we keep adding compost and leaves to compensate for what we remove.

Over time, my dirt has changed to soil. This is most evident in the garden beds, hedgerows, and the thicket, where year after year, we piled up leaves, compost, and mulch. Younger Son can layer on a foot of leaves in November and by June, it has rotted down. Turn over the soil and you will see a looser, more friable layer of humus full of worms and insects. This soil can absorb rainwater better, hold it longer, and not become soggy. Looser soil means better aeration, which leads to healthier root structures, which can grow deeper to reach subsoil water and nutrients.

Interestingly, the soil has also improved in the lawn where we have not put in nearly as much effort. We do not water or fertilize grass. We've spread a thin layer of compost over the grass twice in ten years and use a mulching lawnmower at its highest setting, letting the clippings rot in place. Younger Son also worked over the lawn with the broadfork punching holes into the soil allowing air and water to flow into it.

These actions encouraged the grass to grow deeper roots. But what also seems to have happened is that the exploding population of worms, ants, and other arthropods living in the beds, hedgerows, and the thicket are slowly colonizing the soil desert under the grass. They are doing the work for us, turning and aerating the soil; then fertilizing it with their own waste products.

Good soil building is the single best thing you can do to start and maintain healthy plants. A wide mix of vigorously growing plants will better withstand diseases and pests. Your produce will be more nutritious. It may even taste better. But since fruits and vegetables are removed and eaten, soil building needs to be a regular part of your gardening routine. Feed the soil to feed the plants to feed your family.

FEED FIRST, THEN PLANT

Many of my plant die-offs have been related to not improving the soil *before* planting my expensive baby shrubs and perennials. The hedgerow along the north side is a case in point. It had a straggly forsythia hedge hiding a steep downslope. We installed the four-foot chain-link fence almost as soon as we moved in to contain our toddlers and dog. A few years later, Dear Husband and Oldest Child dug out the forsythias. I wanted to have a mixed shrub border of assorted natives to block the north wind, screen the yard, and provide habitat for native songbirds.

To slow water run-off, I lined the bottom of the fence with com-

Soil Building

posite decking about six inches tall. The decking is rot- and insect-proof, and should last forever. I threw leaves on in the fall and planted my expensive native shrubs in the spring. Six years or so later, almost everything had died. The soil was too heavy, too much like a brick. It would not accept rainwater and had very little organic matter in it. It was dirt and not soil. I tried adding leaves for the last few years, but this was not enough to save the shrubs. The survivors are doing better now that the soil is finally improving.

What I should have done was wait two or three more years after pulling out the forsythias. Each year, I should have laid down thick layers of compost, mulch, and scavenged leaves, let the vegetation grow that wanted to grow, and cut it down every fall to rot in place. Several years of this treatment would have vastly improved the soil.

My shrubs would have had a much better chance at life *and* I would have learned how badly I needed a serious wind barrier along the fence.

The raised vegetable beds have had similar issues. Once built, they are hard to double-dig and spade in loads of leaves and compost. I would layer on compost but it was never enough to compensate for what the lettuces and tomatoes took from the soil.

Soil building has now become a routine part of my annual gardening schedule. When fall comes, I collect every leaf possible. Younger Son lays them thickly on every bed. In the spring, the remaining leaves are turned under and compost spread on top. Only then do we plant seeds and seedlings. Younger Son and I started experimenting with green manure and letting beds lay fallow for a season or two. We are trying no-till as well, which means we pull aside the layers of dead leaves just enough to punch a hole for a single seed or small plant.

We have seriously concentrated on soil building only for the last few years, and with each passing year, it's noticeably better: darker, more crumbly, and able to absorb rainwater. My vegetables seem to be doing better. In addition to adding all this organic material to my soil, I sometimes use bone meal (for phosphorus), greensand (for potassium and trace minerals), and crushed eggshells (for calcium). I make iron water by allowing nails to rust in a bucket of water and apply this very, very sparingly. If I had chickens or rabbits, I would compost their manure and add that to the soil as well. We do not use any other fertilizers or pesticides.

LIVING OFF COMPOST

As we move deeper into a more uncertain future, compost and leaves may become the only affordable soil amendment. Wars have been fought over the great deposits of guano in caves (bat poo) and on small ocean islands (seagull poo) waiting to be mined and spread on farmers' fields. Those deposits have, for the most part, long since been mined out.

Most inorganic fertilizers these days are made from natural gas. Do not expect them to get cheaper. It is cheap enough now to buy a bottle of fish emulsion for one's houseplants, but very few of us can afford to use this product on a large vegetable garden.

So stop throwing away your fertility. Every leaf that falls on your property should stay on it, as should every blade of grass, carrot top, and potato peeling. When your wasteful, profligate neighbors throw away their fertility, collect it at once. If they ask what you are doing, explain that you garden intensively and need the leaves to feed your soil and mulch your beds.

This may inspire them to start gardening, which is a good thing, even if it means fewer leaves for you. The more self-sufficient your neighbors are, the more resilient your community.

LEAVES AND GRASS

Leaves are so easy to handle. They are usually dry and rot very nicely in compost bins or spread out as mulch. In the fall, we spread whatever compost is in the bins on every raised bed, followed by a foot-thick layer of leaves. By the time it is warm enough to plant in the spring, most of them have decayed through weather, time, and insect activity. It is easy to spade under the remaining few inches. We rarely have a problem with them matting and clumping, and if they do, we fluff them with a rake.

The asparagus and rhubarb beds get their foot of leaves as well, but because these plants are perennials, we don't spade in the leaves. Any unrotted leaves in the spring are pulled away from the new growth and left in place as a weed barrier.

The flowerbeds, hedgerows (where the berry bushes are), and the thicket get as many leaves as we can salvage *after* the raised vegetable beds are done. These plants don't require as much compost as the vegetables and they tend to feed themselves in the fall with their own leaf drop. These leaves are never spaded in, but left to rot in place and act as a weed barrier. By late August, the leaves have vanished

Soil Building

into the soil and these areas are ready for their next load.

Sometimes my leaves, especially the giant brown bagfuls I collect in Lancaster County, are full of pine needles, acorns, sweet gum balls, twigs, and other bits. This rots down fine, if slower. If I am not desperate for leaves to cover the vegetable beds, I use the twiggier stuff on the hedgerows and under the berry bushes. Branches and twigs can be turned into mulch by breaking them into smaller pieces with a chipper or by hand. This is another reason to have a wilderness area in your yard; it gives you a place to toss branches and old Christmas trees where they can rot down slowly and undisturbed.

Grass clippings are more problematic. We experimented with using a pickup-truck load of clippings from Denny in the spring as mulch. The clippings matted, got slimy, and putrefied. Great piles of grass clippings don't rot into compost very well unless they are turned and loosened every few days. With little or no air to keep the composting action going, they pack down into a slimy mass. A sullen teenager with a pitchfork is the best remedy. For now, the best method we found with grass clippings is to use a mulching lawnmower and let the clippings rot in place, rather than collecting and managing larger quantities.

HOW TO START BUILDING YOUR SOIL

When laying out your garden, decide where you want to put vegetable beds, permanent beds for perennials like asparagus and rhubarb, flower borders, hedgerows for berries or fruit trees, hedges, and your wilderness areas.

As soon as you know what a stretch of grass will become, set the lawnmower to its lowest setting and mow the area down to nubbins. Leave the clippings in place. Soak with water, then lay on multiple sheets of old newspapers, completely covering the new bed in a thick layer many sheets deep. The newspaper layer helps kill the grass and perennial weeds. Punch holes in the newspaper with a spading fork. Water again. Cover the newspaper layer with a foot or more of leaves or mulch and water well. A year later, turn over the layers and be amazed. This is what soil building does.

If you want raised beds encased in a four-sided box of composite decking, follow the same procedure and finish by building the box. Fill it up with more layers of compost, leaves, and mulch. If you have soil handy from recycled houseplants or other building projects, layer that in, too.

If your soil is dreadful, and you have a sturdy teenager or two at hand, double-dig your vegetable garden. Do not do this for anything else as only annual crops of vegetables really benefit from this exhausting, laborious job.

You should only have to do this once per bed. Begin with the above procedure and wait a year while time and soil critters work their magic. Mark off the area, dig a trench about a foot deep and two feet wide, and dump the contents into a wheelbarrow. With a spading fork, loosen and turn the soil in the bottom of the trench. Work into the soil whatever organic material you have on hand. Move to the second strip and dig out the soil, but put it into the trench you just dug. Loosen the bottom soil of the trench and add more organic amendments. Repeat this process until you reach the end of the bed. You will end up with an empty trench that has been spaded, turned, and loosened. Empty the wheelbarrow into the trench. If you can, cover the double-dug bed with a foot of leaves and compost. Wait another year. The soil will be beautiful, healthy, loose, friable, and full of life.

GROWING COVER CROPS

You can also improve your soil with cover crops. These plants are grown to be chopped up and spaded under to feed the soil. Farmers do this to improve their soil and so can you.

Ever since medieval times, fields were allowed to lie fallow every few years to let the soil recover. Whatever wanted to grow would be left alone. Cows or sheep would fertilize the soil with their manure. After a year or two, the pasture would be plowed and sown with a crop.

For garden beds, don't let Nature decide. Cover crop seed mixtures are sold from catalogs like Johnny's Selected Seeds. They have a wide range of choices depending on your geographic area and soil needs. These cover crops will have plants that will fix nitrogen and extend deep roots to break up hard-packed soil and bring up nutrients from the subsoil. Let the plants grow, chop them up at the first frost, turn them into the soil, and they will enrich the bed in time for next year's tomatoes.

PUT YOUR SOIL TO THE TEST

Plants need many kinds of nutrients. If one nutrient is lacking, then no matter how rich your soil, that one missing element will de-

Soil Building

termine how well your crop grows. To find out if anything is missing from your soil, have it tested.

You can perform the first, basic test with a quart glass jar and water. Fill the jar about one-quarter full with soil. Add water until the jar is nearly full. Shake vigorously until soil and water are fully mixed. Let the jar sit undisturbed for several days.

The contents should settle out in layers, with heavier rocks and sand in the bottom, topped with silt particles, then clay, and any organic matter at the top. If you see a lot of sand, you have sandy soil. If you see a lot of clay, well, you know. You want to see a thick layer of organic humus on top. There probably won't be much. Perform this test in several locations in your yard, as it is very unlikely the soil will be the same everywhere. You want to dig down an inch or two to get your sample, as this is where the plant roots will grow.

To get more in-depth information, you need a soil-testing kit. Every garden center sells them and the directions are easy to follow. You can also get your soil tested by a laboratory. This will give you much more information than the garden center kits. The local county agricultural extension agent will be able to tell you whom to contact in your area. Some states do this free, while others charge a fee.

The test results will tell you if you are low on any of the big three elements: potassium, phosphorus, and nitrogen. You will then get a long discussion of microelements and suggested changes and amendments. Missing micronutrients, like the big three, can be added to your soil by spreading various amendments, and the lab report will tell you which ones to buy at the garden center.

We were low on calcium, which is easy to supply. Save your eggshells, crush them fine, and sprinkle them everywhere. They disappear fast.

The test will also tell you the soil's pH level; that is, how acidic or alkaline it is. The pH level determines what plants will grow joyfully, which will die a lingering, resentful death, and which will struggle along.

Not all plants like the same soil type. Blueberries, for example, insist on a very acid soil. It is hard to change the pH of soil permanently, so your blueberries may have to be grown in containers if your soil is more alkaline. Grass likes a more alkaline soil; spreading lime increases the alkalinity of your soil making the grass happier. Acid-loving plants will not appreciate the lime from your lawn leaching over into their beds every time it rains.

SOIL TYPES

A heavy clay drains poorly and can become waterlogged, drowning plant roots. If, that is, it accepts rainwater in the first place. Clay can harden and bake into a bricklike consistency. Water rolls off it without soaking in. A silty soil is made up of particles larger than clay and smaller than sand. It can be fertile, but it can become waterlogged easily. Unless you live in an area that used to be a riverbank, you probably won't get a true silt soil. Sand drains and drains and holds no moisture at all. Roots get plenty of air but they die from dryness.

Of the three, I like clay. It is hard to amend at first, but it retains moisture better and has more available nutrients and minerals. Silt can amend well, but it won't have clay's fertility. Sandy soils burn through compost at a much higher rate than clay, and the drainage is better, but plants dry out quicker because of that. The cure for both conditions — drainage and water absorption — is compost, leaves, mulches, and other organic material you can layer onto the soil.

Then there is another solution to dealing with poor soil: raised beds. A raised bed completely changes the soil from what is in the surrounding areas. Think of them as giant pots that are open at the bottom. You can build raised beds on a parking lot if you make them deep enough for the roots. If you want to grow blueberries and you do not have very acid soil, a raised bed with custom-mixed soil is the only way to succeed. I tried to grow blueberries and despite regular applications of pine straw, coffee grounds, and Holly-tone (a soil amendment for acid-loving plants like azaleas, hollies, and blueberries), I could not change the soil pH. The blueberries are gone, replaced with hazelnut bushes.

Do not use inorganic mulches like gravel or shredded rubber. They do nothing to improve your soil so what is the point of having them? Any mulch that was once alive will rot and improve your soil, so choose what is locally available, starting with composted grass clippings and free leaves every fall. When landscapers cut down trees, they chip the tree. Ask and most of them will be happy to give you that material so they won't have to dispose of it. Wood ashes can be composted and so can sawdust, nutshells, cocoa pods, Halloween hay bales, straw, seaweed, and spent mushroom compost. Anything that was once alive will rot for you and improve your soil.

Make soil building a regular part of your garden routine and your improved soil will reward you with healthier plants, both in the growing and the eating. Don't ever stop, as you can never add too much organic material to your soil.

Feed your soil and it will feed you.

26

Water Storage

Emergency Storage – Efficiency and Cutting Water Waste – Fixing Faucets, Toilets, and Pipes — Getting On a Water Diet — The Three Types of Water — Collecting Water — Long-Range and Long-Term Water Storage

Y<small>OU CANNOT LIVE WITHOUT WATER. Y</small>OUR GARDEN, everybody's garden, will die without water. Every single living thing on earth has to have water or die. Every industrial product uses water in its processes, sometimes quite a lot of it. Cooling steel after forging? Water. Dyeing the wool from the sheep you sheared? Water. Building a loom from scrap lumber? Those trees grew with water. Mixing concrete? Water. Making adobe bricks? Water. Growing wheat and then shipping it worldwide? Amazing amounts of water. Fracking natural gas? Flushing toilets throughout the western world? Gargantuan, amazing, astounding amounts of water that becomes undrinkable.

On the surface, water does not appear to be a scarce resource. The oceans are full of it and about 70% of the earth's surface is water. However, unless you are a saltwater fish, ocean water is mostly useless. Saltwater is very corrosive so it is not used for industrial purposes. It poisons the soil so it cannot be used for irrigation. You cannot drink it. If you are going to use seawater for anything other than saltwater aquariums and mining sea-salt, it has to be purified at huge costs of energy and money.

Fresh water falls from the sky as rain. The quality can be terrible such as the acid rain in China. Our rain-fed streams and lakes are better, but you should not drink from them without purification due to the bacteria, intestinal parasites, heavy metals, and manure contamination that leach in from farms, factories, cities, and towns. Wherever you are, you are downstream from somebody.

Given a chance, rainwater soaks into the ground into aquifers. These are sort of giant spongy parts of the earth's crust. They are everywhere and can contain billions to trillions of gallons of clean, pure fossil water.

Notice that phrase: fossil water. It takes millions of years for a big aquifer to fill with rainwater and only a few years for industrious people to pump it dry for irrigation and industry. Wells in India and Pakistan that were fifty feet deep fifty years ago now have to be hundreds of feet deep to reach the aquifer. This water was pumped onto the fields, where most of it evaporated or ran off into the sea. Very little actually got to the thirsty plant roots and sank back down into the aquifer.

This is happening in the United States, where there are dozens of aquifers. Some, such as the Edwards in central Texas, are replenished annually from streams, rivers, and lakes. Others are not. One of the largest, the Ogallala, which covers eight states in the Midwest, sees as little as a tenth of its outflow return to its more arid sections.

Then there are the rivers that are completely diverted to serve human needs. Every drop of the Colorado River and the Rio Grande is used for irrigation, industry, toilet flushing, lawns, golf courses, swimming pools, you name it. These rivers no longer reach the ocean.

Weather patterns do not seem to be as reliable anymore. There is some thought that during the last ten thousand years of human life – since the development of agriculture, in fact – the earth's climate was unusually stable, consistent, and calm. This may be changing and not for the better. It may mean bigger, longer, harsher droughts followed by torrential rains that are lost to the seas due to runoff into streams.

Gardens and farms prefer a regular amount of rain falling consistently. An inch or so a week is what the gardening books say. That certainly seems to be true for my garden. This does not have the same effect as four or five inches at once every thirty days. Alternating flood and drought is hard on you, your garden, your community, and your agriculture. Monsoons and dry seasons are manageable with sufficient time, effort, and knowledge, but regular rain, an inch a week, is considerably easier.

Managing your water effectively involves several issues, and we will consider each in turn.

EMERGENCY STORAGE

The first step in managing your water supply is to store enough for emergencies. The Red Cross says a gallon of water per person per day will be enough to drink, and maybe wash your hands or cook a little. This does not include toilets, showers, dishwashing, laundry, pets, pools, plants, livestock, or anything else. In my household of five, plus pets, houseplants, and a large garden, we use about forty gallons of water per person, per day. Most people use more, a lot more in some cases.

The Red Cross says you should have a minimum of three days of water on hand. This means that my household should keep six gallons for one day, five for us and one for the pets. Times three days, this means eighteen gallon jugs of water. This is the rock-bottom minimum. A five-day supply would be better as it provides more margin for error.

When you are at the supermarket, look at those shelves of bottled water in gallon jugs and see how much space storing three days of water would take. Look around at home and decide where you are going to put all that water. As with everything else, the best water storage area is cool, dry, and in the dark.

I have gallon jugs of water tucked away in my basement, still in their original plastic jugs. I have never had them leak or fail and some of them are now ten years old. If we have to use it in an emergency, it should be as clean, pure, and safe as the day I stored it.

Stored water will taste better if it is aerated. After any boiling or bleach treatments, pour the water from container to container a few times to infuse it with air. If it still tastes off, use it to make tea. Flat water is also fine for hand washing or cooking.

You probably won't have the space to store more than twenty or thirty gallons of water. It gets heavy fast, so make sure the shelves are reinforced. Keep them on the bottom shelves, or at least don't put anything breakable underneath the jugs. Check occasionally for leaks.

If you are having a water emergency, remember that the water in your toilet tank — *not the bowl* — is still potable, as is the water in your hot water tank and pipes. Before using, shut off the water coming into your house to prevent potentially contaminated water mixing with your clean water.

If you need to replace your hot water heater, the need to store water is a good reason to get the biggest unit you can afford. Do not get a hot-water-on-demand unit. They store no water at all, and can encourage family members to take longer showers than they already do.

If you are lucky enough to get advance notice that a water emergency is coming, you can temporarily store water. The easiest way is to get a rubber disk to cover the closed drain in your clean bathtub and fill it. The disk will slow down the water leakage, giving you potentially another fifty to sixty gallons of water. Keep away any little ones you have, as the tub is a drowning hazard. You can also get special single-use plastic bags designed to store water in the bathtub. This would keep the water cleaner and less of a safety hazard. Those bags might also be harder to use and drain when the emergency passes. The rubber disk seems easier.

Have clean, empty water containers with lids on standby and when an emergency threatens, fill them up and store in your freezer and fridge. Leave headspace in the containers for the ice to expand. The mass of cold water and ice will help maintain the temperature if you lose power and the water remains drinkable. In fact, if you regularly have freezer space open up with the gardening and hunting seasons, *plan* on filling the empty spaces with jugs of water. It will keep everything colder in the event of a power outage and make your freezer more efficient.

While you are filling the freezer jugs, don't forget to hunt up your camping water storage jugs and fill them with ice and water. This is why I keep a five-gallon Coleman water jug in my basement. In the event of an emergency, it gets filled with ice and water and sits on the counter, ready for use.

If you have a swimming pool, you have thousands of gallons of water at hand. Its drinkability depends on its purity and algae load, and it might need straining, standing, boiling, and aerating, but it is perfectly fine for flushing toilets and washing dishes.

During the emergency, cut back hard on water usage! Stop doing laundry and watering plants, and use paper plates, paper napkins, and disposable flatware. Wash hands only, tell the gentlemen to fertilize the compost bin, and only flush the toilet when feces are present. Toilets can be flushed with stored water from the bathtub. Pour a bucket of water into the toilet bowl, and it will flush. Use up the tabletop storage water first (your camping water jugs) followed by your bathtub, emergency storage water, and water in the hot water heater.

As you empty out the purchased jugs, keep trying to get more water. You may have to save your empty jugs for reuse, if the only source of replacement water is the National Guard water truck. They will not supply you with empty containers.

It is unbelievably inconvenient to not have water, fresh and safe, available at the tap on demand. We experienced this first-hand many years ago in York, S.C. There was a problem in the reservoir and suddenly, with no notice, NO water was available. After a day of panic – every store for miles was immediately stripped clean of water – the city got the reservoir system going again. The water was brown as weak tea and smelled dreadful. You could at least use the toilet, although the water looked so bad, it did not look like you had flushed.

Because this affected only a relatively small area, local stores were able to ship in tons of water to sell. It took two weeks for the water to gradually shift in color and odor. After the first four days, you could wash the laundry without it being permanently stained and the dishes smelling bad afterwards. The city said the water was safe to drink as it was heavily chlorinated (you could tell), although I doubt anyone did.

By about the one-week mark, you could shower again, and after two weeks, everything was back to normal. It was definitely a learning experience. Thank God, we could use our toilets after the first day! Since then, I *always* keep a dozen or so gallon jugs of water on the shelf.

Water emergencies happen more often than you might think. If you are on a well, the electric pump could stop working because of a power outage or a mechanical failure. You should have a backup system to get your water. If your well is too deep for a manual pump, then you need a generator. You should still store emergency water just in case.

So, find a place to store several days worth of gallon jugs of water, keep water frozen in your freezer, get rubber disks for your bathtubs, keep insulated camping jugs for water on hand in your basement and pay attention to news and weather reports. If you do not need these preparations? That's great. If you do need them, you will be grateful you prepared.

EFFICIENCY AND CUTTING WATER WASTE

The next stage in water management is being more efficient with water. The less you use, the less you need. This can save you money

Water Storage

twice over. Water is cheap at about a penny a gallon, but why pay for more than you need? Keep in mind you also pay again with your sewage bill, which is based on your water usage. The sewage company assumes that all the water that comes into the house leaves through the plumbing. People with large swimming pools or who water their lawn religiously often have a second line installed so as to not pay for sewage treatment for water that goes onto the grass or into the pool.

So first, check for leaks in your system. Find the water meter. It will most likely be in a dark corner of your basement. Wipe off the decades of dust and look for the dial that counts your usage. If no water is being used, the meter should not change. The best test is to get everyone out of the house for several hours or more. Before you leave and the meter has stopped spinning after everyone had their last bathroom break, hand wash, and glass of water, write the number down. You can do this overnight, so long as nobody gets up in the middle of the night to use the toilet or get some water before you check the meter in the morning.

When you come back, hours later, the meter reading should be the same. If it is not, you either forgot your automatic sprinkler system or your icemaker, or you have a leak. The difference between the two numbers will tell you how large a leak it is. A pinhole leak may take hours to register on the meter. That may not seem like much, but a leak never stops and runs up your bill. Tiny leaks also have a nasty habit of becoming big, damaging, expensive leaks.

Your water meter should be near the main water shut-off valve into your house. Everyone should know where this is, so anyone can shut the water off in an emergency. This becomes especially important in older houses, where sinks and toilets might not have their own shut-off valves. The next time any of those fixtures need work, you will have to shut off the water to the entire house. This is a great opportunity to have the plumber install a shut-off at whatever he is working on.

If you discover a leak, the next step is locating it. Do any faucets drip? Does the toilet run? Is there a suspicious damp spot that keeps recurring on the basement floor? Stains in the ceiling underneath the upstairs bathroom? Leaks may also show up in the dishwasher lines (a stain on the ceiling below may be your only clue) and the line to your fridge's icemaker.

Once you've found the problem, the next step is to fix it.

FIXING FAUCETS, TOILETS, AND PIPES

A handy person with a plumber's guide from the library can often fix a leaky faucet. If they are in terrible condition, replace them with better quality models that will hold up better. If you replace several faucets, choose a single brand for all of them. That way, they all work the same and share the same repair parts.

Toilets may have very slow leaks. Test by putting a bottle of red food coloring in the toilet tank. Keep everyone away from the toilet being tested. If the water in the bowl turns red on its own (and not with your toddler's help), then there is a slow leak in the toilet tank's guts. A handy person with a plumbing book may be able to repair it.

If your toilet is in poor shape, consider replacing it with a low-flow model. Older toilets use a *lot* of water per flush. Be very careful what you buy as some models work much better than others. A toilet that will only flush liquids will drive you nuts as you flush and flush and flush in a vain attempt to get the solid items down. Moreover, you will use far more clean water.

Toilet technology changes quickly so see what is current before buying. Magazines such as *Consumer Reports, Fine Homebuilding, This Old House,* and *Family Handyman* have plenty of advice to offer. When you choose a toilet, try to get one with a four-inch diameter throat as opposed to the standard three-inch model. Family members who have a larger output will spend less time plunging the toilet.

Traditionally, water usage can be cut in old-style toilets by sinking bricks or half-gallon jugs of water into the tank. This seems of dubious merit as the bricks might crumble over time and mess up the works of the toilet. Anything bumping around in the tank increases the risk of cracking the porcelain and causing a leak. In addition, toilets are designed to use a certain amount of water to flush well and clear the bowl. Reducing the amount of water in the tank may reduce its effectiveness.

Another way to cut water use is to follow the saying: If it's yellow, let it mellow; if it's brown, flush it down. This needs to be agreed on by every member of your household for this process to work at its best. It will be troublesome to guests, toddlers, and pets. It isn't that sanitary. You will save a lot of water, but again, at a penny per gallon — five cents a flush — how much are you saving? If you pay more for your water, you will save more on the water and sewage bills. This option may best be reserved for water emergencies, and if you really need to save every penny.

Pipe leaks should be repaired by a plumber. Don't put it off. Tiny leaks can suddenly become catastrophic leaks that cost you far more than the plumber will.

GETTING ON A WATER DIET

Once the leaks are fixed, you are ready to be more efficient in your water usage. There are loads of ways to cut back, but they all follow the same rule: Don't let unused water run down the drain.

Don't run the water until it is cold. Keep a pitcher in the fridge and drink from that. Don't leave the water running to shave. Fill the sink instead. Run only full loads in the washer and dishwasher. Scrape the dishes into the compost bin before you put them into the dishwasher rather than rinsing them under running water. Wash the car on the lawn or use a car wash that recycles the water. Is it necessary to wash a garment if it has been on your body for less than a day? Underwear and socks? Sure. Pants when the only physical work you did in them was sitting at a desk? Maybe not. Do you need a thirty-minute shower twice a day? If you work in the bilges of a ship, then, oh, yes. In an air-conditioned office? Doubtful.

Every time you turn on the tap, use only what you need. Pay attention to what you are doing and be mindful of your money washing down the drain.

Next, start catching water inside the house before it goes down the drain. If you use a dehumidifier, don't dump that water; use it for houseplants or outside ornamentals. If you hand wash dishes, use rubber tubs to wash and rinse in. Dump the water outside on ornamentals, trees, or grass.

In a more serious situation, such as a drought, plug up the bathtub during a shower. Bail out the water into buckets and use it to flush toilets or water trees and shrubs. Some people shower with a Rubbermaid bin at their feet to catch the extra water. Is it easier to not do this? Sure. Once again, you are using your energy to spend less money and waste less water.

If it helps, think of carrying water as part of your exercise routine. It is also good practice, because if you *have* to cut back on water usage, having the habit of being mindful of how you use water will make it easier.

THE THREE TYPES OF WATER

Water comes in three types. *Clean water* comes out of the tap. It is drinkable, pure, and free of contaminants. Our houses are set up to use this water for everything, including our toilets.

Gray water you do not want to drink. You have washed dishes, your body, or clothes in it; it has detergent residues, food particles, and other stuff you would rather not drink.

Black water comes from your toilet. It is contaminated with urine and feces, and it is not reusable. The way to avoid black water is via composting toilets, a complex subject that requires a book of its own. Read the *Humanure Handbook* before you decide to go this route.

Catching clean or gray water from the sink in a Rubbermaid bin is easy and doesn't involve replumbing your house. Catching gray water from bathtubs, dishwashers, and washing machines for reuse requires more effort. Many municipalities frown on replumbing your house to route used washing machine water onto your lawn. It doesn't meet the building code, and you have to be very careful what detergents and soaps you use as you could contaminate the groundwater or poison your garden.

If you live in a place where it rains regularly, gray water replumbing will be complex, expensive, and not hugely useful. If you live in Arizona, where every drop counts, the thousands of gallons of water your household uses every month may mean a lot to your garden. It may be the only source of irrigation water you can afford. There are books available on the subject, so study up before calling a plumber. You also have to be sure that your retrofitting meets your local building code. Some municipalities don't care. Some municipalities care a lot, and you won't be able to resell your house without returning it to its original condition.

Gray water systems need far more maintenance than just using the sewage system for your household's used water. They are, by definition, more complex. They dump large amounts of water at once in one place, such as when your washer finishes a cycle. Soaps, detergents, hair-care products; anything that goes down the drain has to be biodegradable in a way that regular products may not be. These products cost more and may not clean as well.

Once you have conserved or caught all the water inside your house for reuse, it is time to move outside. Roofs, even small ones, can collect thousands of gallons of water in a heavy rainstorm. This water can be captured and saved to water your garden. There are two ways of dealing with this water to keep it from being lost to the storm drains.

COLLECTING WATER

The first way is to install rain barrels or water cubes at downspouts. The amount of water you collect will vary depending on the size of the collection unit, the amount of rain, and more subtly, the square footage of roof that is being drained. If the gutters and downspouts are draining a small roof area, you won't collect as much rain. If you have a complex roofline with many surfaces, gutters, and downspouts, you can have huge variances in the volume of rain flowing through the downspouts.

You can buy rain barrels readymade or convert Rubbermaid trashcans using online instructions. If you have a choice of location, put larger collection units (like 250-gallon cubes) under larger-flow downspouts and smaller collection units (like fifty-gallon rain barrels) under the lesser-flow spouts. It does not take much of a storm to fill a fifty-gallon rain barrel to overflowing. Install a 250-gallon cube in the same location, and you may discover that a typical rain only delivers 100 gallons to that spot.

Rain barrels and cubes only work when you use them. They require regular management and maintenance. A few days after each rain, you need to have a sullen teenager empty the barrel into buckets and water everything that needs to be watered. If your rains are regular in nature (and you pay close attention to weather forecasts), you can empty the barrel or cube by the midpoint of each rain/dry cycle. Or, you can water the garden with the stored rain when it needs it and hope it rains in time to refill the barrel for the next dry spell.

Rain barrels and cubes *must* have an overflow valve for when the monsoon comes. Make sure the overflows are directed *away* from your house's foundation. If you get huge amounts of rain at irregular intervals, use as many cubes and barrels as you can fit under your downspouts to catch that precious water. Rain barrels and cubes can be chained together to store more water.

The barrels and cubes should have a screen over the gutter opening to keep mosquitoes out. If someone complains that you are running a mosquito farm, point out your screens. Then mention that mosquitoes can breed in a teacup of water in four or five days so the real problem is standing water in sandbox toys, litter, and unmaintained piles of junk. If your climate requires it, rain barrels need to be drained when the temperature goes below freezing. The screens should be cleaned occasionally.

Make your rain barrel or cube easier to empty into a bucket by putting them up on concrete blocks. The faucet is at the very bottom of the container and if you put the barrel on the ground, you will have about two inches of room for a hose or bucket. Don't do this to yourself. Rain barrel water should be strained and purified before drinking (think of what the birds do on your asphalt shingles!) but it will work fine to flush toilets.

There are, apparently, some areas that get nasty about collecting rainwater that lands on your property. Check first! Some homeowners associations dislike rain barrels, vegetable gardens, clotheslines, and compost bins; all items so necessary for fostering your resilience. Either get on the board and change the rules, or sell the house and move somewhere less restrictive. If it is the local government's rules, then be very discreet so the neighbors don't rat you out, move, or run for local office and change the law.

The second way to easily catch rainwater from your downspouts is in the ground. This is *not* going to be drinking water. This water will keep your garden going longer between rains.

Walk around your house and note where the downspouts are. With time and a sullen teenager with a shovel, you can dig shallow, mowable swales to divert that water into your landscaping. The only active part of this method is the digging. Gravity does the rest. Why do this? Because rainwater that drains from the downspout into the neighbor's driveway is lost. Rainwater that drains into a swale (moving it away from your foundation) aimed at the vegetable garden or the berry bushes will soak into the soil. Better water penetration will help your plants last longer between rains. It is much easier to maintain a swale than a rain barrel. This method works hand in hand with improving your soil.

LONG-RANGE AND LONG-TERM WATER STORAGE

In the long term, the easiest, cheapest way to store water is in the ground. There are two ways to go about this. For household water – drinking, laundry, hygiene, cooking, and some irrigation – you need a cistern to catch every drop of rainwater that falls on your property. If you live in dryer portions of the country and you expect to be at least

Water Storage

partially off-grid, a cistern is a must.

A cistern is an enormous tank capable of holding thousands of gallons of rain. They are usually buried to protect the water from contaminants and evaporation and to keep it cooler. Think of it as an underground swimming pool topped with a layer of lawn.

Cisterns are not do-it-yourself projects unless you have an army of sullen teenagers with shovels to dig the gargantuan hole, brick it up, line it with tile, build the cover, drain the downspouts into it, and then landscape over it. A cistern also needs, if you are going to use it for drinking water, a sorting and filtering system so that you don't drink the contaminants that wash off your shingles during the first fifteen minutes of a rainstorm. Cisterns need pumps to get the water out. An electric pump is easy to use but you must have a manual backup for when the power goes out.

Locating the cistern can be challenging, because most, if not all, of your home's gutters need to drain into it to keep it filled. It is probably easier to dig the cistern first, then build the house, rather than retrofitting one into a small yard with trees, driveways, underground pipes and anything else getting in the way. If no space can be found, a cistern can be built above ground.

Do a lot of research before installing a cistern so you know how to use and maintain it. Get plenty of references from the builder and visit his installed cisterns so you can see how big they can be and how they work. Bigger is always better. If you can count on only fifteen inches of rain a year, arriving in one or two big storms, you need to catch every drop.

The second way to store rainwater is in the ground. Soil that catches and holds onto water lets you go longer between waterings when the rains are not reliable. It'll also mean less watering each time. Less runoff and evaporation means more water soaking into the soil for your thirsty vegetables. Improved soil leads to being more drought-proof.

You improve your soil with tons of organic material, deep-rooted plants, no bare soil ever, and never turning over the soil if you can avoid it. You want a deep, rich, humusy loam. You can turn that dead dirt in your yard into every gardener's dream. It takes years but it isn't rocket science. In the fifteen years we have lived at Fortress Peschel, we have gone from standing water and run-off after every rain to no standing water ever. Every drop of precious rainwater soaks into my soil. See Chapter 25, Soil Building, for more on how to do this.

27

Diverting Water From Your Basement

Solving One Problem Revealed Another – Attacking the Problem From Outside – The Magic of Drylok – The Return of the Seepage – Sticking the Landing — Give Your House a Checkup

WATER IN THE BASEMENT IS AGGRAVATING beyond words. This is not, strictly speaking, a resilience topic. It doesn't involve setting goals, food storage tips, or getting out of debt. However, if you do not keep water out of your basement, then your life will become less resilient in a hurry. It will cost you lots of money and time to fix, and all the prepper goods you have stored in your basement will be ruined by the flood.

Water in the basement or crawl space is not a problem that I or my Dear Husband had experienced. My parents live in a house over a century old with a brick foundation, and there has never been a drop of water in that basement. Neither my house in Norfolk nor our home in South Carolina, both built on crawl spaces, ever had a problem.

Then we bought our house in Central Pa., a three-bedroom ranch built over a basement. Every house this far north seems to have a full basement as you have problems with frost heave if you don't. Our house was built in the mid-1950s, of cement block and heavy timbers that you don't see any more.

Our house was owned by the family that built it, and I do not believe they ever paid much attention to routine maintenance, as you will see.

Diverting Water From Your Basement

When Dear Husband visited the house for the first time, the basement was crammed with the owners' possessions, including heaps of old towels. This was a sign we missed, a sinister clue to the coming horror.

The building inspector did the best he could, but the basement was so crammed that he could not get into every corner with a flashlight and a poking stick. DH certainly could not. Nonetheless, we bought the house and in July 2001, we moved in.

It had been a dry spring and summer. But in August, it rained, and it rained hard. I came back from the library that night, kids in tow, to discover an inch of water approaching the basement steps of the finished portion, up onto the carpet! Opening the basement door to the unfinished portion revealed an inch or so of standing water. Only the unevenly sloped floor kept this new branch of the Susquehanna River from damaging our possessions.

I was *not* happy. However, this did explain the heaps of towels. It also explained why the chest freezer left by the previous owners had been placed on skids.

But why was the water coming in? I raced outside, in the pouring rain, and discovered that the house gutters did not have concrete splashes to divert the water away from the house. The old homeowners had installed downspouts at the front of the house that went into the ground. Whatever underground system had been installed had clearly failed.

The rest of the night was spent in a panic. DH was at work and there was nothing he could do. I was in an unfamiliar neighborhood with three kids, 2, 4, and 11. I started mopping, and when DH came home at two in the morning, he joined in until we got all the water.

The next day, closer inspection revealed that there was *no floor drain* in the basement, nor was there a sump pump. This was probably for the best since the previous owners would not have maintained them, anymore than they maintained the rest of the house.

Since that traumatic day, I have done extensive landscaping around the house, and I have never found any evidence of an underground drainage system from the downspouts to the street. Never. Houses with such a system should have drainage pipes sticking out of the lawn by the street. Water should come out of them when it rains. If it doesn't, then the system is clogged. If you don't find any pipes, then your home is probably using French drains in which the water flows into an underground trench filled with gravel, or a pipe filled with holes. In either case, you have serious, hidden trouble.

That same morning, I raced to the hardware store and bought concrete splashes for all six downspouts. DH installed them, disconnecting the two front downspouts from whatever mystery place they ran into. It rained again soon thereafter, and we had no water in the basement. Amazing, no?

This is basic stuff! You don't get more basic than this! Put a freaking concrete splash at every single downspout to lead the water away from the foundations! It works like magic, every single time! I paid about $10 per splash and saved myself untold amounts of aggravation. Installing the splashes was one of the easiest and most effective repairs we made to this house. It took longer to drive to Lowes and buy them than it did to install them. Doing this alone solved 75% of our basement water problems.

Sixty bucks to keep water out of the basement, and the previous owners could not be bothered. They *let* water seep into the basement for decades and mopped up afterwards with their collection of moldy towels. They lived with the problem rather than make an effort, even the most minimal one, to fix the problem.

I am not that kind of a person. There was no way we were going to live with water coming into the basement. Thus began a multi-year evolution with multiple fixes that ended a few years ago, when we finally discovered the main source of the problem.

SOLVING ONE PROBLEM REVEALED ANOTHER

Because the previous owners routinely let water into the basement, we got to fix all kinds of problems. One of our first expenses after moving in was replacing the oil tank. Our house, like many in the northeast, is heated with an oil furnace using forced air. Our oil tank stood on metal legs in the corner of the basement, in what is now the workshop and what had been the original coal bin.

Because of the never-ending moisture issues from flooding, dampness, and condensation, a tank that should have lasted as long as the house had one of its legs rusted through. That was a quick $800.

While we were doing this, we discovered that the roof leaked. A new roof took care of those problems and also kept *more* water out of the basement. Water can work its way into your basement from a tiny hole in the roof, trickle down the inside of a wall where you won't ever see it, and show up as a puddle in the basement. You won't know where that water came from and figuring it out will drive you crazy.

Before we reroofed the house, we also had to rebuild the furnace chimney; the previous owners had neglected to have a chimney cap installed and rain corroded away the inside. That was like two thousand bucks. Time has mercifully softened some of those memories.

Back to the basement. The concrete splashes went a long, long way to keeping routine rain out of the foundation. Occasionally, an especially strong downpour would force a ribbon of water to seep in where the wall met the floor. Even the torrential rains from Hurricane Ivan did not push as much water into the basement as the first awful incident, although it tried.

ATTACKING THE PROBLEM FROM OUTSIDE

But the basement wasn't completely dry. There were two issues to deal with: one inside and one outside. Outside, most of our water problems were coming from the landing by the front door. They had built the sidewalk to slope towards the foundation. If the previous owners had told the builder, "You know, we think our house needs water in the basement," they could not have designed a better system. In addition, the lawn in front of the living room window *also* sloped towards the foundation.

We could not afford to replace the steps and landing right away, so we caulked the crack between the sidewalk and the foundation. This helped, particularly with water that had been infiltrating under the front steps.

Then we changed the landscaping by the front sidewalk by lining each side with dry creek beds. Dear Husband dug a ditch about a foot wide, about eight inches deep at the house end and 18 inches at the street end. This encouraged the water to flow away from the house. He filled these ditches with coarse gravel and topped them with slabs of Pennsylvania bluestone from the building project going on across the street. The contractor was happy to see us cart away his disposal problem. We also replaced the lawn underneath the picture window with flowerbeds, again resculpted to slope away from the foundation.

The dry creeks look decorative, and they work pretty well. Each one is about forty feet long. They eliminated more of the seepage. After they were finished, we only got seepage from rain that ran down the sidewalk and pooled against the foundation, and it took a very heavy, all-day rain for that to happen.

At the other end of the house, the driveway sent water into that corner of the foundation joining water from the downspout. Adding a splash helped there, especially after we added a corrugated vinyl tube to move the water further away from the basement. This did not do anything about the runoff coming from the driveway. To combat this, I dug out a semicircle by the driveway edge, sloped away from the house, and filled it with white marble chips. This diverted water away from the house *and* made it easier to walk up the driveway to the side-gate.

None of the slopes that I am describing can be seen, as they are all underground and filled with gravel. From the surface, they look level.

In that same corner, next to the driveway I dug a rain garden, a deeply dug bed in the hope that water-happy plants could thrive. I originally planted it with a variety of plants, all of which were unhappy. Then my friend and neighbor Lisa gave me ferns, and they took off. The ferns *love* being here, and they soak up amazing amounts of water.

Finally, DH built a sidewalk connecting the driveway to the sidewalk leading to the front door. He dug a ditch twenty-six feet long, forty inches wide, and about a foot deep. This ditch runs parallel to the house and is sloped towards the street. It also slopes from the driveway towards the existing sidewalk where it meets the dry creek. The pavers lay on a thick bed of sand, which helps encourage drainage. The rain garden of ferns drains under this sidewalk and into the flowerbed on the other side.

The final job in the front yard was to improve the rest of the soil's drainage. The goal is to always put rainwater where it belongs: in your soil and not your basement. We have a strip of grass on one side of the existing sidewalk. The rest of the front yard consists of the driveway, two sidewalks, and flowerbeds. The beds are heavily mulched and, over time, the soil has changed its composition from impermeable clay to deep, absorbent, sponge-like topsoil. I go into detail about this process in the soil-building chapter.

To solve these problems, we didn't rely on instruction books. They didn't exist, or we couldn't find them. Instead, we used our simple knowledge about water — it's wet and likes to run downhill —

to create solutions.

Take our backyard. There was a steep slope along the side of the yard that created a stumbling threat as you reached the side-gate. To solve this as well as any potential drainage issues where the slope met the house, DH built a short wall running from the corner into the yard. He dug a ditch several feet deep, several feet wide, and about thirteen feet long. He filled the ditch with more stone from the construction site across the street. He built a dry-stone wall to terrace the slope, and added steps to get up and down. We now have a wall on the sidewalk side that is the same height (three feet) as the ground on the garden side. This drains like a champ, channeling water from the back of the house deep underground and well away from the foundation.

Doing this work took years. We did it ourselves, and spent serious money on concrete splashes, lots and lots of coarse gravel, a ton of sand, and sidewalk pavers. The dry creeks, the concrete splashes, the new sidewalk, the rain garden, the flowerbeds and improved soil work in concert to move the rainwater away from the house and put it into the soil. Removing any one element would make the remaining ones less functional.

THE MAGIC OF DRYLOK

The inside of the basement was the site of another set of projects, taking years, and we still aren't finished.

The worst part of the basement was the inside corner, right by the sloped sidewalk landing on the outside. The hot-water tank is here, along with the main sewage line that sends waste to the street connection. This, along with the wall running parallel to the street behind the washer, dryer, and freezer, is where we got most of the seepage. The wall behind the appliances was not nearly as bad as the wall behind the hot-water tank. Its seepage mostly came in where the wall met the floor.

But the area near the hot-water tank was ground zero. There was so much moisture present that about 90% of the paint had flaked off the concrete-block wall. The bare wall was pitted from moisture damage. Elsewhere, we only have patches of flaking paint and efflorescence, generally at floor level.

We scraped, brushed, and swept down these walls, removed the remaining paint, then repainted with a magic, miracle product called

Drylok. This is paint embedded with ingredients that give it a thick, pudding-y consistency. It is designed to fill the cracks and crevices and bond with the surface of unpainted concrete blocks to create a nearly impenetrable seal.

Drylok is made for dry surfaces, but if water is coming through the wall *at this very minute,* there is a product called Fast-Plug that can seal the holes and gaps. We'll tell you how we know that later.

Drylok has a soap-and-water cleanup. It can be applied even when the concrete block walls are damp. It seals and rebuilds the concrete block, keeping out condensation and seepage. Best of all, it comes in a matte white finish which brightens the basement and makes it look less like a cave.

Drylok cannot hold back a flood, but it can slow it down considerably. It is also expensive. It spreads like pudding, so a gallon doesn't go very far, but it is far cheaper than replacing the foundation wall. Buy it in the five-gallon containers and save a few bucks over the gallon cans.

The paint can comes with directions on how to prepare the walls. If there are efflorescence deposits on the walls, you'll need to get a chemical to clean them first (Drylok won't stick to it).

Drylok works when it is painted on raw concrete block, so take a wire brush and get as much paint off as you can. If the paint is already flaking, this is bad and good news. Bad because it was caused by moisture damage and good because the wire brush will scour most of it off. Just sweep down the remaining bits and you are good to go.

Be meticulous about your prep work and Drylok can work miracles for you. It certainly did for us. DH painted the walls from the outside corner below the front door to the workshop window. The Drylok worked so well that during especially heavy rains, the water that seeped down the foundation wall couldn't enter the basement until it reached a place where there was no Drylok.

Drylok also helped lower the basement's humidity. When we moved in, we had to run the dehumidifier continuously in the summer. After Drylok-ing, the dehumidifier would turn itself off when it reached its set point. It had never done this before. We gradually dried out years of accumulated moisture.

THE RETURN OF THE SEEPAGE

After all this work was done, we thought our water problems

were solved. Like near the end of the horror movie, when the kids think they killed the masked guy who had sliced 'n' diced their friends. Yeah, like that.

Then a tremendous storm came through, accompanied by high winds that slammed water against the front of the house. Down in the basement, there were rows of tiny holes in the concrete block; decades back the exterminator had drilled them to treat a termite infestation, and they were plugged when he was finished.

Apparently, he had used caulk. Because when we checked on the basement, we found several of these holes had opened. Water was leaking in. The force was so strong that these plugs popped out followed by arcs of water. As we watched, horrified, two more came out. *Pop! Pop!* It was a pretty fountain effect, and we would have enjoyed it except we were busy scavenging for buckets to stop the basement from getting flooded (again).

Later, once our personal fountain show shut down, and we were mopping up, we figured that we still did not get as much water infiltration as we had during the first storm. All our work in the basement and the front yard *was* having an effect.

The next day, DH sealed the holes with Fast-Plug. Since he was already sweaty and dirty, he also ran a line of sealant where the wall met the floor, as far as he could reach. No water has tried to come in there since.

And, yet, the worst was still to come. The villainous Leak Monster had been defeated, but not slain.

Meanwhile, we were breathing easy and looking forward to doing preventative maintenance. We want to Drylok the rest of the basement. The remaining walls are painted and the paint is adhering, except behind the oil tank. The old damage caused the paint to flake off but it is not going to be easy to get some skinny, limber person (Hi Younger Son!) to wiggle back there, wire brush paint off the bad spots, and then paint the newly exposed concrete. Eventually, it will happen.

I also want to strip the basement bare and carefully check each wall, from top to bottom, for damage. This would also let us repaint the walls in ultra-high-gloss white enamel, which would make the space lighter and brighter.

The other job we did in the basement was preventative. The previous owners had built a little room outside the back basement wall.

You reached it via the most termite-eaten, horrible wooden door you can imagine, poorly concealing a four-foot by six-foot room floored with sand.

This space was probably used as a root cellar, but to us, it looked like a dungeon. It was filthy, damp, damp, damp, and had neither lighting nor shelves. It *did* have a two-gallon bucket to collect water leaking from the concrete ceiling, on top of which the previous owners had planted eight-foot cedars. The roots of the cedars were guaranteed to break up the concrete ceiling and indeed were doing just that. There was no water damage in this corner, but you could see it coming.

I was not going to live with this. We called Jake the Contractor. He and his crew removed the termite-riddled door (all old damage, thank the Lord), rebuilt and waterproofed the concrete-block foundation, installed a window that lights up that corner, and on the outside, knocked the concrete roof into the hole. The hole was filled with gravel, topped with soil and the area is now home to a set of productive raised beds. Inside, I painted the new, raw concrete block with more Drylok, the seams were sealed, and the floor painted. This corner is now clean, dry storage lit by daylight, with no water seepage problem. The water monster had been beaten.

Or so we thought. There was still one last terrible discovery to make.

STICKING THE LANDING

We had started the last job: leveling the front sidewalk and landing. We rarely saw water in the basement, just some seepage when a hurricane blew over. Most people would have lived with it, but water is a powerful force. It can wear down rock given enough time. The Grand Canyon, for example. We intended to stay in this house for the rest of our lives, and we wanted this problem fixed for good.

Time to call Jake the Contractor; he returned with his crew. They left the porch steps alone, but ripped out the old concrete pad at the foot, along with about twenty feet of sidewalk. When the rubble was removed, they dug. Then they dug a little deeper.

One of the crew called us outside to show us "something you should see." Cue the sinister music. We found them standing around the hole, shaking their heads in disbelief.

"Here's why you were getting so much water in your basement," one of them said. They had dug deep enough to uncover the sewage main that runs from the house to the street. Every house has one. All your waste water — from sinks, toilets, bathtubs, showers, dishwasher and washing machine — feed into this line. It's a big pipe, easily eight inches in diameter or more.

In the basement, the pipe enters the foundation through the middle of a concrete block. Someone had taken a hammer to make the hole, ran the pipe through, and then filled in the gaps, leaving a relatively smooth and unbroken surface.

Not so outside. There, the pipe rested on the concrete block wall, but there was a gap all around it big enough to stick in your fist. The hole in our foundation wall was almost 16 inches across and about as high. No wonder we had a water problem! Concrete block is *hollow*! All the water that ran down the outside of the foundation wall — from the downspout six feet away, and down the sidewalk to pool right above it — ran down the outside of the wall, then inside it, and *filled up the air spaces*! It was like having a concrete-block aquarium until it slowly seeped into the ground, eroding the wall, its humidity forcing the paint to peel.

It is hard to believe that the wall hadn't caved in already. Pure dumb luck on the part of the previous homeowners is all I can say. And if they had installed the damn $10 concrete splashes like any sane homeowner would, they would not have gotten most of the damage that they did get. There would still have been damage, no question, but nothing like what we had.

After they recovered from the shock, the crew closed the gaping hole correctly around the sewage line, waterproofed everything they could reach, and re-poured the concrete slab, this time sloped away from the foundation.

It still bugs me that we did not fix the reverse slope first, but after we had stopped 95% of the water infiltration, it seemed less important to replace the slab than to do all the other rehab projects that had to be done. On the other hand, who would have ever believed that a homebuilder would deliberately *leave a !%@#$#% hole in the foundation wall*?

The acid test of all our work came about a year later. Tropical Storm Lee arrived in Hershey and dumped about a foot of rain in one day. It was a storm of the millennium. This storm topped all our previous storms, even Hurricane Agnes in 1972, which flooded nearby

Harrisburg, and portions of Dauphin County, and remains *the* standard by which every storm is measured in the midstate.

For the first time since we moved here, we saw low-lying sections of Hershey under water. The schools were evacuated and remained closed for several days. Basements were flooded to above their first floor. The Penn Hotel and Sports Bar, down the hill from our house, had not just its basement full of water, but also the first floor. The owners and customers evacuated to the second floor, then anxiously watched to see if the flood would follow them. The houses near it suffered damage from being under nearly twenty feet of water.

At our house, we got a few gallons of water. Despite damage to the foundation wall as a result of fifty-five years of water infiltration, everything we did — concrete splashes, dry creeks, soil improvement, new roof and gutters, plugging all the leaks, plus Drylok — limited the damage from the worst storm to ever pass over Hershey. We got a few gallons of water, easily mopped up with a sponge mop, a bucket, and some towels.

If we had not done any of this work, we would have had to regularly replace our supplies, plus everything else that would be ruined by a flood. The concrete splashes, by themselves, stopped the majority of our water damage, and every correction and repair after that decreased the percentage. Other than filling in the dungeon, replacing the concrete landing, and reroofing the house, we did all the work ourselves.

GIVE YOUR HOUSE A CHECKUP

You can do this too, and if you have *any* water problems, you should get started today. **DO NOT WAIT.**

Walk around your house and make sure all of your downspouts work, the gutters are clean and free flowing (an annual job for a sullen teenager on a ladder) and there's a concrete splash at every downspout. This will solve most of your day-to-day issues.

The key is to always, always, always make the land slope away from your house. Water wants to run downhill, and the correctly angled slope will encourage it to do so.

Inside, plug all the holes, including the tiny ones, and if you have raw concrete walls, Drylok the place from top to bottom.

Fixing your basement's moisture problems will let you use your basement for its intended purpose: storage of your preps. Make it the source of your salvation, not the cause of your problems.

28

Grocery Shopping and Food Storage

Your Ideal Grocery Store – Learning How to Cook – The Recipe For Beating the House – Keeping a Price Book – Relying On the Pantry Principle – The Truth Behind Food Expiration – Basic Grocery Shopping – A Typical Shopping Week – The Devil In the Small Print – Playing the Showcase Game – Win Friends at the Service Desk – Getting Gas – Jedi-Master Shopping – Protecting Yourself – A Place For Your Food – Kitchen Cabinets – A Fresh Look For the Pantry — Rethinking Space

IMPROVING YOUR GROCERY SHOPPING SKILLS is much easier than learning how to grow your food. Good shopping skills give you a tax-free raise; money you can spend other than at the grocery store. You are taxed on what you earn, not on what you do not spend. How you shop demonstrates what matters to you.

I am a firm believer in shopping locally. So, as a dedicated energy saver, conservationist, and locavore, I source all our food from within a ten-mile radius. In our case, I use the Giant, 1½ miles away.

I joke, but for a serious purpose. We moved to Hershey in part because I can walk to my bank, drugstore, office supply store, the post office, etc. This saves me money, gets me out in my community, and I always need the exercise. Plus, in an emergency, I know I can drag groceries or other items home in a kid's wagon instead of my car.

There are people who object that you cannot be a locavore — who gets all their food from within a hundred miles — if you are using a supermarket. Meeting this purity test shows your superior status to lesser mortals. To them, you should grow your food in your huge vegetable garden or get everything from properly documented sources via the local farmer's market. There is also Community Supported Agriculture (CSA) in which local farms deliver their produce weekly to a nearby pickup point. (If you're interested, ask at the local farmer's market or look online for one in your area.)

What I find amusing about the locavore movement is that it puts old wine in new, environmentally safe, bioerodable, PCR plastic bottles.

Before the Industrial Revolution, we all were locavores. We ate well during the summer and fall, and preserved the rest of the harvest for the winter. Animals were born in the spring and some were slaughtered in the fall so you had meat all winter. If you knew how, you preserved your milk by making it into hard cheese. In January, we ate the preserved food, root cellar fare such as rutabagas, potatoes, and turnips, cabbages that were fermented into kimchi and sauerkraut, dried beans, and winter squashes. In the winter, chickens don't lay as much so we could not depend on eggs.

This is why early spring is known in many cultures as the starving time, the thin time. This is true for wildlife as well as people. There just isn't that much left to eat.

This was a common way to live. You had to be rich to not be hungry in early spring.

Traditionally, the foods that did get transported long distances were of high value and unlikely to decay such as tea leaves, spices, and coffee beans, or their huge quantities made them cost-effective to ship such as grains and dried legumes.

Notice that there are no strawberries in January on this list. This was a limited, dull diet. By the time spring rolled around, the peasants were desperate for fresh greens to keep their teeth in. Hence, the popularity of traditional spring tonics made from dandelion leaves. This gave you a shot of vitamin C and warded off scurvy.

We don't have this problem. In the First World, we eat better than the wealthiest Roman emperors did. Strawberries in January. Raspberries in February. Delicate spring greens in August. Apples in May. Today's supermarkets are almost completely divorced from the seasons, something you quickly discover when you grow your own vegetables.

To be a grow-all-your-own-food locavore takes a lot of work, and

I am happy I can choose what I want to do: growing supplemental vegetables and fruit, and buying and cooking with the seasons. I love my refrigerator and freezer. I don't have to worry about spoilage. I love my fully stocked pantry without having to spend hours canning, drying, fermenting, and pickling. These are great privileges, and I appreciate them.

There are many ways to better utilize the wonderful resource that is an American grocery store.

YOUR IDEAL GROCERY STORE

The first step is to choose your store. There are two Giants within five miles of my home. The larger, newer, fancier one is further away. It also has the gas pumps where I buy discounted gas. Do I shop there on a biweekly basis? I do not, yet many of my neighbors do.

I only go to the fancy Giant when I need to redeem my gas points. Those extra three-and-a-half miles one way translates into seven extra miles per trip plus the additional travel time. On a single-trip basis, that isn't much at all. But over a year, at two trips per week, that is 728 miles that I don't put on my car and 728 miles in gas I don't burn.

Since I go to the fancier Giant to redeem my gas points every few weeks, and I do my regular shopping while I am there, we will subtract that mileage and say that I save 600 miles per year by shopping at the closer store. There is also the time I don't spend driving that I put to other uses.

While there are several grocery stores within five miles of my house, I like the Giant best for price, selection, convenience, and the gas points. I spent much time researching my options, using my price book – more on that later – and reading the ads carefully before settling on Giant.

If I wanted to splurge, I could go all the way across the river to the Wegmans. This is a really fancy, high-end grocery store. When they opened near Mechanicsburg, several of my neighbors regularly made the twenty-mile pilgrimage (forty miles roundtrip plus time) to shop there.

I made the trip once, when I wasn't nearly as enlightened (and cheap) as I am now. It's a very nice supermarket, but the prices seemed a little higher, and it was certainly farther away. It was not worth the effort, so I never returned. Even if the Wegmans has some magical product that no one else in the area carried, I would rather live without it.

We have a Sam's Club within a seven-mile radius plus the Walmart. I used to have a Sam's Club card, but careful shopping and the pantry principle — more on that later — worked just as well and meant I spent less money, less gas, and less time. Sam's Club lures you into spending far more money than you planned on. It can have wonderful deals but if you spend more money than you budgeted and you purchase wonderful items you didn't know you wanted until you saw them, you still lose. Same with Costco; there is one twenty miles away so it is even less worth my time and gas money. (We did go there once, to buy a canopy so that Peschel Press could sell books at the local arts festivals.)

This lesson on avoiding impulse purchases was driven home by an anecdote I remember from a book on how to save on your grocery bills. I don't remember the title or the author but I sure remember her story. The author had broken her leg and had to order her groceries from the most expensive grocer in town, the kind that wrapped each piece of fruit in tissue paper. She had no choice – it was the only one that delivered – and she still spent less than she did at the cheaper supermarket.

How could this be? Because the fancy grocer only sent what she ordered. It did not add to her list those wonderful, must-have products that call to us when we cruise the aisles. This was my experience in Sam's Club and Wegmans. I see products I don't need and are not on the list, but I want them, and I buy them.

I do not buy groceries at Walmart. This is a personal choice. Walmart can be cheaper than Giant, enough to possibly pay for the extra gas and time. I do *not* earn gas points at Walmart so the discounted gas available at Giant may still make up the cost difference.

However, I do not like what Walmart does to local communities. I do not like what it does to local businesses, I do not like how Walmart treats its employees, and I really don't like how they handle perishable foods. Since I have good alternatives, I choose not to give my money to Walmart.

If I had to routinely walk to buy groceries, I would use Karns or Pronio's as they are within a mile of my house. That extra distance to Giant adds up when you are pulling a wagon full of groceries in August. Both stores are smaller than Giant. Pronio's is a stand-alone, locally owned operation. Karns is a small midstate chain. Giant is a regional chain, headquartered within twenty miles of my house so it is sort of locally owned and operated.

The deciding issue for which grocery store to chose, *if I had to walk each time*, would be the gas points. You cannot grow gasoline and biofuel has its own sets of problems. If we *had* to have the gas for a regular commute to work, then Giant would win for the gas points, and I would make the hike pulling a wagon or use a bike with panniers. If we were car-free, then I would shop Karns or Pronio's because of the distance and cherry-pick at Giant for products I could not get otherwise.

There is also a Weis grocery store within the one-mile radius. Every time I went there, the floor needed to be mopped and the shelves straightened. It did not strike me as being kept clean or well-maintained and that made me suspicious of their handling of perishable items. This is not to say that the chain is a poor choice; just that the local branch is not for me. I have not been inside this store in years so it could have changed for the better.

LEARNING HOW TO COOK

The second part of better grocery shopping is deciding what you need to cook your family's meals. If most of your meals are from restaurants and take-out, then your family will probably accept brand-name frozen dinners, salad-in-a-bag, and a Sara Lee cheesecake, and it will cost you less per meal. Your time counts here, too. It's faster to microwave a frozen dinner than to drive to Wendy's and back.

If you want to save more, then you need basic cooking skills. Almost *anything* you cook at home will cost less than the comparable item from a store. It's easy to fall into the trap that take-out food and restaurant dollars don't count in your food budget. They do. If you are eating it, then it is part of your food budget.

While I am on the subject of restaurant meals, if you're dining and can't eat it all, *take it home and eat it for lunch the next day*. Huge quantities of partially eaten restaurant meals are thrown out every day. You wanted this meal enough to leave home, order, and pay for it. It isn't shameful or poor to save leftovers. What matters more to you? The opinion of a waitress who already thinks you are rich and wasteful? Or saving a little money so you can pay off debt and build your emergency fund?

You will never minimize your food budget if you don't cook. Paying someone else to do the prep work always costs more. Take potatoes. Regular, whole potatoes can cost as little as 40¢ a pound. Instead of spending much more for microwave-ready baking potatoes, scrub a potato, prick the skin with a fork and microwave it for five minutes. If it isn't done to your liking, nuke it a few minutes more. There. You just saved money.

I'll go into a lot more detail in the chapter on cooking.

THE RECIPE FOR BEATING THE HOUSE

Whether or not you do most of the cooking, you can still save significant money at the grocery store over what you are spending now. It comes down to knowing where the high-priced traps are laid.

This is not a cynical belief, but a practical one: Grocery stores are in business to make money. Their profit margins are razor thin. They are in a highly competitive category, facing competition from rival stores, food vendors, and restaurants. Grocery stores sell to the sharp customers, but they make their real money on shoppers who don't pay attention, who shop with their stomachs, and who shop on autopilot, except when they see something shiny and new.

They are so good at separating customers from their money that they could give Las Vegas casinos a lesson or two.

Products of intense research, supermarkets are designed to encourage you to spend. This is why you have to walk through the entire store to get staples like a loaf of bread and a gallon of milk. This is why the floral department (pretty and colorful), the fresh bakery (smells so good), and the produce department (nutritious and colorful) are near the entrance, forcing you to walk through them on your way to the milk and bread. This is why the checkout lanes are narrow and lined with the most expensive impulse items. Who can resist celebrity magazines and candy bars? It is the last chance the grocery has to siphon more money while you wait for the shopper in front of you to finish up.

So, think of grocery shopping as a challenge. You are betting that your skills can beat the house at its own game. If you are a poor shopper now, you could cut your grocery bill in half. If you are better than average, it won't be as much of a drop, but you'll still spend less. No matter what, the money you save is like getting a tax-free raise.

Here's how to do it.

Grocery Shopping and Food Storage

Start with a list. What foods do you need, and what have you run out of? What do you regularly use, and what do you cook regularly? If you never do another thing, making a shopping list that reflects what you cook and eat and what you have used up — *and sticking to it* — will save you money.

Do not walk through a grocery store and toss random products into your cart. *Oh, that looks good. That might be fun to try. I'll bet everyone will eat that.* This leads to food waste as your purchases don't get used up and they rot or no one will eat so it gets thrown away. Trashing food is like trashing money. If you compost your food waste or feed it to animals, it isn't as much of a waste, but still, why put expensive fancy produce in your compost bin when it is just as happy with carrot peelings?

Suggestion: Keep a running list on the refrigerator so as items run out, they can be added to it. You may be able to train family members to do this; I never could. Having a complete list means that you don't need to go to the supermarket every day. Unless you are extremely disciplined, daily exposure to the come-ons in the grocery store is like asking to have the cash vacuumed out of your wallet. Keeping a list means fewer trips to the store.

I shop twice a week: my big trip on Tuesday and a run on Saturday for milk, cream, and fruit for Sunday breakfast. My family is big on drinking milk, as well as using cream for our daily pot of coffee, hence the second trip. Otherwise, I keep my list for the second trip as small as possible.

If I needed to, I could train the family to drink reconstituted dry milk instead of fresh and use dry milk in our coffee instead of cream. Then, I could store a year's worth of dry milk and never run out. There are people who do this successfully, and they save money, too. We are not that dedicated.

So, shop with a list and go once a week for your main trip. Only go more often if you have to, or if you have run out of a critical item like cat food.

If you have a very large refrigerator and pantry, you may be able to cut your grocery trips to every other week. It means that you don't take advantage of each week's loss leaders, but that may not matter if you spend less overall.

If you are forced to make that emergency trip for cat food (rather than serve your cats expensive canned tuna), then make yourself buy *only* the item you need. Walk into the store, and do *not* get a buggy, not even a small basket. That'll only encourage you to buy stuff you don't need. If you have to hand-carry what you need, you buy less.

Shopping with a list requires organizational skills. You have to know what you use, keep track of it, know what's about to expire in your cupboards, and match them up with the sales. And, of course, you have to remember to bring the list with you.

Knowing what you have and routinely use will let you recognize a real deal when you spot one. If the store is discontinuing Alpo dog food at 50% off and you have a dog that regularly eats it, this impulse purchase can save you money.

KEEPING A PRICE BOOK

This leads us to the price book. Amy Dacyczyn of *The Tightwad Gazette* showed me how to make one. You get a small notebook, and you write down the products you regularly buy. Add to that list the usual prices charged for them. Watch for sales on these items and write down those prices.

Over time, you will get a feel for when a sale price is really a good deal or not. If the price is as low as she'll go, based on your records, then buy a lot of that item.

I used my price book for years. It was not hugely detailed. I didn't spell out the price for each brand and size of cereal or canned fruit. I just marked down the highest price I was willing to pay. If a large box of Raisin Bran — no matter the brand — could be purchased for less than $2, I bought it. Since I own a freezer (highly, highly recommended), I buy my brands of bread only when they are buy one, get one free. Then I buy enough to last for months.

As my cooking skills improved, and I learned how to make products like salad dressing and pasta sauce from scratch, I stopped buying them. I no longer needed to keep track of those prices. I finally retired my price book after over a decade of use when I could rely on my memory to recognize a good price when I saw it.

RELYING ON THE PANTRY PRINCIPLE

Buying on price leads directly to the next major way to save money: the pantry principle. I learned this method from *Cut Your Grocery Bills in Half* by Barbara Salsbury (1982). Salsbury updated her book in 2005 and renamed it *Beating the High Cost of Eating: The Essential*

Guide to Supermarket Survival.

The books reflect their times. Refunding was a lot bigger in 1982 so that edition covers it thoroughly. The worksheets are different too, and the earlier version has an index the revised edition lacks. Read them via interlibrary loan before buying. Both are well worth your time.

What a happy day when I found the 1982 version in the local library twenty-some years ago! The basic idea is that when an item you use regularly goes on sale, buy enough to last your family until the next super sale. If your brand of tuna goes on sale routinely at 99¢ a can, then never buy it at $1.19 a can. If you find a super sale at 79¢ a can, buy much, much more.

If you are using a price book and paying attention to the weekly sales flier from your supermarket, you will quickly learn that the grocery industry rotates what goes on sale regularly. Some items go on sale every other week, some every other month, and others only two or three times a year. Some items get a super sale twice a year, others never do. Becoming familiar with your store's sales pattern over the years will pay back big bucks.

The Pantry Principle stresses eating and cooking only from your pantry and the weekly loss leaders at the supermarket. You only buy on sale and never, ever pay full price. A well-stocked pantry means that if the car falls apart, you have money to throw at the problem. You don't go grocery shopping that week and divert the food dollars to the emergency instead.

THE TRUTH BEHIND FOOD EXPIRATION

Let's talk about food expiration dates. While it is very nice to have them, they can also lead you to throw out perfectly usable food. There is no national standard for manufacturers; they simply make the best guess based on their experience (and maybe their last quarter's profits).

Canned goods can last for decades past their expiration dates. This is also true of food in glass jars like pasta sauce and can be true for paper boxes of dried noodles. How you store your food matters far more than what the date says. Store your food on ventilated shelves in a cool, dark place that is dry and pest-free, and it will last well beyond its expiration date. There may be a loss of vitamins and a poorer appearance, but it will not be unsafe.

Leaving food items where it is damp or in garages where the temperature swings wildly or where bugs and rodents can get at them will make those boxes of spaghetti turn on you much earlier than the date on the label would indicate.

For example, in 2015 I made a batch of sugar cookies from a mix given to me by a friend. The mix had expired in May 2009. The box was sealed and the mix itself was inside a sealed foil bag. It looked fine, no mold or weevils, it smelled fine, it mixed up fine, it baked fine, and the cookies tasted fine, other than the slightly off-chemical taste I notice in packaged cookie mixes.

The correct way to deal with food expiration dates is to rotate your stock. Follow the slogan used in the food industry: FIFO. First in, first out. This is where being organized pays dividends. When you shelve your purchases, label the products with the expiration date. A Sharpie works best; pencil isn't dark enough and pens don't always write on the can's slick paper. Grease pencils work, too. We leave a Sharpie on the laundry table where we sort food for storage. It saves having to hunt up a new one each week.

When you are scanning your shelves, the date *you* write in big letters is much easier to read than the tiny, hidden-away print the manufacturer provided. Put the newest items to the back of the shelf and move the oldest ones to the front. Use the oldest ones first.

The second tip for handling food that expires is learning how fast you use something up. If your family eats three cans of tuna a week, you have a good idea how much tuna you want on hand. If the tuna goes on sale routinely at 99¢ the first week of every month, buy fifteen cans. That gives you three cans a week for five weeks, tiding you over comfortably until the next sale. When you buy more sale-priced tuna, move the newer cans to the back and use the oldest cans first.

If tuna goes on a super sale of 79¢ a can, which you learn it does every six months according to your price book, then you need to decide how many cans you need to carry you over to the next super sale. This would be three cans times four weeks times six months or seventy-two cans of tuna plus a few extra for margin.

When you buy seventy-two cans of tuna at once, it is worth going through the cans at the store looking for the furthest-away expiration dates. Do not assume the store rotates its products as they are supposed to. Grocery store stockers are quite likely to put the newest cans in front and push the older cans to the back. It is far easier to do this than emptying out the shelf, checking each can, and then arranging them by date. *You* have to check the dates to be sure.

In fact, if you are stocking a pantry, you should *always* check the expiration dates. I sometimes run across expired items on the store shelf. They aren't bad but because I am going to store them at home for a long time, I want to get as long of a time window as I can. Expired cans or jars should be passed along to a store clerk; do not leave them on the shelf for a more careless shopper to pick up.

I check the expiration dates on everything that I plan on storing for any length of time and *always* on perishables like cheese, eggs, and dairy products. Cheese, by the way, can have a surprisingly lengthy life span, when unopened, allowing you to stock up at a good sale. The exception is shredded cheese; it will turn on you far faster than brick cheese. For storage purposes, it is better to buy bricks than already shredded. It lasts longer and is sometimes cheaper per pound. Keep eggs in their carton in the coolest part of the fridge to keep them happier.

The grocery industry wants you to throw away expired food, not eat it. They make more money when you do this. They also have to err on the side of caution; they don't know if you are going to be storing your cans of corn in the trunk of your car, in the crawlspace under your house, or in that unheated, leaky, bug-infested toolshed. They choose a worst-case scenario to accommodate idiots. If you aren't an idiot, and use the best food storage procedures, then don't worry too much about expiration dates.

BASIC GROCERY SHOPPING

No reputable supermarket deliberately cheats its customers. Their policies are plain, their sales are promoted, and the prices are marked on every shelf for every item. After that, it is up to you, the consumer, to make the most of the situation. Let's look into how we can best do that.

First, ask at your supermarket for their policy regarding sales, coupons, rain checks, and what they do if they overcharge you for an item. They should have handouts for you to take home and study. This information may also be available on your grocery store's website. Do not rely on the cashiers or stockers for this information. The manager may know, as part of her job, but what counts is what is written down or published online.

Buy the Sunday newspaper, where every week the grocery stores in your area advertise that week's best buys. Most, but not all of them, will advertise in the biggest regional paper. If you do not see weekly ads for the supermarket you like best, ask at the service desk where they do advertise. For example, Karns rarely puts its entire week's worth of ads in our local paper. Instead, they run spot ads of their very best sales in the *Sunday Patriot-News* and *The Sun*, our local weekly. To get their full ad, you have to go to the store or get the *Community Courier*, a freebie weekly newspaper.

Study the circulars at home, with your list and coupon box, before setting foot in the store. This quiet study period will let you become familiar with your store's ads.

First, look for the week's super sales. These items are usually prominently displayed on the front page of the multi-page flier. Study the sales to find the best prices, and then plan your menus around them. This is assuming that you plan menus so you never walk into the kitchen cold and make dinner on the fly.

Menu planning is a standard tactic to make cooking meals more straightforward and less haphazard. I'll be honest. I don't plan menus a week in advance. I generally decide the night before what I am cooking the next day so I can take the meat out of the freezer. I'm a good cook, I rarely use recipes, and I am used to looking over what needs to be used up and making do. I have a fully stocked pantry, an array of cookware, and a range of seasonings, which make this easier for me.

To do this successfully, you need to be able to walk into a kitchen cold and produce a meal for five using only what is on hand. And then those five people have to eat it without carrying on. This demands a high skill level. If you aren't that good a cook, making up basic menus in advance may work better for you. Note that my advice contradicts what home economists have long taught. *Never* plan a week's worth of menus first and then attempt to match up what you want to cook with the week's sales. If you want to cut your grocery bill, then let the sale of the week dictate the menus you will be cooking.

So study the ads to figure out what you want to stock up on and eat that week. It will take time but think of it this way: If it takes me two hours (which is generous) to go through the ads and coupon inserts and match them up with my list and my needs, then I can easily

Grocery Shopping and Food Storage

save more than $20. This is an hourly rate of $10 an hour, tax-free. That is worth my time.

A TYPICAL SHOPPING WEEK

It takes time to become familiar with a grocery ad, so let's look at a circular from Giant (prices as of January 2015) and see the typical grocery store traps. These traps reward the careful shopper (that's me) by penalizing the careless, random shopper (not you, at least not anymore).

> **GET TO KNOW YOUR CASHIER**
>
> I try to choose the same cashier on each visit — Hi Evelyn! — and I always talk to her. It fits me into the community and the cashier is more likely to chat with me about store policy, giving me heads-up on changes, and how other customers do not seem to see the sale staring at them.

For example, every time you don't pick up both items of a Buy One Get One Free pair (or BOGOF) you subsidize my shopping trip. Cashiers have told me people do this a lot.

At the top of the circular is a "Pack Your Pantry" banner promoting Giant's best buys for the week. The first item is Campbell's tomato or chicken noodle soup at 50¢ a can. *But*, the ad says in small type, you must buy ten of them – and *only* ten – to get the sale price. Additional or lesser quantities will ring up at 80¢ a can. Buy nine cans, you'll pay $7.20. Add one more can, and the total price drops to $5.

That is correct: it will cost you $2.20 *less* to buy ten cans rather than nine. If you buy a dozen cans, you will pay $5 plus an additional $1.60 for the two spares, or $6.60! This is not as good a bargain as just ten cans but still less than buying nine. You have to buy thirteen cans for the purchase price to cost *more* than buying nine cans. This is an easy mistake to make.

If you regularly use two cans of Campbell's soup a week, you are best off buying ten and storing most of them to gradually use up over the next few weeks. This is the Pantry Principle in action and demonstrates how much you can save by buying ahead. This also lets you stockpile food until you end up with several weeks worth at all times.

Next, on the same page, Kellogg's cereal is on sale at $1.49 a box. This time, you must buy four boxes to get this special price. As with the Campbell's soup, smaller or larger quantities raise the price per box to $2.50 each. I had two manufacturer's coupons that took $1 off two boxes. Buying four boxes of Raisin Bran at $1.49 each cost $5.96. Applying the two coupons cut my total to $3.96, or 99¢ a box.

This is how I routinely spend $150 per week on groceries for a family of five. And yes, this includes personal care, paper goods, laundry soap, cleaning products, pet food, and anything else you would normally buy at a grocery store.

I do not do a lot of couponing. Most of them are for processed foods, which I don't often use. I do clip coupons, keeping them in a small index card box, filed by categories including cereal, soups, and meat. I don't obsess over it, but I save enough money with them to make it worth my while.

But what about those super couponers you hear about on the news, the ones who were getting those amazing three buggies of groceries for 10 bucks? I looked into their practices, and a number of them are ethically questionable. They traded coupons over the internet, subscribed to coupon websites, bought coupons on eBay, printed out internet coupons (I tried this, and it wasn't worth my time or paper *at all*), and sometimes stole coupon inserts from newspapers in honor boxes and at the newsstand.

Even if you don't want to keep track of a moderate amount of coupons like I do, you can still save money if you use heavily advertised products. For example, if your family uses Dove shampoo, save their high-value coupons. When a sale on Dove shampoo surfaces in your grocery store circular, apply the manufacturer's coupons and buy as many as you can (the Pantry Principle, remember?). The key is being organized enough to save your coupons in an index card-sized

> **DON'T FORGET THE COUPONS**
>
> A common mistake with this kind of sale is forgetting to use manufacturer's coupons for even greater savings. If you have a coupon for Campbell's chicken noodle or tomato soup for $1 off of eight cans, the cashier will subtract this at the register so you will pay $4 for ten cans of soup, or 40¢ a can. You can buy more cans than the coupon stipulates to meet the store's sale requirements. The manufacturer does not care how many you buy, as long as you meet their requirement for each coupon. If you buy eight cans, you will pay $7.20 minus the dollar coupon for a total price of $6.20. Buying the two extra cans will lower each individual price, plus you still get the dollar off, making you pay $4 as your final price.

box, where you can match them to an item when it is on sale.

This is not complicated once you are used to settling down with the circular each week, but it still seems to be beyond many people. My answer to this is: would you pick up a five-dollar bill in the street? How many five-dollar bills do you see in the street? I routinely save five to ten bucks off my total cost using coupons. I *never* see fives or tens in the gutter. Coupon money is free money and worth my time.

Coupon inserts are the other reason to subscribe to the Sunday newspaper, as this is the easiest way to get them. Other ways include Catalina coupons – they are named for the company that provides them – at the checkout counter, the free magazines Giant regularly puts out containing recipes and coupons, I sometimes get them from my neighbors, and I pick coupons up off the ground in the parking lot. When I am finished with my inserts, I pass them along to my neighbors. I use less than 15% of the coupons I find, but I still save enough money to make it worthwhile.

To learn more about super couponing, I recommend Kathy Spencer's book *For Free: Shopping Secrets for Smart Women Who Love Getting Something for Nothing*. This woman turned couponing and shopping strategies into a fulltime job. There are also plenty of other how-to-use-coupons books at any library. Get a recent one as policies and strategies can change fast. Keep in mind that if you don't use products that are routinely couponed, and you don't put in the time and effort, you will never save the money a coupon queen will.

The most important part about using coupons is that they *only* save you money when they are applied to a product *that you were going to buy anyway*. If you buy a product just to redeem the coupon, then you spent cash that could have gone to something else. Only use coupons for what you use routinely, and always stack them with sales. This gives you the biggest discount for the effort involved.

Even if you don't use coupons, you will always save money if you follow these shopping practices: the price book, the Pantry Principle, shopping and cooking only from sales, sticking to a list, staying away from the grocery store other than once a week or less, and knowing your store's policies. You don't need to buy specific brands for these tactics to work. Store brands go on sale just like name brands. You just have to pay attention.

So let's get back to the circular. Snapple Iced Tea 12-pack is on sale, BOGOF. Is this a good deal? Not to me. First, I would never buy this. It is iced tea. It is bothered water in bottles. The day I cannot make it from scratch for pennies is the day my kids shove me into the nursing home. Products like this can be made at home for far less money. If your tap water is contaminated or tastes bad, it still costs you far less money to make iced tea using bottled water than buying it readymade ever will. Moreover, this is far better for the environment as manufacturing bottles, filling bottles, shipping bottles, and throwing away bottles all have their costs.

But back to the Snapple. When something is BOGOF, that means you get the second item free. It does not mean that you pay 50% off on the first item and 50% off on the second. People seem to believe that BOGOF is equivalent to a half-off sale. It is not. A 50%-off sale means you only have to take one item home. BOGOF only gives you the discount when you throw the second item into the cart.

Do people routinely buy only one half of a BOGOF sale? According to the cashiers, they do. My favorite cashier, Evelyn, has told me that she tells customers to go back and get the second item because it is free and the customer says, "Eeh, too much trouble." Are these shoppers made of money or are they bone lazy and stupid? Either way, they subsidize my shopping.

As I said before, manufacturer's coupons can be used with BOGOF purchases. The mechanics vary from store to store, so this is why you want to know your store's policies. Some places let you redeem only one coupon per pair; others let you attach one coupon per item. If you – God forbid – buy the Snapple BOGOF at, say, $6 for the pair, and you redeem two dollar-off coupons, one for each twelve-pack, your final price is $4 for two 12-packs or 17¢ a bottle. It is still cheaper to make your own iced tea.

Next, we see Giant-brand bacon on sale at three for $10. Since it does not say we *must* buy three packages, the true price is $3.33 per package. This is the price that will ring up per package regardless of whether we buy one, two, three, or ten packages. Grocery stores use this kind of offer to get you to buy more than you might otherwise.

Let me repeat this: Unless stated otherwise, ten for ten dollars does not mean you have to buy ten items to get the sale price. It means a dollar apiece.

Ten items for $10 is a good chance to use coupons that ask you to buy four, five, or six of one thing to get an additional dollar off. Match the sale to the coupon and only buy what you need to redeem the coupon. Unless, of course, you are stocking up because, coupon or not, the sale is great, you use the product regularly, and you would buy as many as you could anyway. Coupon usage will improve the Pantry Principle's cost per item a little, but only if you routinely buy and use the product.

Here is how the bacon at $3.33 can become an even better deal. I have a Giant loyalty card, and they send me coupons in the mail. Lo and behold, the last mailer included a dollar-off coupon for store-brand bacon. My final price for a one-pound package of store-brand bacon, normally $4.00, was $2.33. I was happy with my deal.

THE DEVIL IN THE SMALL PRINT

When you study the sales flier, pay special attention to the tiny print alongside each picture and its description. Sometimes, the store will tell you how much you will save. For the bacon, Giant told me that I would save (in type a little bigger than a period) $4.97 on three packages, or $1.66 per package. That is not a bad savings, about one-third off the original price.

Other times, the savings are miniscule. The next page of the circular lists a 12-pack of Giant-brand soda selling for $2.77. In tiny print, we see a savings of 22¢, less than 10% off. Soda can and does regularly get better sales than this, so if you must buy overpriced sugar water, then wait for a better deal. This is where your price book and recognizing a good sale pays off. When this soda is 40% off, buy plenty, enough to wait it out until the next 40%-off sale.

The only reason for buying canned soda is so you can put one in someone's lunch and keep them from hitting the vending machine for $1.50 sodas. Giant-brand soda at $2.77 for twelve works out to 23¢ a can. If you simply must have soda, buy it at the grocery store and not from a vending machine. Remember, if you consume it, wherever you get it from, it's part of your food budget. Food-like substances from vending machines still count.

Looking further into the flier, we see a product advertised as though it is on sale. On the same page as the soda is Finish Dishwasher Tabs, $5.99 for a 20- to 32-count package. Because it is in the circular, it appears to be on sale. It is not.

At the store, I checked the item, and the regular price is $5.99. The product is not on sale. I should have realized it wasn't on sale because in the ad, there is no Bonus Buy arrow next to the item, and no "save xx cents" in tiny type. Since I have dishwasher soap, I can wait for a real sale.

PLAYING THE SHOWCASE GAME

Lately, Giant has been doing a promotion that rewards you for mixing and matching products from the same manufacturer. For example, if you spend ten dollars (or more) on a listed assortment of products, you will pay the sale price and then receive another $3 off your final price.

To maximize this opportunity, we need to play the showcase game from *The Price Is Right*. We want to spend as close to $10 as possible without going under or too far over. Remember to check the fine print in the ad to see if manufacturer's coupons will be subtracted from the minimum spend. In this case, coupons were not counted.

One of the products is Hamburger Helper, regularly priced at $1.49 a box. The sale price is ten for $10. However, because of this special deal, *if* you spend $10, Giant will take another $3 off at the register, bringing your final price for ten boxes not to $10, but to $7, or 70¢ a box. The tiny print tells us that we save $4.90 if we buy ten boxes, or 49¢ a box. But because of the special promotion, you actually saved $7.90 over the cost of ten boxes.

If you make Hamburger Helper once a week, these ten boxes will last ten weeks and cost 70¢ a week, plus the cost of whatever else you add to it. If you buy one box a week as you use it and pay the full price ($1.49), you will spend $14.90 for the ten boxes. Seven dollars is less than half of $14.90 and your savings can be put to use elsewhere, like the hamburger. So you save $7.90 by buying in advance, and storing the Hamburger Helper in your cupboard as opposed to storing it at Giant on their shelf.

This deal can get better. Since Giant does *not* count manufacturer's coupons when tallying up the $10 cost (i.e., for every dollar coupon you redeem, you have to buy another box to make up the difference), you can use your Hamburger Helper coupons, paying still less. You must always check the fine print carefully as you don't want your coupons to keep you from getting the quantity discount.

It is always worth studying this type of ad to see if the items being promoted are ones you use. You don't want to go too far over the minimum spend, as the savings stop there. Spending twice as much ($20 instead of $10) will not net you another three dollars off. Should you buy more stuff under this deal? Only if your price book says the prices are terrific bargains *without* the additional $3 off.

WIN FRIENDS AT THE SERVICE DESK

When you have a question about what, exactally, is on sale or have trouble interpreting the ad, ask at the service desk. The staff can be quite helpful. They would far rather explain how an ad works in advance than void out the cash register after you bought something because you misinterpreted the sale.

The service desk is also where you get rain checks. Often a store will run a sale so good they will run out of merchandise. Even if you get there too late and the shelf is bare, you can still take advantage of the sale. Go to the service desk and ask for a rain check. When those shelves are restocked two weeks later, you can still buy at the sale price. In case any questions arise, staple the ad with the sale item to the rain check. Rain checks are usually good for sixty days, so you should have plenty of time to redeem them. I keep my rain checks in the front of my coupon box, where I won't forget them. You can use manufacturer's coupons with rain checks just as you do any other sale item.

Friendly tip: Tell the cashier you have a rain check when she starts ringing up your groceries. It has to be keyed in differently, and it is easier to do it right the first time, rather than make a mistake and have to call a manager to void out the item.

GETTING GAS

As an additional come-on to lure customers into the store, Giant offers gas points; one point for every dollar spent on everything other than milk, cream, and some other dairy products. Other stores with gas programs will have their own, unique prohibitions, so ask at the service desk for details. Each 100 points gives me a 10¢ a gallon discount at the gas pumps at the fancy Giant on PA39. Because we drive so little, I redeem my gas points about every three to four weeks. I usually receive a discount of 40¢ to 70¢ a gallon, rarely more. Giant gas is competitively priced, so this is a real discount.

How can Giant afford this? First, and most unbelievably, many people who accrue gas points — and Giant gives them to everyone who uses a store loyalty card — never redeem them. They pay full price somewhere else rather than buy discounted gas at the grocery store that they go to anyway. Grocery store gas is not different from other gas, and it comes in different octane ratings like at any service station. To which I can only say: Thank you for subsidizing me.

Second, not every shopper has a loyalty card. Giant gives those shoppers the sale price by using a discount card kept at the cash register. Since these people do not have a loyalty card, they do not receive the gas points. Thank you for subsidizing me.

The loyalty card does mean that Giant tracks my shopping. This is why I receive targeted mailings of coupons from them. Does this put me in yet another database? It does. This is a small price to pay to get the savings. Since I do no social media, and I rarely pay with a credit card, preferring a check, my exposure to data-sucking giant squids is minimal. This is a personal choice, but loyalty cards do reward careful shoppers with greater savings. It is your choice. If you want to balance loyalty card data-mining with privacy, use the loyalty card and always pay cash.

The third way that Giant supports the gas points program is more subtle. They advertise it everywhere: discounted gas! The store *knows* that plenty of people who might shop elsewhere come to Giant and promptly turn into the typical mindless customer. A customer who doesn't bargain hunt, who leaves half of a BOGOF item on the store shelf, who pays full price rather than wait for a sale, who impulse buys, who doesn't fulfill the requirements to get the lowest possible price: This person is a valued shopper as she opens her wallet and lets Giant vacuum out the money. This customer subsidizes me, and then often forgets to redeem her gas points, subsidizing me still further. Thank you is all I can say.

Giant changes their gas point program periodically, matching the ebb and flow of the economy. As an example, they used to let you buy up to thirty gallons at the discount price; now it is a maximum of twenty-five gallons. It's still high enough to encourage people to bring gas cans to fill up, that they then use to top off their tank later in the week.

We don't use that much gas, so this is a way in which I subsidize more organized gas users who show up at the pump with their five-gallon gas cans. Many of these people also have massive pickup trucks whilst I have a small sedan. They need to fill additional five-gallon gas cans every time they buy gas. I don't have to. Nevertheless, if we were still commuting to work or using a gas-powered lawnmower, I would fill up a five-gallon gas can or two every time I bought discounted gas.

Giant also runs special sales tied to their gas points program. They give you a list of products, some on sale and some not, and if you buy seven items on the list, you earn an additional 40¢ off per gallon. The products and minimum purchase requirement varies from week to week. It tends to lean towards heavily processed foods, health & beauty, and toxic cleaning products. If you use many of these items, it can be worth it to stock up when they are on sale like this. Remember to apply any coupons you have.

Another way that Giant offers extra gas points, in a way that subsidizes me, is the gas points coupon. They will offer in the Sunday paper a coupon where, if you buy at least $50 in groceries, they will double your gas points. Sometimes, they give you points for a minimum spend as in 300 additional gas points if you spend $100. That is 30¢ a gallon more for spending what you might spend anyway. Even if you don't use any other coupons, this one deal can regularly save you a couple of bucks. Yet I routinely see customers spend much more than the minimum and not hand over a gas coupon.

JEDI-MASTER SHOPPING

Grocery stores train you to be a loyal customer. Loyalty cards, mailers, and house brands encourage you to not wander off the reservation. Which is why you should consider doing just that.

If you want to maximize your savings and minimize your costs *and* you have the time and gas, study *all* the supermarket fliers. With your trusty price book, figure out who has the rock-bottom price that week on products you use a lot. If the Weis, where you normally never go, is offering a great deal on peanut butter, buy as much of it as you can. Then leave.

What you are doing is taking advantage of a *loss leader*. This is not just a low price, but a price so low that the store loses money selling it. Loss leaders are designed to get people into the store, where they will buy full-price products on their list, more than making up the difference. Buying only the loss leader is a tactic called cherry picking. Grocery stores hate cherry pickers. They have no store loyalty and buy only the very best deals, but there's nothing the stores can do to stop it.

Cherry picking requires time to read every ad and more time and gas to travel among the stores. You have to be very disciplined. The minute you start impulse buying, you spend more money than the cherry picking saved you.

If you are concerned about what the managers and cashiers think about you coming in to regularly buy one or two products, think about it this way. Cashiers don't care. As long as you are a friendly customer ready to pay when asked, it doesn't matter to them what you are buying. Neither do the managers care. When devising their sales, grocery stores expect to see cherry pickers. They factor it into their prices. It is a part of doing business, and if they balance their sales and prices correctly, the disadvantages of cherry-picking shoppers are outweighed by the shoppers who don't look at the prices at all.

If you live in a densely populated area, with several highly competitive supermarket chains, cherry picking can work really well. I used to do this until I realized that it wasn't worth my time and gas. My area isn't competitive enough. Following the Pantry Principle means that I can wait until that item goes on sale at my price at my store.

PROTECTING YOURSELF

There is one last step to take before leaving the store. As I put items in the buggy, I keep track of my prices, writing them down on my list, rounding to the nearest dollar. This makes the adding easier, and I am not usually off by too much. I also note any coupons and subtract them as I go.

This does two things.

First, I know approximately what I am going to pay at the checkout. I have a limited budget, so I am perfectly willing to put products back if I cannot afford them. I have to prioritize, and if that means not coming home with mint double-stuffed Oreos, Dear Husband will understand.

Second, if the cash register amount is way off, then I know that there is a mistake. As I've gotten better at this, the mistake nearly always turns out to be on the part of the grocery store. Not every item is rung up at the marked price. Not every coupon is taken off.

When that happens, I pay the cashier, find a quiet place to stop and go over my receipt item by item. It takes about five minutes to compare the price of each item on the receipt with what I wrote on my list. I know what coupons I gave to the cashier. When I find the mistake, I get it fixed right away at the service counter.

It is important to get this done immediately. If the cash register refused to ring up the 50¢-off coupon on any CareOne product (which happened to me today), I am the only person who cares. If you don't get it fixed right away, while it is fresh in your mind and you have the receipt handy, you never will. You won't remember to bring back the receipt the next time you shop. So I spend five minutes going over my receipt, and over the years, it has earned me a nice chunk of change. Because I have the receipt, the service desk has never, ever had a problem with giving me my money.

Don't worry about getting the cashier into trouble. It is very rarely his fault unless he rings up an item twice. The computerized cash register makes the error because the product's price wasn't entered into the system correctly. With more than 50,000 items in a standard supermarket, and prices changing weekly, it is a wonder that there aren't more errors.

Pay attention as your groceries are being rung up. No one else will. No one else cares. Then bag your groceries and go over the receipt.

Maximizing your food dollar at the grocery store is simple: learn the store's policies, learn how to read ads, develop a price book, and follow the Pantry Principle. Once you get those groceries home, you move onto the next part: food storage.

A PLACE FOR YOUR FOOD

Proper food storage consists of following two rules. There's First In, First Out (FIFO), where you store your food so that you use the oldest items first. The second rule is to store your food in a cool, dry, pest-free, and dark space.

Effective storage begins with effective food buying. First, don't buy anything that you and your family won't eat. It does not matter if that candied squash was 29¢ a pound or that those whole-wheat berries and MREs are incredibly shelf-stable. If you don't know how to cook it, and your family would not eat it anyway, that is money down the drain. In addition, you wasted precious time, storage space, and life energy.

Whole-wheat berries can be stored until the next ice age. However, you need a grain grinder and know how to cook them. Before you store large quantities of anything new, practice cooking and eating small quantities. You may love grinding the berries for porridge and bread. Your family may love it, or maybe not. Practice first before shelling out serious bucks and storage space.

KITCHEN CABINETS

The second component of good food storage is your storage facility. The goal is to create a place that is cool, dry, pest-free, with good air circulation, and in the dark. Anything will last longer under those conditions. The enemy of food is pests, humidity, heat, temperature swings, and light. Even canned goods can be affected.

To do this, start with the kitchen cabinets. Do you get bugs there? Do they look dirty? They may need refurbishing. This is a big project and is best done either all at once – so you get it over with – or one cabinet at a time as you work up the energy and enthusiasm. Sand the interiors, paint the surfaces with a coat of primer, caulk the joints, paint the walls with ultra-high-gloss white latex enamel, and glue a layer of white sheet vinyl on each shelf, including the bottom one.

The caulking seals the corner seams, making it harder for bugs to infiltrate. The high-gloss white paint makes interiors less cave-like and easier to see into. It is also easier to clean. The sheet vinyl gives you a wipe-clean, padded surface. Glasses and jars won't stick to sheet vinyl, unlike a painted surface. Since the vinyl is glued down with floor adhesive, bugs won't get underneath, unlike shelf paper.

Do this for all your cabinets. The sheet vinyl flooring is especially nice in the cabinet under the sink. In addition to being wipe-clean, it is also water-resistant.

Next, do the kitchen drawers. They are tedious and fussy to do-over, much more so than the cabinets, but they will be pristine and fully functional when the job is finished. As you rehab cabinets and drawers, make repairs and reinforcements.

While you are redoing the cabinets, consider installing organizers after the sand / prime / caulk / paint cycle. This is where you can get creative. For example, we modified one drawer to hold spice jars by adding dowels to angle the jars (we pulled this idea from *Martha Stewart Living*). This drawer holds my forty-four jars; easy to find, easy to use, and readily available without being exposed to light, air, moisture, and bugs. Over the stove is the worst possible place to store spices and herbs, closely followed by racks on countertops and walls

Grocery Shopping and Food Storage

where they are always exposed to light, heat, and moisture.

Other miracle organizers need to be carefully evaluated. We installed a pull-down knife block, a pull-out cleaning caddy under the sink, a holder for tinfoil and plastic wrap, and added vertical dividers in a cabinet to store cookie sheets and other tall, skinny stuff. Organizers like this only work if you use them. If they prove troublesome — everything has to be stacked just so — you won't use them and they turn into another piece of annoying, junky plastic.

The best way I have found to organize kitchen cabinets for food storage is to segregate like with like and to *not* mix dishes with food. I store my food over the sink and stove, and my dishes in a cabinet by the fridge.

A FRESH LOOK FOR THE PANTRY

There is pantry space in many homes, but it does not necessarily start out that way. It may have started as a closet, or a wall in the unfinished basement, but it took a little imagination and the will to create it.

If you don't have a pantry, it may take a fresh look around to find it. For example, do your kitchen cabinets go all the way to the ceiling? What is in those topmost spaces? They should hold what you rarely use, and if you don't use them, maybe you should discard them.

What if above your cabinets you have that dreadful dead air space? The one that decorator magazines fill with objects that within a week collect greasy dust? Toss the *objets d'art,* and you have found space. If you are handy, installing small doors will turn this dead space into cabinet space. Even ceiling-mounted curtain rods and valances will conceal your new storage location for paper goods and laundry soap. A valance is washable and will cut down on the greasy dust that would build up there.

Those with more advanced carpentry skills can turn soffits into cabinets. Or, when you replace cabinets in a kitchen, install the ones that go all the way to the ceiling.

In our 1,200-square-foot ranch in South Carolina, we added a pantry when we redid the former enclosed porch. This space was much larger than it needed to be, so we cut it in half, leaving one half as a home office. On the other side, we added a much-needed half-bath, leaving a narrow, deep closet. That became the pantry. The back was lined, floor to ceiling, with 18-inch deep ClosetMaid shelves. On the left wall, we hung pegboard and hooks to hold mops, brooms, dustpans, and anything else that could be hung up.

On the right side, my DH took ClosetMaid shelves that were designed for hanging clothes. He trimmed them so the shelves were four inches deep, turned them upside down (so the hang-bar side was turned up) and ran them from floor to ceiling. Not deep enough, you say? Four inches holds a 40-oz. peanut butter jar perfectly as well as all kinds of cans, boxes, and what have you. The bent side provided a lip to keep food in place.

We lost seven inches of side-to-side space, a minor inconvenience compared to the two walls of storage space we gained.

Here's another example: My brother redid his kitchen and since he was handy, he opened up a wall in a hallway access to his kitchen. He installed shelves between the studs, painted and caulked, and installed cabinet doors. The result was built-in, low-profile cabinets that run floor to ceiling and hold dozens of products in what would otherwise be wasted space. The shelves were about four inches deep, the depth of a standard 2-by-4 stud cavity.

A friend did the same thing when he renovated a narrow bathroom. He opened the wall, installed shelves between the studs, hung cabinet doors, and that bathroom suddenly had storage space for all the personal care items he could want. He could even store rolls of toilet paper once they were removed from the bigger bags. Four-inch deep shelves leave room for a single layer of a lot of stuff.

Do you have space over your washer and dryer? Install cabinets and shelves to hold laundry products, cleaning supplies, and paper goods. Do you have alcoves tucked behind doors? This is another spot for narrow shelves.

One of our better obtainium finds was a wooden butcher-block breakfast table that the neighbors were throwing away. My DH set the table on a platform made from a ¾-inch sheet of plywood, then raised it six inches using feet made from salvaged bits of wood. He added a shelf to the back of the table. Placed next to the dryer, across from the pantry, it serves as a combination laundry-sorting, grocery-sorting table with plenty of storage underneath.

I have salvaged shelving units to put in the unfinished basement, and I have bought and had my DH modify particleboard storage cabinets. We put all the storage units up on skids to allow for airflow and discourage dampness.

Our biggest project was remaking the basement pantry. This originally consisted of three rough wooden shelves, ten feet long, running the length of a bare-stud wall, each shelf being about two feet apart. There was a lot of wasted space.

My DH dismantled it, saving the wood for reuse, insulated the wall, and covered it with plywood. He installed plywood dividers about three feet apart, creating three bays. He caulked every seam, painted everything ultra-high-gloss white, and installed floor to ceiling ClosetMaid ventilated shelving, six shelves in two bays and eight in the third (room enough to stack two cans per shelf). The ClosetMaid shelving determined the depth of the plywood bays and provided airflow, which is very important in a basement. The finished shelves are much easier to use and organize. This job more than doubled the usable space and made the area easier to keep clean.

RETHINKING SPACE

Once you run out of wall space for shelves, then you get creative. Can you put cans of tuna under the bed in slide-out Rubbermaid bins? Will extra toilet paper fit into the topmost shelf of a closet? As you look over your home, think carefully about where you could store what you need.

Organization is always your friend and organizing your home to take better advantage of the Pantry Principle can free up money to pay for shelving systems. At the same time, sorting your possessions can help you to get rid of what you no longer need or want. As you examine what's in those closets, cabinets, and under-the-bed storage units, you may decide to sell unused video games on eBay, donate unwanted clothes to the thrift shop, and recycle that heap of scrap metal in the basement. This frees up still more space.

When you are looking for storage space, unfinished basements – as long as they don't have water issues – can be ideal. Basements are naturally cool and dark. Their issues are dampness (fatal to food storage), lack of air circulation, and pests. Ventilated wire shelving helps to overcome these problems as does making sure there is an inch of airspace under the bottom shelf. Cleanliness and regular cleaning will curtail pest problems.

Attics are not as easy to access, and they are vulnerable to wild temperature swings from summer to winter. If you have to use an attic, store things that do not need a consistent temperature like paper towels or toilet paper. If you have something that could be stored in the attic like seasonal decorations, move them there and free up the space for your canned fruit.

Garages, depending on how they were built, can suffer from wild temperature swings, too, especially when you open the garage door in January. Garages are also on display to the neighborhood whenever you open the door. You may not want the neighbors seeing your lifetime supply of laundry soap. Garages have the potentially loads of space but they are usually used to store cars, automotive products, home improvement and maintenance supplies, and gardening tools. Moving the gardening equipment to a toolshed can free up space for paper towels and toilet paper.

Toolsheds are terrible for food storage. They are out of sight and out of mind, suffer from wild temperature and moisture swings and are guaranteed to have bugs and critters.

To use the Pantry Principle to its fullest extent, save the most money, and build up a few weeks of food storage, you have to work out where to put all the cans and boxes. Shopping awareness, learning how to read the grocery ads, keeping and using shopping lists, cooking with the food you have on hand, and using a price book are vital strategies to cut your grocery bill. The Pantry Principle takes you to the next level of organization and money management. This is the level that lets you start saving some serious money and prepare for rainy days.

29

Cooking From Scratch

The Curse of Uncrustables – Scratch Cooking – Learning How to Cook – Expanding Your Repertoire – Not All You Cook You Will Eat

COOKING IS ONE OF THOSE IMMENSELY USEFUL skills because everyone has to eat, two or three times a day, every day, 365 days per year. There is no escaping the demands of the body. The stomach, like the bladder and bowels, makes slaves of us all.

Learning to cook saves money and time, and adds another layer of resiliency to your life. Unless you are preparing elaborate gourmet meals, something quick from your kitchen will always cost less and take less time than going out.

Let's use McDonald's as a measuring device. Does a home-cooked meal cost less per person and take less time than driving to the local chain store, waiting in line, and driving home? We aren't even talking about health issues here, but it is pretty darn hard to make a saltier, greasier meal than McD's, and they are not bad.

So here we are in the McD's drive-through. If you get one of their value meals, you will spend about $5 per person. Order five of them and you have spent $25 plus about forty minutes. That is how long it takes for me to find shoes and cash, walk out the door, drive to McD's, wait in line, get my order, drive home, and unpack the now-lukewarm food so the piranhas can attack it. There will be no leftovers.

I spend about $150 a week on groceries for a household of five. Every member of my household is over fifteen. This covers our twenty-one meals — ranging from breakfast (yogurt for Dear Husband; oatmeal for myself) to a blowout dinner or two — and includes my health, beauty, cleaning, and paper goods products, along with dog and cat food for my 45-lb. dog, Muffy, and our two useless cats.

Assuming $25 a trip, my grocery budget would pay for *six* meals from McD's, with no leftovers, no animal chow, and no other necessaries.

Not such a bargain, is it?

Basic cooking from scratch will always cost less than eating out, three meals a day, seven days a week. Basic cooking tends to take less time, but not always. The question here is hands-on time versus ignore time. Food in a crock-pot takes hours to cook, but once the meat and veg are simmering, you stop paying attention to it and go do something else.

SCRATCH COOKING

So what is scratch cooking? To me, it is when you do some or most of the work yourself. You use raw ingredients and transform them, via heat and mixing, into a meal.

You don't need to start with a live chicken to claim that you made your chicken dinner from scratch. You don't need to grow your own grains and mill them to bake your own bread. If you have the time and inclination to do them, well, I am deeply impressed. You will have far better quality food, you will know exactly where it came from and what went into it, you will undoubtedly save money, and

---

THE CURSE OF UNCRUSTABLES

Smucker's Uncrustables represents a triumph of food marketing. Making a PB&J sandwich is easy. All you need is a flat surface and a plastic knife. Bread and peanut butter are reasonably shelf-stable. You can get several days of sandwiches from the bread and peanut butter lasts for weeks.

And yet, Uncrustables exist.

Consider the price. A box of ten costs $7. Each sandwich is two ounces. That is 70¢ apiece and those sandwiches are *tiny*. For the cost of two boxes, I can easily buy more than one loaf of bread, a big jar of peanut butter, and a jar of grape jelly. I will make *more* sandwiches, bigger and fresher than what comes in the box, and they are ready to eat. I don't need to defrost them, unlike Uncrustables.

Uncrustables are a stellar example of the industrial-agricultural food complex's ability to sell you food that you could do better and cheaper yourself. In this case, you don't even save time.

you'll be able to survive most of what the universe sends your way. You will also be devoting a whole lot of time to this endeavor.

Everybody used to start with a pile of grain, a live chicken, and a heap of vegetables with dirt clinging to them. This is time-consuming work. I've spent plenty of time preparing root vegetables I grew (beets, carrots, parsnips) and, boy, do they take time to scrub clean, first outside with the hose to get the worst of the dirt off and then again inside. If you save the carrot tops for soup, you will spend more time to wash and inspect the greens for bugs and dirt.

Women did the overwhelming majority of this work, either for their own families – we used to call them housewives – or for other families, when we called them cooks. It always took time. Lots of time. If you're interested in reading about the history of the industrial-agricultural food complex and why so many women ran with open arms into modern grocery stores, read *Perfection Salad* by Laura Shapiro. Other titles on this subject that I've read and enjoyed are Shapiro's *Something from the Oven*, Barbara Haber's *From Hardtack to Home Fries*, and Carolyn Wyman's *Better than Homemade*.

These are great books if you want to explore why grocery stores look like they do now. They have their axes to grind, so read them carefully and see what isn't being spelled out. Yes, the food industry wants to pay their employees and amortize their expensive equipment and sell you stuff that you could make yourself. They also save you oodles of time that you can use for something else, like spending eight hours a day outside your home in a paying job.

Columnist Megan McArdle sometimes writes interesting articles about food, previously at *The Atlantic* and now online at *Bloomberg View*. She is always fun to read, and she does cook from scratch. She has also considered how long it takes to do so, and the change between a woman cooking for her family back in the 1920s (thirty hours a week) versus today (six hours or less) is amazing. When I think about how long it takes to make a thoroughly scratch meal – just one – and extrapolate that time to three meals a day, seven days a week, I can believe it.

The key is to find the balance between homemade and time-consuming. Cake is a good example. I can make a cake from scratch using the *Joy of Cooking* (1972), or I can use Duncan Hines. Duncan Hines costs way less, takes way less time, and we like it fine. I cannot say that the taste difference is worth the extra work or cost. I do make my frosting from scratch, as frosting from a can is so vile that I wouldn't use it even if it were free. A Duncan Hines cake, filled and frosted, will cost less than a store-bought sheet cake, and it will taste better. I will have far more choice in flavor and styling, and it will take less time to make than the time I would have to spend at work to earn the money to buy the sheet cake.

Do I make soup from scratch? You bet, as I can use up stuff that has to be eaten, I am far more inventive than any soup company is, I control the salt levels, and I make a lot at one time, leaving leftovers for the next few days.

Do I buy canned soup? Yes, I do. They make a convenient dinner when I'm blurry with fatigue and no one can be persuaded to get into the kitchen. For us, canned soup and buttered toast is fast food. It is cheap, easy, quick, and I doubt if the salt content is higher than a McD's meal.

What is scratch? Is it opening a jar of Ragu? I make my spaghetti sauce. It tastes far better, I season it the way we like it, I make a lot, and Dear Husband turns the excess into homemade pizzas. But opening a jar of Ragu and cooking a pound of dried spaghetti is still cooking compared to opening a can of Spaghetti-Os, which are vile. It isn't that hard to open a jar of sauce and heat it up while boiling water for pasta.

What is scratch? Growing leafy greens in your backyard and turning them into salad? Buying heads of lettuce and tearing them into shreds? Buying salad-in-a-bag, ready to go? They all qualify, compared to going to a chain-gang restaurant and buying chemically freshened lettuce that you don't know how many people sneezed on.

We do make our own salad dressing to go on those greens. It is pathetically easy to make vinaigrette. Get a small jar with a tight lid, pour in two fingers of any kind of vinegar, add two more fingers of any kind of oil and add salt, pepper, and a pinch of whatever herbs and spices you have at hand. Shake. That's it. Shake with every use, as this does not have the mysterious magic emulsifiers that keep supermarket salad dressing shelf-stable and cohesive. Emulsifiers don't add to the flavor, but they do add to the cost. Vary the oil and vinegar, and you will never eat the same dressing twice. It keeps for weeks in the fridge, too.

What is scratch? Is it opening a bag of frozen chicken tenders? Is it taking a pile of raw chicken breasts, cutting them up, and tossing them with seasoned cornmeal? They both end up in the oven alongside the sliced, seasoned potato wedges.

I have made chicken tenders both ways and, I have to say, Perdue is easier and quicker. It is not cheaper, even when bought buy-one-get-one-free with coupons. Store-brand chicken breasts with cornmeal and spices will always cost less. Here, I determine how much money I have versus time versus life energy. Perdue chicken tenders rest quietly in my freezer, ready when I need them. Homemade chicken tenders have to be planned for, either buying the chicken breasts and making them right away or remembering to take them out of the freezer early enough so they can thaw. Then there is the time to prep raw chicken and clean up afterwards.

I make the potatoes from scratch. It is not that hard to peel and cut up potatoes, season them well, and roast them in the oven although Ore-Ida might like you to think so. Is it worth paying $2 a pound for fancy, seasoned French fries versus 40¢ a pound for regular potatoes and doing the work yourself? If you want to save some money, the choice is obvious.

What is scratch? Is it growing Brussels sprouts, checking them for cabbageworm damage, harvesting, cleaning, and cooking them? Getting them from someone else who spent all summer staking them and fussing over them? Opening a bag of Hanover Gold frozen sprouts and pan-frying them in bacon grease with plenty of garlic? I've done sprouts all of these ways, and Hanover Gold is easier, quicker, and cheaper. Let me add that you shouldn't buy any other brand. I have, and they head rapidly into "green balls of death" territory.

When you know how to cook, you have far more choices. You can customize your meals to suit your diet, your family's persnicketiness, your budget, and your time. If you cannot cook, you are hostage to restaurants and what they choose to sell you.

Restaurants, whether family-run, chain gang, or a Michelin four-star bucket-list destination, always balance the cost of ingredients and labor plus time against what they can charge and make a profit. Do not think for one minute that everything you are eating was actually prepared in the kitchen. It may not have been. Many "fast casual" places don't cook much. The food comes in freezer bags from a central, industrial kitchen and is reheated to order. That hole-in-the-wall Chinese place may do more scratch cooking to order than TGI Friday's. You cannot always tell.

I learned some of this from a book by Tracie McMillan called *The American Way of Eating: Undercover at Walmart, Applebee's, Farm Fields and the Dinner Table.* This book reminded me of something I had not thought of in years. A roommate I had decades ago worked at a family owned ski resort. She would sometimes bring home huge trays of frozen chicken enchiladas and the like, made for the restaurant trade. I had always thought that stuff was made from scratch in a restaurant kitchen. It is, but not necessarily the kitchen you are eating next to and paying a premium for. It is an industrial kitchen somewhere else, packaged, frozen, shipped, stored, until you, the customer, order it from the waitress.

The biggest hurdle with cooking from scratch is the time involved. Canned soup and buttered toast make a fast dinner when I am fainting with fatigue and out of time. But plain, unfancy cooking can take less time than stopping at the drive-through and coming home. When you make it yourself, you also have a much better idea of what you are eating and can control how much salt and grease is in your food.

Over time, your cooking skills will improve. You will learn to cook a wider variety of food, and you will get faster at it. You will probably never get as fast as a professional chef is unless you take lessons, but with practice, you will improve. The better you can cook, the more you can get out of what is hanging around in your kitchen. This saves you money, using what you already paid for. More skill means you can take advantage of sales at the grocery store, such as larger cuts of meat or whole chickens. You can use what is the best price versus what is the only thing you know how to cook.

LEARNING HOW TO COOK

So you've decided to learn how to cook. Do not start with gourmet magazines or cooking shows. That's festival, special-occasion food. This is not the food that your mother or grandmother routinely put on the table, three times a day, seven days a week. You want basic, utilitarian cooking. It doesn't cost that much to learn, and it doesn't involve exotic cookware, strange ingredients, or specialty skills.

The best place to start is with your family and friends. See if someone can show you the basics of eggs and stoves.

If your mother or grandmother aren't around (or they don't cook either) go back into the past and look for "teach yourself how to cook" books. A half-century back or more, quite a few people learned how to cook from books. They didn't learn at Grandma's knee. I know I didn't. I am mostly self-taught. The advantage to old books is that they don't expect you to have a fish poacher, five kinds of oil, or cilantro.

A very nice book to start with is *Cooking for Absolute Beginners* by Muriel Fitzsimmons and Cortland Fitzsimmons. It is a Dover Publications reprint from a 1946 book called *You Can Cook If You Can Read* and the book proves it with every page. Yes, it is dated. It doesn't have any pictures, not even a line drawing. However, it has a sense of humor, and it assumes you know nothing about cooking

There are other cookbooks that will teach you the basics. Betty Crocker has published nice ones over the years. If you don't feel like buying a book right away (and you don't have Aunt Sukey on speed-dial) go down to the library. Look for words like basic and beginner and "learn how to" in the title. Children's cookbooks can be good too, but watch out for trendy or cutesy recipes such as sandwiches looking like clown faces.

You can even look for help from the industrial-agricultural food complex. Your grocery store is full of "make a meal" products, both shelf-stable standbys like Hamburger Helper and modern freezer-case products with vegetables in them. They get you used to standing while facing the stove and seeing what happens as the food simmers, boils, and bakes. Follow the directions exactly as you get used to using a stove and a pan. When you can cook Hamburger Helper without stumbling over the directions, try adding new ingredients, like onions and peppers, cooking them with the meat.

Don't expect to eat Hamburger Helper the rest of your life (unless you want to). This exercise is designed to get you comfortable with turning raw food into cooked food with a high chance of success. It won't take long to notice that a can of sauce and a box of dried pasta cost far less per pound than HH does, and they are less salty and processed tasting. Again, the grocery store is jammed full of alternatives, most of which can be combined and recombined in new and inventive ways.

As for cookware, the grocery store will usually sell basic items. Otherwise, go down to Walmart and pick up a two-quart saucepan with a lid, a one-quart saucepan with a lid, and a non-stick frying pan. After that, add what you need as you come across it.

Despite accumulating a number of pots and pans, I use the same ones over and over. I have two non-stick frying pans (ideal for scrambling eggs), several saucepans in various sizes, a Dutch oven, and a stockpot. I use those the most. One of my cast-iron skillets is seasoned so well it only gets used for cornbread. I use my double boiler less than once a year. If you buy a big set of cookware, you may discover that you never use some of the pieces. On the other hand, if someone gives you one, take it joyfully and add to the set as you discover what else you need.

All the "teach yourself how to cook" books will have lists of suggested pots, pans, mixing bowls, utensils, measuring cups, and other equipment. Read over them to see what you already have or can get from well-stocked relatives before you buy anything. Even a list as basic as the one in *Cooking for Absolute Beginners* has items on it that I don't own, such as pudding molds and food mills. I have been cooking for more than thirty years, and I have never felt the need for either of them.

Before spending the money on more pots and pans, start cooking using simple recipes and find out what you will use. Keep in mind your storage space when considering a new purchase. Plenty of lists recommend candy thermometers, but if you aren't going to make fudge, you don't need one.

Baking, as in cakes and pies, is a skill to work on *after* you have become comfortable cooking on the stovetop. A casserole, although it is baked in the oven, is basically stew with a topping and tends to be similar in how it is mixed and assembled to many meals you cook on the stove. For casseroles and oven-fried potatoes, you will need a 9-by-13-inch baking dish and a cookie sheet with low sides.

As you cook, you will develop a list of easy-to-make foods that your family will eat. Stick with easy and quick at first. There is no reason to learn how to make Beef Wellington. There are plenty of cookbooks that specialize in simple food with few ingredients. The ones to be wary of are those that claim to be few ingredients and they turn out to be pricy or weird, leaving you stuck with leftovers that no one will eat.

If you find that you like only a few recipes in a book, it may be better to copy them and leave the book at the library. If you find yourself checking out the book repeatedly and using many of the recipes, then buy the book.

Another old book that I like to cook from is Peg Bracken's *The Complete I Hate to Cook Book*. These recipes date back to the early 1960s and are simple, basic, and unconcerned with fat, calories, or salt. Most of them are delicious, too. The book is a hoot to read, and it shows that plenty of women never liked or wanted to cook, no matter what you've been told about ye olden days. They did it because they had to, and they did utilitarian cooking only. This is still a worthwhile goal.

EXPANDING YOUR REPERTOIRE

As you get better at cooking, try fancier dishes on holidays and weekends. Plan some meals that allow for leftovers (or "planned overs" as twee foodie writers call them). I like to make plenty, so I don't have to cook every day. Does this mean that we eat the same thing several days in a row? Yes, it does. It also means that if I cook intensively for several days, we get a fridge packed with a smorgasbord of leftovers, offering variety at the evening meal. Just make sure to use your leftovers. They don't save you time or money if they are shoved back to the far corners of your fridge. If I see too many containers in the fridge, I don't cook until all the leftovers are eaten.

Leftovers also mean cheap lunches to take to work and easy breakfasts if you don't feel like cereal, boiled eggs or toast. There is no rule that says you cannot eat leftover spaghetti for breakfast.

Another part of cooking from scratch is challenging the idea of what constitutes a meal. Omelets, sautéed vegetables, and toast for dinner? We do that. Pancakes, bacon, and heaps of fruit, canned or fresh? You bet. If you don't feel up to omelets for dinner, substitute scrambled eggs.

As you expand your repertoire, look at basic cooking from other traditions. I do a lot of vaguely oriental cooking. I sauté chopped vegetables – onions, peppers, celery, carrots, whatever is around, chopped meat (except ground meat as it doesn't work well for this), add a jar of Asian sauce from the supermarket, and serve over fresh rice. Is it authentic Chinese cooking? Not on your life. Nevertheless, it's easy to make and different every time, depending on what I throw in and how I season it.

If you need inspiration, there are "learn to cook fast and easy" books for every cooking tradition in the world. I have one that promises to teach French cooking fast, a reprint of a 1930 book by Edouard de Pomaine called *French Cooking in Ten Minutes, or Adapting to the Rhythm of Modern Life*. The recipes are basic, and they put food on the table in a hurry.

What you'll learn from ethnic and regional cookbooks is that it is the seasonings and side dishes that change chicken from something Italian to German to Indian to Chinese to Mexican. Chinese cooking doesn't come with a side of fries, but French cooking can (pomme frites). Pasta sends an Italian signal, not a Mexican one. Rice, depending on how it is prepared, says Asian, Italian, or Spanish. It doesn't say German.

When you're searching for recipes, look for short lists of recognizable ingredients. Be wary of recipes that call for exotic foodstuffs. Half a tin of smoked baby octopus can sit in the back of the fridge for a long, long time before you compost it. Capers are another item you use half the container in one recipe and then see the jar in the fridge for the rest of your life.

As your cooking skills improve, branch out into desserts. After store-brand ice cream, the easiest dessert for variety, low cost, number of servings, and ease of preparation is instant pudding and jello. Add canned fruit to jello to improve it.

If you buy ready-to-eat jello or pudding, check out the rack of tiny boxes over in the baking aisle. You have to boil water to make jello but you can do that in the microwave. Instant pudding, chockfull of bizarre ingredients not found in nature, is as easy as it comes. Don't pay extra to have it prepared by someone else.

Should you make your own cookies? I make an array of cookies and all of them, hands down, are better than anything I can buy. They cost less, sometimes far less per pound, than the commercial variety but they take considerably more time than ripping open a box of Keeblers. There are exceptions. We made Faux-reos from *The King Arthur Flour Baker's Companion*. They were terrific. The ingredients weren't expensive but it took hours to make them and the kitchen was trashed. Buy Oreos instead. Chocolate chip cookies? Use the recipe on the bag (with butter, not margarine or shortening) and the resulting cookie is superior to everything from the cookie aisle, including those gaspingly expensive Pepperidge Farm cookies.

I do not make every kind of dessert. I don't make traditional piecrusts, using the refrigerated ones from Pillsbury instead. I do make graham cracker crusts for cheesecake. They are easy, cost less, and taste far better than those stale ones from the store.

As you explore the world of cooking, compare what you are learning to do with what is available readymade in the supermarket. Almost every item in a supermarket started out as real food from a real kitchen, even snack foods like pretzels and tortilla chips. This leads to making things you thought you had to buy. There are many books on this topic, old and new. A recent one that we really enjoy is *Make the Bread, Buy the Butter* by Jennifer Reese.

There are plenty of others such as *Make Your Own Groceries* by Daphne Metaxas and *Cheaper and Better* by Nancy Birnes. You'll discover that you can make your own granola (easy and cheap), tortilla chips, big fat pretzels, pancake syrup, pastrami, marshmallows, chocolate syrup, cream cheese, ginger ale, and Fig Newtons.

Your big, fat "cook everything" book will have some of this stuff as well. Read the index and see what is hiding. Every basic cookbook has numerous recipes for pancakes. You do not have to buy pour-out-of-a-spout ready-mixed pancake batter, or (shudder) frozen pancakes. If you have flour, butter, eggs, leavening, and milk, you have pancakes. It is not hard.

Drop biscuits are similar. They are much, much easier than southern-style flaky ones with the steep learning curve that have to be patted out and cut with a biscuit cutter. Drop biscuits are so easy that you won't want the whack-em-on-the-counter variety ever again. As with everything else you make yourself, you will not eat an extensive list of stabilizers and preservatives that allowed a biscuit to be made in a factory months ago, stored in a warehouse, stored at the store, sold to you, and then wait in your fridge before baking and come out, well, not fresh, exactly. Something like it though, thanks to the miracles of modern food chemistry.

NOT ALL YOU COOK YOU WILL EAT

As you branch out into this new world of cookery, you also get recipes for products like liquid soap. It is amazingly cheap to make compared to even the cheapest bargain brand.

You will need a box grater, several one-quart glass canning jars, and a small bar of soap (any kind will do, even the small bars of hotel soap). Grate the soap and scrape the bits into the jar. Cover the contents with boiling water. Let it cool, and shake. The grated soap dissolves into the boiling water and you get liquid soap. Depending on how thick the mixture is, you may want to split the soap between two jars, adding more boiling water to thin it.

A small bar of soap, on sale, is about 25¢. This will make a quart or more of liquid hand soap, suitable for refilling the fancy container or using it in the shower. Since even a small container of liquid soap is $1 or more, you can see the savings. It is quick to make, too.

The "make your own groceries" books are full of this kind of recipe for everyday products. It is surprising to see what you can do yourself. Will you do it all? Probably not, as it all takes time. But if you have time and not much money, you can make the money go further.

And, at a minimum, by learning how to prepare groceries yourself, you can take control of what you and your family are eating and using. When you make it yourself, you know what you are eating. When you can cook, you aren't at the mercy of what other people want to feed you.

30

Sewing and Mending

The Way We Used to Sew — The Price of Cheap – The Case For Sewing – Start With Repairs – The Next Stage: Creative Sewing – Making Clothes – Sew What? – The Hunt For Fabric – Sewing As Personal Expression – Why You Should Sew

SEWING, LIKE BASIC HOME COOKING, has become a lost art; a skill that in two generations went from the vast majority of women knowing at least how to repair a hem and put meals on the table three times a day, to most women barely recognizing a needle and thimble and relying on the miracle of pre-fab convenience food cookery. Sewing, like cooking, is time-consuming work and both can quickly turn into drudgery.

If you cannot find the Zen of bending over a sewing machine for hours on end or making a meal in an hour that gets eaten in five minutes and then repeating the process for the rest of your life, three times a day, you start resenting the work. Why wouldn't you?

This is especially true if you maintain a sixty-hour-a-week career and use some of that money to pay lower-class women to do the same work. My sister the programmer works at least that many hours every week. During sick days and vacations, she is expected to check her email faithfully *and* make up every missed hour of work when she gets back. You simply cannot maintain that pace and spend three hours a day cooking and cleaning *and* doing all the sewing of garments, household linens, plus repair work and mending.

This doesn't cover the work needed to run a house well, nor time spent on exercise and other body maintenance, commuting, community service, church work, housekeeping, personal time with children, spouse, and friends, and food growing and preservation. That "only twenty-four hours in a day" pesky time management issue reappears with a vengeance. With super cheap clothing available and all the other demands on our time, it is no surprise that sewing fell off the radar. Your time matters a lot.

So, again, why sew at all? We'll get into that, but first, a history lesson.

THE WAY WE USED TO SEW

I learned how to sew decades ago, partly from my mother and partly in the home economics classes that every girl used to take in school. According to my children, those classes are called Family Consumer Sciences now, and everybody, boys and girls alike, takes them.

Shop class seems to have gone by the wayside, at least here in our school district in the Sweetest Place on Earth. The reasoning must be that you don't need to know how to fix your house and repair your car, but you still need to eat and run a household. Most of the graduates from Hershey High will be able to pay for carpenters and mechanics but not full-time, live-in cooks and housekeepers. This might keep the Family Consumer Science program alive for a few more years.

The goal of home-ec was to get us used to the real world. That meant learning to cook on working stoves in a fully equipped kitchen. We even had knives! Sewing was taught using real machines, one for each girl. I have a vague memory of working my way around a fabric-cutting table with sharp dressmaking shears, ten inches long and as dangerous as any knife. With these tools, I made clothes: a dress with a back zipper, a blouse with multiple buttonholes, collar, and cuffs, and a zippered skirt with a set-in waistband. I even wore them.

Today, the sewing portion of Family Consumer Science that my children took consisted of making either a small, square pillow or a drawstring bag. The pillow concealed its unfinished seams inside itself. The drawstring bag showed every defect of its design and construction.

That's it.

If you want to learn more than that, even a basic skill such as sewing on a button, you have to go elsewhere. You certainly don't learn how to pick out a pattern and cloth, select, lay out, and cut the fashion fabric, and then sew the pieces together, fitting as you go, and inserting zippers or making buttonholes.

At home, my mother made most of our everyday dresses, back when girls in small towns still wore dresses to school every day. She made curtains and bedspreads, and repaired everything to make it last longer and save money. When you do not have money, you spend time.

Clothing was more expensive then, relative to income, and every retailer, from dime stores like Woolworth to department stores like Sears, carried fabric for home sewers. The Sears catalog also sold notions to go along with its fabrics.

Nowadays, it is damn difficult to find a place that sells fabric outside of a fabric store. Those are becoming scarce, as craft stores replace them and sometimes, quilt shops. Quilt shops do sell fabric that you can use for clothing, but it tends to be expensive. They also do not sell specialty fabric like flannel-back satin, fleece, interfacing, or home-dec. They do not sell patterns or garment notions. You can buy thread and needles, though.

THE PRICE OF CHEAP

This changed because clothing is now very cheap. We take it for granted that you can walk into any store and find heaps of clothing. The price has nothing to do with the fabric, notions, or the workmanship.

A shirt that has two front pieces, back, yoke, two set-in sleeves, a placket with ten buttonholes and ten buttons, plus collar and cuffs (with more buttonholes and buttons) can cost less than a T-shirt which consists of four pieces of fabric serged together (in other words, a sized tube with no side seams, two sleeves, and a collar). T-shirts these days may not even have hems. The sleeve and bottom edges are raw and unfinished for that in your face, edgy look; an edgy look that will not hold up in the wearing or the wash.

I saw this fact of construction versus cost demonstrated the other day in Boscov's. I looked over a pair of Isotoner gloves. Each glove consisted of a front, back, and thumb piece. There were three fourchettes (the inner piece between each finger that connects the glove's front and back) plus decorative trim panels, lining, and an interlining of Thinsulate. The price was less than half of a nearby shawl made of polar fleece that consisted of a rectangle bound in bias tape, with a narrow slit cut to allow it to fit around the neck better.

How can this possibly be? The shawl's construction made it a basic home-ec project. It consisted of a yard of cheap fleece with a few yards of cheap bias tape. Well-sewn gloves are one of the fiddliest, most detail-oriented projects imaginable where there is no margin for error and the seam margins have to be one-eighth of an inch (or less) and yet still hold tightly, while remaining flexible.

Whenever I look at the clothing in stores, I am amazed at how *little* is being charged for basic garments. Yes, many of them are not that well sewn (quarter-inch seam margins) and made from the cheapest fabric. However, I know how long it takes to make a basic shirt and that unless I am given the fabric, the pattern, and the notions, I will rarely spend less than $10 to $15 on the supplies. After several hours, I will have a plain cotton shirt that won't look much different from the Walmart special. I will sew it better, it will wear better, and it will fit better, but is that worth my money and time?

If you want even cheaper clothes, check out the consignment stores, thrift shops, and yard sales. Not cheap enough? Pull your clothes from open trashcans, Dumpsters (especially in apartment complexes), and piled up on the sidewalk with a free sign on them. I have found good clothes in all of these places. Do not let the dirt and moisture stop you. Clothing can always be washed.

The second-hand clothing market is so enormous that there is no reason to ever buy new clothes. The exceptions are socks, undergarments, and sleepwear. Those items tend to not show up at all, or they are worn almost to rags. Otherwise, some time spent shopping at Goodwill will produce whatever you want: scarves and neckties by the bushel basket, handbags, coats, ball gowns, Fair Isle sweaters, wedding dresses, tuxedos, jeans, jeans, jeans, khakis, velvet, satin, suits, and leather jackets.

If the Goodwill isn't cheap enough for you, then look for their Bargain Bin and Outlet Center stores. Pawing through the bins, you will find Ralph Lauren and Tommy Hilfiger garments mixed in with the Old Navy and Faded Glory. You pay for them by the pound. These stores also carry bedding, tablecloths, and draperies. This can become an important source of raw material for projects, so keep an open eye and an open mind when you rummage through a bin.

Lowest in cost, and far more reliable than getting lucky in the street, is playing pass-along and hand-me-down with family and friends. We have been part of several hand-me-down networks in

South Carolina and Hershey. Oldest Child was once given a huge bag of cotton summer shorts by an older relative that I would swear had never been worn. There were so many pairs of shorts that I split them with a friend and both our kids ended up with twelve new pairs each.

Of course, when we are finished with a garment, I clean and repair it and pass it along to live in someone else's closet. Any age person can participate in a pass-along loop, from babies to adults. Never say no to a garment; just pass it along if it doesn't suit you.

There is rarely a reason to spend your scarce money on new clothes.

THE CASE FOR SEWING

So with this wealth of clothing out there, why sew? Because if you want something unique, something well made, something that fits will, you have to do it yourself. If your body type is anything other than a standard size and height, or you are not built like a clothes hanger, and you want attractive, well-made, properly fitted garments, you have to go with custom-made.

If you have unusual needs, such as maternity wear that doesn't look like what a five-year-old would wear, with Peter Pan collars and cutesy designs, if you are breastfeeding fulltime and on demand; if you have a handicap that prevents you from using zippers or buttons; if you need costumes for your steampunk cosplay, then custom is the way to go.

You can have this clothing custom-made by the local seamstress or tailor. You may have to look hard to find this service, but these people still exist. Just remember to ask first how much it will cost. If the price shocks you, remember that the local seamstress or tailor wants more than the 27¢ an hour that a sewing machine operator was paid to make Gap clothes in India (source: *The Guardian*, 2012). The local seamstress cannot cut her fabric costs by buying in 100,000-yard increments. The local tailor has rent, Social Security taxes, federal, state, and local taxes, and utilities to pay.

Third World sweatshops and prison labor are the reasons why new clothes in the United States cost so little.

How do you solve this problem of cost? By doing it yourself, starting with a needle, thread, thimble, and sewing scissors. You teach yourself to make basic repairs, such as sewing buttons back on and closing split seams. Thanks to *Project Runway*, sewing became hip again, so you can find basic how-to-mend and repair books with loads of pictures that aren't sixty years old or older.

A current book is *Mend It Better: Creative Patching, Darning, and Stitching* by Kristin M. Roach. A really excellent older book is *The Mender's Manual: Repairing and Preserving Garments and Bedding* by Estelle Foote, M.D. The difference between the two books is that Dr. Foote assumes you know how to sew. Ms. Roach assumes you have never held a needle and gives you plenty of photographs to demonstrate how to thread and hold one.

As your how-to-sew books get older and older, the basic information and directions become sparser with many fewer illustrations. Nevertheless, older books can be *more* useful as they assume you do not have money to spare. They give instructions that you wouldn't get today such as how to replace a lining in a jacket. Older books also assume that you have an older relative whom you can ask. If you have a mother, grandmother, or aunt who still mends, repairs, and sews, you have a stunningly valuable resource, so ask for help. I have learned a lot from books but being shown a technique by someone who knows what she is doing is far better than trying to interpret cryptic instructions and tiny line drawings.

START WITH REPAIRS

Repair work is easy to understand. It is crazy and wasteful to discard a blouse because a button is missing or a seam has opened up. These are both easy fixes and take far less time and money than shopping for a new blouse. If, of course, you have a needle, thread, thimble, scissors, and a jar of buttons and you know how to use them.

Every household that plans to repair clothing should have a button jar. Take a clean, clear peanut butter jar and save the loose buttons you find in the washer, on the floor, and attached as replacements to the clothes you bought. When you have to buy a packet of buttons to replace the one missing shirt button, put the extras into the jar.

Since I sew a lot, I have collected thousands of buttons. I sort my buttons by type (shank or hole) and color. For basic repairs, you won't need nearly this many. What makes button replacement hard is that you rarely find an *exact* match of even a plain, half-inch white shirt button. This most basic of buttons comes in dozens of variations. Fancy types are impossible to match. Therefore, I save every button I come across, and joyfully accept unwanted buttons from other people. If I find a jarful of buttons at a thrift shop or yard sale, I'll buy it and add it to the stash. This way, I can come pretty close to a match *or* I replace all the buttons on the garment. I always keep in mind that most people don't examine buttons closely so a close-enough match is good enough.

To complete your basic repair kit, you will need a few spools of thread: white, black, cream, and three shades of gray (light, medium, dark). The gray thread will let you get reasonably close to the color tone of the item you are fixing the seam on. Since this stitching is hidden, you don't need an exact color match. If the thread is going to show, you may want to visit the fabric store and buy an exact match. I use Coats and Clark or Gütermann's thread; both are widely available and work very nicely. You can no longer use the super-cheap no-name thread you sometimes see in dime stores. This thread is so poorly made it is not suitable for anything but hand basting, as it may break apart when the garment is washed.

A book of hand needles in various sizes, a thimble that fits, a pair of sewing scissors, and a small box of straight pins and safety pins will round out your repair kit. These items are widely available; even grocery stores carry some of this stuff tucked away in the aisle with the household cleansers and mops.

The thimble is the hardest item to get, as you have to try them on. Yes, thimbles come in sizes. You want one that fits snugly over your middle finger on your dominant hand but not so snugly that it pinches. It has to fit well so it doesn't come off as you sew. The thimble lets you push the needle through the fabric without puncturing your flesh. It is absolutely worth the trouble to learn how to hand sew with a thimble if you are going to do repair work. It increases your speed and saves your skin.

Get a decent pair of sewing scissors and mark them as such. *Do not ever let anyone cut paper with your sewing scissors.* Paper cutting ruins the blade for fabric and you will then have to cut out the heart and liver of whoever ruined your good scissors. Damaged scissors have to be resharpened; fabric stores sometimes offer this service. You can sometimes find someone who sharpens scissors at farmer's markets; I got my scissors redone at the Hershey farmer's market and what a joy they were to use afterwards.

Then you get a basic mending book such as *Hand Mending Made Easy: Save Time and Money Repairing Your Own Clothes* by Nan L. Ides, and you are ready to start fixing simple stuff. Once you learn to sew on buttons and close opened seams, you can move on to repairing hems. When you have learned to repair a hem, you can start altering a hem.

I do some sewing for money and a simple job I do often is shortening the hems on pants. Depending on the type of pants, I alter them by hand or by machine. *Any* sewing job that can be done by machine can be done by hand and hems are an easy place to learn. There are some jobs that should still be done by hand, even if you can do them by machine. It works better, it looks better, or it just takes less time. Yes, hand sewing can sometimes be faster than machine sewing. It can make just as strong a seam.

Learning basic mending is empowering. You no longer have to discard a garment because of an easily repaired seam. As you get better at it, you'll learn to do harder, more complex jobs. This saves you time and money; the time spent shopping for replacements and the money spent on buying new garments. Doing basic repairs will also free up cash to pay a tailor or seamstress for the harder jobs such as relining or taking in a suit jacket or replacing a complex coat zipper.

As you start repairing garments, you will run across snaps. They are a bit more involved than replacing a button, but not much. Very rarely, a snap needs the touch of a hammer to flatten it so it fits better into its other half. More often, it has to be replaced. You replace snaps one of two ways: sew-on snaps are replaced in kind. You carefully pick off the damaged or missing snaps and sew on the replacements.

The second kind, a snap that is held onto a garment with tiny, invisible teeth, must be replaced with a snap replacer. This is a giant specialty set of pliers from Dritz. Purchase one and plenty of replacement snaps in various sizes and colors at a fabric store in the notions department. A snap replacer and a jar of snaps makes an excellent baby gift as missing snaps make that onesie useless. And yet, it is an amazingly simple repair to make. I have salvaged many baby clothes with this gadget.

Zippers can sometimes be repaired. A missing pull can be replaced with a paper clip or a circle key holder. Sometimes the slide doesn't quite grip anymore and a very gentle squeeze with pliers will tighten it. Sometimes the teeth can be lubricated with a wax crayon or a bit of bar soap to make the zipper slide easily.

However, if teeth are missing, the slide is missing, or the zipper is torn, you have a catastrophic failure and the zipper must be replaced, a far more difficult task. You can never replace half a zipper as they come in a huge array of sizes and types of teeth and you will never find an exact match. Zippers, even separating ones, are always sold as a set for this reason.

Just about any garment can be repaired to get more use out of it, just as any sock or knitted garment can be darned. The question is whether the garment is worth the time spent repairing it. If so, the next issue is deciding if the repair will show and does that matter. Knee patches on pants are a good example. I have put replacement patches on all kinds of pants – including sweats, jeans, khakis, and knits – on the outside or on the inside of the garment. The repair always shows, sometimes quite a lot. It is very worthwhile to patch kid's pants. Your kids will outgrow them long before the garment collapses from overuse. Knee patches will let a pair of jeans last through multiple children.

If having the repair show does matter, then get new clothes or sew on the patches so it looks like a fashion statement. Cover the holes in your plaid flannel shirt with large flowers cut from a floral fabric in a contrasting color. Add trim to the cuffs and collar and swap out the buttons to reflect the beautiful cabbage roses you sewed onto your worn-out flannel shirt. Now, instead of telling the world you are poor and thrifty because your shirt is patched, you become artistic and crafty because you *appliquéd* it. The end result is the same: The hole in the garment was covered up.

This can be time-consuming work, and only you can decide if it is worth it. There are benefits to consider. You will improve your skills with each elaborate repair job, and you will learn more about how a garment is put together. You will keep a piece of clothing from the landfill. You will save hard cash. The repaired garment becomes a unique fashion statement.

Clothing that is terminally worn, when the fabric has holes all over it, may not be salvageable. If a garment has no life left in it, or if it is unwearable, then please don't give it to the thrift shop to discard. Recycle it for usable parts. Always save the buttons, interesting patches, and any other notions you think you can use before turning a garment into a shop rag. Buttons never wear out. The larger your stash, the easier it is to match a missing one.

Once you are comfortable making basic repairs, you can level up with an iron and an ironing board. Ironing a hem to the correct length makes the sewing much easier. It took me years to learn that you need to spend as much time at the ironing board as you do at the sewing machine. Pressing as you sew (by hand or machine) makes the finished work look smoother and more professional.

The leading cause of failure in irons is being knocked over onto the floor by bad cats, so always put your iron away when it is not in use, and it will serve you for years.

If you expand the range of your repair work, a sewing machine will be next. Look for new and used models, pass-alongs, and thrift shop buys. If you want a new one, shop carefully and check to see if you really need its features. Many places that sell sewing machines throw in free lessons. If your shop does this, take advantage of it.

If you are fortunate enough to get a pass-along machine, take it into the sewing repair shop (ask at the fabric store) and have the machine cleaned and tuned up. Get a manual so you know what it can do and how to thread it. The shop might be able to order you one, or you can find them online by typing in the machine's brand and model name plus the word "manual."

THE NEXT STAGE: CREATIVE SEWING

Repair work on clothes easily segues into the wonderful, amazing, eye-popping, and fascinating world of altered couture. Ye olde sewing books called it remaking old clothes into new clothes, back when people did this because they were thrifty instead of trendy.

Once you have learned how to sew big cabbage roses over holes in a flannel shirt, it is an easy mental step to removing and swapping the sleeves from the blue flannel shirt with the green flannel shirt. This work, both the ripping and the resewing, can and should be done by hand. It is much easier to make the tiny tucks needed to fit one nearly the same size edge against another when sewing by hand. When you do this work by machine, you have to hand baste it completely to make the edges line up right; so you might as well do it completely by hand.

If you live in central Pennsylvania, you can see altered couture for yourself. Suze Moll is a long-time, local practitioner. She has small stands at various places in the area, and she sells on the local craft circuit. Go to her Facebook page (https://www.facebook.com/Remix-Art-to-Wear-1383822328518220/) to find her stuff. She does the best thing I have ever seen to upcycle fancy colored bras: she turns them into tiny evening bags! They are just the cutest things ever, and each one is unique.

There are tons of online resources for altered couture and plenty of books and magazines on the topic to get you started. With their help, you'll see the possibilities. You'll become braver about taking apart and putting together clothes. You'll learn how garments are constructed, and since the raw materials come from the back of the closet or the bargain bin at Goodwill, very little money is involved. Only time and the nerve to take a pair of scissors to an old prom dress are needed.

I have recycled many old prom dresses and bridesmaid dresses into new items. Those big skirts have a lot of fabric that was only worn once. I upcycled several of these dresses into nursing tops for me. On-demand breastfeeding is much easier when you wear a nursing top. The ones you can buy are very expensive and tend to be boringly utilitarian. Get the patterns, learn to sew (or have them sewn for you) and you can have summer- and winter-weight nursing tops in a variety of colors. I even color blocked some of mine, using the black skirt from one prom dress as the underlayer and the bright pink skirt of another dress for the overlayer. I made them to last, and it is quite possible that someone is still using them over fifteen years later.

Prom and bridesmaid dresses upcycle beautifully into princess costumes for little girls. The easiest method is to cut off the spaghetti straps and resew the new shoulder seams closed where you cut off the straps at the top of the bodice. The dress is now magically a foot shorter. Try it on your little princess and decide if you need to chop some of the hem off or take in the side seams. Or not, as little girls get taller fast.

Dear Daughter ended up with a huge assortment of princess attire that she and her friends wore for years as they enacted complex psychodramas in our living room. Each prom dress has to be handled differently but since they are free or almost free for the asking, it is worth the risk of mistakes. Remember to save any unneeded notions. The butt bow, for example, can be made over into a massive Halloween hat.

Repairing and remaking the clothes you acquire secondhand gives you, at the cost of only your time and thread, a custom wardrobe and a better understanding of garment construction. You will get far more life out of your clothes. As your skills progress, you can make your readymade garments fit better; shortening too-long hems, moving over buttons, and taking in side seams or adding darts.

MAKING CLOTHES

Your improved skill set will let you move naturally and easily onto making clothes out of whole cloth. Once you move into clothing construction from scratch, you will have to have a sewing machine, an iron, and an ironing board if you haven't already acquired them.

A sewing machine is an enormous timesaver for those long seams. Changing from hand sewing to a sewing machine is the equivalent of going from writing a novel in longhand to using a typewriter. It is that much of a change. This is why, after purchasing a James hand washer with a wringer, the second appliance every 19th-century woman bought was a Singer sewing machine.

Any piece of clothing much more complex than a poncho requires a pattern. However, you can learn to make your own patterns if you don't want to use the ones from Simplicity or Vogue. Making patterns is empowering, and it lets you see how you can more easily adapt commercial sewing patterns. Homemade patterns tend to be for simpler, less tailored garments but when you are learning to sew a garment from scratch, that is what you will be making anyway. I do not recommend starting with a complex three-piece suit from Vogue. Start small with a pullover-style top or an elastic-waist skirt.

To start, get a very basic book like *Design It, Sew It, and Wear It* by Duane Bradley and work through the variations. When you are finished, you'll have a small wardrobe, some sewing chops, and a much better understanding of fit and making two-dimensional pieces of cloth shape themselves around a three-dimensional body. Moreover, these garments were made with fabric you liked as opposed to what the clothing factory thought was cheapest and would sell.

Then move up to a slightly harder book like *The Illustrated Hassle-Free Make Your Own Clothes Book* by Joan Weiner Bordow and Sharon Rosenberg. Overcome your distaste for the hippy-dippy text and the very dated fashions and see that underneath those distractions are complete instructions to make skirts, pants, tops, dresses, etc., using your body measurements and copying clothes you already own.

If you work your way through contemporary books like *DIY Couture: Create Your Own Fashion Collection* by Rosie Martin or *Dressmaking: The Complete Step-By-Step Guide to Making Your Own Clothes* by Alison Smith, you will end up with quite a wardrobe.

Consider your fabric choices carefully. You can make the exact same pattern several times in different fabrics and get very different results. The illustrations tend to be drawn as though everything is made of lightweight cotton that will be worn only in the summer. If you use heavier fabric like fleece, make the sleeves long and raise the neckline, the pattern you learned to make for a summer-weight top becomes a winter-weight garment. The models in these books tend to look like twenty-four-year-old coat hangers, but don't let that stop you. Since you are making the patterns to fit *your* body, and you are choosing fabrics to suit *your* taste, the end results don't have to be teenager wear.

Before you buy any of these books, get them from the library and read them to see if you can use them. If you really like a book, you may want to buy it, particularly if it comes with patterns, either paper or on CD. The library won't thank you if you cut up the patterns. Make copies so the original patterns remain untouched. You may want to do this even if you buy the book so that someone else of a different dress size can reuse the patterns.

If you decide to go the commercial pattern route, do not be thrown by the price. Few of us pay full retail for Vogue patterns. We buy them when Joann's or Hancock Fabric runs a $3.99 sale. Simplicity, McCall, and Butterick patterns go on sale regularly for $1.99 or even 99¢ each. A good pattern sale lets you stock up on patterns that you think you might use later one. Just be warned that you could end up with a filing cabinet of patterns that you never use.

Other commercial patterns like Burda or KwikSew rarely go on sale. You have to pay full price. Independent pattern companies that advertise in the back of sewing magazines never go on sale, but they are often the most interesting. If you really like the pattern that an independent is offering, just pay for it and use it several times over to get your money's worth.

Other places to find patterns include the stashes of any sewing friends and relatives, thrift shops, yard sales, and eBay. Just make sure your purchases have all the pieces and instructions. I don't buy patterns that have been cut, as there is always a chance that some of the pieces never made it back into the envelope.

Since clothing goes in and out of style, the patterns also change. The age of your pattern sort of matters; a Nehru jacket with no lapels and high mandarin collar is firmly locked in its era. However, if you make the jacket exactly as the pattern calls for but use a modern fabric like fleece, it won't look so dated.

Fabric also goes in and out of style so a modern pattern in a vintage fabric doesn't quite look the same as if you used a period-appropriate fabric. Lapel shapes, sleeves, collars, cuffs, pockets, plackets, yokes: They can be style markers and change as the fashion industry changes. Even how a sleeve is set in can change, but the pattern is still usable. The real difficulty with using old patterns is that the directions may not be as thorough. Like old cookbooks, the old patterns, even the very easy ones, assume you know the basics.

When you buy patterns, you need to know your real body measurements. Any decent sewing book will tell you how to do this, as do the make-your-own clothes books. Patterns are sized by actual tape measurements, not whatever the garment industry is currently calling a size ten. If you have a forty-two-inch bust, look at the back of the pattern envelope for that measurement and that is your size. Never, never, never assume that if you wear a size twelve from Dress Barn that your pattern size will be a size 12. It won't be even close. Your pattern size may be an eighteen or even larger. Buy and cut out the pattern that actually fits your body.

The most expensive part of making your own clothes is the fabric. A basic long-sleeved shirt with two front panels, back, collar, cuffs, yoke, and placket will use about three yards of forty-five-inch-wide fabric. If you spend $5 a yard, then the cloth alone will run you $15, not including the thread, any pattern, interfacing, and buttons. Once you factor in your time, that thrift shop shirt for three bucks starts looking pretty good.

SEW WHAT?

So once again, why sew your own clothes?

I do it because I want something that no one else has. I want my clothes to fit reasonably well, not always easy with ready-to-wear and my nonstandard body, and I want them well made and to not fall apart in the wash. Clothing is an expression of my self; an artistic statement.

My clothes also show that I know how to sew, which is useful when someone asks, "Who can mend my garment? Sew my custom costume? Rehem my prom dress? Make my kitchen curtains?" My clothing becomes my advertisement for my home sewing business.

When I got tired of wearing boring old T-shirts, I made an assortment of surgical scrubs using McCall's pattern 3253. A surgical scrub pattern lets you make a v-neck pull-on T-shirt-type top with no buttons, zippers, snaps, collars, or set-in sleeves out of a woven fabric. It is, other than the pivot point at the base of the v-neck, fast and easy to make. The first few tries took a little practice and some hand basting; fifty shirts later, I zip right through that part. Moreover, because the garment design keeps the fashion fabric as a single uncut piece, I could take advantage of huge, all-over design repeats, the kind where the design motif is eighteen or even twenty-four inches across.

The point of making the scrubs was not to replicate what dental hygienists and LPNs wear. It was to show off amazing, wow, look-at-me, fabulous fabrics. It is very showy to wear a scrub printed with a flowing stream inhabited by life-size, accurately colored koi. This shirt pattern was so successful that I made fourteen of them for me, plus plenty more for Dear Husband, Oldest Child, Younger Son, Nephew R, Nephew B, and various friends. The shirts are unique and one-of-a-kind, just like the people wearing them.

THE HUNT FOR FABRIC

So if you want this unique look, then how do you find affordable fabric to make it happen? First, get on the Joann's mailing list. They run regular sales on all kinds of fabric and regularly provide a 40%-off coupon to use on other merchandise. Check the weekly sales flier in the newspaper or go online to their website and think carefully about what you want to make before you set foot in the store.

Spread the word that you will take unwanted fabric and sewing notions from relatives, friends, and neighbors. This is the fabric they cannot use, won't use, don't know why they bought it, someone gave it to them or they had stopped sewing.

The important thing is to take everything, no matter how repellant that orangey-brown double-knit polyester is. The minute you say, "I don't want those grungy old shop rags," the offering person will think, "I guess you don't want that seven-yard piece of Thai silk, either."

But I do want that Thai silk! I do want that five-yard piece of brocade home-dec so suitable for tote bags! I do want the Christmas-patterned cottons! I do, I do, I do! Say yes to everything and the universe will give you more than you bargained for. This is how you receive the pickup-truck load of material when the elderly sewing relative dies and you get her stash.

Occasionally, I have even found fabric being thrown away. I have picked up dressmaking cottons, home-dec upholsteries, and bags of scraps. I wash my finds and give them a home in my stash or pass them along.

Other fabric sources are yard sales and thrift shops. Cloth here is sometimes yardage that someone did not want. More often, it is yardage already made into tablecloths, shower curtains, sheets, curtains and drapes, ball gowns, or wool coats. A lightly used tablecloth or queen-size sheet will provide a lot of fabric, excellent for making a practice garment before you cut up the expensive fashion fabric. A set of draperies can sometimes offer two pieces of material for the price of one: the fashion fabric and the Roc-lon blackout lining, which alone regularly costs seven bucks a yard at Joann's.

To turn a set of pinch-pleated draperies into yard goods, you need a seam ripper and time. Rip out the hems and the pinch pleating, iron the press marks flat, wash it, iron the piece again, and you will have some seriously large yardage to work with. I don't generally rip the seams in the skirts of prom dresses and ball gowns unless I need every inch possible, as the margins are too narrow to bother with. Drapery hems and pinch-pleats, however, can offer as much as ten extra inches of material. I rip the hems in sheets and tablecloths for the same reason.

It is well worth pawing through the bargain bins at Goodwill looking for draperies. Remember that you need never tell anyone where the material came from; let them guess how you could have afforded that lovely ivory fabric with the pattern of woven squares that you turned into a stylish coat. They will never guess it started life as a cloth shower curtain.

Then you find all the other places in your area that sell fabric and notions. Walmart sometimes sells fabric in addition to notions, patterns, and thread. The Walmarts that carry fabric usually have a bargain bin with dollar-a-yard fabric and up. I have bought fabric on spec if the price is right and I really like it. Every once in a while, the Walmart dollar bin has been very good to me, so I always check it out.

There are many fabric stores besides Joann's and Hancock's, many of them locally owned and operated. Look around, ask around, and you may be rewarded. You may have a quilting shop in your area. Quilt shops don't, as a rule, sell clothing patterns, buttons, interfacing, or anything else to make garments, but they do carry very nice cottons and cotton blends. There is no reason why you cannot make a shirt out of fabric sold for quilting. If you like how the material looks and feels, then use it.

Whatever shop I am in, I always check the bargain bins. You never know what you will find. I used to, as I said, buy fabric on spec if the price was right and I really liked it. I don't do this anymore now that I am dedicated to using up the enormous amount of material I have. That pickup truck load of cloth will take me years to work through it.

Many people buy their fabric online. I very rarely do this as I have real fabric stores in my area, and I like to see and feel what I buy before I spend money. However, if you want a specialty item like Cordura or zippers by the foot and you don't live in a major city, you will have to go online. Try to get samples first, so you can see before you buy, and make sure you know the return policy.

But no matter what, do not spend money on cloth when you are unsure of what you will make with it even if you absolutely love the fabric and cannot imagine living without it. You can fill up a lot of Rubbermaid storage bins this way if you aren't very careful about saying no to great buys.

When we recarpeted our finished basement, including the sewing closet, I had the interesting experience of Dear Husband discovering just how much fabric I had, when he had to move all the Rubbermaid bins. It did not make him happier that at least half of the bins were full of fabric that had been given to me. Gradually, gradually, I am using up those hundreds of yards of cloth.

The only control to buying more fabric is shopping your own stash first. If you have sewing friends, then shop their stash and let them shop yours before you go shopping. This saves money and gets that fabric sewn into the beautiful garment that it wants to be.

SEWING AS PERSONAL EXPRESSION

So what else do I sew, and what do I dream of sewing? One-of-a-kind garments I cannot buy or cannot afford to buy. I want a collection of stylish coats, as that is what everyone sees me in for much of the year. What I want is not likely to turn up at the thrift shop, and I certainly cannot afford to pay retail for what I envision.

I buy basic sweaters that are the right color and fit at the Jubilee Thrift Shop, then trim them out to make them special and unique. I am not keen on sewing knits, and I cannot knit a sweater so this is my work-around. I also make my curtains, drapes, window quilts, pillows, bed quilts, shopping bags, lingerie bags for fine washables in the washer, and potholders with heat-resistant fabric.

I want to sew a Roman shade for the dining room window to save heating energy. Like other unusual home-dec items, I can make this for far less than I would pay retail. Another item on the list is a fabric bag to put a cooking pot into – similar to a hay box. I can, for damn sure, make a cloth cooking bag for far less than Amazon charges. A salvaged ironing board cover and pad, which I already have, plus batting and fashion fabric from the stash, and I am good to go.

When the kids were younger, I sewed complex Halloween costumes. These were worn both for trick-or-treating and at the annual Hershey Halloween Parade and Costume Contest. Sometimes I even won prize money, but never enough to cover my costs.

On the other hand, some of the garment sewing I do really does save money compared to commonly available ready-to-wear. I like good quality flannel or fleece pjs for me and the family as we keep the heat low in the winter (64 degrees during the day and 55 degrees at night). Better quality flannel goods such as Lantz of Salzburg are gaspingly expensive, and I don't like the patterns they come in. However, if I shop for a good sale on flannel, I can make simple pajamas for far less money than I can buy them. I reuse the same pattern over and over, so I only pay for the pattern once.

Sewing pajamas is an easy way to learn garment construction. Fit is relatively unimportant and nobody outside the home will ever see your efforts.

WHY YOU SHOULD SEW

This is why *I* sew. I sew to repair and reuse garments until I have extracted every minute of use out of them. That saves me cash, suits my philosophy, and keeps resources out of the waste stream.

I sew to remake old clothes into new, personal garments. This saves me more money and lets me express myself.

I sew new garments from whole cloth to advertise my design and sewing chops. I sew to get exactly what I want, at a price I am willing to pay, for me, my family, and my house. I get clothes that are unique.

So should *you* sew?

At a minimum, learn to do basic mending and repair work, and learn to rehem pants. That alone will save money and prolong the life of your clothing.

After that, it gets harder. Everyone has to eat, so everyone should learn basic cooking. Sewing clothing and household items is a more complex choice. Clothes are readily available and very cheap. Drapes and bedding range in price from thrift shop and Walmart cheap to the sky's-the-limit. Sewing them from scratch takes time away from other tasks that have to be done.

The answer depends on what you want from it. If you want to keep your body covered while saving money, use yard sales, thrift shops, consignment stores, and the clearance racks. Participate in pass-along and hand-me-down circles.

However, if you want one-of-a-kind clothes for you or your family, or one of you doesn't fit into anything readymade, then you will either pay big bucks or learn to do it yourself. Start with altered couture, remaking old clothes into new ones. As you learn how garments are constructed, think about making some of your own clothes from patterns you design or select and fabrics you choose. Begin small with a top or an elastic-waist skirt and see how you like it. Progress to simple fleece or flannel pajamas and see if you enjoy the work. If you do, you may have found a new, useful hobby/skill that shows off your design abilities and may even make you a little money when you do sewing work for non-sewing people.

If you don't like sewing, you can still do basic repair work and you will have a better understanding of how a garment should be made when you purchase ready-to-wear.

31

Sleep

The Need for Sleep – The Best Way to Sleep – The Problem With Partners – More Ways to Fall Asleep

IT HAS BEEN YEARS SINCE I LAST GOT on an airplane – and I probably never will again for a host of reasons – but I remember the flight attendant's safety demonstration. They emphasized that in an emergency you should take care of yourself with your seatbelt and your oxygen mask *before* you took care of children or invalids traveling with you. The rationale was obvious: You cannot help anyone if you had not ensured your safety first.

This is what sleep and exercise do for you. They make you healthier and more resilient so you can take better care of the people around you. You become better able to do the work *you* have to do, and *you* can recover faster when bad events happen. You cannot take care of anyone else if you don't take care of yourself first.

THE NEED FOR SLEEP

You see these ridiculous T-shirts that say, "I'll sleep when I'm dead". The truth is that if you don't get enough sleep, you *will* be dead. Sleep deprivation is an effective way to hurt yourself. It is so powerful a weapon that it is a time-honored torture technique and one that does not leave any marks.

Sleep is so necessary to our existence that it runs counter to our survival instinct. When we're asleep, we are vulnerable and unaware of everything that is happening around us. We are easy prey for any predator.

And yet, every living creature with a brain sleeps.

At the bottom of the food chain, fat, juicy little mousies and rabbits sleep. Fish sleep with half of their brain and then sleep with the other half. Dolphins and whales do this, too, taking naps with one eye open to look for predators while the opposite side of their brain sleeps. Birds sleep, lined up on branches. When brown tree snakes were accidentally introduced into Guam years ago, they took advantage of sleep and devoured whole branches full of sleeping birds that did not evolve in an environment with snakes. There are not many birds left on Guam.

You don't get many evolutionary traits that lead directly to being eaten before reproducing. Afterwards, sure. The job got done. Nevertheless, sleep stays. This tells us that sleep must be of vital importance.

Sleep is difficult to study, so for a long time nobody knew why it was needed. Empirical evidence told us that we function poorly when we are sleep-deprived. This seemed true of animals as well. Thanks to improvements in brain studies, we have a better idea of what happens when we sleep and why we need it so desperately. Sleep seems to be vital to the functioning of the brain — which is active all day — filling up with junk thoughts and junk chemicals. When we sleep, our body does its housekeeping on the brain, getting it ready for another day. If we don't get enough sleep, the brain isn't fully cleaned and ready to go.

Think of it as rinsing your dinner dishes instead of scraping and washing them. Keep eating your meals off those dirty, unscraped plates, and problems will arise. It is icky, unsanitary, and leads to food poisoning or intestinal parasites. This is why we wash our dishes before reusing them.

You have to sleep to keep your brain at its best.

Sleep affects all our body processes. Even your weight is affected by your lack of sleep. More sleep lets your body maintain its weight, and not just because if you are asleep, you cannot eat. Many types of hormones are adversely affected by not sleeping and research keeps discovering more. Are your children diagnosed with ADD? Maybe they need far more sleep than they are getting. Does your depression lead to insomnia or does your insomnia make you depressed? More and more, it seems like the latter. Everywhere you look, you find more body issues that are related to sleep.

Sleep seems, as well, to act like a checking account. That is to say, you cannot make up sleep deprivation with a few extra hours of sleeping in. Like any other debt, you have to pay it *all* back, before you can start over. Thus, years of sleep deprivation – the product of being told we have too much to do to waste precious time sleeping – can mean years of catching up.

Studies show that sleep-deprived people will, if given the chance, sleep 14 hours a night for weeks and weeks until they fall back to the more normal seven to nine hours a night. They had to make up that time.

My Dear Husband experienced this when he was working, alone, for six months in Central Pa., while the kids, animals, and I stayed in S.C. trying to sell our house. DH did nothing *but* sleep and work for the first few months he was up here. As he caught up, he started feeling like a new person; an alert, high-functioning person.

Sleep studies also show that if you follow the sun's schedule – going to bed when it gets dark and getting up when it gets light – you are down for more hours, sometimes many more than eight. That is when your sleep divides into two parts: first sleep, then wakefulness of an hour or so, followed by second sleep. A great book on this subject, *At Day's Close: Night in Times Past* by A. Roger Ekirch, describes this now-forgotten world without artificial light. Diaries and letters dating back to when people only had candles reflect this very different style of sleep. During the waking period, people would talk quietly, daydream, pray, write by candlelight, and even spend quality time with their partner.

I suffer from chronic, unrelenting insomnia. It is hard for me to fall asleep, and I wake up easily. I do all the sleep hygiene stuff, and I probably know more than most doctors about the subject. Nonetheless, it has taken me almost two years of sleeping ten hours or more a night to start feeling like a real person and not a zombie. Years and years of not enough sleep and interrupted sleep left me borderline psychotic and suicidal. I feel much better now, thank you, but if you want to see fear, suggest to my children that I cut back on my sleep.

What changed for me? The kids got older. Younger Son stopped the endless nighttime coughing fits from dust mite allergies. We improved our locks and got Muffy so I felt more comfortable alone at night. And best of all, my DH got his golden ticket and stopped working weird evening shifts whereby he would come home any time from midnight to 3 a.m. and waking me up. Once he was home full time, *he* started getting up at 6 a.m. to get the offspring off to school.

In previous years, I got up at 6 a.m. to get the kids moving, no matter how little I slept the night before, and he slept in. DH had to in order to function at work, but even so, it was still hard for him to focus during the day. My DH always had the gift of being able to go back to sleep and take naps. He still suffered from no-sleep headaches regularly. He doesn't anymore. I was never able to go back to bed and sleep, which did not make my life better. Instead, I got more and more zombified, affecting how well I functioned, spoke, felt, thought, everything.

I had a sleep study done and found out that, as suspected, I had garden-variety insomnia. The only therapy that treats this condition is rigorous sleep hygiene. These are boring and time-consuming procedures to follow. They have to be done faithfully, night after night, without making a mistake. They do help, with time and effort. Drugs only work in the short term and none of them worked for me. At all.

The pharmaceutical industry makes truckloads of money selling sleep aids, so these are promoted. Yet most sleep doctors agree that sleep hygiene techniques, which take far more time and effort than popping a pill, work much better. Since these methods are free and no one makes money on them, sleep hygiene is ignored far more than it should be.

THE BEST WAY TO SLEEP

Sleep hygiene consists of, first, admitting that you need to sleep. That you most likely need seven to nine hours of sleep *every single night without fail*. Then, you rearrange your schedule and say no to a host of activities so you go to bed *with the lights out* at 10 p.m. in order to get up at 6 a.m. Ten p.m. to 6 a.m. is eight hours. If you have to get up at 5 a.m., then you have to go to bed, lights out, at 9 p.m.

And then you sleep. You don't keep your smartphone by your bedside, you don't read, you don't watch TV, you don't keep checking your email, you lay quietly in the dark and wait for sleep. Do not have any electronic devices with alarms or blinking lights that keep you awake near you.

Keeping to a lights-out routine can be challenging. All that work left undone calls to you. All that must-see TV, books, web surfing, and games that you want to see, read, watch and play; you lay awake hearing them calling for your attention. Block them out as best you can and stick to a schedule.

Sleep specialists say that you should get up at the same time on weekends as you do on weekdays. We still don't do this, even though we stick pretty well to lights out at 10:30 p.m. My DH will get up if he doesn't feel the need to sleep. I nearly always want more sleep so I tend to sleep in until – gasp – 8 a.m. or even 9 a.m. on weekends.

Darkness matters. You don't want any lights. Room-darkening shades and room-darkening drapes help immensely to block outside light. They make it possible to sleep during the day if you are doing shift work. They also muffle sound and act as insulation against the cold. See the chapter on the Window Dance for details on window treatments.

Next, get rid of the blinky lights in the bedroom that can distract you. The only lights in our bedroom at night are the red numbers on the clock radio. It is on top of the dresser, not in line with my eyes, and I have to make a conscious effort to look at the time. There was a blinking light on the carbon monoxide detector, a tiny strobe that flashed every minute. A piece of black electrical tape took care of that problem.

My whole house is done up with room-darkening shades and heavy drapes. This provides much-needed insulation against the cold and outside noise, plus it keeps sunlight from filtering into the rooms when I don't want it to. Early morning? It stays dark. Have to go to bed before it gets dark outside? No longer a problem. We have these shades in parts of the house that don't seem to need them, such as the kitchen and living rooms. However, our house is designed to bounce light from room to room via mirrors and high-gloss painted walls, so if the drapes are open in the living room, light spills down the hall into the bedrooms, waking us up.

I keep a nightlight in the bathroom to make it safer to navigate at 3 a.m. I get the lowest wattage bulb I can find and keep the door ajar to reduce the amount of light leaving the room. It is slaved to a photocell, so the light turns itself off during the day.

Humans are creatures of habit. Walk into the kitchen, and we look for something to eat, even if we are not hungry. How many times do we walk into the family room and turn on the TV, even if we didn't intend to do so? We can use this human trait to our advantage in the bedroom by reserving it for two functions: sleep and sex. No home offices, no libraries, no TV watching, no craft stations, no exercise equipment. None of that stuff. Clutter is distracting too, whether it is the pile of laundry on the floor, an unfinished project, or stacks of junk mail.

Sleep

I admit that we do read in bed. This can be a no-no for many people. Your reading material does matter. Stimulating books like Stephen King horror novels do not make the best bedtime reading. I tend to read sewing magazines and soil-management books before lights out. They are not what you call hugely exciting. In fact, since we read regularly before turning the light out, it acts as a trigger to the body. Once we settle in for a read, we relax and are ready for sleep. It does make a difference how you read. Real books don't stimulate the eye and keep us from relaxing. Smartphones, iPads, and laptop computers keep us "up," and it takes longer for us to get to sleep. As for eBook readers, the models that are not backlit are fine. Their only problem is that it is so easy to buy new books, it may be difficult to stop reading.

In addition to the room-darkening shades and removing distractions, I've decorated our bedroom to make it more conducive to sleep. The walls are a deep midnight blue with sparkly silver and gold stars. I cut them out of contact paper and stuck them up all over the walls. I spattered the walls with silver model-airplane paint. It looks a lot like the Milky Way. The designs on the drapes, rug, and bedding reflect this nighttime sky theme. The original idea was to help my DH sleep when he worked evening shifts. A darker room is easier to sleep in. It turned out to help my insomnia a little. So even if you paint the rest of your house sunshine yellow and arrest-me-red, keep those colors away from your bedroom. Your goal is to create a soothing, serene, calming, cool, and dark environment.

Other things you can do:
- Don't eat after dinner. This cuts down on the risk of acid reflux. Do you like ice cream right before bed? The sugar buzz can keep you awake.
- No coffee or any other caffeinated products after noon. Cut way back on caffeine. It stays with you far longer than is widely realized.
- Alcohol doesn't help you sleep. A glass of wine can be soothing and relaxing but after you go to sleep, a few hours later you may be restless, wake up, and then be unable to fall back asleep. More alcohol will not make it better.

THE PROBLEM WITH PARTNERS

Consider how your partner affects your sleep hygiene. If he or she snores, has restless legs, coughs all night long, mumbles, sleepwalks, thrashes about like a gaffed fish, wants the bedroom the opposite temperature you need, works bizarre hours, comes to bed at random intervals, insists on having the smartphone on all night and totally denies they are contributing to *your* sleep deprivation, then you have a real problem.

Sleep studies always ask about your partner because they are so often the reason you cannot sleep. They also ask if you sleep better when away from home for the same reason. What keeps you from sleeping at home and can you fix it so you *can* sleep at home? Good sleep hygiene depends on having a partner who does not sabotage your efforts.

If your partner won't change, then you suffer. This is the reason for separate bedrooms. This solution has its own drawbacks — where are you going to put your snoring husband, especially if you can hear him throughout the house? — but it may be your only hope if you can't stand earplugs.

Some of the above conditions can be fixed. Sleep apnea treatment, for example, can cure snoring. Others are predicaments that have to be managed, such as irregular work hours. Keep in mind that eliminating interruptions, such as lighting and electronic devices, may make the other issues easier to cope with.

MORE WAYS TO FALL ASLEEP

Another area to look at is your bed. Is the mattress collapsing? More than two decades old? Is it big enough for you, your partner, your four cats, and the dog? The dog can be trained to sleep in his own bed or on the floor, thus freeing up some space. Training cats is a lost cause so close the door – and listen to them meow on the other side all night long – get a bigger bed, or live with it.

If you wake up every day with a backache, a new mattress may help. Unfortunately, you won't know for sure until after you purchase one. If you sleep better when you are not at home, the mattress may be the culprit, or one of them.

When you shop for mattresses, take your time and do your homework. Expect to spend serious money to get a better mattress and box spring. Get a warranty so if the new mattress doesn't make your sleep better, then you have a faint chance of getting your money back. New bedding is expensive, so do the easier sleep hygiene stuff first.

If noise or tinnitus is a distraction, then a white noise machine can help. I have tinnitus; that constant ringing static in the ears. There is little to be done about it, other than maintaining a healthy blood pressure. The white noise machine helps mask the never-ending buzz and outside noises, too. We bought one about five years ago, and it really helps. We listen to ocean waves all night long. DH loves it, and I don't hear as much of the endless buzz and crackle in my ears. If you are concerned that a white noise machine will keep you from hearing prowlers or other potential problems, set the sound at the lowest level that works for you, upgrade your locks, and get a dog.

I like our white noise machine so much we will replace it within seconds of our current model failing. I might even pay for next-day shipping from Amazon; it means that much to me.

Lastly, train your mind to go to sleep when the lights are off. I attended a sleep doctor's lecture, and he said that we have a kind of switch in the brain, on for awake, off for asleep. However, it isn't always easy for the brain to realize that it needs to turn off. Therefore, you give it a pattern to recognize that tells your brain, "It is time to shut down."

I make word lists. This sounds dopey but it really works.

One list consists of fruits and vegetables, recited in alphabetical order: apples, apricots, artichokes, arugula, asparagus, avocados, bamboo shoots, bananas, basil, beans, beets, blackberries, blueberries, bok choy, boysenberries, breadfruit, broccoli, Brussels sprouts. I continue until I reach the end with yams, yucca root, and zucchini. Do this every night and after a few weeks, you train your brain to say, "Oh, I recognize this list. It's time to sleep."

When I want a change, I use the animal list: aardvark, aardwolf, adder, Afghan hound, Airedale, Akita, akula, albatross, alligator, alpaca, anaconda, anchovy, ants, anteaters, antelopes, apes, armadillo, asp, ass, and aye-ayes, down to yaks and zebras. When I started with animals, I could go through the entire list and then start over. After months of training, I tend to fall asleep long before I reach panther and Pikachu.

When I wake up in the night, which I do routinely, I start the list again. And I tend to fall back asleep quicker.

Any word list will do, but it should be complex enough to keep you from losing focus, and boring and soothing enough to encourage your mind to shut down. This list routine works best if you do it faithfully. It needs to become a habit to combat insomnia.

The word list was my last step in improving my sleep hygiene, and it really helped. I learned it from one of the many books out there on sleep. The library is full of them, and there are many more resources online. I look at them all, even though there isn't much that is new to me anymore.

So why keep studying sleep hygiene? It reminds me how important my sleep is, and, sometimes, I come across something I had never thought of. I had never heard of the word list trick before and so that book full of otherwise duplicate information (for me) was absolutely worth reviewing.

Good sleep hygiene is so important. Better sleep will make you feel so much better. When you are awake, you will be more focused, more even-tempered, and better able to perform every job on your list. Your health will improve. Your weight may even be a little easier to manage. There aren't many downsides to sleeping better, other than having to say no to things you want to do. However, if sleeping more forces you to be better organized during the day to get everything done, then how did you lose? Good quality of life is more important than quantity.

32

Exercise

Getting Serious – Adding Exercises to Your Chores – Time to Exercise – Is a Gym Worth It? – A Year Later – Another Year Later

Just as our bodies are meant to sleep, our bodies are meant to move. Most of us don't spend hours and hours in a field hoeing beets or weeding. We don't walk for miles every day. We don't haul water, look after livestock, chop trees, tend fires, or cook chicken stew with dumplings starting with a live chicken, a vegetable garden and a pile of flour that you ground yourself.

Our ancestors lived far more strenuous lives, involving huge amounts of work and exertion. This change is not a bad thing: very few of us in the First World drop dead of exhaustion by fifty anymore. It does mean that since physical fitness is no longer built into our day-to-day routine, we have to work at it.

I am not talking about being model thin, either. There are plenty of thin people who cannot run a mile without gasping for breath. Being thin does *not* equate to being fit. It is perfectly possible to be overweight (but not obese) and yet have better cardiovascular fitness than that skinny person who cannot walk five miles or spade over a garden bed.

By using your body every day, you get a stronger heart, better wind, more endurance, more strength, and more flexibility. A stronger body is healthier and more resilient. If you are already in shape, you are better able to move when you have to, such as running down 55 flights of stairs after a terrorist attack. If you take care of yourself, you are better able to take care of your loved ones.

Dear Husband and I are entering our late fifties. Time and miles are leaving their marks upon us. Yet I am in far better physical shape than I was ten years ago. I've lost forty pounds, and I exercise every day. I incorporate movement throughout my day.

Why did I do this? It was hurting too much to *not* exercise. My hips hurt. My knees hurt. My joints hurt. I couldn't do the things I used to do. Strenuous gardening would leave me crippled the next day.

I was left with a choice: decline, bitching all the way, or change how I lived.

GETTING SERIOUS

Declining would have been easier by far; also far more painful. It was reaching the point where every staircase was becoming an effort to use as it hurt my knees so much. I could not lie down because my hips hurt. I took a lot of over-the-counter pain meds. My weight led directly to gallbladder disease, and I had surgery. That was painful and unpleasant too. I didn't like the way I felt, I didn't like the way I looked, and I didn't like the way I was aging.

So I got serious about food and exercise. I walked more. I tried to eat less and better. I bought a Wii Fit Plus and started using it. I got a pedometer and a dog to encourage still more walking. Muffy really is multi-functional: security, varmint control, company, and exercise equipment all in one.

Am I still overweight? You bet! I would like to lose another twenty to thirty pounds. This is a goal I might achieve. I will never come close to that perfect weight for my height without the help of a zombie apocalypse, but if they come shambling, I can outrun fatter people and isn't that what counts?

Moreover, I feel so much better. My knees don't hurt, my hips don't hurt. I sleep better. I can work outside without crippling myself. My baby-step simple yoga routine means my joints don't hurt, and I am far more flexible. My incredibly basic aerobic routine means I don't get out of breath as quickly. My stupidly basic strength training means I can do heavy yard work. My back doesn't routinely hurt. I can walk a mile or two with my dog. I take far fewer pain meds.

All this wonderfulness only cost me time and effort. It didn't cost very much money, except for the Wii Fit Plus game and balance board. I bought a good pair of sneakers and a pedometer to remind me to keep moving. I check my steps throughout the day and that keeps me motivated to keep moving.

Exercise

Spending time and effort are far harder than spending the money. I don't like parting with my hard-earned bucks. But the time! The effort! Spending cash is a onetime evolution. Fitness is earned, an hour at a time, day after day after day.

The time needed to work out requires more of that pesky time management. I exercise about an hour a day. I do not count dog walking or any of my work around my home and yard towards this dedicated hour. I do my routine and get on with the day.

Because we only get twenty-four hours a day, it is guaranteed that you will have to sacrifice something else to find the time to exercise. If you spend a few hours a day watching TV or aimlessly web surfing, you'll find the time. You just need to get motivated. However, if you already use all of your time productively (be honest), you have to make hard choices as to what activities to give up.

The other hard part of exercise is making the effort. You block out the time and then you get hot, sticky, and sweaty. There are people who will tell you that magical endorphins will appear and you will genuinely love how you feel while you are exercising. This has not been true for me. I feel better while I exercise, but it is not ever rainbows and unicorns, blue sky, and candy canes fun.

Instead, I put on the mindset that I need to exercise to feel better in every part of my life. What finally worked for me was a) finding a routine that I could stick to, and b) focusing on how my muscles stretched as I moved through it. It has to be kind of Zen for me. This mental discipline has taken a lot of work. It certainly did not come naturally.

So I exercise every day, both dedicated time and whatever I can incorporate into my day. My example has even led to Dear Husband working out. He was never a gym rat, but like me, he was discovering as he aged, that he did not like how he felt. Exercising for him was a mental as well as a physical struggle.

In the last year, DH has lost twenty pounds. He tries to walk twice a day. He has his own exercise routine. He feels much better. He looks better. He had to learn that he had to do body maintenance every day. He had to make time for his program, time that he could not spend doing something else. He has to be more focused when he is writing as he has less time overall

Is it worth it to him? Absolutely. Is it worth it to me? Yes, totally. In addition, we encourage each other to keep at it. Better health, better focus, better flexibility, better shape. So we exercise. Every day, both dedicated time and as part of our daily routine.

ADDING EXERCISES TO YOUR CHORES

You can improve your fitness two ways. Both require effort, time, and thought. The first way is to incorporate movement into your daily routine. The second way is to dedicate time to working out.

If you can be moving around while doing something, then move around. When you are on the phone, walk back and forth while talking. Park your car as far away from the building as you can and walk in. Use the stairs (up and down) instead of elevators and escalators. Knowing where the staircases are is also useful if there is a fire emergency. When you run errands, park in a central location and walk to as many of them as feasible. This saves gas, too.

Walk your dog every day; twice a day if you can spare the time. And give your dog long walks, not just in and out, so your dog can do its business. Your dog will be so grateful and you will learn your area, meet your neighbors, and get into shape.

Wear a pedometer. I put mine on an elastic band around my ankle because it did not work to wear it at my waist. Get the cheapest one you can find at Walmart. The more expensive ones don't work any better and they are more complicated to operate. It is also more upsetting to lose a $45 pedometer than a $5 one. If all you want to do is count steps, you don't need a pedometer that will calculate calories, act as a stopwatch, tell time, and keep short-term and long-term goals.

The pedometer reminds you to keep moving. I check mine throughout the day to see how many steps I have walked. The short goal is 5,000 steps a day. The long goal is to make 10,000 steps each day. The super goal is to break 12,500 or even 15,000 steps. You will quickly discover how much you have to move to hit 10,000 steps. Two long dog walks daily – of a mile or so each – will help considerably in reaching this goal.

If your pedometer tells you that you only walk a thousand or so steps per day, then you need to get up and move around a lot more.

Pick the more strenuous option, whether mixing a cake with a wooden spoon instead of a hand mixer or spading over a garden bed versus using a rotary tiller. Do it by hand, using your body, and you improve your fitness and save energy dollars. A clothesline is a fine example: It costs you nothing but time to hang the wash, and you get to walk back and forth in the sun. A dryer costs money to run and does nothing to improve your health.

A treadmill can be more useful if you incorporate it with another activity. A treadmill desk lets you walk and type at the same time. You can buy one, or if you are handy, build one yourself. A treadmill in front of your TV set will encourage you to use it, instead of sitting down while watching a show.

If you feel particularly inspired (or cruel), hook up your TV set to a bicycle. If you or your children want to watch TV, then somebody has to bicycle enough to generate the electricity needed to run the TV. This will both improve family fitness *and* cut down on TV viewing. Clearly, a win all around.

There are many ways to use bikes to generate power for small and not-so-small appliances. Check out *The Human Powered Home: Choosing Muscles Over Motors* by Tamara Dean. Every idea in this book will improve your fitness and save precious energy dollars.

But these ideas only work if you do them. So start small. Whenever you can, do it the manual way. Get a push mower instead of a power mower. Use manual hedge clippers instead of a gasoline hedge trimmer. Try a rake instead of firing up a leaf blower. Walk whenever and wherever you can.

Yeah, it's more work; way more in many cases. But it costs less, saving both energy dollars and gym membership dollars and builds exercise into your daily routine.

If you are genuinely concerned about a difficult and challenging future, you will need to be prepared to do your chores manually anyway. Energy costs money. Power tools cost money. No matter what else you do, you are going to be eating and generating energy, so learn to do what you can with your muscles now, while it is easy. While you can visit a doctor if you injure yourself. While there is aspirin in drug stores and chiropractors on every corner. While there are resources available to help you.

TIME TO EXERCISE

The second half of exercising involves creating a dedicated routine. The best routine is the one you are willing to do every day or every other day. It doesn't matter that much what the routine is, unless you are training for a triathlon (and you wouldn't be here reading this anyway; you're off swimming with sharks or lifting Jersey walls).

I am talking to all of us couch potatoes. If the thought of exercise makes you lie down with a damp tea towel over your eyes until the urge goes away, then the routine that works best is the one you will actually do. If it's old Richard Simmons tapes that work, then dust them off and start moving.

In the case of me and Dear Husband, it was getting a Wii Fit Plus game and balance board. We have had it for more than five years, and I can perform the various yoga, strength, and aerobic routines for an hour a day. I had to work up to this level over the years, learning the exercises and building up my stamina.

The Wii Fit Plus works for me. It is convenient. I know what to do. I can make my routine longer as I get stronger. Recently, I added wrist and ankle weights to add intensity to the workout. Does this make me able to run mini-marathons? Dear me, no. Have I lost weight, gotten much more toned, and taken care of several physical problems? Absolutely.

I have discovered that I have to alternate among strength training (what we used to call calisthenics), yoga, and aerobics. I would focus exclusively on yoga for weeks and notice that I was losing strength in my arms while gaining in flexibility. If I concentrated on strength training, then I lost some of the yoga flexibility and my joints would hurt more. If I focused on aerobics, I lost strength and flexibility.

The Wii keeps track of what I do, so I check each day and see what I haven't done recently and do that routine. If I will be walking around all day, I will choose a flexibility or strength routine. If I'll be sitting at the desk or sewing machine all day, then aerobics it is. If my back hurts or my joints bother me more than usual, yoga will stretch and sooth me.

A wide variety of exercise is very important, especially as you get older. My elderly parents (mom is seventy-six and dad is eight) walk several miles a day and maintain their big house and yard. They also complain that their joints hurt and they are losing their strength. I say to them: find that yoga or tai chi class at the senior center and sign up. Do they listen? They do not. Aerobic activity like long daily walks is important but you still have to be flexible and strong. You are moving a different set of muscles and tendons along with all those other body parts when you change your exercise pattern.

I weigh in every day. This reminds me to not eat everything in sight like I want to. The Wii keeps track of my weight over the years so I can look back and see my progress. I try very hard to make the time to do a full fifty-minute session, but if I cannot squeeze out the time, I aim for half an hour. When I can only manage fifteen minutes, I do the more strenuous exercises to maximize my effectiveness.

I like to think that if I didn't have time in the morning, I would make up for it in the afternoon. That very rarely happens. I have to get the exercise done, first thing in the morning. Again, you have to discover what works best for you.

In the end, what matters is doing the exercises. If it hurts, then scale back. That no-pain, no-gain mantra only buys boats for orthopedic surgeons. Don't pay any attention to it. And don't pay any attention to those gym rats who tell you that you aren't doing enough. Or shaming you because of how you look and how you jiggle. This is another reason to exercise in the privacy of your own home.

Start where you are and gradually, gently, do more. It is far easier to criticize than it is to do, so some of the people who say rude things about your baby steps into fitness may be secretly jealous that you are exercising and they are not.

There are plenty of exercise videos at any library so you can try out a routine for free. Many game platforms have exercise games. Again, it matters more that you find a routine you like and are willing to do on a daily basis. So go down to the library and try out the books and tapes they have. Watch YouTube videos to get an idea of what a crunch is and how to do one correctly. Books are not always as clear as you could want.

When you find a routine you like, then buy the video. If you get bored with the same old thing, find a few routines that you like and alternate them. The key is doing it every day. Don't forget to incorporate all three types of movement into your routine: flexibility, strength, and aerobics. Really, the hardest part by far in exercising is overcoming your own inertia and then, even harder, is making the time. That pesky time management rears its head and you have to sacrifice some other thing that you do in order to find the time to exercise.

IS A GYM WORTH IT?

Eventually, you may want to venture into a gym. Before you do this, you should already be working out daily. Gyms cost money, and you have to spend even more time driving there and back, changing your clothes, and showering afterwards. Your living room does not have these issues. On the other hand, a well-equipped gym has far more options available, such as classes and specialized equipment, and people who can guide you through them.

If you go the gym route, then ask around. What are the facilities like? Does anyone you know use and recommend them? Go for a visit. Get a short-term trial membership. Do not spend any money until you are sure you will use the gym regularly. If the gym or its staff and patrons make you feel uncomfortable, fat, out-of-shape, or feeling bad, I guarantee that you won't ever go back. So shop around before you lay out the cash.

There may be other options in your area, such as yoga and tai chi classes to improve your flexibility and strengthen your joints, or martial arts and self-defense classes to improve your personal safety. Again, shop around and try them out before laying down a lot of money and a major commitment. If you won't do the work, or you can't or won't spend the time, then the finest gym or aerobics class in the world isn't worth the money.

If you have an employer that offers exercise classes, gym memberships, or other fitness programs, then take advantage of them. If your employer doesn't, stop by human resources and ask if they can be made available. If enough of your co-workers ask for dedicated time to work out, then even Catbert might be persuaded to add health and fitness programs to the company's benefits.

It is especially important that you spell out to human resources how a healthier, fitter workforce will tend to need less medical care. A fatter, sicklier workforce will cost more and be less productive. Knowing this might be enough to get your employer to offer a companywide fitness benefit package. If your company does add a program, after you have asked for one, then sign up right away and use it. Show through your actions that you meant what you said.

So look over your options. Add exercise to your daily routine by doing tasks the manual way. Then add an exercise routine to your day. Aerobics, lifting weights, yoga, tai chi, calisthenics, swimming, bicycling, ballroom dancing, martial arts: it doesn't matter as long as you start exercising. Pick what you like and get moving. And as you get fitter, add more exercise and keep stretching yourself.

A YEAR LATER

I'd been doing my exercise routine for several years. I'd been feeling much better, tighter, and more toned. My weight loss seemed to have stabilized but I wasn't gaining so I considered this a win. I was (and am) still overweight but I am so much better than I was. My clothes fit better, I look better, I feel better.

Then two changes in my life threw me for a loop. I started to write much more, taking up far more of my time. This put pressure on getting my usual tasks done. As you know, I *have* to get enough sleep. Without it, I become crazy.

I had already cut back on my housekeeping, gardening, community activities, and from-scratch cooking. I do very little online surfing, I don't shop for recreation, and I don't watch TV. A boring life, I know, but it suits me. I wanted to exercise more intensely to burn more calories in less time.

This led to the second stumble: I injured myself exercising. I had been doing sit-ups faithfully, working myself up to seventy of them. This had been going on every day for months. I didn't want to do more of them, so I started doing them faster.

Then I developed tremendous pain in my right hip. It was painful to walk, painful to move, painful to sleep. A nerve tingle developed from hip to toes as if my right leg was asleep. I stopped doing most of the sit-ups and other exercises because they hurt. I could not perform certain yoga poses anymore. They hurt.

When I didn't heal after some weeks, I dragged myself to the doctor. The doctor suggested sciatica and bursitis, and I asked for physical therapy. I needed to keep exercising, and I wanted to know how to do it safely and with less pain.

Physical therapy can work wonders. A good therapist and your own dedication and hard work can rebuild your body. Dear Husband had physical therapy years ago for a frozen shoulder, and it saved him from surgery. Dear Daughter had physical therapy when she broke her leg at age six. She would have made a full recovery anyway, due to the magical resilience of youth, but the exercises she practiced certainly did not hurt.

The physical therapist looked me over, listened to my symptoms, and decided the doctor was wrong. I did not have bursitis in my hip or sciatica. Although the pain was in my right hip and leg, she said I had injured a disc in my spine. She gave me a series of back exercises that worked wonders.

An MRI confirmed what the physical therapist thought. I had a herniated disc, below the waist. Two spinal epidurals worked miracles in pain relief but I will have to be careful for the rest of my life. My other recourse is more, gentle exercise and trying harder with my diet to take the weight off.

The physical therapist also told me that I had probably injured my spine by doing sit-ups. She told me to *never* do them. I never will again, because it hurts too much. Apparently, I should have been doing something else that doesn't involve flexing the spine as much. The physical therapist showed me how to do modified crunches, by laying flat on the floor and lifting my shoulders.

The therapist also told me one of the important rules of exercise, one that I had never heard of. If you bend one way, repeatedly, **you need to bend in the opposite way, repeatedly**. A bend-forward motion for an exercise should be alternated with a bend-backward motion. Moving your arms in forward circles should be followed by backward circles. If you routinely bend your spine forward, as in sit-ups or crunches, then you need to bend backwards as much.

There were two problems with my sit-ups. I was doing them too fast. More importantly, if I had done them in sets of ten, and followed each set with ten press-ups (which she insisted that I do for my spine), I probably would not be having an issue today. Ten sit-ups followed by ten press-ups. Repeat until you get to seventy. My spine would have been flexed both ways, allowing the discs to recover, and I would not have injured myself.

The irritating thing about all this is that I didn't work out that strenuously to begin with! I was never a gym rat. Any hard-core exerciser would sneer at my routine of baby steps and light workouts.

But I still hurt myself.

Doing less exercise also meant that my weight is creeping back up. That doesn't help one little bit. If you have joint pain, any doctor will tell you to *lose weight*. Your joints don't care about fat acceptance, only about the weight you are putting on them. Better fitness means that the muscles surrounding those joints are stronger. However, you still have to weigh less.

So you still have to exercise. Slow, gentle, gradual, and if what you are doing really hurts, stop and do something else. You have to do strength exercises, flexibility exercises, and aerobic exercises. The tricky part is doing enough to improve your health without injuring yourself. If you do nothing, you still lose. Your health will decline even faster.

Argh.

So persevere. Don't push too hard, back off it hurts, and if you have a physical therapist or personal trainer at hand, find out what you can do to make your exercise routine safer. The consequences of not exercising are worse. Go to Walmart and people-watch in the aisles for a few hours and you will see what I mean. Just do it a little smarter than I did.

ANOTHER YEAR LATER

Because of the epidurals, the pain and nerve damage have gone away. Yay, modern medicine! I still exercise every day, but I changed my routine again to manage pain and time.

I discovered the Royal Canadian Air Force Workout. This was a program developed in the mid-1950s by Dr. Bill Orban for Canadian Air Force members, male and female. This is an easy program to find. It was extremely popular and was published in dozens of editions and there is plenty of material about it online.

It has been working quite well for me. I don't use the Wii anymore for exercise, only to weigh in on every morning. I am holding steady on my weight. Damn, but weight loss is hard.

The RCAF program is not very difficult at the beginner levels, which is what I do. If you work your way to the upper levels, expect a very strenuous workout. It is intense enough that it could lead to injuries but so could bicycling or long-distance running.

That means, with this or any other exercise program, you should listen to your body. If you hurt doing something, find out why. Also, remember to bend the other way to compensate for each exercise. In my case, I modified the routine so that I do not do the sit-ups or jumping. I do the crunches and follow them with the press-ups my physical therapist recommended.

I like the RCAF program. Since I have memorized the routine, I can do it anywhere. It combines all three aspects of fitness: strength, flexibility, and aerobics. The back exercises that the physical therapist recommended add a level as well.

I spend less time than I did previously, as the RCAF routine is more intense than the Wii program. I run in place, up to fifteen minutes a day, after I do the full routine. This takes me about forty-five minutes. I exercise like this, barring illness, five or six days a week. I take Sundays off. I don't even get on the scale on Sundays anymore. I give my body a full day of rest, other than walking Muffy.

I have slowly increased the weight in the wrist and ankle weights. The wrist weights are standard, one-and-a-half pounds per wrist. Each ankle weight can carry as little as a half-pound up to five pounds. I can manage, after well over a year of working up to it, four pounds per ankle. Another year will get me up to the full five pounds, but I won't push it.

Part of my exercise routine involves walking Muffy every day. Sometimes we walk more and sometimes less, depending on the weather, how I feel (she is always game), and how close I am to my goal of 10,000 steps. It is a really nice feeling to pass 12,500 steps in a day, but you have to walk several miles to get that far. I try very hard to keep up the walking since if I walk less for several days, I can tell. I lose my stamina quickly if I don't keep up with the program.

It is very easy to lose fitness and much harder to gain it.

The key to exercise is finding something that you like and then do it. Don't be afraid to change your routine. If it isn't working, then find something that works better. I keep trying, and that is all you can do: keep trying.

33

Dental Care

How to Brush Your Teeth – Visit the Dentist – Your Teeth and Your Future

ONE OF THE GREAT MIRACLES OF MODERN LIFE is dental care. Think back to those Dickensian miseries of tooth decay that could not be treated other than by yanking out a rotted tooth with pliers. Dental care has improved so much in the last twenty years that it is no longer a marvel when your kids leave the dentist saying, "Look, mom. No cavities!"

For those of you not old enough to remember, that was the slogan back in the '60s for Crest toothpaste. Think about it: Isn't that what toothpaste is supposed to do? And yet, even if you brushed faithfully, it did not prevent them very well.

By the time I was eighteen, I had a cavity (filled with shiny silver) in every single flat-topped tooth in my mouth. I was consistent with my brushing; every night and generally before I left the house for school. Despite that care, in my early teens one tooth was so rotted that it had to be pulled.

On one memorable occasion, my brother's dentist announced to my mother that he had *seven* cavities. My brother was not a fan of tooth brushing and it showed. It cost quite a bit of money to fill those cavities, at a time when my mother did not have the cash to spare.

Today, my three kids (as of this writing from eighteen to twenty-seven) have a grand total of one cavity between them. One cavity. Is their oral hygiene that much better than mine? Not at all.

It was the technology that changed. Toothbrushes are better. Hard toothbrushes damaged teeth in a way that soft brushes do not. Save the hard toothbrushes (you can still buy them) for scrubbing the grout between your tiles. Do not use them on your teeth.

Toothpaste has improved, with better mild abrasives, better fluoride, better everything. Find a brand you like, use it consistently, and you will be fine.

Fluoride is added to the water. Many people are suspicious of fluoride in drinking water, but it does harden tooth enamel. The key is getting enough, but not too much.

Flossing. Nobody flossed when I was growing up. I don't think even dentists flossed. Yet flossing saves the enamel between your teeth. You will never get a toothbrush to go where the floss goes.

Rinsing. You can do this with plain water (which I do), with water with a touch of salt or baking soda or peroxide mixed in or you can spend good money on fluoride products. This can be useful if your water doesn't have fluoride in it.

HOW TO BRUSH YOUR TEETH

There is even a specific order to brushing your teeth, which will vastly improve your oral health. It also shows why you do not necessarily need to use a fluoride product.

First, rinse the mouth. This removes the loose junk from your teeth. A mouthful of warm water swished around is fine.

Then floss. The rinsing removed the bigger bits so the floss can reach into the crevices and get at the finer sludge that builds up. Floss every tooth you want to keep. Be thorough. You can use floss sticks, floss in a floss holder, or hold the floss with your fingers.

Rinse again, removing the sludge from your mouth that the flossing kicked up. Then brush the surfaces, cleaning, polishing, and adding that microscopic layer of fluoride. If you floss *after* you brush, you remove the fluoride you just put onto your teeth. So don't do that.

When you brush, take your time. A lick and a promise won't do the job nearly as well as taking several minutes of careful work, getting every tooth surface you can reach. Swish the fluoride foam around when you finish, but don't swallow it. Rinsing with water will remove some of the fluoride that you carefully applied. This is where a fluoride rinse makes sense, if your water doesn't contain it.

So: rinse, floss, rinse, brush. Do this after every meal and before you go to bed every single day of your life, and you will have a fighting chance of having your teeth outlive you. Start today. If you are out in public and cannot brush your teeth, you can still rinse your mouth in the bathroom. That will at least remove some of the food particles and the sludgy film from your teeth until you can brush them.

VISIT THE DENTIST

You can do more. Get a dental checkup every six months to make sure there aren't any problems hiding in your mouth. The more rigorous your oral hygiene, the easier it is for the dental hygienist to do her work. By the way, brush before you visit the dentist. That way, the hygienist does not have to do the basic work you could have done at home.

At the dentist, get the magic sealants. They are one of the greatest inventions in dental care. Sealants are why none of my kids have cavities (except Oldest Child with his lone specimen). I cannot recommend sealants highly enough. They are such a miracle that if your insurance does not cover them, pay for them yourself. They will save you the big bucks you would spend from fixing cavities later along with the pain.

This careful work will help avoid gum disease too. Healthier gums mean your teeth are less susceptible to decay and will last longer. They will also look better than having people see the roots of your teeth.

YOUR TEETH AND YOUR FUTURE

By this time, you're wondering what better oral hygiene has to do with an uncertain future.

It will save you big bucks. I could have purchased two very nice, full-immersion Disney vacation packages for my family for what I have paid to repair my teeth. Even if I did not need the root canals, the infills, and the gum care, my fillings had to be replaced as they age. I was surprised when the dentist told me fillings don't last forever. Those cavities that were repaired when you were thirteen will need to be redone when you are fifty. Good oral hygiene costs only about fifteen minutes out of your day, plus floss, toothbrushes, toothpaste, and water. Your dentist may even give you a new toothbrush with every visit, along with some floss and toothpaste. Mine does.

You will also save on pain, and there is no pain like dental pain. It can affect every aspect of your life, as you attempt to function while miserable with agony. I have had fillings fall out, I have had root canals, I have had braces, and I have had cracked teeth. The pain is awful.

Your teeth, like your eyes and your ears, never get better on their own. Broken bones will heal, cuts will leave scars. A surgeon can remove your appendix and gallbladder, and you'll recover good as new.

Not teeth. You don't grow new ones to replace the ones you have to have pulled. They don't heal from trauma. They don't knit themselves together like a bone does. The purpose of the dental work you do at home and your dentist does in his office is to stem the tide of entropy and decay.

Besides being astonishingly painful, bad teeth can kill you. People have died from abscessed teeth. Think about that pocket of black decay rotting in your mouth, so close to your sinuses, eyes, ears, and brain. Good oral care prevents this.

Dental care in the future may be unavailable. You may not be able to afford a dentist, or there may not be one you can reach. A daily habit of fastidious dental care will go a long ways towards ensuring that if you are forced to go without professional attention, you can manage until you can get to a dentist.

My tooth care is far better than it was. I have had to change my lax ways to prevent future pain and expense. When I watch my elderly parents struggling every day with dentures, partial plates, and routine pain, it reminds me that I do not want to suffer the same thing. So I make myself rinse, floss, rinse, and brush.

There are two other things you can do to improve your dental hygiene. Stop smoking, and don't use any other kind of tobacco product. They are terrible for your teeth and gums. The other thing is to stop drinking sugary beverages. Nothing lays down a layer of enamel-dissolving chemicals between your teeth like a carbonated soda.

So remember: rinse, floss, rinse, and brush. Repeat after every meal and before you go to bed. Do this over a lifetime, and your teeth will last you a lifetime. Get your family into the habit, and save them a lifetime of pain as well.

34

In-Depth Goal Setting

So HERE I AM, ON A SUNDAY AFTERNOON, and undecided on which of the many, many jobs I should do next. I could waste time playing Spider – I play the two-deck version, and I am very good at it, too – but does that help me meet my goals? Probably not. Sigh.

Goals have to be reviewed regularly, and they can change over time. Ours have. When we moved into Fortress Peschel, it was Chez Peschel. We had thought about and planned for an uncertain future, but not to the extent that we do now.

Financial Independence and ease of operations had always been a priority for both of us and while I was holding down the fort in South Carolina, Dear Husband was in Pa., learning his new job at the newspaper and house hunting. He found our current residence, and it met our goals of being something that we could afford without financial stress, large enough to hold the family and the animals, had a yard, and was in the Hershey school district, within walking distance of some stores, and an easy commute to work.

Once we had the house, our goals changed again. We had to pay it off (did that), fix everything wrong with it (still working on that), paint the house (90% done), design and redesign the yard, and become part of our new community. We are working on all of that, too.

I kept the goal of paying off the house in plain sight in the dining room. I made a paper thermometer, like what you see in fundraising campaigns, and every payment was marked on it. It moved soooo slowly to zero cash owed to the bank, but it did move. It moved faster than it would have otherwise, because all our extra cash went to the mortgage, if we didn't have other debt to pay off first. Even an extra $10 a month counts.

If this seems like nickels and dimes, it is. What we have found, over and over, and every thrift writer in the world agrees on this, is that it all adds up. An extra cookie a day equals a few extra pounds at the end of the year. Extra money every month at the beginning of a mortgage when the principal payment is tiny and the interest payment is huge, will lop a year or more off the mortgage at the far end.

If you have a financial goal such as an emergency fund, paying off credit card debt, student loans, medical bills, mortgage, or money owed to anyone, I highly recommend a thermometer on graph paper. With each payment, fill it in and watch your progress. When you reach the top, success! Then choose another goal and make a new chart.

When you are out of debt, your financial goals change. Do you want to become a debt slave again? How about focusing on that goal of a year's living expenses in your emergency fund? This is not your retirement fund, by the way. The year's salary in your emergency fund will let you weather storms like job loss, major health issues, and having your house blown to bits by the tornado.

The year's income in a savings account *will not make your problems go away*. It will make them easier to cope with. Money is freedom from hassle. Less money in an emergency fund means that smaller emergencies can be crippling. If all your cars die at once and you have $30,000 in your emergency fund, you can buy two used cars and pay cash. If all your cars die and you have only $300, you are stuck.

An emergency fund should always be one of your goals, and the bigger the better

Do you live in a fixer-upper? Then one of your goals should be to fix up the old dump. I've done three houses: my house in Norfolk, our house in South Carolina, and our current house. In addition, I have made improvements to various rented apartments, and I watched my parents improve two houses. It can be done. You don't have to be a contractor or an expert carpenter. We are not.

All it takes is time, patience, money, and the willingness to learn new skills. The goal of fixing up your house has an end date. Every room is painted, the electrical systems meet code, the plumbing is watertight, and the roof doesn't leak. The basement stays dry. That one is vital to achieve many other goals, such as where to store months of groceries.

The purpose of fixing up a house is to make it so you don't have to do anything but routine maintenance afterwards. Once I have a room painted, the rugs installed, and the drapes hung, I don't change

In-Depth Goal Setting

it. I don't periodically redecorate because I am tired of how the place looks. That is a waste of my money, time, and energy.

There are jobs still on the list. The basement walls need to be coated with Drylok, and then topped with ultra-high-gloss white paint. The crumbling sheet vinyl floors in the kitchen and bathrooms are waiting to be replaced as time, money, and energy permit.

The second half of our home improvement goal was to make the house one where we could age in place. Thus the closets, the lever doorknobs, the grab bars, and the added staircase railings. We chose long-lasting finishes, and extended-life carpets and shingles so we would *not* have to do it again later.

Think about it. You are in the hardware store looking at tubes of caulk. You can buy five-year caulk or fifty-year caulk. It costs two bucks more per tube to get the fifty-year caulk. Spend the money! Do you like caulking that much? I don't. Do it right the first time and save yourself oodles of aggravation.

Our landscaping choices were made with the same goals in mind. We wanted easy-to-maintain sidewalks that sloped (no tripping hazards), raised beds (easier to weed), wilderness areas that could be ignored, and clearly defined small lawns that could be easily mowed by an old lady (that's me) with a rotary push mower.

We had the chain-link fence installed. Done, and done for good. Chain-link lasts essentially forever. We planned ahead and installed three gates; two for pedestrians, and one doublewide to allow a vehicle into the yard. The cost of that gate was repaid many times over. The second side gate was installed to allow easier access for DD to visit her friend next door. The convenience was well worth the cost.

We also wanted to ensure privacy. We planted a row of columnar shrubs around most of the property. We have yews, thuja, columnar apple trees, and columnar hollies. I've detailed our travails with hedges and fences in an earlier chapter, and most of what we've planted is growing nicely. The hollies' eventual fate remains to be seen.

The neighbors behind us recently removed their huge privet hedge, demonstrating why you need a hedge of your own. The yews, in the ground now for over a decade, proved their worth. We cannot see the neighbors, the Reese factory or the highway, and they cannot see us. Hedges take time to grow so if you want them, plant them right after you install the chain-link fence. They work together and have to be done in the correct order. It is much harder to retrofit a fence into an overgrown mass of shrubbery than it is to install the fence first and then plant the hedge.

The landscaping goal on the north side never changed from the day we ripped out the forsythia and replaced them with a hedgerow of native shrubs. I wanted privacy and protection from the north wind. But things didn't work out like I thought they would, and so I had to keep going back. If the columnar hollies fail – we'll know in ten years – then it is going to be yews. I know those will thrive. Will we like planting yews in our late sixties? I doubt it so I hope the hollies perform as the catalog claimed they will.

After a few years of flailing around with the yard, I came across the concept of permaculture. This was not the original goal. We started with restoring the yard to an Eastern deciduous woodland. This was a separate goal from privacy and security via the hedge and fence system, but they work together. A native shagbark hickory tree screens and shades just as well as a Norway maple.

As I became more concerned with being resilient in the face of an uncertain future, my vision for the yard changed dramatically. Food production took a more important role and that meant raised vegetable beds. At its heart, permaculture means gardening in concert with nature and making natural systems do most of the work. One of the goals of permaculture is to successfully integrate privacy, food production, work zones, play zones, and wilderness areas to provide habitat for beneficial insects and birds.

Zone your yard so the parts you use the most, like the herb bed, are close to the back door. You are much more likely to use your herbs and vegetables if you don't have to traipse to the far edge of the yard to fetch the parsley and carrots. The same is true of your clothesline. It needs to be close enough that you don't avoid using it.

Our compost bins are at the far end of the yard tucked in by the toolshed. Their appearance and structure has changed quite a bit over the years. Pallet-sided bins gave way to wire for better airflow. This area was not originally fenced off from the rest of the yard. Getting Muffy meant that we had to do it and fast. She would have been regularly digging in the bins, enthusiastically looking for rodents or interesting-smelling stuff and making a huge mess. The ground was grass, which turned into a weedy, muddy mess, awkward to mow. Wood chips and mulch didn't work, either. Eventually, we got lucky

In-Depth Goal Setting

when a neighbor discarded a big pile of bricks. Younger Son brought them home, cleaned out the weeds, leveled the ground, and laid the bricks tightly on the dirt. This flooring is far better than what we had, even if it still has to be weeded or weed-whacked regularly.

If I had planned better from the beginning, I would have made the area easier to maintain. The location has always been a problem. You want your productive vegetable beds close to the house, same as your patios and clotheslines. Compost bins, while necessary, shouldn't be located on your most valuable real estate. Therefore, they are shoved off to the far corner, out of sight and out of mind, and not always convenient to use.

Permaculture led us to putting the fruit trees, nut trees, and berry bushes around the edges of the yard, inside the hedge walls. That seems to be working out. The plants that died, like the blueberries, generally did because I didn't pay enough attention to soil conditions, light levels, and spacing. Blueberries demand a highly acidic soil, one I do not have, and I should have realized that they would never grow. I wasted time and money because I did not pay attention to what they needed.

One of the goals of permaculture is to interplant your food plants leading to the wonderful, final structure of a layered food forest. This hasn't worked out very well. Is it because I haven't put in enough work? Enough knowledge? Did I make poor choices of plants for the soil and light conditions? I don't know. This has led, over time, to changing our planting goals. If something won't grow, like the blueberries, then I stop killing myself. Instead, I buy blueberries at the grocery store when they are in season.

I grow currants (three kinds) and gooseberries. The original, vague goal was to grow fruit. The birds took a few years to discover the bushes, and they just love them. Gooseberries turned out to be surrounded by vicious thorns and they are seedy. Currants need to be perfectly ripe to be edible, they are seedy, and like gooseberries, are probably best suited for making jam.

So do I make jam? I do not. I don't have much free time, and I discovered I have the wrong kind of stove. The glass-topped model that came with the house cannot take the weight of a canner. There are horror stories of glass-top stoves shattering under the weight of a fully loaded canner.

Another goal gone by the wayside. I have a canner and multiple canning jars, and I don't use them. It is a lot more expensive to replace a stove than it is to buy readymade jam. I may still learn canning when the stove has to be replaced. I may not purchase another glass-topped stove. On the other hand, my kitchen has extremely limited counter space and we have to use the stove as a workspace.

So I'm confronted with contradictory goals. What do I really want to do? To learn how to can the fruit I grow? To avoid replacing an expensive stove? To lose more of my precious counter space in a small kitchen? The canning project is on hold, but I could try another route. What if I traded my canning equipment, my currants, and my gooseberries to a neighbor in exchange for the use of her stove? We could can together, and my neighbor would be paid with half of the finished jams. That could work and it would tighten up the relationship between us. On the other hand, we could drive each other crazy, fighting over currants in a small, hot kitchen where the knives are close at hand. Do I want this? Would this meet my goals of growing and preserving my own food and being part of a tight-knit community?

The point I want to get across is this: Goals change over time. They are not static. Some don't work out. A goal may look like it fulfills one objective, but often, it fulfills multiple objectives, so even a partial success is still a success. Fruit growing hasn't worked out, but my soil has improved, I learned a lot, and I keep the birds well fed.

The goal of improving your fitness also works on multiple levels. You get healthier, your clothes fit better, you become more able to tolerate a wide range of stresses, you can work better at all kinds of physical projects without injuring yourself, you save some money on healthcare, and you meet your neighbors when they see you trotting around the neighborhood with your dog. Multiple goals are achieved with what looks like one single goal: getting physically fit.

Periodically, we look around and check to see if we are on track with our goals. We update and change them when needed. We ask ourselves: Is what we are doing helping us to meet our goals?

If the answer is no, and it is no repeatedly, then you have to ask the harder question of why not. Financial Independence is a terrific example. If you're serious about getting out of debt and not being a slave to your creditors, then why aren't you working harder to do so? Maybe you aren't doing the time-consuming, hard work of selling your excess stuff on eBay because you don't care, and you don't want

In-Depth Goal Setting

to be bothered. Maybe you want to buy what you want, when you want, and the future be damned. If this is true, then you need a different goal.

But if you truly do want to be out of debt, then you need to figure out why you are sabotaging yourself.

The same is true of food gardening, self-education, your exercise program, and any other improvement efforts that are on your list. Exercising every day takes time and effort and the payoff takes forever. Planting an extensive garden means you have to take care of it, learn to cook with the produce, preserve the excess for the winter, and train the family to eat what you grow. Is that what you want?

It is very important to revisit your goals regularly. That way, you can see if you are achieving them, you can update your goals, and if you don't do something that you say you want to do, you can figure out why not. Maybe the answer is that you should be doing something else. That happens. I used to do a lot more cooking from scratch and serious food and wilderness gardening. I don't do nearly as much now as I don't have the time when I'm trying to write several thousand words a day.

My updated goals include finishing *Fed, Safe & Sheltered* and releasing it through Peschel Press; the book you are holding in your hands now. Editing these essays into a coherent whole was a challenge and took plenty of time.

Sewing is important to me so I've been thinking seriously about writing a series of instructional books; the kind I would have liked to buy when I was starting out. One would be on making cloth grocery bags, something that gets used regularly, taking the place of plastic ones. Another would be on making nightgowns and pajamas. Most of us wear them, they are easy to sew, and fit is unimportant. I make something that I call a NotQuilt. It's hard to explain but they are not hard to make. It's easier than piecing and quilting a real one, you make them from the scrap cloth you have on hand, you recycle dead electric blankets and ugly bedspreads as the batting layer, and the finished product looks and functions just like a quilt. These books are all in the future, as I have to sew the examples, writing and photographing as I go.

I am also writing a series of novels set on a terraformed Mars. This will allow me to work out my thoughts on resource depletion, sustainability, class, and status issues, with plenty of sex and violence to cushion the ride. Does this take time away from all my other efforts? You bet it does. But I want to do this and not just because I have something to say about the management of limited resources. I want to make some money.

In order to meet my new goal of writing thousands of words every day, other goals have gone by the wayside. Fortunately, the underlying goals of Fortress Peschel have long been Financial Independence and sustainability. Having no debt and emergency money in the bank lets us do this. Having spent years of our precious life energy to make our house low-maintenance means we don't have to do it as much anymore. This frees up time and money for the writing project.

Knowing how to cook from scratch and having a fridge means I can cook large meals every few days, and we eat leftovers the other days. Your family can be trained to do this. You are not a short-order cook. Your time is valuable.

The garden has, for the most part, been put aside. Many of the raised beds are fallow. That means we pile them high with leaves every fall and ignore them. The soil critters break down the leaves and improve the soil, and we don't do a thing. When we get back to serious food production, I expect that the soil will be in far better shape. We keep up with the mowing, pruning, and weeding, and it has been working out.

My sewing emphasis has shifted to the aforementioned projects. I no longer make elaborate Halloween costumes for the offspring. They've aged out of the system. I do plenty of mending, because as with home cooking, it is very cost-effective. Sometimes the mending pile gets big before I have the time to visit it, but you cannot have everything.

Many of the systems here at Fortress Peschel like the clothesline, drying racks, and the heavy window quilts, were put in use so long ago that we cannot imagine doing anything else. They are part of the daily routine, just like exercising, jobbing my errands together, and writing. They never stop saving us time and money. They became maintenance and are no longer goals to achieve.

I cannot suggest how often you should examine your goals. Only you can do that. but when you do, ask yourself: Are you going in the right direction? Are you getting done what you want to? Are you managing your time so that you achieve what you want, rather than binge-watching TV?

In-Depth Goal Setting

Your goals announce what matters to you. Managing your time so you achieve them says that you really mean it. Your accomplishments make you more adaptable and more confident. The universe will throw curve balls that change your goals, sometimes very suddenly. But if you have no goals, no skills, no resiliency, you will never be able to do anything other than drift and react. The future will not make itself easier to suit you or me.

Bibliography

These are the books mentioned in the text. They guided me on my journey and are all worth reading.

FOOD AND SHOPPING

Bracken, Peg. *The Compleat I Hate to Cook Book.* New York: Galahad Books, 1960.

Fitzsimmons, Muriel and Cortland. *Cooking for Absolute Beginners.* New York: Dover Publications, 1976.

Haber, Barbara. *From Hardtack to Home Fries: An Uncommon History of American Cooks and Meals.* New York: Penguin Books, 2003.

Hartwig, Daphne Metaxas. *Make Your Own Groceries.* Indianapolis: Bobbs-Merrill, 1979.

Hertzberg, Ruth. *Putting Food By.* Lexington, Mass.: Stephen Greene Press, 1982.

Jeavons, John. *How to Grow More Vegetables: Than You Ever Thought Possible on Less Land Than You Can Imagine.* Berkeley, Calif.: Ten Speed, 2017.

King Arthur Flour. *The King Arthur Flour Baker's Companion: The All-Purpose Baking Cookbook.* Woodstock, Vt.: The Countryman Press, 2012.

McMillan, Tracie and Hillary Huber. *The American Way of Eating: Undercover at Walmart, Applebee's, Farm Fields, and the Dinner Table.* New York: Scribner, 2012.

Pomiane, Edouard de. *French Cooking in Ten Minutes: Or, Adapting to the Rhythm of Modern Life.* New York: North Point Press, 1994.

Reese, Jennifer. *Make the Bread, Buy the Butter: What You Should and Shouldn't Cook from Scratch – Over 120 For the Best Homemade Foods.* New York: Atria Books, 2014.

Rombauer, Irma S. and Marion Rombauer Becker. *The Joy of Cooking.* New York: Scribner, 1975 and New York: Scribner, 1997.

Salsbury, Barbara, and Cheri Loveless. *Cut Your Grocery Bills in Half!: Supermarket Survival.* Washington, D.C.: Acropolis Books, 1983.

Shapiro, Laura. *Perfection Salad.* New York: Random House, 2001.

Shapiro, Laura. *Something From the Oven: Reinventing Dinner in 1950s America.* New York: Penguin Books, 2005.

Wyman, Carolyn. *Better Than Homemade: Amazing Foods that Changed the Way We Eat*. New York: Bristol Park Books, 2010.

GARDENING

Bartholomew, Mel. *Square Foot Gardening*. Emmaus, Pa.: Rodale Press, 1981.

Deppe, Carol. *The Resilient Gardener: Food Production and Self-Reliance in Uncertain Times*. White River Junction, Vt.: Chelsea Green, 2011.

Jenkins, Joseph C. *The Humanure Handbook: A Guide to Composting Human Manure: Emphasizing Minimum Technology and Maximum Hygienic Safety*. Grove City, Pa.: Jenkins Publishing, 1994.

Solomon, Steve. *Gardening When It Counts: Growing Food in Hard Times*. Gabriola Island, British Columbia: New Society Publishers, 2008.

HEALTH, HOME AND CLUTTER

Aslett, Don. *Don Aslett's Clutter Free!: Finally and Forever*. Pocatello, Idaho: Marsh Creek Press, 1995.

Dean, Tamara. *The Human-Powered Home: Choosing Muscles Over Motors*. Gabriola Island, B.C.: New Society Publishers, 2008.

Roizen, Michael F. *You: The Owner's Manual*. New York: HarperCollins, 2008.

Webb, Martha, and Sarah Parsons Zackheim. *Dress Your House for Success: Five Fast, Easy Steps to Selling Your House, Apartment, or Condo For the Highest Possible Price*. New York: Three Rivers Press, 1997.

Wilder, Laura Ingalls. *Little House on the Prairie*. New York: Scholastic, 1953.

HISTORY

Ekirch, A. Roger. *At Day's Close: A History of Nighttime*. London: Phoenix, 2006.

Goodman, Ruth. *How to Be a Tudor: A Dawn-to-Dusk Guide to Everyday Life*. London: Penguin Books, 2016.

MONEY AND THRIFT

Dacyscyn, Amy. *The Complete Tightwad Gazette*. New York: Villard Books, 1999.

Economides, Steve, and Annette Economides. *America's Cheapest Family Gets You Right on the Money*. New York: Three Rivers Press, 2007.

Robin, Vicki and Joseph R. Dominguez. *Your Money Or Your Life: Nine Steps to Transforming Your Relationship With Money and Achieving Financial Independence*. New York: Penguin Books, 2008.

Spencer, Kathy and Samantha Rose. *How to Shop for Free: Shopping Secrets for Smart Women Who Love to Get Something for Nothing*. Cambridge, Mass.: Da Capo Lifelong, 2011.

PREPPER

Harrison, Kathy. *Just In Case: How to be Self-Sufficient When the Unexpected Happens*. North Adams, Mass.: Storey Pub., 2008.

Kunstler, James Howard. *The Long Emergency: Surviving the End of Oil, Climate Change, and Other Converging Catastrophes of the Twenty-First Century*. New York: Grove Press, 2009.

SECURITY

De Becker, Gavin. *The Gift of Fear: And Other Survival Signals That Protect Us From Violence*. New York: Dell, 1997.

Kilcommons, Brian, and Sarah Wilson. *Paws to Consider: Choosing the Right Dog for You and Your Family*. New York: Warner Books, 1999.

SEWING

Bordow, Joan Wiener and Sharon Rosenberg. *The Illustrated Hassle-Free Make Your Own Clothes Book*. New York: Skyhorse Publishing, 2008. This is a reprint of a 1971 edition.

Bradley, Duane and Judith Hoffman Corwin. *Design It, Sew It, and Wear It: How to Make Yourself a Super Wardrobe Without Commercial Patterns*. New York: Crowell, 1979.

Brewbaker, Paula. *Clothing Care and Repair* (The Singer Sewing Reference Library). Minnetonka, Minn.: Cy DeCosse Inc., 1985.

Foote, Estelle J. *The Mender's Manual: Repairing and Preserving Garments and Bedding*. New York: Harcourt Brace Jovanovich, 1977.

Ides, Nan L. *Hand Mending Made Easy: Save Time and Money Repairing Your Own Clothes.* Salem, Ore.: Palmer Pletsch, 2008.
Martin, Rosie. *DIY Couture: Create Your Own Fashion Collection.* London: Laurence King Publishing, 2012.
Roach, Kristin M. *Mend It Better.* North Adams, Mass.: Storey Pub., 2012.
Smith, Alison. *Dressmaking: The Complete Step-by-step Guide to Making Your Own Clothes.* New York: DK Publishing, 2012.

WEBSITES

Ecosophia, www.ecosophia.net/.
Resilience, www.resilience.org. This prepper site's politics are left-wing, and acts as a clearinghouse for similar sites.
Survival Blog. www.survivalblog.com. Its politics are right-wing, but like Resilience it can lead you to a whole 'nother set of websites. What's most fascinating to watch is where the two sites agree.

About the Author

Teresa Peschel lives with her family in the Sweetest Place on Earth. She has long been interested in sustainability, resource depletion, and finding a balanced life, not too much and not too little. This led her to write *Fed, Safe, & Sheltered.* (formerly Suburban Stockade). Her next book, *Sew Cloth Grocery Bag,* follows in the same vein.

Teresa also explores these issues, as Odessa Moon, in her science-fiction romances on a terraformed Mars. Visit Teresa at the Peschel Press (https://peschelpress.com/Peschel Press) or Odessa Moon websites (https://odessamoon.com/).

www.ingramcontent.com/pod-product-compliance
Lightning Source LLC
Chambersburg PA
CBHW030146100526
44592CB00009B/141